British Bus Publishing

Body codes used in the Bus Handbook series:

Type:
A	Articulated vehicle
B	Bus, either single-deck or double-deck
BC	Suburban - high-back seated bus
C	Coach
M	Minibus with design capacity of 16 seats or less
N	Low-floor bus (*Niederflur*), either single-deck or double-deck
O	Open-top bus (CO = convertible - PO = partial open-top)

Seating capacity is then shown. For double-decks the upper deck quantity is followed by the lower deck.

Door position:-
C	Centre entrance/exit
D	Dual doorway.
F	Front entrance/exit
R	Rear entrance/exit (no distinction between doored and open)
T	Three or more access points

Equipment:-
L	Lift for wheelchair	TV	Training vehicle.
M	Mail compartment	RV	Used as tow bus or engineers vehicle.
T	Toilet	w	Vehicle is withdrawn from service.

e.g. - B32/28F is a double-deck bus with thirty-two seats upstairs, twenty-eight down and a front entrance/exit.
N43D is a low-floor bus with two doorways.

Re-registrations:-
Where a vehicle has gained new index marks the details are listed at the end of each fleet showing the current mark, followed in sequence by those previously carried starting with the original mark.

Regional books in the series:

The Scottish Bus Handbook
The Ireland & Islands Bus Handbook
The North East Bus Handbook
The Yorkshire Bus Handbook
The Lancashire, Cumbria and Manchester Bus Handbook
The Merseyside and Cheshire Bus Handbook
The East Midlands Bus Handbook
The West Midlands Bus Handbook
The Welsh Bus Handbook
The Chilterns and West Anglia Bus Handbook
The East Anglia Bus Handbook
The South East Bus Handbook
The South West Bus Handbook

Annual books are produced for the major groups:

The Stagecoach Bus Handbook
The FirstBus Bus Handbook
The Arriva Bus Handbook
The National Express Handbook
Editions for earlier years are available. Please contact the publisher.

Associated series:

The Hong Kong Bus Handbook
The Leyland Lynx Handbook
The Model Bus Handbook
The Postbus Handbook
The Overall Advertisment Bus Handbook - Volume 1
The Toy & Model Bus Handbook - Volume 1 - Early Diecasts
The Fire Brigade Handbook (fleet list of each local authority fire brigade)
The Fire Brigade Handbook - Special Appliances Volume 1
The Fire Brigade Handbook - Special Appliances Volume 2
The Police Range Rover Handbook

Contents

The South West Bus Handbook

This second edition of the Bus Handbook covering England's South West region and is part of a series that details the fleets of bus and express coach operators from across Britain. A list of current editions is shown on page 2. The operators included in this edition cover those who provide tendered and commercial services in the counties and unitary area within the region. Also included are a number of operators who provide significant coaching activities.

Quality photographs for inclusion in the series are welcome, for which a fee is payable. The publishers unfortunately cannot accept responsibility for any loss and request you show your name on each picture or slide.

To keep the fleet information up to date we recommend the Ian Allan publication, Buses, published monthly, or for more detailed information, the PSV Circle monthly news sheets.

The writer and publisher would be glad to hear from readers should any information be available which corrects or enhances that given in this publication.

Series Editor: Bill Potter
Principal Editor for *The South West Bus Handbook*: Simon Nicholas and David Donati

Acknowledgments:
We are grateful to John Madge, John Burch, Keith Grimes, Steve White, the PSV Circle and the operating companies for their assistance in the compilation of this book.

The cover photographs are by Bill Potter and Mark Lyons

Earlier editions of the area covered by the South West Bus Handbook:

1st Edition - 1997-   ISBN 1-897990-42-1
This Edition - 2001   ISBN 1-897990-64-2

ISBN 1 897990 64 2 (2nd Edition)
Published by *British Bus Publishing Ltd*
16 St Margaret's Drive, Wellington, Telford, TF1 3PH

Telephone: 01952 255669 - Facsimile 01952 222397 - www.britishbuspublishing.co.uk
© British Bus Publishing Ltd, September 2001

A BUS / CROWN COACHES

L C Munden & Son Ltd, 6-7 Freestone Road, St Phillips, Bristol, BS2 0QN
A J Peters, 104 Winchester Road, Brislington, Bristol, BS4 3NL

NFB113R	Bristol VRT/SL3/6LXB	Eastern Coach Works	B43/33F	1977	City Line, 1993
OHR184R	Leyland Fleetline FE30AGR	Eastern Coach Works	B43/31F	1977	Westward, Kingswood, 1997
MOU747R	Bristol VRT/SL3/6LXB	Eastern Coach Works	B43/27D	1977	First Cityline, 2000
KOO792V	Bristol VRT/SL3/6LXB	Eastern Coach Works	B39/31F	1980	First Cityline, 2000
AHW198V	Bristol VRT/SL3/6LXB	Eastern Coach Works	B43/27D	1980	First Bristol, 2000
KOO791V	Bristol VRT/SL3/6LXB	Eastern Coach Works	B39/31F	1980	First Bristol, 1998
KOO793V	Bristol VRT/SL3/6LXB	Eastern Coach Works	B39/31F	1980	First Bristol, 1998
STW33W	Bristol VRT/SL3/6LXB	Eastern Coach Works	B39/31F	1980	First Bristol, 2000
EWS739W	Bristol VRT/SL3/6LXB	Eastern Coach Works	B43/31F	1981	First Cityline, 2000
EWS741W	Bristol VRT/SL3/6LXB	Eastern Coach Works	B43/31F	1981	First Cityline, 2000
EWS742W	Bristol VRT/SL3/6LXB	Eastern Coach Works	B43/31F	1981	First Cityline, 2000
XHK221X	Bristol VRT/SL3/6LXB	Eastern Coach Works	B39/31F	1981	First Cityline, 2000
XHK222X	Bristol VRT/SL3/6LXB	Eastern Coach Works	B39/31F	1981	First Cityline, 2000
RBO506Y	Leyland Olympian ONLXB/1R	East Lancashire	B43/31F	1983	Cardiff Bus, 1998
RBO508Y	Leyland Olympian ONLXB/1R	East Lancashire	B43/31F	1983	Cardiff Bus, 1998
B823YTC	Leyland Tiger TRCTL11/3L	Wadham Stringer Vanguard	B54F	1985	MoD (37 KC 39), 1998
TAZ4992	Leyland Royal Tiger RTC	Leyland Doyen	C49FT	1987	Merthyr Tydfil, 1989
TAZ4993	Leyland Tiger TRCTL11/3RH	Plaxton Paramount 3500 II	C51FT	1987	Merthyr Tydfil, 1989
D283XCX	DAF SB2305DHTD585	Plaxton Paramount 3200 III	C53F	1987	Bennetts, Gloucester, 1992
E211JDD	DAF SB2305DHTD585	Plaxton Paramount 3200 III	C53F	1987	Bennetts, Gloucester, 1992
P985OTP	LDV Convoy	LDV	M16	1997	Churchfields, 2001
R222AJP	DAF DE02RSDB250	Optare Spectra	N51/30F	1998	
S111AJP	DAF DE02RSDB250	Optare Spectra	N50/27F	1998	
V444AJP	DAF DE02RSDB250	Alexander ALX400	N45/24F	1999	

Special event vehicles:

UHY384	Bristol KSW6G	Eastern Coach Works	B32/28RD	1955	New to Bristol
969EHW	Bristol Lodekka LD6G	Eastern Coach Works	B33/25RD	1959	New to Bath Tramways
972EHW	Bristol Lodekka LD6B	Eastern Coach Works	B33/25R	1959	New to Bristol
HHW920L	Bristol RELL6L	Eastern Coach Works	B44D	1973	New to Bristol
OAE954M	Bristol RELL6L	Eastern Coach Worls	B50F	1973	New to Bristol
PPH471R	Bristol VRT/SL3/501	Eastern Coach Works	B43/31F	1977	New to Bristol

Previous Registrations:

TAZ4992	D801NBO	TAZ4993	D802NBO

Livery: Cream and white (double-decks) replacing blue and white/cream

A Bus has the distinction of being the first operator in Britain to operate a low-floor double-deck when they placed R222AJP into service. This has been joined by two further low-floor DAF double-decks, including Alexander-bodied V444AJP, seen in Bristol.
Richard Godfrey

ALANSWAY

Alansway Coaches Ltd, 61 Queens Street, Newton Abbot, TQ12 2AU

5	C500BFB	Ford Transit 190	Dormobile	B16F	1985	Badgerline, 1994
2	C165VRE	Ford Transit 190	PMT	B16F	1986	Fosseway, Grittleton, 1993
6	C561BHY	Ford Transit 190	Dormobile	B16F	1986	Badgerline, 1994
	C671FFJ	Ford Transit 190	Carlyle	B16F	1986	Southern National, 1998
12	C672FFJ	Ford Transit 190	Carlyle	B16F	1986	Bayline, 1996
15	C694FFJ	Ford Transit 190	Carlyle	B16F	1986	Bayline, 1997
8	C695FFJ	Ford Transit 190	Carlyle	B16F	1986	Bayline, 1996
9	C705FFJ	Ford Transit 190	Robin Hood	B16F	1986	Devon General, 1996
14	C746FFJ	Ford Transit 190	Carlyle	B16F	1986	Devon General, 1997
16	C745FFJ	Ford Transit 190	Carlyle	B16F	1986	Devon General, 1997
	C752FFJ	Ford Transit 190	Carlyle	B16F	1986	Stagecoach Devon, 1998
	C759FFJ	Ford Transit 190	Carlyle	B16F	1986	Stagecoach Devon, 1998
	C833CVX	Iveco Daily 49.10	Dormobile	B16FL	1986	private owner, 1998
11	D910HOU	Iveco Daily 49.10	Robin Hood City Nippy	B19F	1987	City Line, 1995
10	D914HOU	Iveco Daily 49.10	Robin Hood City Nippy	B19F	1987	City Line, 1995
	D759PTU	Freight Rover Sherpa	Dormobile	B16F	1986	Harratt, Kingsteignton, 1998
	CCZ8927	Ford Transit VE6	Dormobile	B16F	1987	Cooks Coaches, Wellington, 2000
	D98CFA	Ford Transit VE6	Dormobile	B16F	1987	Cooks Coaches, Wellington, 2000
	D102CFA	Ford Transit VE6	Dormobile	B16F	1987	Cooks Coaches, Wellington, 2000
19	E486ONX	Iveco Daily 49-10	Carlyle Dailybus 2	B25F	1987	West Midlands Travel, 1997
	E202HRY	Iveco Daily 49-10	Carlyle Dailybus 2	B25F	1988	Arriva Fox County, 1998
	E203HRY	Iveco Daily 49-10	Carlyle Dailybus 2	B25F	1988	Arriva Fox County, 1998
	CCZ3164	Ford Transit VE6	Mellor	B16F	1988	Southern National, 1999
	CCZ3165	Ford Transit VE6	Mellor	B16F	1988	Southern National, 1999
	F751FDV	Ford Transit VE6	Mellor	B16F	1988	First Southern National, 2000
	F753FDV	Ford Transit VE6	Mellor	B16F	1988	First Southern National, 2000
	F871UAC	Iveco Daily 49-10	Robin Hood City Nippy	B25F	1989	Brown, Churchdown, 1999
	F590OHT	Iveco Daily 49-10	Dormobile	B25F	1988	First Southern National, 2000
	F905FHE	Iveco Daily 40-08	Carlyle Dailybus 2	B19F	1989	Southern National, 1998
	F906FHE	Iveco Daily 40-08	Carlyle Dailybus 2	B19F	1989	Southern National, 1998
	G230EOA	Iveco Daily 49-10	Carlyle Dailybus 2	B16F	1989	Arriva Fox County, 1998
	G127TJA	Mercedes-Benz 811D	Carlyle	B33F	1990	Arriva North Midlands, 2001
	H132CDB	Mercedes-Benz 811	LHE Commuter	B31F	1990	Arriva North Midlands, 2001
	K989TOD	Renault Master T35D	Renault	M8	1993	private owner, 1998

Previous Registrations:

CCZ3164	E219BDV	CCZ8927	D92CFA
CCZ3165	D788NDV		

Livery: White and orange

Route 50 plies between The Willows and Torquay centre. Dormobile-bodied Iveco F590OHT is seen on the service. This example is one of three Iveco 49-10s operated, each featuring a different body.
Mark Bailey

ALEXCARS

Alexcars Ltd, 11 Love Lane, Cirencester, GL7 1YG

516ACH	MAN SR280	MAN	C49FT	1983	MAN demonstrator, 1983
SIL1823	ACE Puma	Wright Contour	C35F	1985	Flanagan, Grappenhall, 2000
ACH69A	Bedford YNV Venturer	Plaxton Pararmount 3200 II	C57F	1985	Rambler, Hastings, 1992
RIL3702	Hestair Duple SDAK1503	Duple 425	C57F	1985	Star, Birmingham, 1999
RIL3701	Hestair Duple SDA1510	Duple 425	C55F	1987	Coach Team, Chippenham, 1999
ACH80A	Volkswagen LT55	Optare City Pacer	B25F	1988	Prestwood Travel, 1998
H39VNH	MAN 10.180 HOCL-R	Jonckheere Deauville P599	C37F	1990	Travel Taylor's, Sutton Scotney, '95
ACH53A	MAN 10.180 HOCL-R	Caetano Algarve	C35F	1991	Wray's, Harrogate, 1999
672DYA	Toyota Coaster HDB30R	Caetano Optimo II	C21F	1991	Hearn, Harrow Weald, 2001
TIL1858	Toyota Coaster HDB30R	Caetano Optimo II	C21F	1991	Peruffo, Kimbolton, 2000
SJI5028	Dennis Javelin 12SDA1929	Berkhof Excellence 1000	C53F	1991	Lucketts, Fareham, 1998
SJI5027	Dennis Javelin 12SDA1929	Berkhof Excellence 1000	C53F	1992	Lucketts, Fareham, 1998
HIB275	Volkswagen Transporter	Volkswagen	M8	1992	Reed, Windsor, 1997
LUI5601	Dennis Javelin 12SDA2122	Wadham Stringer Vanguard II	BC70F	1992	MoD ( ), 2001
ODW459*	Dennis Javelin GX	Neoplan Transliner	C49FT	1996	Coach Stop, Leigh, 2000
R851SDT	MAN 11.220 HOCL-R	Irizar MidiCentury	C35F	1997	Channel Coachways, Bow, 2001
T446HRV	Dennis Dart SLF	SCC Compass	N44F	1999	
Y69HHE	Scania L94IB	Irizar InterCentury 12.32	C53F	2001	

Previous Registrations:

516ACH	UAM932Y		ODW449	P969HWF
672DYA	J310KFP		RIL3701	E453CGM
ACH53A	H172EJF		RIL3702	C152PAB
ACH80A	E901LVE		SIL1823	B938BVH, 466YGM, B938BVH, 836FUS
ACH69A	B888PDY		SJI5027	J10DJM
HIB275	J124VDP		SJI5028	J20BCK
LUI5601	K279PHT		TIL1858	J303KFP, FIW748, J990JKN

Livery: Two tone blue; yellow (school buses)

Alexcars' vehicles dedicated to school transport duties carry a yellow livery and appropriate lettering. K279PHT is shown here and, as the lettering shows, seats 70, these being 3+2 high-back seating. The vehicle was new to the British Army and was re-registered LUI5601 in Augist 2001. *P J Stockwell*

ANDY JAMES

A R James, Priory Industrial Estate, London Road, Tetbury, GL8 8HZ

UWY83X	Leyland Leopard PSU3F/4R	Duple Dominant IV Express	C49F	1981	Harrogate & District, 1994
C113JCS	Leyland Tiger TRCLXC/2RH	Duple 340	C49FT	1986	West, Northallerton, 2000
D726VAM	Dodge Commando G13	Marshall Campaigner	B39F	1986	MoD (80KF63), 1996
E204YGC	Mercedes-Benz 709D	Reeve Burgess	C25F	1988	Rover, Horsley, 2000
F891TOY	Setra S210HI	Setra	C28FT	1989	Wings Executive Travel, Hayes, 2000
G42SSR	Iveco Daily 49.10	Robin Hood City Nippy	B23F	1989	Houston Ramm, 2001
J228JJR	Renault S75	Plaxton Beaver	B28F	1991	Bodman & Heath, Worton, 2000
N3ARJ	Bova FLC12.280	Bova Futura Club	C53F	1995	
TIL6877	Optare Excel L1000	Optare	N32F	1997	Tillingbourne, 2001
N222LFR	MAN NL222FR	East Lancashire Spryte	N42F	1995	MAN, Swindon, 2001
R30ARJ	Dennis Javelin GX	Neoplan Transliner	C53F	1997	
R57JSG	Mercedes-Benz Vario O810	Plaxton Beaver 2	B33F	1998	
R252SDT	Mercedes-Benz Vario O814	Plaxton Beaver 2	B33F	1998	Mercedes-Benz demonstrator, 1999
R807HWS	Mercedes-Benz Vario O814	Plaxton Beaver 2	B33F	1998	
R808HWS	Mercedes-Benz Vario O814	Plaxton Beaver 2	B33F	1998	
T30ARJ	Mercedes-Benz Vario O814	Autobus Nouvelle	C33F	1999	

Previous Registrations:

F891TOY	F82GGC, RIB6198, WET880	T30ARJ	T436TEU

Livery: Cream and yellow (coaches); orange and white (buses)

The current production minibus from Mercedes-Benz is the Vario, availble with two engine ratings, the O810 and more powerful O814. Fitted with Plaxton's Beaver 2 body, R807HWS is seen in Chippenham while heading for Malmesbury. This model will continue to be built within the Transbus group at the East Midlands site. *Richard Godfrey*

APPLEGATES

E F Applegate, Heathfield Garage, Heathfield, Alkington, Berkeley, GL13 9PL

MGL953P	Bedford YMT	Plaxton Supreme III	C49F	1976	Gill & Munden, Wadebridge, 1980
YPL420T	Leyland National 10351B/1R (Cummins)		B41F	1978	Arriva Southern Counties, 2000
GYE277W	Leyland Titan TNLXB2RR	Leyland	B44/28F	1981	Sovereign, 1997
OHV707Y	Leyland Titan TNLXB2RR	Leyland	B44/26D	1983	Sovereign, 1997
OHV768Y	Leyland Titan TNLXB2RR	Leyland	B44/26D	1983	London Central, 2000
BFR958Y	Mercedes-Benz L307D	Cheshire Conversions	M12	1983	Grantley & Cole, Sharpness, 1998
PHT885Y	Setra S215HD	Setra Tornado	C49FT	1983	Ball, Felixstowe, 1994
A19EFA	Neoplan N722/3	Plaxton Paramount 4000 II	C53/18CT	1986	Durham Travel, Hetton-le-Hole, 1995
A17EFA	Volvo B10M-61	Jonckheere Deauville P599	C51FT	1988	Len Wright, Watford, 1998
A20EFA	Volvo B10M-60	Jonckheere Deauville P599	C48FT	1989	Yellow Bus, Stoke Mandeville, 1998
G340KWE	Neoplan N122/3	Neoplan Skyliner	C57/18CT	1990	Home James, Totton, 2000
G485KBD	LAG G355Z	LAG Panoramic	C49FT	1990	Streets Coachways, Chivenor, 2001
A18EFA	Scania K113TRB	Irizar Century 12.37	C51FT	1995	Silver Choice, East Kilbride, 1997
R477CKN	Mercedes-Benz Vario O814	Robin Hood	C24F	1997	
V2EFA	Mercedes-Benz Vario O814	Robin Hood	C25F	1999	

Previous registrations:

A16EFA	-	A20EFA	F103CBD
A17EFA	F959RNV	G485KBD	WJI3814
A18EFA	M26XSC	G340KWE	G340KWE, HJI8686
A19EFA	C220CWW, RIB4320	PHT885Y	CPA477Y, 6348ED

Livery: White, green, yellow and red

Applegates operate two double-deck coaches, both based on Neoplan sub-frames. One was bodied by Plaxton while G340KWE, illustrated here, is an integral Neoplan Skyliner coach. During the summer of 2001, Neoplan, which builds around 2140 units per year merged with another German-based company, MAN, who built 4740 units in 2000. The new company has been called Neoman Bus GmbH. P J Stockwell

AXE VALLEY MINI TRAVEL

F M Searle, Bus Depot, 26 Harbour Road, Seaton, EX12 2NA

GBU8V	MCW Metrobus DR101/6	MCW	B43/30F	1979	Arriva The Shires, 2000
DVK489W	MCW Metrobus DR101/11	MCW	B46/30F	1980	Go-Northern, 2000
KEP829X	Leyland National 2 NL116AL11/1R		B52FL	1981	First Eastern Counties, 1999
NMW329X	Bedford YNT	Duple Dominant IV	C53F	1982	Brixham Travel, 1994
B87WUV	Leyland Titan TNLXB/2RR	Leyland	B44/26D	1984	London Central, 2001
D134LTA	Renault-Dodge S56	Reeve Burgess	B23F	1986	Plymouth Citybus, 1991
D144LTA	Renault-Dodge S56	Reeve Burgess	B23F	1986	Plymouth Citybus, 1991
E358KPO	Iveco Daily 49-10	Robin Hood City Nippy	B25F	1987	Mike Halford, Bridport, 2000
K331RCN	Iveco TurboDaily 59-12	Dormobile Routemaker	B29F	1992	Mike Halford, Bridport, 2001
K332RCN	Iveco TurboDaily 59-12	Dormobile Routemaker	B29F	1992	Phil Anslow, Pontypool, 1999

Livery: Cream and maroon

The Axe Valley fleet includes two Renault-Dodge S56 minibuses that were new to Plymouth. Now carrying the cream and maroon colours. D114LTA has migrates up the Channel to Sidmouth where it was photographed. *Robert Edworthy*

BAKERS DOLPHIN

Bakers Coaches Ltd, 88 High Street, Weston-super-Mare, BS23 1HT

1	P725JYA	Volvo B10M-62	Van Hool Alizée	C44FT	1997	
2	R372XYD	Volvo B10M-62	Van Hool T9 Alizée	C46FT	1998	
3	R373XYD	Volvo B10M-62	Van Hool T9 Alizée	C46FT	1998	
4	Y227NYA	Volvo B10M-62	Van Hool T9 Alizée	C48FT	2001	
5	T761JYB	Volvo B10M-62	Van Hool T9 Alizée	C48FT	1999	
6	T762JYB	Volvo B10M-62	Van Hool T9 Alizée	C48FT	1999	
7	340MYA	Volvo B10M-60	Van Hool Alizée	C49FT	1990	Shearings, 1993
8	SIL6716	Volvo B10M-62	Jonckheere Deauville 45	C49FT	1994	Wallace Arnold, 1999
9	SIL6715	Volvo B10M-62	Jonckheere Deauville 45	C49FT	1994	Wallace Arnold, 1999
10	Y228NYA	Volvo B10M-62	Van Hool T9 Alizée	C48FT	2001	
11	7740KO	Volvo B10M-61	Van Hool Alizée	C49FT	1983	Rowe, Muirkirk, 1986
12	Y229NYA	Bova FDD 12.370	Bova Futura	C48FT	2001	
14	791WHT	Volvo B10M-62	Van Hool Alizée	C46FT	1996	
15	UJI3791	Volvo B10M-61	Van Hool Alizée	C49FT	1988	Bow Belle of Devon, 1997
16	UPV487	Volvo B10M-62	Van Hool Alizée	C46FT	1996	
17	WJI6880	Volvo B10M-60	Van Hool Alizée	C49FT	1992	Metroline (Brents), Watford, 1996
18	NIL4981	Volvo B10M-61	Van Hool Alizée	C49FT	1988	Edwards Bros, Tiers Cross, 1997
19	L917NWW	Volvo B10M-60	Van Hool Alizée	C49FT	1994	Wallace Arnold, 2001
21	WJI2321	Volvo B10M-60	Van Hool Alizée	C53F	1989	Clarkes of London, 1998
22	958VKM	Volvo B10M-61	Van Hool Alizée	C53F	1989	Park's of Hamilton, 1994
23	NIL4982	Volvo B10M-61	Van Hool Alizée	C53F	1988	Clarkes of London, 1997
24	NIL5381	Volvo B10M-61	Van Hool Alizée	C53F	1988	Clarkes of London, 1997
25	NIL5382	Volvo B10M-61	Van Hool Alizée	C53F	1988	Clarkes of London, 1997
26	YXI2730	Volvo B10M-61	Van Hool Alizée	C53F	1989	Shearings, 1996
27	YXI2732	Volvo B10M-61	Van Hool Alizée	C53F	1989	Shearings, 1996
29	WJI6879	Volvo B10M-60	Van Hool Alizée	C53F	1989	Clarkes of London, 1998
31	NIL4983	Volvo B10M-61	Plaxton Paramount 3200 II	C53F	1986	Shearings, 1993
32	NIL4984	Volvo B10M-61	Plaxton Paramount 3200 II	C53F	1986	Whitehead, Conisbrough, 1993
33	NIL4985	Volvo B10M-61	Plaxton Paramount 3200 II	C53F	1986	East Surrey, Godstone, 1993
34	NIL4986	Volvo B10M-61	Plaxton Paramount 3200 II	C53F	1986	Shearings, 1993
41	WJI3491	Leyland Tiger TRCTL11/3LZM	Plaxton Derwent	BC52F	1987	MoD (82KF26), 1998
42	WJI3492	Leyland Tiger TRCTL11/3LZM	Plaxton Derwent	BC52F	1987	MoD ( ), 1998
43	WJI3493	Leyland Tiger TRCTL11/3LZM	Plaxton Derwent	BC52F	1987	MoD (82KF19), 1998
44	WJI3490	Leyland Tiger TRCTL11/3LZM	Plaxton Derwent	BC52F	1987	MoD (82KF24), 1998
45	XJI6331	Leyland Tiger TRCTL11/3LZM	Plaxton Derwent	BC54F	1987	Beeline, Warminster, 1999
46	WJI3496	Leyland Tiger TRCTL11/3LZM	Plaxton Derwent	BC52F	1987	MoD (82KF23), 1998
48	XJI6330	Leyland Tiger TRCTL11/3LZM	Plaxton Derwent	BC52F	1987	MoD (87KF48), 1998

Bakers Dolphin has taken many former former Army buses for use on school duties. Showing the high-back seating fitted to these buses, WJI3490 was initially built in left-hand drive layout for duties in Germany having its Plaxton body converted after disposal by the Ministry.
David Heath

52	XJI5459	Leyland Tiger TRCTL11/3LZM	Plaxton Derwent	BC68F	1987	MoD ( ), 1998
53	XJI5458	Leyland Tiger TRCTL11/3LZM	Plaxton Derwent	BC68F	1987	MoD (82KF37), 1998
54	XJI6332	Leyland Tiger TRCTL11/3LZM	Plaxton Derwent	BC68F	1987	Turner, Bristol, 1999
55	XJI6333	Leyland Tiger TRCTL11/3LZM	Plaxton Derwent	BC68F	1987	MoD (87KF42), 1998
57	XJI5457	Leyland Tiger TRCTL11/3LZM	Plaxton Derwent	BC68F	1987	MoD (87KF48), 1998
58	WJI3494	Leyland Tiger TRCTL11/3LZM	Plaxton Derwent	BC68F	1987	MoD (82KF18), 1998
59	WJI3495	Leyland Tiger TRCTL11/3LZM	Plaxton Derwent	BC68F	1987	MoD (82KF31), 1998
60	WJI3497	Leyland Tiger TRCTL11/3LZM	Plaxton Derwent	BC68F	1987	MoD (82KF30), 1998
61	RJI5716	Volvo B10M-53	Van Hool Astral	C51/25CT	1985	
65	P726JYA	Volvo B12T	Van Hool Astrobel	C53/14CT	1997	
66	R632VYB	Volvo B12T	Van Hool Astrobel	C51/16CT	1998	
72	R778MFH	Mercedes-Benz O1120L	Ferqui Solera	C35F	1998	
73	C432VGX	Mercedes-Benz L608D	Rootes	C19F	1985	Crystals, Dartford, 1990
75	IUI4360	Mercedes-Benz 609D	Olympus	C24F	2000	MCH, Uxbridge, 1997
81	YRY1Y	Bedford YMT	Plaxton Supreme IV	C53F	1982	King of the Road, Worthing, 1991
82	TAY888X	Bedford YMT	Plaxton Supreme IV	C53F	1981	King of the Road, Worthing, 1991
83	HHU146V	Bedford YMT	Plaxton Supreme IV	C53F	1980	Barnes, Puriton, 1991
84	ERB548T	Bedford YMT	Plaxton Supreme IV Express	C53F	1979	Barnes, Puriton, 1991
85	PHT114Y	Bedford YNT	Plaxton Supreme IV	C53F	1982	Stuart Palmer, Dunstable, 1992
86	KAU573V	Bedford YMT	Plaxton Supreme IV Express	C53F	1980	Barton, 1988
87	XEL542X	Bedford YMT	Plaxton Supreme V	C53F	1982	Beeline, Warminster, 1992
88	VBC984X	Bedford YNT	Plaxton Supreme IV	C53F	1982	Mountford, Manchester, 1992
89	SLH42W	Bedford YMT	Plaxton Supreme IV	C53F	1981	Capital, West Drayton, 1992
91	LTY551X	Bedford YNT	Plaxton Supreme V Express	C53F	1982	Rochester & Marshall, 1990
92	LTY552X	Bedford YNT	Plaxton Supreme V Express	C53F	1982	Rochester & Marshall, 1990
93	LTY553X	Bedford YNT	Plaxton Supreme V Express	C53F	1982	Rochester & Marshall, 1990
94	FTO552V	Bedford YMT	Plaxton Supreme IV Express	C53F	1979	Barton, 1988
96	LNU578W	Bedford YMT	Plaxton Supreme IV	C53F	1980	Barton, 1988
97	LNU579W	Bedford YMT	Plaxton Supreme IV	C53F	1980	Barton, 1988
98	LNU582W	Bedford YMT	Plaxton Supreme IV	C53F	1980	Barton, 1988
99	VNT18S	Bedford YLQ	Duple Dominant II	C45F	1976	Herring, Burnham, 1986
102	XLH570	Volvo B10M-61	Van Hool Alizée	C57F	1989	Park's of Hamilton, 1994
104	T920LEU	Volvo B7R	Plaxton Prima	C57F	1999	
105	315MWL	Volvo B10M-62	Van Hool Alizée	C53F	1996	
106	HHU31V	Volvo B58-61	Plaxton Supreme IV	C57F	1980	
107	HPL422V	Volvo B58-61	Plaxton Supreme IV	C57F	1980	Syway, Cranleigh, 1983
108	VJY921V	Volvo B58-61	Plaxton Supreme IV	C57F	1980	Smith, Buntingford, 1991
109	OUF359W	Volvo B58-61	Plaxton Supreme IV	C57F	1981	Crawley Luxury Coaches, 1991

Previous Registrations:

315MWL	N203DYB	OUF359W	FTH991W, 789CLC
340MYA	C342GSD, RJI5716	PHT114Y	DNK107Y, 6108BT
791WHT	N804DYB	RJI5716	G868RNC, 340MYA
958VKM	F758ENE	SIL6715	L962NWW
7740KO	USD224Y	SIL6716	L956NWW
HHU31V	BEU817V, 340 MYA	UJI3791	E634BFJ
HHU146V	DKG271V, 315MWL	UPV487	N205DYB
IUI4360	N698SPK	WJI2321	F672TFH
NIL4981	E622UNE	WJI6879	F552TMH
NIL4982	E220JJF	WJI6880	J461HDS, KSK501, J690LGE
NIL4983	C345DND	XLH570	F276MGB
NIL4984	C347DND	XEL542X	WFX74X, YBK605
NIL4985	C349DND	XJI6331	03KJ22
NIL4986	C355DND	XJI6332	82KF28
NIL5381	E222LBC	YXI2730	F730ENE
NIL5382	E224LBC	YXI2732	F732ENE

Livery: Blue, white, yellow and green
Depots: Locking Road, Weston; Esplanade, Weston; Cattle Market, Bridgwater; Outstation: Nalbea

BATH BUS COMPANY

Bath Bus Company Ltd, Mark House, Brassmill Lane, Bath, BA1 3JE

783DYE	AEC Routemaster R2RH	Park Royal	O36/26R	1964	London Coaches, 1997
NFB115R	Bristol VRT/SL3/6LXB	Eastern Coach Works	O43/27F	1976	Stringer, Pontefract, 1997
WOI8022	Bristol VRT/SL3/501(6LXB)	Eastern Coach Works	B43/31F	1977	Dunn Line, Nottingham, 1997
UFX857S	Bristol VRT/SL3/6LXB	Eastern Coach Works	CO43/31F	1977	Southern Vectis, 1998
BCL213T	Bristol VRT/SL3/6LXB	Eastern Coach Works	O43/31F	1978	Thorn, Rayleigh, 1997
WTG360T	Bristol VRT/SL3/6LXB	Alexander AL	CO44/31F	1979	Cardiff Bus, 1999
JWV252W	Bristol VRT/SL3/6LXB	Eastern Coach Works	B43/31F	1980	Stagecoach South, 1997
BBZ8051	Leyland-DAB 07-1735L	Leyland-DAB	ABC67D	1983	First Mainline, 2000
BBZ8027	Leyland-DAB 07-1735L	Leyland-DAB	ABC67D	1983	First Mainline, 2000
BBZ6818	Leyland-DAB 07-1735L	Leyland-DAB	ABC67D	1983	First Mainline, 2000
A931SUL	MCW Metrobus DR101/16	MCW	O43/32F	1983	London General, 2001
A940SUL	MCW Metrobus DR101/16	MCW	O43/32F	1983	London General, 2001
A947SUL	MCW Metrobus DR101/16	MCW	O43/32F	1983	London General, 2001
A740THV	MCW Metrobus DR101/17	MCW	B43/28D	1984	Metroline, 2001
E461CGM	Mercedes-Benz 609D	Robin Hood	B20F	1987	Express Travel, Speke, 1999
E471CGM	Mercedes-Benz 609D	Robin Hood	B20F	1987	Express Travel, Speke, 1999
E477CGM	Mercedes-Benz 609D	Robin Hood	B20F	1987	Express Travel, Speke, 1999
F982EDS	Mercedes-Benz 609D	North West Coach Sales	C24F	1988	Shuttle, Fleur de Lys, 2000
J601WHJ	Mercedes-Benz 811D	Reeve Burgess Beaver	B28F	1991	Arriva London, 2001
J608WHJ	Mercedes-Benz 811D	Reeve Burgess Beaver	B28F	1991	Arriva London, 2001
J611WHJ	Mercedes-Benz 811D	Reeve Burgess Beaver	B28F	1991	Arriva London, 2001
P741HND	Dennis Dart SLF	Plaxton Pointer	N39F	1996	Red Arrow, Smethwick, 1999
P742HND	Dennis Dart SLF	Plaxton Pointer	N39F	1996	Red Arrow, Smethwick, 1999
P748HND	Dennis Dart SLF	Plaxton Pointer	N39F	1996	Red Arrow, Smethwick, 1999

Previous Registrations:

783DYE	from new	BBZ8051	C111HDT
BBZ6818	C113HDT	E282OMG	E282OMG, 354CHU
BBZ8027	C112HDT	WOI8022	PVO818R

Livery: Cream and red; red (City Sightseeing).

The use of articulated buses in Britain has been slow to gain acceptance, with city services in Sheffield being the only early schemes. Three buses from that source, now known as First Mainline, have entered service with the Bath Bus Company. Pictured on a return journey from Midsomer Norton, BBZ6818 shows the Danish styling of the unit which was assembled by Leyland at Lillyhall. *Paul Stockwell*

K W BEARD LTD

K W Beard Ltd, Valley Road, Cinderford, GL14 2PD

WDD17X	Bedford YNT	Plaxton Supreme VI Express	C53F	1982	
RIL9865	DAF MB230DKVL615	Duple 340	C49FT	1986	Yorkshire European, 1997
C355ALJ	Bedford Venturer YNV	Plaxton Paramount 3200 II	C57F	1986	Newbury Coaches, Ledbury, 1999
E318UUB	Volvo B10M-61	Plaxton Paramount 3500 III	C53F	1987	Ashton, St Helens, 1995
F715RDG	Freight Rover Sherpa	Crystals	M16	1988	
F167UDG	Leyland Tiger TRCTL11/3RZ	Plaxton Paramount 3200 III	C53F	1989	
J813KHD	DAF SB3000DKV601	Van Hool Alizeé DH	C51FT	1992	Moxon's, Oldcotes, 2001
K321AUX	Volvo B10M-60	Jonckheere Deauville	C51FT	1992	Elcock Reisen, Telford, 2000
X564CUY	Mercedes-Benz Vario O814	Onyx	C24F	2000	

Previous Registrations:

J813KHD	J813KND, 5711MT	RIL9864	B502UNB
PJI7755	A332PFJ	RIL9865	C645LVH, A2YET, C604FWW

Livery: White and two-tone blue

Recently acquired from Elcock Reisen is Jonckheere Deauville-bodied Volvo K321AUX. *Robert Edworthy*

BEELINE

R&R Coaches Ltd, Bishopstrow Road, Warminster, BA12 9HQ

TIL3383	Bedford YNT (Cummins)	Plaxton Paramount 3200 I	C53F	1984	
ANZ3607	Volvo B10M-61	Plaxton Paramount 3500 II	C53F	1986	Cropley, 20
NIL9886	Volvo B10M-61	Plaxton Paramount 3500 II	C53F	1986	Eastbourne, 1997
XIB1907	Volvo B10M-56	Plaxton Paramount 3200 II	C53F	1986	Smith's, Tring, 1998
XJI6233	Bedford YNT (Cummins)	Plaxton Paramount 3200 III	C53F	1987	
JUI3073	Bedford YNT (Cummins)	Plaxton Paramount 3200 III	C53F	1987	
NIL1387	Bedford YNT (Cummins)	Plaxton Paramount 3200 III	C53F	1987	Leathers Cs, Maiden Bradley, 1998
WJI5152	Bedford YNV Venturer	Plaxton Paramount 3200 III	C53F	1987	Leathers Cs, Maiden Bradley, 1998
IIL1353	Bedford YNT (Cummins)	Plaxton Paramount 3200 III	C53F	1987	East Surrey, Godstone, 1997
RIL1203	Volvo B10M-61	Plaxton Paramount 3500 III	C50FT	1987	Bluebird, Weymouth, 20
832JYA	Volvo B10M-61	Plaxton Paramount 3500 II	C50FT	1987	Burtons
TJI6312	Volvo B10M-61	Plaxton Paramount 3500 III	C50FT	1987	Wickes
BNZ4922	Volvo B10M-61	Plaxton Paramount 3500 III	C50FT	1987	Burtons
YAZ8922	Volvo B10M-61	Plaxton Paramount 3500 III	C50FT	1987	Goodwin, Witheridge, 1997
RJI8602	Volvo B10M-61	Plaxton Paramount 3500 III	C53FT	1988	Allison's Coaches, Dunfermline, 1997
6220WY	Volvo B10M-60	Plaxton Paramount 3200 III	C53F	1989	First Eastern Counties, 2000
L694JEC	Mercedes-Benz 609D	Concept	C24F	1993	Perruzza & Daughters, Kendal, 1998
N270KAM	Mercedes-Benz 811D	Plaxton Beaver	B33F	1995	
N271KAM	Mercedes-Benz 811D	Plaxton Beaver	B33F	1995	
N272KAM	Mercedes-Benz 811D	Plaxton Beaver	B33F	1995	
N273KAM	Mercedes-Benz 811D	Plaxton Beaver	B33F	1995	
N274KAM	Mercedes-Benz 811D	Plaxton Beaver	B33F	1995	
N275KAM	Mercedes-Benz 811D	Plaxton Beaver	B33F	1995	
N276KAM	Mercedes-Benz 814D	Plaxton Beaver	B33F	1995	
N123DNV	Mercedes-Benz 711D	Plaxton Beaver	C25F	1995	Country Lion, Northampton, 1998
N460KMW	Mercedes-Benz 814D	Autobus Classique Nouvelle	C33F	1995	Maynes, Buckie, 1997
N604ADC	Mercedes-Benz 814D	Autobus Classique Nouvelle	C33F	1996	Costello, Dundee, 1997
P689VHU	LDV Convoy	LDV	M16	1997	
R767HOY	LDV Convoy	LDV	M16	1997	
V116GWP	Mercedes-Benz Vario O814		C24F	2000	

Previous Registrations:

832JYA	D68VJC	RIL1203	E312OMG
6220WY	F486LHO, 1879RU, F947WFA	RJI8602	E828EUT
ANZ3607	B505CGP	TIL3383	B448CMC
BNZ4922	D287UDM, VLT229, VLT149, D328UTU	TJI6312	D575MVR
IIL1353	D380BNR	WJI2839	C288NFV, XMR558, C288NFV
JUI3073	B692JAU, 748COF, 8327OPH, COV5V,YTT1,B512BFJ	WJI5152	
N123DNV	A19CLN, L10NKK	XIB1907	C24KBH
NIL1387	HWV904, D913JHW	XJI6233	D551NUA
NIL9886	C580KNO	YAZ8922	D202LWX, WVT818, D326GCD

Livery: White, black and tan; blue and cream(former Leathers coaches)

Bedford JUI3073
has Plaxton
Paramount 3200
express bodywork
and has been
converted to a
Cummins engine
Robert Edworthy

BELLE VUE TRAVEL

Belle Vue - Riveira Coaches

D J Folland, 2 Miglo Industrial Estate, Yalberton Road, Paignton, TQ4 7QW

PBZ9154	Leyland Leopard PSU5C/4R	Duple Dominant II	C57F	1981	Reg's, Hertford, 2001
C911DVF	Ford R1115 (8-metre)	Plaxton Paramount 3200 II	C35F	1985	Andrews, Trudoxhill, 1993
C208FFJ	Ford Transit 190	Robin Hood	B16F	1986	Hills Services, Stibb Cross, 2001
C631BEX	Freight Rover Sherpa	Dormobile	B16F	1986	Belle Vue, Torquay, 1998
D75YRF	Freight Rover Sherpa	Dormobile	B16F	1986	Belle Vue, Torquay, 1998
D586EWS	Freight Rover Sherpa	Dormobile	B16F	1986	Searle, Seaton, 2001
F212LOD	Ford Transit VE6	Ford	M8	1988	private owner, 2001
F737HFJ	Freight Rover Sherpa	Freight Rover	M8	1989	Marks, Plymouth, 1998
G264GKG	Freight Rover Sherpa	Carlyle Citibus 2	B20F	1989	Duchy Travel, Newton Abbot, 2001
H621AEE	Ford Transit VE6	Ford	M14	1991	private owner, 2000

Prevous registration:
C911DVF	KAC1	PBZ9154	HHG193W

Livery: Blue and cream

The Freight Rover Sherpa played an important role in the expansion of the minibus during the final years of National Bus. Now the oldest unit with Belle Vue, C631BEX carries a Dormobile conversion and is seen in Torquay while on a local service to Barton in April 2001. *Mark Bailey*

BENNETTS

P, R A, & D Bennett and P A Lane, Eastern Avenue, Gloucester, GL4 4LP

Reg	Chassis	Body	Layout	Year	History
RUA458W	Bristol VRT/SL3/6LXB	Eastern Coach Works	B43/31F	1981	Yorkshire Buses, 1993
EEH902Y	Leyland Olympian ONLXB/1R	Eastern Coach Works	B43/32F	1983	Arriva Midlands North, 2001
SJR617Y	Leyland Olympian ONLXB/1R	Eastern Coach Works	B43/32F	1983	Go Tyneside, 2000
OFS701Y	Leyland Olympian ONTL11/2R	Eastern Coach Works	B50/31D	1983	Lothian Buses, 2000
OFS702Y	Leyland Olympian ONTL11/2R	Eastern Coach Works	B50/31D	1983	Lothian Buses, 2000
B7BEN	Leyland Olympian ONLXB/1R	Eastern Coach Works	B45/32F	1985	Arriva North East, 2000
F318EWF	DAF SB220LC550	Optare Delta	BC49F	1988	Wall's, Northenden, 1995
F607JSS	DAF SB2305DHS585	Caetano Algarve	C53F	1989	Whyte's, Newmachar, 1994
G382RCW	DAF SB2305DHS585	Van Hool Alizée	C53F	1990	Armchair, Brentford, 1994
G247CLE	DAF SB220LC590	Hispano	B66F	1990	Capital, West Drayton, 1999
G293CLE	DAF SB220LC590	Hispano	B66F	1990	Capital, West Drayton, 1999
J21GCX	DAF SB2305DHS585	Plaxton Paramount 3200 III	C53F	1991	Yorkshire European, Harrogate, 1992
K2BCC	DAF MB230LT615	Plaxton Paramount 3500 III	C53F	1992	
J518LRY	DAF SB2305DHS585	Caetano Algarve II	C53F	1992	Bland, Cottesmore, 1997
K302FYG	DAF DB250WB505	Optare Spectra	B44/23D	1992	Stagecoach East London, 1997
K712RNR	DAF SB2700HDS585	Caetano Algarve II	C53F	1993	Perrett, Shipton Oliffe, 2000
K424WUT	DAF SB2700HDS585	Caetano Algarve II	C53F	1993	Paul S Winson, Loughborough, 1997
K34VFV	DAF SB2700HDS585	Van Hool Alizée	C51FT	1993	Jack Jackson, Blackpool, 1998
L519EHD	DAF SB2700HDS585	Van Hool Alizée	C53F	1994	Enfield Transport, Co Meath, 1998
L463RDN	DAF SB2700HS585	Van Hool Alizée	C51F	1994	Deros, Killarney, 1995
M809RCP	DAF SB3000WS601	Van Hool Alizée	C53F	1995	Redwood, Hemyock, 1996
R400BEN	Optare Excel L1150	Optare	N40F	1998	
R500BEN	Optare Excel L1150	Optare	N40F	1998	
R600BEN	Optare Excel L1150	Optare	N40F	1998	
T419PDG	DAF DE02GSSB220	Ikarus Citibus	N43F	1999	
T59AUA	DAF DE33WSSB300	Van Hool T9 Alizée	C49FT	1999	
Y200BCC	Neoplan N316SHD	Neoplan Euroliner	C49FT	2001	
Y300BCC	Neoplan N316SHD	Neoplan Euroliner	C49FT	2001	
Y400BCC	Neoplan N316SHD	Neoplan Euroliner	C49FT	2001	

Previous Registrations:

B7BEN	B256RAJ	K424WUT	K10PSW
G247CLE	TIB395T (Singapore)	L519EHD	L519EHD, 94MH3061(EI)
G293CLE	TIB...J(Singapore)	L463RDN	94KY1609 (EI)
G382RCW	G973KJX, BIB5491		

Livery: Blue, grey and orange

As the number of Bristol VRs and Leyland Atlanteans and Fleetlines declines the Olympian is now entering service with more independents who undertake school contracts. Shown fitted with the yellow school-bus plate is B7BEN which was new to United.
Robert Edworthy

BERRYS

Berry's Coaches (Taunton) Ltd, Cornishway West, Galmington, Taunton, TA1 5NA

JYA941N	Bedford YRQ	Plaxton Panorama Elite III	C45F	1975	
PYA646P	AEC Reliance 6U3ZR	Plaxton Supreme III	C51F	1976	
TVD862R	Bedford YLQ	Duple Dominant	C45F	1977	Coombs, Bracknell, 1999
UYC860R	Bedford YLQ	Plaxton Supreme III	C45F	1977	
AYA912S	Bedford YLQ	Plaxton Supreme III	C45F	1978	
XAN48T	Bristol VRT/SL3/6LXB	Eastern Coach Works	B43/31F	1978	Roselyn Coaches, Par, 1990
AJH854T	Bristol VRT/SL3/6LXB	Eastern Coach Works	B43/31F	1978	Eagle Coaches, Bristol, 1991
PIB5767	Volvo B10M-61	Van Hool Alizée	C49FT	1982	
B910SPR	Volvo B10M-61	Plaxton Paramount 3200 II	C53F	1985	Excelsior, Bournemouth, 1987
C308FYA	Volvo B10M-53	Plaxton Paramount 4000 II	C52/9FT	1985	
SIB9313	Volvo B10M-61	Jonckheere Jubilee P599	C51FT	1986	
D260HFX	Volvo B10M-61	Plaxton Paramount 3200 III	C53F	1987	Excelsior, Bournemouth, 1989
PIB4019	Volvo B10M-61	Van Hool Alizée	C53FT	1987	
E272XYA	Volvo B10M-61	Van Hool Alizée	C55F	1988	Avalon Coaches, Glastonbury, 1995
PIB2470	Volvo B10M-53	Van Hool Astral	C51/13DT	1988	
PIB3360	Volvo B10M-61	Van Hool Alizée	C49FT	1988	
F476WFX	Volvo B10M-60	Plaxton Paramount 3200 III	C53F	1989	Excelsior, Bournemouth, 1989
SIB9309	Volvo B10M-60	Van Hool Alizée	C49FT	1989	
J819EYC	Volvo B10M-60	Jonckheere Deauville	C51FT	1992	
L116NYB	Volvo B12(T)	Van Hool Astrobel	C57/14CT	1993	
L238OYC	Volvo B10M-60	Van Hool Alizée HE	C49FT	1993	
L920NWW	Volvo B10M-60	Van Hool Alizée HE	C48FT	1994	Wallace Arnold, 1997
M201TYB	Volvo B12(T)	Van Hool Astrobel	C57/14CT	1994	
N320BYA	Volvo B12(T)	Van Hool Astrobel	C57/14CT	1995	
N758CYA	Volvo B10M-62	Van Hool Alizée HE	C53F	1996	
N199DYB	Volvo B10M-62	Van Hool Alizée HE	C53F	1996	
P727JYA	Volvo B12(T)	Van Hool Astrobel	C57/14CT	1997	
R380XYD	Volvo B12(T)	Van Hool Astrobel	C57/14CT	1998	
R199WYD	Volvo B10M-62	Van Hool T9 Alizée	C49FT	1998	
R202WYD	Volvo B10M-62	Van Hool T9 Alizée	C49FT	1998	
T766JYB	Volvo B10M-62	Van Hool T9 Alizée	C49FT	1999	
W161RYB	Volvo B10M-62	Van Hool T9 Alizée	C49FT	2000	

Previous Registrations:

PIB2470	E22XYD		PIB5767	JYC794Y
PIB3360	E63XYC		SIB9309	F121GYB
PIB4019	D547OYD		SIB9313	C785HYA

Livery: White, red and orange

Displaying the lines of the T9 version of Van Hool coach product is R199WYD, the first of four for Berrys. For the British market, which traditionally builds onto chassis the Alizée continues, though an integral product is the more popular choice for mainland Europe and North American markets.
David Heath

BLUEBIRD

Bluebird Coaches (Weymouth) Ltd, 83 The Esplanade, Weymouth, DT4 7AA

CEL919T	Bedford YMT	Plaxton Supreme IV	C53F	1979	
LUA287V	Leyland Leopard PSU3F/4R	Plaxton Supreme IV	C53F	1980	Newton, Guildford, 1999
HIL2146	Leyland Leopard PSU3G/4R	Duple Dominant	B53F	1982	Court, Fillongley, 1998
UCT838	Volvo B10M-61	Duple Dominant IV	C57F	1982	Jacobs, Horton Heath, 1999
A693TPO	Volvo B10M-56	Plaxton Paramount 3200 Express	C53F	1984	Tillingbourne, Cranleigh, 2000
A191MNE	Volvo B10M-61	Van Hool Alizée	C53F	1984	Black Prince, Morley, 1991
317LDV	Volvo B10M-61	Van Hool Alizée	C53F	1985	Tellings-Golden Miller, Byfleet, 1989
654JHU	Volvo B10M-61	Van Hool Alizée	C53F	1985	Tellings-Golden Miller, Byfleet, 1988
C680KDS	Volvo B10M-61	Caetano Algarve	C49FT	1986	AERE, Winfrith, 1993
E768HJF	Dennis Javelin 8.5SDL1903	Plaxton Paramount 3200 III	C35F	1988	Lucketts, Fareham, 1992
YJI8595	Volvo B10M-61	Plaxton Paramount 3200 III	C53F	1988	Sovereign, 1995
F157DBO	Ford Transit VE6	Ford	M14	1989	van conversion, 1994
G955EUH	Leyland-DAF 400	Jubilee	M16	1990	van conversion, 1992
YJI8594	Volvo B10M-62	Plaxton Première 350	C49FT	1994	
YJI8596	Volvo B10M-62	Plaxton Première 350	C49FT	1994	
M740RCP	DAF DE33WSSB3000	Van Hool Alizée HE	C55F	1995	North Kent Express, 2001
M741RCP	DAF DE33WSSB3000	Van Hool Alizée HE	C55F	1995	North Kent Express, 2001
N859XMO	Dennis Javelin 12SDA2159	Berkhof Excellence 1000	C53F	1996	Limebourne, Battersea, 1999
P4BBC	Volvo B10M-62	Van Hool Alizée HE	C49FT	1997	
R9BBC	Volvo B10M-62	Van Hool T9 Alizée	C49FT	1998	
S659ETT	LDV Convoy	G&M	M16	1998	
T7BBC	Bova FHD 12.340	Bova Futura	C49FT	1999	
W2BBC	MAN 18.350 HOCL-R	Neoplan Transliner	C49FT	2000	

Previous Registrations:

317LDV	C334FSU	UCT838	KRV878Y
654JHU	C335FSU	YJI8594	L947CRU
A693TPO	A489YGL, TBC658, A475JPB, HFB89, MIL4687	YJI8595	E310OMG
HIL2146	OWO233Y	YJI8596	L948CRU

Livery: White, orange and blue; Travelsphere W2BBC.
Depot: 450A Chickerell Road, Chickerell, Weymouth, Dorset

The Hoare family's Blurbird Coaches business has operated local excursions since 1924. Though diversification has seen British and mainland European tours eveolve a local programme continues. Seen in Swanage on Easter Monday is Dennis Javelin N859XMO. *Simon Nicholas*

BOOMERANG BUS CO

Boomerang Bus Co Ltd, Oldbury Buildings, Northway Lane, Tewkesbury, GL20 8JG

PSO178W	Leyland Tiger TRCTL11/3R	currently being rebodied		1981	Phil Anslow, Pontypool, 2000
4529WF	Leyland Tiger TRCTL11/3R	Van Hool Alizée	C49FT	1982	Leyland Motors, Leyland, 1984
LIL9270	Leyland Tiger TRCTL11/3R	Plaxton Paramount 3200	C53F	1983	Yorkshire Rider, 1995
WLT713	Leyland Olympian ONLXB/1R	East Lancashire	B43/31F	1984	Cardiff Bus, 1999
5904WF	Leyland Tiger TRCTL11/3R	Berkhof Everest 370	C53F	1984	County (Sampson), 1996
B150ACK	Leyland Tiger TRCTL11/3Rz	currently being rebodied		1985	MC, Melksham, 2000
AAL520A	Freight Rover Sherpa (Isuzu)	Carlyle Citybus 2	B20F	1989	Carlyle, Birmingham, 1991
LIL9271	Leyland Tiger TRCL10/3RZA	Plaxton Paramount 3200 III	C53F	1989	Blackpool Buses (Seagull), 2000
G100VMM	Leyland Tiger TRCL10/3ARZA	Plaxton Paramount 3200 III	C57F	1990	Reading, 2000
RIL9773	Dennis Dart 8.5SDL3003	Carlyle Dartline	BC28F	1990	Metroline, 1998
RIL9774	Dennis Dart 8.5SDL3003	Duple Dartline	BC28F	1990	London United, 1999
RIL9775	Dennis Dart 8.5SDL3003	Carlyle Dartline	BC28F	1990	London United, 1999
RIL9776	Dennis Dart 8.5SDL3003	Duple Dartline	BC28F	1990	London United, 1999
LIL3066	Mercedes-Benz 811D	Phoenix	B31F	1990	Daisy, Broughton, 1998
LIL9267	Mercedes-Benz 811D	Phoenix	B31F	1990	Solent Blue Line, 1996
LIL9268	Mercedes-Benz 811D	Phoenix	B31F	1990	Solent Blue Line, 1996
BAZ7386	Mercedes-Benz 811D	Autobus Classique	C29F	1992	Stevenson, South Kirkby, 1998
RIL9772	Dennis Dart 9.8SDL3035	Plaxton Pointer	B40F	1994	Catch-a-Bus, East Boldon, 1998

Special event vehicles

RL2727	Thornycroft A1	Mumford	Ch20	1926	preservation
ABH358	Leyland Cub KP3	Duple	C20F	1932	preservation

Previous Registrations:

4529WF	WBV541Y, 6449WF, 8921WF	LIL9271	F700ENE
5904WF	B110KPF	PSO178W	BSG547W, WLT741, WGB176W, CSU921, PSO178W, IIB9140
AAL520A	F418BOP, 4529WF	RIL9772	L881YVK
BAZ7386	J566DJV	RIL9773	H135MOB
LIL3066	G208YDL	RIL9774	G506VYE
LIL9267	G209YDL	RIL9775	G44TGM
LIL9268	G210YDL	RIL9776	G508VYE
LIL9270	EWW947Y	WLT713	A516VKG

Livery: Yellow

Carrying a 'traditional' index mark associated with an LT Routemaster, WLT713 is now allocated to a yellow Leyland Olympian new to Cardiff. This East Lancashire-bodied bus is now used primarily on school duties, being pictured en route for Tewkesbury.
Robert Edworthy

BUGLERS

R A & S J Bugler, 100 School Road, Brislington, Bristol, BS4 4NF

PHY698S	Bristol VRT/SL3/6LXB	Eastern Coach Works	B43/33F	1977	City Line, 1993
SIB8357	Volvo B10M-61	Van Hool Alizée	C53F	1987	Premier Travel, 1993
TRX615	Dennis Javelin 11SDL1905	Plaxton Paramount 3200 III	C53F	1988	Snowdon, Easington Colliery, 1990
F432OBK	Mercedes-Benz 811D	Robin Hood	BC28FL	1988	
586PHU	Mercedes-Benz 811D	Robin Hood	C29F	1988	
HIL3471	Dennis Javelin 12SDA1907	Plaxton Paramount 3200 III	C45DL	1988	Mayne's, Buckie, 1991
TAZ6963	Volvo B10M-60	Van Hool Alizée	C53F	1989	Clarke's of London, 1998
280OHT	Leyland Swift ST2R44C97T5	Elme Orion	C37DL	1990	Gosling, Redbourn, 1991
426VNU	Dennis Javelin 12SDA1912	Plaxton Paramount 3200 III	C41DL	1990	Denslow, Chard, 1992
HAZ2963	Dennis Javelin 12SDA1919	Plaxton Paramount 3200 III	C57F	1990	Bakers, Biddulph, 1994
WDR145	Volvo B10M-62	Van Hool Alizée HE	C53F	1995	Apcoa, Copthorne, 2000
M845CWS	Mercedes-Benz 711D	Marshall C19	C18FL	1995	
P536YEU	Dennis Javelin	UVG Cutlass	C53F	1997	?, 2001
T565RFS	Mercedes-Benz Vario O814	Plaxton Beaver 2	B27F	1999	

Previous Registrations:

280OHT	G647KBV		SIB8357	D344KVE
426VNU	G366PYB		TAZ6963	F167RJF
586PHU	F251OPX		TRX615	E843EUT
HAZ2963	G653EBF, 3379RU, G143FRF		WDR145	M210UYD
HIL3471	F640PSE			

Livery: White, red and orange

The newest minibus in Buglers' fleet operates the Baltic Wharf Loop in Bristol. T565RFS was pictured as it crossed St Augustine Parade. Buglers have been long-established in the provision of special needs transport in the city. *Richard Godfrey*

CARADON RIVIERA TOURS

E J & J K Deeble, Deeble Garage, Upton Cross, Liskeard, PL14 5AX

NWW163K	Bristol LH6L	Plaxton Supreme III	C45F	1972	Bassetts, Tittensop, 2001
31907(GB-G)	Bristol LHS6L	Plaxton Supreme V	C37F	1975	Guernseybus, 2001
GHV504N	Bristol LHS6L	Eastern Coach Works	B29F	1975	LB Richmond, 1993
JSV983	Bristol LHL6L	Plaxton Supreme III	C51F	1978	Lewis, Cwmaman, 1992
DAD256T	Leyland Leopard PSU5C/4R	Plaxton Supreme IV	C57F	1979	Millmans Cs, Newton Abbot, 2001
DSD950V	Seddon Pennine 7	Alexander AT	BC49F	1979	Western Buses, 1997
DSD953V	Seddon Pennine 7	Alexander AT	BC49F	1979	Western Buses, 1997
FTO550V	Bedford YMT	Plaxton Supreme IV Express	C53F	1979	Stagecoach East Midland, 2001
BVA787V	Leyland Leopard PSU3F/5R	Plaxton Supreme IV Express	C49F	1980	Millmans Cs, Newton Abbot, 2001
751CRT	Leyland Leopard PSU3E/4RT	Plaxton Supreme IV	C53F	1980	Ford, Street, 1994
JWE244W	Leyland Leopard PSU5D/4R	Plaxton Supreme IV Express	C49FT	1980	Llynfi Coaches, Maesteg, 1998
HIL2379	Leyland Tiger TRCTL11/3R	Duple Dominant IV	C57F	1982	Procter, Fenton, 2001
CLJ413Y	Bristol LHS6L	Plaxton Supreme V	C33F	1983	MacEwans, Amisfield, 1991
GSU344	Leyland Tiger TRCTL11/2RH	Alexander TC	C47F	1985	Stagecoach Fife Buses, 1999
924CRT	Leyland Tiger TRCTL11/1RH	Reeve Burgess	C35F	1985	Chambers, Stevenage, 1999
C849CSN	Leyland Royal Tiger RTC	Leyland Doyen	C49FT	1986	Meadway, Birmingham, 2001
D241OOJ	Freight Rover Sherpa	Carlyle	B20F	1987	Henderson, Penygraig, 1998
D309PEJ	Freight Rover Sherpa	Optare	B16F	1987	Childs, Kiveton Park, 2001
E402TVC	MCW MetroRider MF150/52	MCW	B23F	1988	Llynfi Coaches, Maesteg, 1997
F92XBV	Leyland Tiger TRBTL11/2RP	East Lancashire	BC47F	1989	Rossendale, 2001
F93XBV	Leyland Tiger TRBTL11/2RP	East Lancashire	B51F	1989	Rossendale, 2001
F94XBV	Leyland Tiger TRBTL11/2RP	East Lancashire	B51F	1989	Rossendale, 2001
F95XBV	Leyland Tiger TRBTL11/2RP	East Lancashire	B51F	1989	Rossendale, 2001

Previous Registrations:

751CRT	LUA267V	GSU344	B210FFS
924CRT	B833VSR, EUE489, B276YSL	HIL2379	ARE508Y
31907(GB-G)	31909, JFH473N	JSV983	DCA766S
C849CSN	C816BTS, WLT784	MUY25X	VRJ594X, 954GAT
D309PEJ	D309PEJ, TJI6875		

Livery: White and blue

Alexander T-type bodies are fitted to a pair of Seddon Pennine vehicles purchased from the Stagecoach Group member Western Buses in 1997. Now mostly confined to contract work GSU344 was pictured at its base in Upton Cross.
Robert Edworthy

CARMEL

A G Hazell, Station Road, Northlew, Okehampton, EX20 3BN

Reg	Chassis	Body	Seating	Year	History
LSK527	Dennis Javelin 8.5SDL1903	Duple 320	C35F	1988	First Northampton, 1999
F680CYC	Dennis Javelin 11SDA1905	Duple 320	C53F	1988	Coombs, Weston-super-Mare, 1996
RJI8611	Dennis Javelin 12SDA1907	Plaxton Paramount 3200 III	C53F	1988	Bakers, Weston-super Mare, 1996
F487WPR	Dennis Javelin 11SDA2159	Duple 320	C55F	1989	Vince Coaches, Burghclere, 2000
G218SWL	Dennis Javelin 12SDA1907	Duple 320	C57F	1989	Grey, Witchford, 2000
PIL6501	Hestair-Duple SDA1512	Duple 425	C55FT	1990	Redwood, Hemyock, 1999
J2EST	Hestair-Duple SDA1512	Duple 425	C53FT	1991	Bailey, Hucknall, 1999
UJI1765	Toyota Coaster HDB30R	Caetano Optimo II	C21F	1992	Nelson, Glynneath, 2000
J877LRG	Mercedes-Benz 814D	Autobus Classique	C33F	1993	Wilksons Travel, Walsall, 1998
K807EET	Bova FHD 12.290	Bova Futura	C49FT	1993	Priory, Gosport, 2000
L225BUT	Dennis Javelin 12SDA2125	Plaxton Première 320	C53F	1994	Epsom Coaches, 2000
M505XFY	Mercedes-Benz 814L	North West Buffalo	C35F	1995	Jordan, Stourport, 1999
M582KTG	Mercedes-Benz 811D	G&M	C24F	1995	van, 1999
S18RED	Mercedes-Benz Vario O814	Plaxton Beaver 2	B27F	1999	Redline, Penwortham, 2000

Special event vehicles

Reg	Chassis	Body	Seating	Year	History
LOD495	Albion Victor FT39N	Duple	FC31F	1950	preservation, 1994
JFJ875	Daimler CVD650	Weymann	B35F	1950	preservation, 1995

Previous Registrations:

LSK527	E151XHS	RJI8611	F129TRU
PIL6501	G981OGJ, USV630	UJI1765	K999GSM

Livery Red and cream
Web: www.carmelcoaches.co.uk

The fleet of Carmel is famous for its two vintage buses that operate the Dartmoor service during the season. Normally the Albion provides the main service. Besides these buses, the fleet has gathered a number of Dennis Javelins. Pictured at their attractive Devon base is Duple 320 F487WPR. *Bill Potter*

CASTLEWAYS

Castleways (Winchcombe) Ltd, Castle House, Greet Road, Winchcombe, Cheltenham, GL54 5PU

FAD708T	Bedford YMT	Plaxton Supreme IV Express	C49F	1979	
LFH719V	Leyland Leopard PSU3E/4R	Plaxton Supreme IV Express	C49F	1980	
LFH720V	Leyland Leopard PSU3E/4R	Plaxton Supreme IV Express	C49F	1980	
G82BHP	Peugeot Talbot Pullman	Talbot	C20F	1990	Sapwell, Ashton, 1993
J362BNW	Mercedes-Benz 811D	Optare StarRider	C29F	1991	
J688MFE	Setra S215HR	Setra Rational	C53F	1992	
J689MFE	Setra S215HR	Setra Rational	C53F	1992	
86JBF	Setra S210HD	Setra Tornado	C35F	1995	
M151KDD	Dennis Dart 9.8SDL3054	Plaxton Pointer	BC40F	1995	
M139LNP	Mercedes-Benz 814D	Plaxton Beaver	BC33F	1996	Rose, Blackminster, 1999
TJF757	Setra S250	Setra Special	C53F	1996	Travellers, Hounslow, 1998
P200TCC	Setra S250	Setra Special	C48FT	1997	Travellers, Hounslow, 1999
V200DCC	Setra S315GT-HD	Setra	C48FT	2000	
W391JOG	Toyota Coaster BB50R	Caetano Optimo IV	C22F	2000	

Previous Registrations:

86JBF	N325MFE	TJF757	N205PUL

Livery: Navy blue, grey and gold

Photographed passing through Broadway while heading for Cheltenham is LFH720V, a Leyland Leopard with Plaxton Supreme bodywork that has been with Castleways for more than twenty years. *David Donati*

CITYTOUR / RYANS

M J & C Ryan, Watersmeet Cottage, Langridge, Bath, BA1 8AJ

Reg	Chassis	Body	Type	Year	History
NUD106L	Bristol VRT/SL2/6LX	Eastern Coach Works	O41/27F	1973	Thames Transit, 1989
TNJ995S	Bristol VRT/SL3/6LXB	Eastern Coach Works	CO43/27D	1977	Stephenson, Rochford, 1994
TNJ996S	Bristol VRT/SL3/6LXB	Eastern Coach Works	CO43/27D	1977	Brighton & Hove, 1990
TNJ998S	Bristol VRT/SL3/6LXB	Eastern Coach Works	CO43/27D	1977	Stephenson, Rochford, 1994
UWV619S	Bristol VRT/SL3/6LXB	Eastern Coach Works	CO43/31F	1978	Brighton & Hove, 1999
AHW199V	Bristol VRT/SL3/6LXB	Eastern Coach Works	B43/27D	1980	Brewers, 1994
NXI608	Leyland Tiger TRCTL11/2R	Plaxton Supreme VI Express	C53F	1982	Jorvik, Market Weighton, 1992
ANA565Y	Leyland Atleantean AN68D/1R	Northern Counties	O43/32F	1982	GM Buses, 1991
HIL3451	Leyland Tiger TRCTL11/3RZ	Plaxton Paramount 3500 III	C53F	1987	Shearings, 1992
RIL2102	DAF MB230LB615	Plaxton Paramount 3500 III	C53F	1988	Metroline (Brents), 1997
RIL2103	DAF MB230LB615	Plaxton Paramount 3500 III	C53F	1988	Metroline (Brents), 1997
JIL6902	DAF SB2305DHD585	Plaxton Paramount 3200 III	C57F	1988	Smith-Ivins, High Wycombe, 1997
H380XHG	Mercedes-Benz 814D	Reeve Burgess Beaver	C33F	1990	
J243MFP	Dennis Javelin 11SDA1921	Plaxton Paramount 3200 III	C53F	1992	Smith, Liss, 1998
R275LDE	Dennis Javelin	Plaxton Première 320	C57F	1998	Davies Bros, Pencader, 1999
Y446AUY	Mercedes-Benz Vario O814	?	BC F	2001	
Y138RDG	Mercedes-Benz Vario O814	Onyx	C F	2001	
Y139RDG	Mercedes-Benz Vario O814	Onyx	C F	2001	

Previous Registrations:

HIL3451	D595MVR	RIL2102	E647KCX
JIL6902	F214RJK	RIL2103	E64SJS
NXI608	NDW145X		

Livery: Red (Citytour) open-top buses; white, blue and red (Ryans) coaches.
Depot: Lockswood Road, Bath

Five Bristol VRs and an Atlantean form the Citytour open-top fleet in Bath. Pictured rounding The Circus is NUD106L, a now rare mark 2 version of the Bristol. During conversion to open-top, the vehicle retained high-back seating in the lower deck, while all-weather seats were installed onto the upper deck.
Richard Godfrey

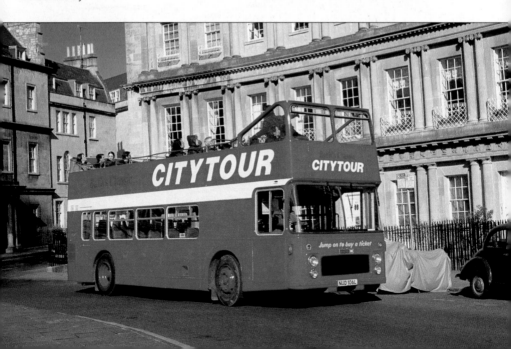

COOMBS TRAVEL

B F Coombs, Coombs House, Searle Crescent, Weston-super-Mare, BS23 3YX

UPK138S	Leyland Atlantean AN68A/1R	Park Royal	B43/30F	1978	North Western, 1997
FDV793V	Bristol LHS6L	Eastern Coach Works	B35F	1979	Mancunian, Bradford, 1993
A158EPA	Leyland Tiger TRCTL11/3R	Plaxton Paramount 3200 E	C57F	1984	London & Country, 1997
KAZ4504	Dennis Lancet SDA516	Alexander P	B53F	1984	Redby, Sunderland, 1994
KAZ4505	Dennis Lancet SDA516	Alexander P	B53F	1984	Redby, Sunderland, 1994
B289KPF	Leyland Tiger TRCTL11/3RH	Plaxton Paramount 3200 IIE	C53F	1985	London & Country, 1997
D21CTR	Bedford YMT	Wadham Stringer Vanguard	B53F	1986	Cambus, 1992
D22CTR	Bedford YMT	Wadham Stringer Vanguard	B53F	1986	Somerbus, Paulton, 1992
D23CTR	Bedford YMT	Wadham Stringer Vanguard	B53F	1986	Cambus, 1992
D60NOF	Freight Rover Sherpa	Carlyle	B18F	1987	Crown Coaches, Bristol, 1997
D327TRN	Mercedes-Benz 709D	Reeve Burgess	BC19F	1987	Miles, Stratton St Margaret, 1999
D401TMW	Renault-Dodge S56	Reeve Burgess	BC25F	1987	
G693NUB	Renault-Dodge S56	Optare	B13FL	1990	Leeds MB, 1998
G699NUB	Renault-Dodge S56	Optare	B8FL	1990	Leeds MB, 1998
H642GRO	Leyland Tiger TRCL10/3ARZA	Plaxton Paramount 3200 III	C53F	1991	Stagecoach East London, 1995
J271TTX	Ford Transit VE6	Ford	M8	1992	private owner, 1994
J272NNC	Scania K93CRB	Plaxton Première 320	C53F	1992	Shearings, 1997
J275NNC	Scania K93CRB	Plaxton Première 320	C53F	1992	Shearings, 1997
J278NNC	Scania K93CRB	Plaxton Première 320	C53F	1992	Shearings, 1997
K721HYA	Mercedes-Benz 709D	Dormobile Routemaker	C29F	1992	
K722HYA	Scania K93CRB	Plaxton Première 320	C53F	1993	
L860NYC	Dennis Javelin 12SDA2131	Plaxton Première 320	C53F	1994	

The last double-deck buses to enter service that are not low floor are from a batch of thirty Scania N113DRB with East Lancashire bodywork. This view of W372PHY was taken at its base in Weston-Super-Mare. The batch all went to smaller independent operators where a modern, seat-belted double-deck was seen to be an asset. *Paul Stockwell*

The South West Bus Handbook

Another Scania operated by Coombs Travel is N970BYC and this carries Van Hool Alizée coachwork. It is seen in Parliament Square while on a visit to London. *Colin Lloyd*

L110UHF	Ford Transit VE6	Ford	M11	1994	Pink Elephant, Heathrow, 1996
L691WHY	Ford Transit VE6	Ford	M14	1994	private owner, 1994
L692WHY	Ford Transit VE6	Ford	M14	1994	private owner, 1994
M745ARP	Ford Transit VE6	Ford	M14	1994	Scot Hire, Exeter, 1995
M572TYB	Scania K93CRB	Van Hool Alizée	C57F	1995	
M573TYB	Scania K93CRB	Van Hool Alizée	C57F	1995	
N410WJL	Mercedes-Benz 814D	Autobus Nouvelle	C29F	1995	Aztec, Bristol, 1998
N605DOR	Ford Transit VE6	Robin Hood	M9L	1996	private owner, 1998
N541CYA	Ford Transit VE6	Ford	M8L	1996	private owner, 2000
N967BYC	Dennis Javelin	UVG Unistar	C57F	1996	
N970BYC	Scania K113CRB	Van Hool Alizée	C57F	1996	
P87JYC	Toyota Coaster HZB50R	Caetano Optimo III	C21F	1996	
P89JYC	Dennis Javelin	Plaxton Premiére 320	C55F	1997	
V448DYB	LDV Convoy	Concept	M16	1999	
W371PHY	Mercedes-Benz Vario O814	Autobus Nouvelle II	C31F	2000	
W372PHY	Scania N113DRB	East Lancashire Cityzen	BC47/31F	2000	

Previous Registrations:

KAZ4504	A504FSS		L110UHF	L110SKB
KAZ4505	A505FSS			

Livery: White and lemon

COTTRELL'S

ER Cottrell, Mill End Street, Mitcheldean, GL17 0HP

GBU2V	MCW Metrobus DR101/6	MCW	B43/30F	1979	GM Buses, 1986
GBU6V	MCW Metrobus DR101/6	MCW	B43/30F	1979	GM Buses, 1986
GBU7V	MCW Metrobus DR101/6	MCW	B43/30F	1979	GM Buses, 1986
NDE147Y	Leyland Tiger TRCTL11/2R	Plaxton Paramount 3200E	C53F	1983	Horlock, Northfleet, 1988
D803NBO	Leyland Tiger TRCTL11/3RH	Plaxton Paramount 3200 II	C51FT	1987	Crown Coaches, Bristol, 1989
D160UDA	Leyland Lion LDTL11/1R	Alexander RH	BC49/23F	1987	Clydeside 2000, 1994
E478AFJ	Leyland Tiger TRCTL11/3RZ	Plaxton Paramount 3500 III	C53F	1988	Loverings, Combe Martin, 1995
F309RMH	Leyland Tiger TRBTL11/2RP	Duple 300	B55F	1989	Rover Bus Service, Chesham, 1993
F66SMC	Leyland Cub LBM6T/2RA	Wadham Stringer Vanguard 2I	B39F	1989	Arrow Coaches, Bristol, 1993
F183UFH	Leyland Tiger TRCTL11/3ARZ	Plaxton Paramount 3200 III	C57F	1989	
H651UWR	Volvo B10M-60	Plaxton Paramount 3500 III	C53F	1991	Machin, Ashby, 1998
H932DRJ	Volvo B10M-60	Plaxton Paramount 3200 III	C53F	1991	Capital, West Drayton, 1997
M9FUG	Dennis Dart 9.8SDL3032	Wadham Stringer Portsdown	B43F	1994	Fuggles, Benenden, 1999

Previous Registrations:

C474CAP	YDG616	D160UGA	D852RDS, 705DYE

Livery: Maroon and cream

The Leyland Titan and Olympian and MCW Metrobus are now being displaced by many operators. Cottrell's now use three MCW Metrobuses including GBU7V, pictured on route 24 to Cinderford while departing Gloucester bus station. These were new to Greater Manchester Transport joining this Gloucestershire fleet in as long ago as 1986. *Robert Edworthy*

The South West Bus Handbook

CURRIAN

TJ, JT & KJ Stoneman, Currian Road Garage, Nanpean, St Austell, PL26 7YD

SNJ590R	Bristol VRT/SL3/6LXB	Eastern Coach Works	B43/31F	1977	Reading Buses, 1995
SNJ593R	Bristol VRT/SL3/6LXB	Eastern Coach Works	B43/31F	1977	Reading Buses, 1995
AAP648T	Bristol VRT/SL3/6LXB	Eastern Coach Works	B43/31F	1978	Stephensons, Rochford, 1998
222FCH	Van Hool T815H	Van Hool Alizée	C49FT	1983	Waterhouse, Polegate, 1995
A600XGL	Bedford YNT	Plaxton Paramount 3200	C53F	1984	Cornishman, 1997
NIW8794	Volvo B10M-61	Plaxton Paramount 3500	C53F	1984	Kingdom, Tiverton, 1999
513SRL	Volvo B10M-61	Duple 340	C49FT	1985	Tracks, Brookland, 2000
971CYB	Bova FHD12.280	Bova Futura	C49FT	1986	Prairie, Hounslow, 1997
RIL5088	DAF MB230DKFL615	Caetano Algarve	C51F	1987	Bodman & Heath, Worton, 1998
P137XFW	Setra S250	Setra Special	C48FT	1997	Clarkes of London, 2001
R455YDT	Scania K113TRB	Irizar Century 12.37	C51FT	1998	Top Travel, Stafford, 2000
V10SAF	Bova FHD12.340	Bova Futura	C49FT	1999	

Previous Registrations:

222FCH	from new	NIW8794	A656UGD
513SRL	C770SGU	RIL5088	E704GNH, A3NBT, E237DMR
971CYB	C972TPV, FIL7665		

Livery: White; white and blue (Leger Travel) R455SDT.

Displaying Currian Holidays as it pays a visit to Legoland is Bova Futura 971CYB. Home for this fleet is the Cornish china clay country near St Austell, itself becoming a tourist attraction with the opening of the Eden Project in 2001. *David Heath*

D A C COACHES

DAC Coaches Ltd, Rylands Garage, St Ann's Chapel, Gunnislake, PL18 9HW

TWS914T	Bristol VRT/SL3/6LXB	Eastern Coach Works	B39/31F	1979	City Line, 2000
WNL382A	Volvo B58-56	Caetano Alpha	C53F	1979	Long, Heanor, 1997
WSV529	Volvo B58-56	Plaxton Supreme IV	C53F	1980	Dunn Line, Nottingham, 1992
RUE300W	Bedford YMQ	Plaxton Supreme IV	C35F	1980	Dalybus, Eccles, 1995
ENF573Y	Volvo B10M-61	Duple Dominant IV	C57F	1983	West Dorset, Dorchester, 1998
228FHT	Volvo B10M-61	Van Hool Alizée	C50FT	1984	Phillips, Crediton, 1999
C526FFJ	Ford Transit 190D	Carlyle	BC16F	1985	Guscott, Halwill, 1997
D930LYC	Bedford YNV Venturer (Cum)	Duple 320	C57F	1987	Caring Coaches, St Athan, 1998
D574SUS	Ford Transit VE6	Deansgate	M12	1987	Western Private Hire, Plymouth, 1996
E782RAF	Ford Transit VE6	Dormobile	C16F	1987	Carriage Compary, Callington, 1990
F476EOD	Mercedes-Benz 410D	Mercedes-Benz	M12	1989	St Lukes Hospice, Plymouth, 1998
G165NAG	Mercedes-Benz 609D	Coachcraft	C24F	1989	Sands Minicoaches, Shepshed, 1994
NIL5652	Volvo B10M-60	Van Hool Alizée	C49FT	1990	Wood, Buckfastleigh, 1999
H437BVU	Mercedes-Benz 709D	Cunliffe	B24FL	1990	Webber, Wheddon Cross, 1999
NIL5651	Volvo B9M	Plaxton Paramount 3200 III	C43F	1991	Dochertys Midland Coaches, 2000
N988KUS	Mercedes-Benz 814D	Mellor	C33F	1996	Lofty, Bridge Trafford, 1997
M38KAX	Volvo B10M-62	Plaxton Première 350	C51FT	1995	Caring Coaches, Llantwit Major, 2001
M41KAX	Volvo B10M-62	Plaxton Première 350	C51FT	1995	Caring Coaches, Llantwit Major, 2001
T979OGA	Mercedes-Benz Vario O814	Mellor	C33F	1999	
V54MOD	Toyota Coaster HZB50R	Caetano Optimo III	C24F	2000	

Previous Registrations:

228FHT	YWD687, A239LFH	RJI5709	G823YJF
D930LYC	D930LYC, PIL7046	WNL382A	AWB319T
NIL5651	H717FLD	WSV529	DYW169V
NIL5652	H487FGL, WIA69, H487FGL		

Livery: White, blue and yellow

Bedford YMQ RUE300W is one of the petite 35-seat Plaxton Supreme IVs that were quite common to rural fleets in the early 1980s. It is seen at the companies home in Gunnislake. *Bill Potter*

DARTLINE

Dealtop Ltd, 4 Goshawk Units, Osprey Road, Sowton, Exeter, EX2 7JG

GAF69V	Volvo B58-56	Duple Dominant II	C53F	1979	Roselyn Coaches, Par, 1997
CSU926	Volvo B10M-61	Duple Caribbean	C49FT	1984	Park's of Hamilton, 1987
LIL7802	Volvo B10M-61	Van Hool Alizée	C51FT	1984	Leons, Stafford, 1996
LIL6537	Volvo B10M-61	Plaxton Paramount 3200 III	C53F	1987	Shearings, 1993
XFJ466	Volvo B10M-61	Plaxton Paramount 3200 III	C53F	1987	Docherty's Midland Coaches, 1998
LIL8052	Volvo B10M-61	Plaxton Paramount 3500 III	C53F	1987	Phillips, Crediton, 1999
UJI3794	Van Hool T815	Van Hool Acron	C51FT	1987	Phillips, Crediton, 1999
LBZ2571	DAF SB3000DKV601	Van Hool Alizée	C53F	1987	Stagecoach Cheltenham, 1998
LIL8557	Bova FHD12.290	Bova Futura	C53F	1988	Phillips, Crediton, 1999
LIL8823	Volvo B10M-61	Van Hool Alizée	C53F	1988	Shearings, 1996
F951HTT	Mercedes-Benz 609D	Devon Conversions	C23F	1988	
KIW4489	Mercedes-Benz 709D	Robin Hood	C24FL	1989	West Glamorgan CC, 1997
F484MTA	Mercedes-Benz 408D	Crystals	M15	1989	
G800PTT	Mercedes-Benz 408D	Crystals	M15	1989	
LIL6538	Volvo B10M-60	Plaxton Paramount 3500 III	C47FT	1989	St Buryan Garage, St Buryan, 1994
G998OKK	Volvo B10M-60	Caetano Algarve	C53F	1989	Phillips, Crediton, 1999
G958VBC	DAF SB2305DHS585	Caetano Algarve	C53F	1989	Phillips, Crediton, 1999
LIL8876	Volvo B10M-60	Plaxton Paramount 3500 III	C48FT	1990	Wray's, Harrogate, 1998
LIL9017	Volvo B10M-60	Plaxton Paramount 3500 III	C49FT	1990	Stagecoach Cheltenham, 1998
J870FGX	Mercedes-Benz 609D	Crystals	C24F	1991	Crystals demonstrator, 1991
J824MOD	Mercedes-Benz 609D	Crystals	C24F	1991	
J825MOD	Mercedes-Benz 609D	Crystals	C24F	1991	
LIL9990	Volvo B10M-60	Caetano Algarve 2	C31FT	1991	Chauffeurline, Melbourne, 1995
J86LLA	Mercedes-Benz 410D	Devon Conversions	M15	1992	Peoples Insurance, London, 1994
K775UTT	Mercedes-Benz 609D	Crystals	C24F	1992	
L345ATA	Mercedes-Benz 609D	G&M	C24F	1993	
L422WHR	Mercedes-Benz 609D	Autobus Classique	C19F	1993	Shayler, Blunsden, 1994
L858COD	Mercedes-Benz 811D	Marshall C16	BC33F	1994	
M646HFJ	LDV 400	LDV	M8L	1994	private owner, 1995
M158KOD	Mercedes-Benz 609D	G&M	C24F	1995	
N1FOR	Bova FHD12.340	Bova Futura	C49FT	1995	Forestdale Coaches, 2000

Carrying a striking green and yellow livery is Dartline Coaches LIL7802, a Volvo B10M with Van Hool Alizée bodywork.
David Heath

Pictured in Exeter while waiting time before a journey to Newton Abbot, is Dartline L858COD, an example of the longer Mercedes-Benz 811D with Marshall bodywork. *Mark Bailey*

N40TCC	Dennis Javelin GX	Plaxton Première 350	C53F	1996	Stort Valley, Stanstead, 2001
P429JDT	Dennis Javelin	Plaxton Première 320	C53F	1996	JGS, Rotherham, 2001
P934KYC	Bova FHD12.233	Bova Futura	C51FT	1997	Phillips, Crediton, 1999
R964MDV	Mercedes-Benz Vario O810	Robin Hood	C25F	1997	
S671ETT	LDV Convoy	G&M	M16	1998	
S944WYB	Volvo B10M-62	Jonckheere Mistral	C51FT	1998	
S923KOD	Iveco TurboDaily 59-12	Mellor	B29F	1998	
S924KOD	Iveco TurboDaily 59-12	Mellor	B29F	1998	
S925KOD	Iveco TurboDaily 59-12	Mellor	B29F	1998	
S926KOD	Iveco TurboDaily 59-12	Mellor	B29F	1998	
W259WRV	Mercedes-Benz Vario O814	Robin Hood	C25F	2000	
Y14DLC	Bova FHD12.370	Bova Futura	C51FT	2001	

Previous Registrations:

CSU926	A728HFP	LIL7802	A644UGD, LOI9772, A149MFA
G238VYJ	G168ODH	LIL8052	E556UHS, UJI3792
GAF69V	FVO661V, 4009SC, ESN640V, 728FDV	LIL8557	E114GBB, OSU895, MIL9746
KIW4489	F896BCY	LIL8823	F738ENE, YXI4971
LBZ2571	E341EVH	LIL8876	G503LWU, A20MCW, G293PUB
LIL6537	D568MVR	LIL9990	J304KFP, 491NFC
LIL6538	F23HGG	XFJ466	D573MVR

Named Vehicles:

CSU926 *Sarah Jane*; F484MTA *Sandra*; G800PTT *Emma*; J824MOD *Caroline*; J825MOD *Muriel*; J86 LLA *Rachel*; J870FGX *Katie*; K775UTT *Sylvia*; KIW4489 *Samantha*; L345ATA *Helen*; L422WHR *Jean Stella*; L858COD *Claire Marie*; LIL6537 *Ezme*; LIL6538 *Jade Georgeina*; LIL7802 *Eileen Mary*; LIL9017 *Barbara Patricia*; LIL9990 *Tasmin Josephine*; M158KOD *Michaela Denise*; M646HFJ *Luanne*; P934KYC *Laura Naomi*; R964MDV *Denise*; S923KOD *Emma Louise*; S924KOD *Holly Kathleen*; S925KOD *June Teresa*; S926KOD *Sharon Louise*; S944WYB *Jean Daphne*; W259WRV *Helliena Victoria*; XFJ466 *Mary Ann*.

Livery: White, navy and lime; white(Majestic Holidays) LBZ2571, LIL8557, LIL8052, G958VBC, N40TCC, P429JDT

DAWLISH COACHES

Dawlish Coaches Ltd, Shutterton Industrial Estate, Dawlish, EX7 0NH

EWW212T	Leyland Leopard PSU3E/4R	Plaxton Supreme IV	C53F	1979	Kiwi, Newton Stewart, 1994
A168PAE	Volvo B10M-61	Duple Laser	C57F	1984	Turners, Bristol, 1992
A169PAE	Volvo B10M-61	Duple Laser	C57F	1984	Turners, Bristol, 1992
E181BTT	Mercedes-Benz 609D	Devon Conversions	C23F	1988	
E296OMG	Volvo B10M-61	Van Hool Alizée	C49FT	1988	North Mymms, Potters Bar, 1992
GIL1683	Volvo B10M-61	Van Hool Alizée	C53F	1988	Park's of Hamilton, 1994
F564HPP	MCW MetroRider MF158/9	MCW	B33F	1988	Stagecoach South, 1996
F512LTT	Volvo B10M-60	Van Hool Alizée	C49FT	1989	
F77MFJ	Volvo B10M-60	Van Hool Alizée	C53F	1989	
F276WAF	Volvo B10M-60	Van Hool Alizée	C49FT	1989	Ford's Coaches, Gunnislake, 1992
H920BPN	Van Hool T815H	Van Hool Alizée	C49FT	1990	Brighton, 1993
8RDV	Van Hool T815H	Van Hool Alizée	C49FT	1990	Brighton, 1993
K922UFX	Mercedes-Benz 811D	Plaxton Beaver	C33F	1992	Amport & District, Thruxton, 1994
K427HWY	Optare MetroRider MR03	Optare	B26F	1993	London Central, 1999
L182PMX	Bova FHD12.340	Bova Futura	C53F	1994	Limebourne, Battersea, 1998
L796DTT	Bova FHD12.340	Bova Futura	C53F	1994	
M587KTT	Bova FHD12.340	Bova Futura	C53F	1995	
M421VYD	Volvo B10M-62	Van Hool Alizée HE	C55F	1995	Avalon, Glastonbury, 2001
M12BUS	Volvo B10M-62	Van Hool Alizée	C53F	1995	Irving, Carlisle, 2000
M252LFJ	Toyota Coaster HZB50R	Caetano Optimo III	C21F	1995	
N201DYB	Bova FHD12.340	Bova Futura	C49FT	1996	
N202DYB	Bova FHD12.340	Bova Futura	C49FT	1996	
N231YCT	Mercedes-Benz 814D	Autobus Classique 2	C29F	1996	
P928KYC	Bova FHD12.333	Bova Futura	C49FT	1997	
P929KYC	Bova FHD12.333	Bova Futura	C49FT	1997	
R208WYD	Bova FHD12.333	Bova Futura	C53F	1998	
R209WYD	Bova FHD12.333	Bova Futura	C53F	1998	
R913ULA	Volvo B10M-62	Berkhof Axial 50	C49FT	1998	Limebourne, Battersea, 1998
R920ULA	Volvo B10M-62	Berkhof Axial 50	C49FT	1998	Limebourne, Battersea, 1998
V483XJV	Mercedes-Benz Vario O814	Autobus Neuvelle 2	C29F	2000	
W157RYB	Bova FHD12.370	Bova Futura	C53F	2000	
W562RYC	Bova FHD12.370	Bova Futura	C49FT	2000	
X424CFJ	Mercedes-Benz Vario O814	Plaxton Beaver 2	B27F	2000	
Y818NAY	Iveco EuroRider 391.12.35	Beulas Stergo E	C49FT	2001	
Y835NAY	Iveco EuroRider 391.12.35	Beulas Stergo E	C49FT	2001	

Previous Registrations:

8RDV	H921BPN		A169PAE	A880UHY, 2170MV
A168PAE	A879UHY, 3138DP		GIL1683	E629UNE, LSK808

Livery: White, red and blue; white (Majestic Holidays) F276WAF, 8RDV and W157RYB; white and blue (Leger Travel) W562RYC

Dawlish Coaches operate minibus *Devon Bus* tendered services for the local Council. Pictured in Starcross is **X424CFJ**, a Mercedes-Benz Vario fitted with Plaxton Beaver 2 bodywork on a servie 186 to Dawlish. The bus carries Shopper lettering.
Mark Bailey

DUCHY TRAVEL

Duchy Travel Ltd, 8B Silverhills Road, Decoy Industrial Estate, Newton Abbot, TQ12 5ND

PGP201L	Bedford VAS5	Plaxton Panorama IV	C29F	1973	Millward, Newton Abbot, 1999
MOU739R	Bristol VRT/SL3/6LXB	Eastern Coach Works	B43/28F	1976	Stagecoach Cheltenham, 2001
ESC847S	Seddon Pennine 7	Alexander AY	B53F	1978	?,?
XCT251T	Bedford YLQ	Plaxton Supreme IV	C45F	1978	Millward, Newton Abbot, 1999
KIW8606	Ford R1114	Van Hool A300	C53F	1979	Coyne, Redruth, 2001
LAK304W	Leyland Leopard PSU3E/4R	Duple Dominant II	C53F	1981	Treneary, Paignton, 1999
LAK310W	Iveco 55-10	Caetano Beja	B18F	1981	Millward, Newton Abbot, 1999
MIJ9795	Bova EL26/581	Bova Europa	C53F	1983	Priory, Gosport, 1999
A531MVU	Ford Transit 190	Made-to-Measure	C16F	1984	Millward, Newton Abbot, 1999
MIL3292	Volvo B10M-61	Plaxton Paramount 3500 II	C49FT	1987	Stratford Blue, 2000
E920HAR	Ford Transit VE6	Duchy	M8	1988	van, 2000
LIL6536	LAG G355Z	LAG Panoramic	C49FT	1988	Redwood, Hemyock, 1999
E222BDV	Ford Transit VE6	Mellor	B16F	1988	First Southern National, 1999
F444ENB	Freight Rover Sherpa	Made-to-Measure	M16	1988	Harratt, Kingsteignton, 1996
F71FKK	Iveco Daily 49-10	Robin Hood City Nippy	B23F	1989	East Devon, Crediton, 1998
F72EKK	Iveco Daily 49-10	Robin Hood City Nippy	B23F	1989	East Devon, Crediton, 1998
JJI5614	Mercedes-Benz 709D	G&M	BC20F	1989	West Glamorgan CC, 1997
G265GKG	Freight Rover Sherpa	Carlyle Citybus 2	B20F	1989	Orion Autobus, Wemyss Bay, 1996
G113PGT	Mercedes-Benz 811D	Alexander Sprint	B28F	1990	Arriva Cymru, 2000
G837UDV	Mercedes-Benz 811D	Carlyle	B33F	1990	Stagecoach Oxford, 2001
WDZ5236	LAG G355Z	LAG Panoramic	C49FT	1990	AJC, Leeds, 2000
H652DOD	Ford Transit VE6	Dormobile	M8L	1991	private, 1998
H987FTT	Mercedes-Benz 811D	Carlyle	B29F	1991	Stagecoach Scotland East, 2001
H989FTT	Mercedes-Benz 811D	Carlyle	B29F	1991	Stagecoach Scotland East, 2001
H176DVM	Volvo B10M-60	Van Hool Alizée	C49FT	1991	Chariots, Stanford-le-Hope, 2000
K597EKU	Iveco Daily 49-10	G&M	B24FL	1993	Smith Self Drive, Thrybergh, 1997
M829HNS	Volvo B10M-62	Van Hool Alizée	C53F	1995	Wood, Buckfastleigh, 2000

Previous registrations:

JJI5614	F892BCY	MIJ9795	CAY212Y
KIW8606	FHK496T, 214TRT, HVW991T	MIL3292	D450CSH, LS8411, D100GSG
LIL6536	F618VNH, A8SOL, USV577, F864OFJ	WDZ5236	G957GRP

The sole double-deck operated by Duchy Travel is Bristol VR MOU739R. It is seen on its usual route, the 12D from Torquay to Brixham.
Paul Stockwell

DUKES TRAVEL

Dukes Travel Ltd, Lakers Road Garage, Lakers Road, Five Acres, Coleford, GL16 7QT

TAD24W	Leyland Tiger TRCTL11/3R	Plaxton Supreme IV	C50F	1981	Warner, Tewkesbury, 1991
FSU803	Volvo B10M-61	Van Hool Alizée	C53F	1984	Barratt, Nantwich, 1995
116XYD	Leyland Tiger TRCTL11/3R	Plaxton Paramount 3500	C55F	1984	Lewis, Greenwich, 1988
H4GBD	Leyland Royal Tiger RT	Van Hool Alizée	C53F	1984	Tellings Golden Miller, Byfleet, 1992
B6GBD	Volvo B10M-61	Jonckheere Jubilee	C51FT	1987	John Morrow, Glasgow, 1995
F293AWW	Leyland Lynx LX112L10ZR1S	Leyland Lynx	B49F	1989	Arriva Cymru, 2000
H141UUA	Optare MetroRider MR03	Optare	B31F	1990	Stagecoach London, 1997
H156UUA	Optare MetroRider MR03	Optare	B26F	1991	London Central, 1998
H158UUA	Optare MetroRider MR03	Optare	B26F	1991	London Central, 1998
H175UUA	Optare MetroRider MR03	Optare	B26F	1991	Stagecoach London, 1998
H9GBD	Mercedes-Benz 811D	Autobus Classique	C33F	1991	Taylor, Nine Wells, 1999
J177MCW	Optare MetroRider MR09	Optare	B23F	1992	Stagecoach Ribble, 1998
H5GBD	Volvo B10M-62	Plaxton Excalibur	C53FT	1992	?, 1999
H6GBD	Volvo B12R	Jonckheere Deauville 65	C49FT	1994	The Kings Ferry, Gillingham, 2001
H7GBD	Volvo B12R	Jonckheere Deauville 65	C49FT	1994	The Kings Ferry, Gillingham, 2001
676GBD	Volvo B10M-62	Jonckheere Deauville	C53F	1994	Landtourers, Farnham, 1998
J302BVO	DAF SB220LC550	Optare Delta	B49F	1990	Trent (Barton), 2001
J303BVO	DAF SB220LC550	Optare Delta	B49F	1990	Trent (Barton), 2001
J304BVO	DAF SB220LC550	Optare Delta	B49F	1990	Trent (Barton), 2001
J305BVO	DAF SB220LC550	Optare Delta	B49F	1990	Trent (Barton), 2001
N201LCK	Optare Excel L1070	Optare	N40F	1996	Blackpool Buses, 2001
N206LCK	Optare Excel L1070	Optare	N40F	1996	Blackpool Buses, 2001
S750RNE	Mercedes-Benz Vario O814	Plaxton Beaver 2	B27F	1998	
Y201KMB	Dennis Dart SLF	Alexander ALX200	N38F	2001	
Y189KMB	Optare Solo M850	Optare	N34F	2001	
51	Mercedes-Benz Vario O814	Plaxton Beaver 2	B27F	2001	
51	Mercedes-Benz Vario O814	Plaxton Beaver 2	B27F	2001	

Previous Registrations:

116XYD	A614HGY	*H4GBD*	*L754YGE, 676GBD*
216TYC	E218GNV	H5GBD	J427HDS
666VHU	B551TWR	H6GBD	M26HNY
B6GBD	E218GNV, 216TYC	H7GBD	M27HNY
FSU803	A643UGD	H9GBD	J673MFH
H4GBD	B551TWR, 666VHU	TAD24W	SDG25W, 4529WF

Livery: White, green and orange
Depot: Laker's Road, Berry Hill

Two new arrivals with Dukes Travel are an Optare Solo and an Alexander-bodied Dennis Dart, the latter, shown here.
Robert Edworthy

EASTVILLE

Eastville Coaches Ltd, 15 Ashgrove Road, Redland, Bristol, BS6 6NA

LHT730P	Bristol VRT/SL3/6LXB	Eastern Coach Works	B43/33F	1976	City Line, 1993
GTX751W	Bristol VRT/SL3/501	Eastern Coach Works	BC40/34F	1980	Lewis, Long Ashton, 2000
TPD112X	Leyland Olympian ONTL11/1R	Roe	B43/29F	1982	Londonlinks, 1997
TPD120X	Leyland Olympian ONTL11/1R	Roe	B43/29F	1982	Londonlinks, 1997
TPD125X	Leyland Olympian ONTL11/1R	Roe	B43/29F	1982	Londonlinks, 1997
BPF131Y	Leyland Olympian ONTL11/1R	Roe	B43/29F	1983	?, 1998
C30EUH	Leyland Olympian ONTL11/1R	East Lancashire	BC47/31F	1985	Stevenson, Rochford, 1998
PJI5013	Volvo B10M-60	Van Hool Alizée	C57F	1989	Roselyn Coaches, Par, 1992
PJI5016	Volvo B10M-60	Van Hool Alizée	C57F	1989	
A11HOU	Volvo B10M-53	Plaxton Paramount 4000 III RS	C55/12DT	1990	Bennett, Hayes End, 1999
M862TYC	Volvo B10M-62	Van Hool Alizée HE	C53F	1994	Chalfont, Southall, 2001
M861TYC	Volvo B10M-62	Van Hool Alizée HE	C53F	1995	Chalfont, Southall, 1998
M419VYD	Volvo B10M-62	Van Hool Alizée HE	C53F	1995	
N24EYB	Volvo B10M-62	Van Hool Alizée HE	C53F	1996	

Previous Registrations:

A11HOU	A3FTG, FTG5, G717JOG	PJI5013	F533WGL
IBZ2955	E354EVH	PJI5016	G965UHU

Livery: White and blue
Depot: Albert Crescent, St Phillips

Eastville operate a number of double-deck vehicles. Pictured in Cardiff is recently-withdrawn KUI8150, a Van Hool Astromega-bodied Volvo. Buses are employed on Bristol school contracts while coaches can often be found on National Express duties. *Robert Edworthy*

EBLEY

G A Jones & C C Levitt, 158 Westward Road, Ebley, Stroud, GL5 4ST

Reg	Chassis	Body	Type	Year	Previous owner
AFH186T	Leyland Leopard PSU5C/4R	Duple Dominant II	C53F	1979	Hoskins& Davis, Eastington, 2000
LSJ872W	Leyland National 2 NL116AL11/1R		B52F	1981	Western Buses, 1998
IIB8903	Leyland Leopard PSU3F/5R	Duple Dominant II	C53F	1981	Boulton, Cardington, 1999
JEO587X	DAF MB200DKTL600	Duple Goldliner IV	C52FT	1982	Andy James, Sherston, 1993
XFG25Y	Leyland National 2 NL116LHB/1R		B52F	1983	Bygone, Smarden, 1998
XFG30Y	Leyland National 2 NL116LHB/1R		B47F	1983	Bygone, Smarden, 1998
A523YSD	Leyland National 2 NL116HLXCT/1R		B52F	1984	Western Buses, 1998
A9ECS	DAF MB200DKFL600	Berkhof Esprite	C53F	1986	Watts, Gillingham, 1996
B21AUS	DAF MB200DKFL600	Van Hool Alizée	C50FT	1985	Stagecoach Midland Red, 1996
D33FYH	Renault-Dodge S56	Locomotors	B27F	1987	Maun, Sutton-in-Ashfield, 1994
E453WJK	Renault-Dodge S56	Alexander AM	B25F	1987	Brighton, 1995
BUI4646	DAF SB3000DKV601	Jonckheere Deauville	C51FT	1988	Buddens, Romsey, 1997
G451XJH	Ford Transit VE6	Ford	M8	1988	private owner, 2000
H24GRE	Ford Transit VE6	Ford	M11	1990	Rover, Horsley, 2001
J229JJR	Renault S75	Plaxton Beaver	B28F	1991	Green Triangle, Atherton, 2000
J230JJR	Renault S75	Plaxton Beaver	B28F	1991	Green Triangle, Atherton, 2000
A6ECS	DAF SB3000DKV601	Van Hool Alizée	C51FT	1992	Hallmark, Luton, 2000

Previous Registrations:

A6ECS	J63GCX, HC6422, J63GCX	IIB8903	TUM980W
A9ECS	C588KTW	JEO587X	PFR835X, 2428WW
BUI4646	F955RNV		

Named vehicles: A9ECS *Tiger*; A523YSD *Boss Cat*; BUI4646 *Lion*; D33FYH *Pink Panther*; E453WJK *Minx*; G451XJH *Kitten*; IIB8903 *Leopard*; JEO857X *Cheetah*; LSJ872W *Felix*; XFG25Y *Whiskers*; XFG30Y *Sylvester*;
Livery: Red and black
Web:
Depot: 11 Ebley Trading Estate, Stroud

A striking red and black livery is applied to Ebley Bus Services' XFG30Y, one of four Leyland National 2s currently in use by the firm. Three are fitted with Gardner engines. *Robert Edworthy*

EXCELSIOR HOLIDAYS

Excelsior Holidays Ltd; Excelsior Coachways Ltd;
22 Sea Road, Bournemouth, BH5 1DD

Part of Flights Travel Group

352	XEL24	Volvo B10M-62	Plaxton Première 320	C53F	1999
353	XEL158	Volvo B10M-62	Plaxton Première 320	C53F	1999
354	XEL254	Volvo B10M-62	Plaxton Première 320	C53F	1999
355	XEL606	Volvo B10M-62	Plaxton Panther	C53F	2000
356	A7EXC	Volvo B10M-62	Plaxton Panther	C53F	2000
357	A16EXC	Volvo B10M-62	Plaxton Panther	C53F	2000
358	A14EXC	Volvo B10M-62	Plaxton Panther	C53F	2000
437	XEL31	Volvo B10M-62	Plaxton Excalibur	C36FT	1998
438	A2EXC	Volvo B10M-62	Plaxton Excalibur	C45FT	1999
439	A3EXC	Volvo B10M-62	Plaxton Excalibur	C49FT	1999
440	A4EXC	Volvo B10M-62	Plaxton Excalibur	C49FT	1999
441	A6EXC	Volvo B10M-62	Plaxton Excalibur	C49FT	1999
442	A1XEL	Volvo B10M-62	Plaxton Excalibur	C49FT	1999
601	A2XEL	Volvo B10M-62	Plaxton Panther	C49FT	2000
602	A3XEL	Volvo B10M-62	Plaxton Panther	C49FT	2000
603	A4XEL	Volvo B10M-62	Plaxton Panther	C49FT	2000
604	A5XEL	Volvo B10M-62	Plaxton Panther	C49FT	2000
605	A6XEL	Volvo B10M-62	Plaxton Panther	C49FT	2000
606	A7XEL	Volvo B10M-62	Plaxton Panther	C49FT	2000
607	A8XEL	Volvo B10M-62	Plaxton Panther	C49FT	2000
608	A9XEL	Volvo B10M-62	Plaxton Panther	C49FT	2000
704	A13XEL	Volvo B10M-62	Plaxton Excalibur	C53F	1997

Excelsior Holidays became part of the Flight Group in 1997 and have since adopted the group's colours. A modern fleet is maintained with Volvo being the main chassis supplier with Plaxton providing bodywork. Illustrating the Première 320 style is 353, XEL158. *Robert Edworthy*

The Plaxton Panther was introduced in 1999 and several joined the Excelsior fleet in 2000. In the summer of 2001, A3EXC is seen at rest at the Ascot Race meeting. *David Heath*

729	A10EXC	Volvo B10M-62	Plaxton Première 320	C49FT	1999	
730	A14EXC	Volvo B10M-62	Plaxton Première 320	C49FT	1999	
731	A17EXC	Volvo B10M-62	Plaxton Première 320	C49FT	1999	
805	A9XCL	Volvo B10M-62	Plaxton Paragon	C44FT	2000	
901	XEL4	Volvo B10M-62	Plaxton Excalibur	C49FT	1998	
902	N7FTG	Volvo B10M-66SE	Plaxton Excalibur	C49FT	1996	Flight's, Birmingham, 1998
903	N8FTG	Volvo B10M-66SE	Plaxton Excalibur	C49FT	1996	Flight's, Birmingham, 1998
904	N9FTG	Volvo B10M-66SE	Plaxton Excalibur	C49FT	1996	Flight's, Birmingham, 1998
905	A7XCL	Volvo B10M-62	Plaxton Paragon	C44FT	2000	
906	A8XCL	Volvo B10M-62	Plaxton Paragon	C44FT	2000	
M10	A19XEL	Toyota Coaster BB50R	Caetano Optimo IV	C18F	1997	
M11	A20XEL	Toyota Coaster BB50R	Caetano Optimo IV	C18F	1997	
M12	A18EXC	Toyota Coaster BB50R	Caetano Optimo IV	C18F	1999	
M13	A19EXC	Toyota Coaster BB50R	Caetano Optimo IV	C18F	1999	
M14	A20EXC	Toyota Coaster BB50R	Caetano Optimo IV	C18F	1999	

Previous Registrations:

N7FTG	N7FTG, XEL31	N8FTG	N8FTG, XEL55S	N9FTG	N9FTG, XEL941

Livery: Cream and black
Note: 437 is the Bournemouth FC team coach.

FILER'S

R J & I H Filer, Slade Lodge, Slade Road, Ilfracombe, EX34 8LB

JYD877Y	Volvo B10M-56	Plaxton Paramount 3200 E	C53F	1983	Hardings, Bagborough, 1995
C681KDS	Volvo B10M-61	Caetano Algarve	C53F	1986	AERE, Winfrith, 1998
C307VMX	DAF MB200DKFL600	Plaxton Paramount 3500 II	C53F	1986	Lewis, Greenwich, 1998
D128HML	Mercedes-Benz 709D	Reeve Burgess	B24F	1987	Skinners of Oxted, 1994
F404CKU	Mercedes-Benz 609D	Whittaker Europa	C24F	1988	
F32HGG	Volvo B10M-60	Plaxton Paramount 3500 III	C47FT	1989	Trathens, Plymouth, 1996
F141KDV	Ford Transit VE6	G&M	M12	1989	Couch, Plymouth, 2000
F751PPU	Mercedes-Benz 407D	Adams	M14	1989	Capital, West Drayton, 1996
RJI8606	Volvo B10M-60	Plaxton Paramount 3200 III	C53F	1989	Baker, Weston-super-Mare, 1999
MIL9750	Bova FHD 12.290	Bova Futura	C53FT	1990	Heaton, Mayford, 2000
MIL9751	Bova FHD 12.290	Bova Futura	C53FT	1990	Heaton, Mayford, 2000
K339EJV	Mercedes-Benz 609D	Autobus Classique	C21F	1992	Harvey, North Bovey, 1995
K332YDW	Bova FHD 12.290	Bova Futura	C53FT	1993	Thomas, Rhondda, 1999
L336DTG	Bova FHD 12.290	Bova Futura	C53FT	1994	Thomas, Rhondda, 1999
N751DAK	Bova FHD 12.340	Bova Futura	C49FT	1996	Dunn-Line, 2001
S139ATA	Volkswagen Transporter	G&M	M12	1998	
V957EOD	Mercedes-Benz 614D	G&M	C24F	1999	

Previous Registrations:

C307VMX	C770MVH, TJL800		MIL9751	G337HBO
MIL9750	G336HBO		RJI8606	G261JCY

Livery: various

Much of Filer's bus work has been sold to First Western National's Red Bus operation allowing the Filer family to concentrate on coaching work. Pictured outside Liverpool Street station in London is L336DTG, one of five Bova Futura coaches currently in the fleet. *David Heath*

FIRST BADGERLINE

Badgerline - Streamline

First Badgerline, Badger House, Oldmixon, Weston-super-Mare, BS24 9AY.

100-113			Volvo B10M-56			Alexander P			BC53F	1987		
100	D100GHY	103	D103GHY	106	D106GHY	109	D109GHY	112	D112GHY
101	D101GHY	104	D104GHY	107	D107GHY	110	D110GHY	113	D113GHY
102	D102GHY	105	D105GHY	108	D108GHY	111	D111GHY		

122-136			Dennis Lance 11SDA3112			Plaxton Verde			B49F	1993-94		
122	L122TFB	125	L125TFB	128	L128TFB	131	L131TFB	134	L134TFB
123	L123TFB	126	L126TFB	129	L129TFB	132	L132TFB	135	L135TFB
124	L124TFB	127	L127TFB	130	L130TFB	133	L133TFB	136	L136TFB

137-142			Dennis Lance SLF			Wright Pathfinder 320			N37F	1995		
137	M137FAE	138	M138FAE	140	M140FAE	141	M141FAE	142	M142FAE

203-225			Dennis Dart 9.8SDL3035			Plaxton Pointer			B40F	1993-94		
203	L203SHW	208	L208SHW	213	L213VHU	217	L217VHU	221	L221VHU
204	L204SHW	209	L209SHW	214	L214VHU	218	L218VHU	223	L223VHU
205	L205SHW	211	L211VHU	215	L215VHU	219	L219VHU	224	L224VHU
206	L206SHW	212	L212VHU	216	L216VHU	220	L220VHU	225	L225VHU
207	L207SHW								

228-242			Dennis Dart 9.8SDL3054			Plaxton Pointer			B40F	1995		
228	N228KAE	231	N231KAE	234	N234KAE	237	N237KAE	240	N240KAE
229	N229KAE	232	N232KAE	235	N235KAE	238	N238KAE	241	N241KAE
230	N230KAE	233	N233KAE	236	N236KAE	239	N239KAE	242	N242KAE

243-250			Dennis Dart 9.8SDL3054			Plaxton Pointer			B40F	1996		
243	N243LHT	245	N245LHT	247	N247LHT	249	N249LHT	250	N250LHT
244	N244LHT	246	N246LHT	248	N248LHT				

Reapints into the new national colours for First Group are now becoming more common. One of the early Dennis Darts, 249, N249LHT, illustrates the scheme as it works route 349 in Bristol. Low-floor versions of the Pointer carry the 'Willow Leaf' version of *Barbie*.
David Heath

251-257 Dennis Dart — Plaxton Pointer — B40F — 1996

| 251 | P251PAE | 253 | P253PAE | 255 | P255PAE | 256 | P256PAE | 257 | P257PAE |
| 252 | P252PAE | 254 | P254PAE | | | | | | |

258-264 Dennis Dart SLF — Plaxton Pointer — N39F — 1996

| 258 | P258PAE | 260 | P260PAE | 262 | P262PAE | 263 | P263PAE | 264 | P264PAE |
| 259 | P259PAE | 261 | P261PAE | | | | | | |

290-299 Dennis Javelin GX 12SDA2153 — Plaxton Expressliner 2 — C46FT* — 1995-98 — *297-9 are C49FT

| 290 | M290FAE | 292 | M292FAE | 297 | R297AYB | 298 | R298AYB | 299 | R299AYB |
| 291 | M291FAE | 293 | M293FAE | | | | | | |

1221-1230 Dennis Lance 11SDA3107 — Plaxton Verde — B49F — 1994 — Midland Red West, 1997

| 1221 | L221AAB | 1223 | L223AAB | 1225 | L225AAB | 1227 | L227AAB | 1229 | L229AAB |
| 1222 | L322AAB | 1224 | L224AAB | 1226 | L226AAB | 1228 | L228AAB | 1230 | L230AAB |

| 1505 | L505VHU | Dennis Dart 9SDL3034 | Plaxton Pointer | B35F | 1994 |

1609-1662 Leyland Lynx LX2R11C15Z4R — Leyland Lynx — B49F — 1989-90 — 1609-13 City Line, 2001

1609	F609RTC	1612	F612RTC	1631	F631RTC	1642	H642YHT	1644	H644YHT
1610	F610RTC	1613	F613RTC	1640	H640YHT	1643	H643YHT	1645	H645YHT
1611	F611RTC	1630	F630RTC	1641	H641YHT				

1714	R714BAE	Dennis Dart SLF	Plaxton Pointer 2	N29F	1997	
1715	R715BAE	Dennis Dart SLF	Plaxton Pointer 2	N29F	1997	
1716	R716BAE	Dennis Dart SLF	Plaxton Pointer 2	N29F	1997	
1717	R717BAE	Dennis Dart SLF	Plaxton Pointer 2	N29F	1997	
1728	T728REU	Dennis Dart SLF	Plaxton Pointer SPD	N35F	1999	
1729	T729REU	Dennis Dart SLF	Plaxton Pointer SPD	N35F	1999	
1730	T730REU	Dennis Dart SLF	Alexander ALX200	N37F	1999	
1731	T731REU	Dennis Dart SLF	Alexander ALX200	N37F	1999	
1741	R221MSA	Dennis Dart SLF	Plaxton Pointer 2	N37F	1998	First Aberdeen, 2001
1742	R222MSA	Dennis Dart SLF	Plaxton Pointer 2	N37F	1998	First Aberdeen, 2001

1901-1910 Volvo B10BLE — Wright Renown — N47F — 1998

| 1901 | R901BOU | 1903 | R903BOU | 1905 | R905BOU | 1907 | R907BOU | 1909 | R909BOU |
| 1902 | R902BOU | 1904 | R904BOU | 1906 | R906BOU | 1908 | R908BOU | 1910 | R910BOU |

| 1911 | R460VOP | Volvo B10BLE | Wright Renown | N44F | 1997 | Volvo demonstrator, 1999 |

1912-1920 Volvo B10BLE — Wright Renown — N47F — 1998

| 1912 | R912BOU | 1914 | R914BOU | 1916 | R916BOU | 1918 | R918BOU | 1920 | R920COU |
| 1913 | R913BOU | 1915 | R915BOU | 1917 | R917BOU | 1919 | R919BOU | | |

2500	D500GHY	Volvo B10M-61	Van Hool Alizée	C48FT	1987	
2501	D501GHY	Volvo B10M-61	Van Hool Alizée	C53F	1987	
2503	D503GHY	Volvo B10M-61	Van Hool Alizée	C48FT	1987	
2564	TDZ3265	Volvo B10M-60	Plaxton Expressliner 2	C46FT	1993	First Wessex, 2001
2567	865GAT	Volvo B10M-60	Plaxton Expressliner 2	C46FT	1993	First Wessex, 2001
2600	WYY752	Volvo B10M-61	Van Hool Alizée	C57F	1987	First Cityline, 2001
2601	LSU788	Volvo B10M-61	Van Hool Alizée	C57F	1987	First Cityline, 2001

3610-3616 Leyland Lynx LX2R11C15Z4R — Leyland Lynx — B49F — 1990 — First Cityline, 2001

| 3610 | H610YTC | 3612 | H612YTC | 3614 | H614YTC | 3615 | H615YTC | 3616 | H616YTC |
| 3611 | H611YTC | 3613 | H613YTC | | | | | | |

3800-3822 Mercedes-Benz 811D — Optare StarRider — B31F* — 1988 — *3819 is BC29F

| 3801 | E801MOU | 3806 | E806MOU | 3811w | E811MOU | 3814w | E814MOU | 3819w | E819MOU |
| 3802 | E802MOU | 3810w | E810MOU | 3813w | E813MOU | 3816w | E816MOU | | |

The Dennis Lance with Plaxton Verde bodywork was purchased by the Badgerline group for its fleets just prior to the merger with GRT and the formation of FirstBus. New to Midland Red West, 1223, L223AAB is seen in Bath carrying Badgerline green and yellow. *Richard Godfrey*

3850-3866

	Mercedes-Benz 709D			Reeve Burgess Beaver		B23F		1991-92	
3850	J850FTC	3854	J854FTC	3858	J858FTC	3861	J861HWS	3864	J864HWS
3851	J851FTC	3855	J855FTC	3859	J859FTC	3862	J862HWS	3865	J865HWS
3852	J852FTC	3857	J857FTC	3860	J860HWS	3863	J863HWS	3866	J866HWS
3853	J853FTC								

3867-3876

	Mercedes-Benz 709D			Plaxton Beaver		B23F		1993	
3867	K867NEU	3869	K869NEU	3871	K871NEU	3873	K873NEU	3875	K875NEU
3868	K868NEU	3870	K870NEU	3872	K872NEU	3874	K874NEU	3876	K876NEU

3877	L877TFB	Mercedes-Benz 711D	Plaxton Beaver	B23F	1993	

3878-3908

	Mercedes-Benz 709D			Plaxton Beaver		B23F		1994	
3878	L878VHT	3884	L884VHT	3891	L891VHT	3897	L897VHT	3904	L904VHT
3879	L879VHT	3885	L885VHT	3892	L892VHT	3899	L899VHT	3905	L905VHT
3880	L880VHT	3886	L886VHT	3893	L893VHT	3901	L901VHT	3906	L906VHT
3881	L881VHT	3887	L887VHT	3894	L894VHT	3902	L902VHT	3907	L907VHT
3882	M882BEU	3889	L889VHT	3895	L895VHT	3903	L903VHT	3908	L908VHT
3883	L883VHT	3890	L890VHT	3896	L896VHT				

3912	E694UND	Mercedes-Benz 609D	Made-to-Measure	B21F	1987	Durbin, 1996
3913	F850TCW	Mercedes-Benz 609D	Reeve Burgess Beaver	B20F	1988	Clapton Cs, Radstock, 1994
3914	J850OBV	Mercedes-Benz 709D	Plaxton Beaver	B23F	1992	Clapton Cs, Radstock, 1994
3915	L390UHU	Mercedes-Benz 709D	Plaxton Beaver	B23F	1993	Clapton Cs, Radstock, 1994
3916	K29OEU	Mercedes-Benz 709D	Wright NimBus	B29F	1993	Somerbus, Poulton, 1994
3917	K922VDV	Iveco TurboDaily 59-12	Mellor Duet	B26F	1993	First Hampshire, 2000
3934	L434XRF	Mercedes-Benz 709D	Plaxton Beaver	B24F	1992	First PMT. 2001
3936	Y36HBT	Optare Solo M850	Optare	N29F	2001	
3937	Y37HBT	Optare Solo M850	Optare	N29F	2001	
3938	Y38HBT	Optare Solo M850	Optare	N29F	2001	
3939	Y39HBT	Optare Solo M850	Optare	N29F	2001	
3941	L441XRF	Mercedes-Benz 709D	Plaxton Beaver	B24F	1992	First PMT. 2001
3942	L442XRF	Mercedes-Benz 709D	Plaxton Beaver	B24F	1992	First PMT. 2001
3954	L554LVT	Mercedes-Benz 709D	Marshall C19	B23F	1994	First PMT. 2001
3955	L455LVT	Mercedes-Benz 709D	Marshall C19	B23F	1994	First PMT. 2001
3956	L556LVT	Mercedes-Benz 709D	Marshall C19	B23F	1994	First PMT. 2001
3957	L557LVT	Mercedes-Benz 709D	Marshall C19	B23F	1994	First PMT. 2001

3974	N574CEH	Mercedes-Benz 709D	Plaxton Beaver	B22F	1995	First PMT. 2001
3994	L494HRE	Mercedes-Benz 709D	Dormobile Routemaker	B24F	1993	First PMT. 2001
3995	L495HRE	Mercedes-Benz 709D	Dormobile Routemaker	B24F	1993	First PMT. 2001

5700-5711   Volvo Citybus B10M-50   Alexander RH   BC47/35F 1987

5700	D700GHY	5703	D703GHY	5706	D706GHY	5708	D708GHY	5710	D710GHY
5701	D701GHY	5704	D704GHY	5707	D707GHY	5709	D709GHY	5711	D711GHY
5702	D702GHY	5705	D705GHY						

5714	E217BTA	Volvo Citybus B10M-50	Alexander RH	BC47/35F	1988	Western National, 1989
7801	L801SAE	Mercedes-Benz 709D	Plaxton Beaver	B22F	1994	First City Line, 2001
7802	L802SAE	Mercedes-Benz 709D	Plaxton Beaver	B22F	1994	First City Line, 2001
7835	M835ATC	Mercedes-Benz 709D	Plaxton Beaver	B22F	1994	
7836	M836ATC	Mercedes-Benz 709D	Plaxton Beaver	B22F	1994	
7843	M843ATC	Mercedes-Benz 709D	Plaxton Beaver	B22F	1994	
7858	M858ATC	Mercedes-Benz 709D	Plaxton Beaver	B22F	1994	First City Line, 2001
8201	X201HAE	Dennis Dart SLF	Plaxton Pointer MPD	N29F	2000	
8202	X202HAE	Dennis Dart SLF	Plaxton Pointer MPD	N29F	2000	
8203	X203HAE	Dennis Dart SLF	Plaxton Pointer MPD	N29F	2000	
8300	P829KTP	Iveco TurboDaily 59-12	UVG CitiStar	B25F	1996	Streamline, Bath, 1997
8301	P828KTP	Iveco TurboDaily 59-12	UVG CitiStar	B25F	1996	Streamline, Bath, 1997
8302	N34FWU	DAF DE02LTSB220	Ikarus Citibus	B49F	1996	Streamline, Bath, 1997
8303	N28FWU	DAF DE02LTSB220	Ikarus Citibus	B49F	1996	Streamline, Bath, 1997
8304	N29FWU	DAF DE02LTSB220	Ikarus Citibus	B49F	1996	Streamline, Bath, 1997
8305	M606RCP	DAF SB220LT550	Ikarus Citibus	B49F	1995	Streamline, Bath, 1997
8306	M968USC	Mercedes-Benz 814D	Plaxton Beaver	C33F	1994	Streamline, Bath, 1997
8307	M45BEG	Mercedes-Benz 811D	Marshall C16	B31F	1994	Streamline, Bath, 1997
8308	M46BEG	Mercedes-Benz 811D	Marshall C16	B31F	1994	Streamline, Bath, 1997
8309	M857XHY	Mercedes-Benz 811D	Marshall C16	B31F	1994	Streamline, Bath, 1997
8310	M48BEG	Mercedes-Benz 811D	Marshall C16	B31F	1994	Streamline, Bath, 1997
8311	K690UFV	Mercedes-Benz 709D	Plaxton Beaver	B23F	1993	Streamline, Bath, 1997
8312	K691UFV	Mercedes-Benz 709D	Plaxton Beaver	B23F	1993	Streamline, Bath, 1997
8313	K692UFV	Mercedes-Benz 709D	Plaxton Beaver	B23F	1993	Streamline, Bath, 1997
8314	K693UFV	Mercedes-Benz 709D	Plaxton Beaver	B23F	1993	Streamline, Bath, 1997
8315	K694UFV	Mercedes-Benz 709D	Plaxton Beaver	B23F	1993	Streamline, Bath, 1997
8600	RTH931S	Bristol VRT/SL3/501(6LXB)	Eastern Coach Works	CO43/31F	1977	SWT, 1991
8605	VDV143S	Bristol VRT/SL3/6LXB	Eastern Coach Works	CO43/31F	1978	Western National, 1993
8606	VDV137S	Bristol VRT/SL3/6LXB	Eastern Coach Works	CO43/31F	1977	Western National, 1990
8608	UFX860S	Bristol VRT/SL3/6LXB	Eastern Coach Works	CO43/31F	1977	Southern Vectis, 1983

8609-8614   Leyland Olympian ONLXB/1R   Roe   CO47/29F 1984

8609	A809THW	8611	A811THW	8612	A812THW	8613	A813THW	8614	A814THW
8610	A810THW								

8615	JHW107P	Bristol VRT/SL3/6LXB	Eastern Coach Works	O43/29F	1975	
8616	JHW108P	Bristol VRT/SL3/6LXB	Eastern Coach Works	O43/29F	1975	
8617	JHW109P	Bristol VRT/SL3/6LXB	Eastern Coach Works	O43/29F	1975	
8620	LEU256P	Bristol VRT/SL3/6LXB	Eastern Coach Works	O43/27D	1976	
8621	LEU269P	Bristol VRT/SL3/6LXB	Eastern Coach Works	O43/27D	1976	
8656	A756VAF	Leyland Olympian ONLXB/1R	Eastern Coach Works	BC43/31F	1983	Western National, 1997
8657	A757VAF	Leyland Olympian ONLXB/1R	Eastern Coach Works	BC43/31F	1983	Western National, 1997
8980	V980XUB	Optare Solo M850	Optare	N30F	2000	

9005-9010   Leyland Olympian ONCL10/1RZ   Leyland   B47/31F* 1989   *9009/10 are BC43/29F

9005	G905TWS	9007	G907TWS	9008	G908TWS	9009	G909TWS	9010	G910TWS
9006	G906TWS								

9501-9568   Leyland Olympian ONLXB/1R   Roe   B47/29F 1982-84

9501	JHU900X	9509	JHU908X	9515	JHU914X	9532	NTC131Y	9538	NTC137Y
9502	JHU901X	9510	JHU909X	9516	LWS32Y	9534	NTC133Y	9564w	A964THW
9506	JHU905X	9511	JHU910X	9530	NTC129Y	9535	NTC134Y	9566	A966THW
9507	JHU906X	9512	JHU911X	9531	NTC130Y	9536	NTC135Y	9568w	A968THW
9508	JHU907X	9514	JHU913X						

9649-9654   Volvo Olympian YN2RC16Z4   Northern Counties Palatine II B47/29F   1994   First City LIne, 2001

9649	L649SEU	9651	L651SEU	9652	L652SEU	9653	L653SEU	9654	L654SEU
9650	L650SEU								

Bath is the location for this view of Northern Counties Palatine-bodied Volvo Olympian 9651, L651SEU. New to City Line, the vehicle was re-allocated to Badgerline duties under First Bristol. *Richard Godfrey*

9655-9660

Volvo Olympian | Northern Counties Palatine II | B43/29F | 1997

9655	P655UFB	9657	P657UFB	9658	P658UFB	9659	P659UFB	9660	P660UFB
9656	P656UFB							

9688	S688AAE	Volvo Olympian	Northern Counties Palatine II BC47/29F	1998
9689	S689AAE	Volvo Olympian	Northern Counties Palatine II BC47/29F	1998
9690	S690AAE	Volvo Olympian	Northern Counties Palatine II BC47/29F	1998
9691	S691AAE	Volvo Olympian	Northern Counties Palatine II BC47/29F	1998

9709-9717

Dennis Trident | East Lancashire Lolyne | N49/30F | 2000

9709	W709RHT	9712	W712RHT	9714	W714RHT	9716	W716RHT	9717	W717RHT
9711	W711RHT	9713	W713RHT	9715	W715RHT			

Ancillary vehicles:-

43	HRO987V	Bedford YMT	Duple Dominant II	TV	1979	
45	KKW525W	Bedford YMT	Duple Dominant II	TV	1981	
46	EKU75V	Bedford YMT	Duple Dominant II	TV	1980	Billies, Mexborough, 1992
4944	E944LAE	Iveco Daily 49.10	Robin Hood City Nippy	TV	1987	Wessex, 1998
7468	C468BHY	Mercedes-Benz L608D	Reeve Burgess	TV	1986	
8158	C158TLF	Volvo B9M	Plaxton Paramount 3200 II	TV	1985	Capital, West Drayton, 1997
8159	C159TLF	Volvo B9M	Plaxton Paramount 3200 II	TV	1985	Capital, West Drayton, 1997
8317	G229EOA	Iveco Daily 49.10	Carlyle Dailybus 2	TV	1989	
8752	E752YDY	Volvo B9M	Plaxton Paramount 3200 III	TV	1988	Hallmark, 1998

Heritage vehicle:-

8583	GHT127	Bristol K5G	Eastern Coach Works	O33/26R	1941

Previous Registrations:

LSU788	D601GHY	TDZ3265	L64UOU
865GAT	L67UOU	WYY752	D600GHY

Badgerline 1904, R804BOU is seen leaving Wells bus station as it heads for Yeovil. Over three hundred of this low floor variant of the B10 are now in FirstGroup service. *Bill Potter*

Allocations:

Bath (Western Island, Lower Bristol Road)

Outstations:	Chippenham, Colerne, Devizes, Frome, Melksham, Radstock and Trowbridge						
Iveco	8300	8301					
Mercedes-Benz	3801	3806	3850	3867	3868	3870	3871	3872
	3873	3874	3875	3876	3877	3878	3879	3880
	3881	3882	3883	3884	3885	3886	3887	3889
	3890	3891	3892	3893	3894	3895	3896	3912
	3913	3915	3916	3955	3957	3974	7901	7802
	7835	8306	8310	8315				
Solo	8980							
Dart	203	209	211	212	213	214	215	216
	217	218	219	220	221	223	224	225
	232	233	234	235	236	237	238	239
	240	1714	1715	1716	1717	1726	1727	1728
	1729	1730	1731	1741	1742	8201	8202	8203
Lance	134	135	136	142	1221	1222	1223	1225
	1229	1230						
Lynx	1630	1640	1641	1642				
Volvo B10M bus	105	106	107	108	109	110		
Volvo B10B	1911	1914	1916	1917	1918	1919	1920	
DAF/Ikarus	8302	8303	8304	8305				
Javelin Expressliner	290	291	292	293	297	298	299	
Volvo B10M coach	2501	2503	2564	2567				
Bristol K	8583							
Bristol VR	8600	8605	8606	8608	8615	8616	8620	8621
Olympian	8656	8657	9005	9006	9007	9008	9009	9010
	9506	9515	9535	9536	9538	9650	9651	9652
	9654							
Trident	9709	9711	9712	9713	9714	9715	9716	9717

Bristol (Marlborough Street)

Mercedes-Benz	3897	3941	3954	3956	3994	3995	7858	8307
	8308	8309	8313	8314				
Solo	3936	3937	3938	3939				
Dart	204	205	207	208	242	244	245	246
	247	248	249	250	251	252	253	254
	255	1505						
Volvo B10M bus	102	113						
Lance	124	125	126	127	128	129	130	131
	132	133	1224	1226	1227	1228		
Lynx	1609	1610	1612	1613				
Volvo B10B	1901	1910	1912	1913				
Volvo B10M coach	2500	2600						
Olympian	8614	9507	9510	9511	9512	9514	9516	9530
	9531	9532	9534	9564	9566	9653	9655	9656
	9657	9658	9659	9660				

Wells (Prior Road)

Mercedes-Benz	3899	3904	3906	3907	3908			
Dart	206	228						
Lynx	3615	3616						
Volvo B10M bus	100	101						
Volvo B10B	1902	1903	1904	1905	1906	1907	1908	1909
	1915							

Weston-super-Mare (Searle Crescent)

Mercedes-Benz	3802	3851	3852	3853	3854	3855	3857	3858
	3859	3860	3861	3862	3863	3864	3865	3866
	3869	3901	3902	3903	3905	3934	3942	7836
	7843							
Dart	204	229	230	231	241	243	256	257
	258	259	260	261	262	263	264	
Lance	122	123	137	138	140	141		
Lynx	1611	1631	1643	1644	1645	3610	3611	3612
	3613	3614						
Volvo B10M bus	103	104	111	112				
Bristol VR	8617							
Volvo Citybus	5700	5701	5702	5703	5704	5705	5706	5707
	5708	5709	5710	5711	5714			
Olympian	8609	8610	8611	8612	8613	9501	9502	9508
	9509	9688	9689	9690	9691			

Unallocated

Mercedes-Benz	3819	3914	8311	8312
Volvo B10M coach	2601			

FIRST CITY LINE

City Line

First Bristol Buses Ltd, Enterprise House, Easton Road, Bristol, BS5 0DZ

1503-1508	Dennis Dart 9SDL3034	Plaxton Pointer	B35F	1994	
1503 L503VHU	1504 L504VHU	1506 L506VHU	1507 L507VHU	1508 L508VHU	

1509-1547	Dennis Dart 9SDL3053	Plaxton Pointer	B35F	1995	
1509 M509DHU	1517 M517DHU	1525 M525FFB	1533 M533FFB	1541 N541HAE	
1510 M510DHU	1518 M518DHU	1526 M526FFB	1534 M534FFB	1542 N542HAE	
1511 M511DHU	1519 M519DHU	1527 M527FFB	1535 M535FFB	1543 N543HAE	
1512 M512DHU	1520 M520FFB	1528 M528FFB	1536 M536FFB	1544 N544HAE	
1513 M513DHU	1521 M521FFB	1529 M529FFB	1537 M537FFB	1545 N545HAE	
1514 M514DHU	1522 M522FFB	1530 M530FFB	1538 M538FFB	1546 N546HAE	
1515 M515DHU	1523 M523FFB	1531 M531FFB	1539 N539HAE	1547 N547HAE	
1516 M516DHU	1524 M524FFB	1532 M532FFB	1540 N540HAE		

1548	N548HAE	Dennis Dart 9SDL3053	Plaxton Pointer	B35F	1996	CNG development unit.

1549-1559	Dennis Dart	Plaxton Pointer	B35F	1996	
1549 N549LHU	1551 N551LHU	1553 N553LHU	1556 N556LHU	1558 N558LHU	
1550 N550LHU	1552 N552LHU	1554 N554LHU	1557 N557LHU	1559 N559LHU	

1600-1662	Leyland Lynx LX2R11C15Z4R	Leyland Lynx	B49F	1989-90	
1600 F600RTC	1621 F621RTC	1636 H636YHT	1649 H649YHT	1656 H656YHT	
1614 F614RTC	1622 F622RTC	1637 H637YHT	1650 H650YHT	1657 H657YHT	
1615 F615RTC	1623 F623RTC	1638 H638YHT	1651 H651YHT	1658 H658YHT	
1616 F616RTC	1624 F624RTC	1639 H639YHT	1652 H652YHT	1659 H659YHT	
1617 F617RTC	1625 F625RTC	1646 H646YHT	1653 H653YHT	1660 H660YHT	
1618 F618RTC	1632 F632RTC	1647 H647YHT	1654 H654YHT	1661 H661YHT	
1619 F619RTC	1633 H633YHT	1648 H648YHT	1655 H655YHT	1662 H662YHT	
1620 F621RTC	1634 H634YHT				

Along with the Dennis dart, FirstGroup have also purchased the Volvo B6 to meet its midi-bus needs. Twenty-two with Wright Crusader 2 bodywork joined the City Line fleet in 2000, and 1813, W813PFB, is seen passing along The Haymarket in Bristol while heading for Cribbs Causeway.
Mark Lyons

An early example of a City Line Lynx to receive the new colours is 1615, F615RTC. The Lynx are allocated to all the Bristol depots including Hengrove where this example is based. *Paul Stockwell*

1701-1718

	Dennis Dart SLF		Plaxton Pointer 2		N29F	1997		

1701	R701BAE	**1704**	R704BAE	**1707**	R707BAE	**1710**	R710BAE	**1713**	R713BAE
1702	R702BAE	**1705**	R705BAE	**1708**	R708BAE	**1711**	R711BAE	**1718**	R718BAE
1703	R703BAE	**1706**	R706BAE	**1709**	R709BAE	**1712**	R712BAE		

1719	R719RAD	Dennis Dart SLF (CNG)	Plaxton Pointer MPD	N29F	1998	

1720-1725

	Dennis Dart SLF		Plaxton Pointer SPD	N35F	1998-99	

1720	S720AFB	**1722**	S722AFB	**1723**	S723AFB	**1724**	S724AFB	**1725**	S725AFB
1721	S721AFB								

1732-1738

	Dennis Dart SLF		Alexander ALX200	N36F	2000	

1732	V732FAE	**1734**	V734FAE	**1736**	V736FAE	**1737**	V737FAE	**1738**	V738FAE
1733	V733FAE	**1735**	V735FAE						

1801	T801RHW	Volvo B6BLE	Wright Crusader 2	N36F	1999	
1810	V810EFB	Volvo B6BLE	Wright Crusader 2	N36F	1999	Badgerline, 2001

1811-1834

	Volvo B6BLE		Wright Crusader 2	N36F	2000	

1811	W811PFB	**1816**	W816PFB	**1822**	W822PFB	**1826**	W826PFB	**1831**	W831PFB
1812	W812PFB	**1817**	W817PFB	**1823**	W823PFB	**1827**	W827PFB	**1832**	W832PFB
1813	W813PFB	**1818**	W818PFB	**1824**	W824PFB	**1828**	W828PFB	**1833**	W833PFB
1814	W814PFB	**1819**	W819PFB	**1825**	W825PFB	**1829**	W829PFB	**1834**	W834PFB
1815	W815PFB	**1821**	W821PFB						

2326-2332

	Dennis Dart 8.5SDL3003		Wright Handybus	B30F	1991	First London, 2001

2326	JDZ2326	**2328**	JDZ2328	**2330**	JDZ2330	**2331**	JDZ2331	**2332**	JDZ2332
2327	JDZ2327	**2329**	JDZ2329						

3898	L898VHT	Mercedes-Benz 709D	Plaxton Beaver	B23F	1994	
3909	L909VHT	Mercedes-Benz 709D	Plaxton Beaver	B23F	1994	
3910	L910VHT	Mercedes-Benz 709D	Plaxton Beaver	B23F	1994	
3911	L911VHT	Mercedes-Benz 709D	Plaxton Beaver	B23F	1994	
7615	M411RND	Iveco TurboDaily 59-12	Marshall C31	B25F	1995	Greater Manchester, 1997
7618	M414RND	Iveco TurboDaily 59-12	Marshall C31	B20F	1995	Greater Manchester, 1997

7803-7826   Mercedes-Benz 709D   Plaxton Beaver   B22F   1993

7803	L801SAE	7808	L808SAE	7813	L813SAE	7818	L818SAE	7823	L823SAE
7804	L802SAE	7809	L809SAE	7814	L814SAE	7819	L819SAE	7824	L824SAE
7805	L803SAE	7810	L810SAE	7815	L815SAE	7820	L820SAE	7825	L825SAE
7806	L804SAE	7811	L811SAE	7816	L816SAE	7821	L821SAE	7826	L826SAE
7807	L805SAE	7812	L812SAE	7817	L817SAE	7822	L822SAE		

7827-7874   Mercedes-Benz 709D   Plaxton Beaver   B22F   1994

7827	L827WHY	7840	M840ATC	7850	M850ATC	7859	M859ATC	7867	M867ATC
7828	L828WHY	7841	M841ATC	7851	M851ATC	7860	M860ATC	7868	M868ATC
7829	L829WHY	7842	M842ATC	7852	M852ATC	7861	M861ATC	7869	M869ATC
7830	L830WHY	7844	M844ATC	7853	M853ATC	7862	M862ATC	7870	M870ATC
7833	M833ATC	7845	M845ATC	7854	M854ATC	7863	M863ATC	7871	M871ATC
7834	M834ATC	7846	M846ATC	7855	M855ATC	7864	M864ATC	7872	M872ATC
7837	M837ATC	7847	M847ATC	7856	M856ATC	7865	M865ATC	7873	M873ATC
7838	M838ATC	7848	M848ATC	7857	M857ATC	7866	M866ATC	7874	M874ATC
7839	M839ATC	7849	M849ATC						

7875-7879   Mercedes-Benz 709D   Plaxton Beaver   B22F   1995

7875	N875HWS	7876	N876HWS	7877	N877HWS	7878	N878HWS	7879	N879HWS

8916-8924   Dennis Lance SLF   Wright Pathfinder 320   N34D   1994   First Centrewest, 2001

8916	ODZ8916	8918	ODZ8918	8920	ODZ8920	8922	ODZ8922	8924	ODZ8924
8917	ODZ8917	8919	ODZ8919	8921	ODZ8921	8923	ODZ8923		

9424	CUB24Y	Leyland Olympian ONLXB/1R	Roe	B47/29F	1983	First Yorkshire, 2000
9425	CUB25Y	Leyland Olympian ONLXB/1R	Roe	B47/29F	1983	First Yorkshire, 2000
9428	CUB28Y	Leyland Olympian ONLXB/1R	Roe	B47/29F	1983	First Yorkshire, 2000
9431	CUB31Y	Leyland Olympian ONLXB/1R	Roe	B47/29F	1983	First Yorkshire, 2000
9440	CUB40Y	Leyland Olympian ONLXB/1R	Roe	B47/29F	1983	First Yorkshire, 2000
9445	CUB45Y	Leyland Olympian ONLXB/1R	Roe	B47/29F	1983	First Yorkshire, 2000
9477	EWR77Y	Leyland Olympian ONLXB/1R	Roe	B47/29F	1983	First Yorkshire, 2000
9528	LWS44Y	Leyland Olympian ONLXB/1R	Roe	B47/29F	1982	
9529	LWS45Y	Leyland Olympian ONLXB/1R	Roe	B47/29F	1982	
9537	NTC136Y	Leyland Olympian ONLXB/1R	Roe	B47/29F	1982	
9539	NTC138Y	Leyland Olympian ONLXB/1R	Roe	B47/29F	1982	
9543	NTC142Y	Leyland Olympian ONLXB/1R	Roe	B47/29F	1982	

9545-9568   Leyland Olympian ONLXB/1R   Roe   B47/29F   1983-84

9545	A945SAE	9549	A949SAE	9554	A954SAE	9559	A959THW	9563	A963THW
9546	A946SAE	9550	A950SAE	9555	A955THW	9560	A960THW	9565	A965THW
9547	A947SAE	9552	A952SAE	9556	A956THW	9561	A961THW	9567	A967THW
9548	A948SAE	9553	A953SAE	9557	A957THW	9562	A962THW	9568	A968THW

9606-9630   Leyland Olympian ON2R56C16Z4   Northern Counties Palatine   B44/32F   1993

9606	K606LAE	9611	K611LAE	9616	K616LAE	9621	K621LAE	9626	K626LAE
9607	K607LAE	9612	K612LAE	9617	K617LAE	9622	K622LAE	9627	K627LAE
9608	K608LAE	9613	K613LAE	9618	K618LAE	9623	K623LAE	9628	K628LAE
9609	K609LAE	9614	K614LAE	9619	K619LAE	9624	K624LAE	9629	K629LAE
9610	K610LAE	9615	K615LAE	9620	K620LAE	9625	K625LAE	9630	K630LAE

9631-9648   Volvo Olympian YN2RC16Z4*   Northern Counties Palatine II   B47/29F   1993-94   *9645-8 are YN2RC16Z5

9631	L631SEU	9635	L635SEU	9639	L639SEU	9643	L643SEU	9646	L646SEU
9632	L632SEU	9636	L636SEU	9640	L640SEU	9644	L644SEU	9647	L647SEU
9633	L633SEU	9637	L637SEU	9641	L641SEU	9645	L645SEU	9648	L648SEU
9634	L634SEU	9638	L638SEU	9642	L642SEU				

9661	R661NHY	Volvo Olympian	Northern Counties Palatine II	B43/29F	1997
9662	R662NHY	Volvo Olympian	Northern Counties Palatine II	B43/29F	1997
9663	R663NHY	Volvo Olympian	Northern Counties Palatine II	B43/29F	1997
9664	R664NHY	Volvo Olympian	Northern Counties Palatine II	B43/29F	1997

First Cityline operate both Dennis and Volvo low-floor double-deck buses. The Volvo carry Alexander ALX400 bodies while the Dennis, represented here by 9702, W702PHT, feature the East Lancashire Lolyne product. These buses carry Park and Ride livery. *Tim Hall*

9665-9687

Volvo Olympian — Northern Counties Palatine II — B43/29F — 1998

9665	S665AAE	9671	S671AAE	9676	S676AAE	9680	S680AAE	9684	S684AAE
9667	S667AAE	9672	S672AAE	9677	S677AAE	9681	S681AAE	9685	S685AAE
9668	S668AAE	9673	S673AAE	9678	S678AAE	9682	S682AAE	9686	S686AAE
9669	S669AAE	9674	S674AAE	9679	S679AAE	9683	S683AAE	9687	S687AAE
9670	S670AAE	9675	S675AAE						

9701-9708

Dennis Trident — East Lancashire Lolyne — N49/30F — 2000

9701	V701FFB	9703	W703PHT	9705	W705PHT	9707	W707PHT	9708	W708PHT
9702	W702PHT	9704	W704PHT	9706	W706PHT				

9801-9824

Volvo B7TL — Alexander ALX400 — N49/29F — 2000

9801	W801PAE	9806	W806PAE	9812	W812PAE	9816	W816PAE	9821	W821PAE
9802	W802PAE	9807	W807PAE	9813	W813PAE	9817	W817PAE	9822	W822PAE
9803	W803PAE	9808	W808PAE	9814	W814PAE	9818	W818PAE	9823	W823PAE
9804	W804PAE	9809	W809PAE	9815	W815PAE	9819	W819PAE	9824	W824PAE
9805	W805PAE	9811	W811PAE						

Ancillary vehicles:-

3804	E804MOU	Mercedes-Benz 811D	Optare StarRider	TV	1988	First Badgerline, 2000
3805	E805MOU	Mercedes-Benz 811D	Optare StarRider	TV	1988	First Badgerline, 2001
3809	E809MOU	Mercedes-Benz 811D	Optare StarRider	TV	1988	First Badgerline, 2000
3817	E817MOU	Mercedes-Benz 811D	Optare StarRider	TV	1988	First Badgerline, 2000
8152	E202BDV	Ford Transit VE6	Mellor	B7F	1988	Provincial, 1996
8154	E204BDV	Ford Transit VE6	Mellor	B7F	1988	Provincial, 1996
8256	C256CFG	Volvo B9M	Plaxton Paramount 3200 II	TV	1984	
8208	A105EBC	Ford R1115	Plaxton Paramount 3200	TV	1983	
7473	C473BHY	Mercedes-Benz L608D	Reeve Burgess	TV	1986	

Allocations:

Bristol (Easton Road, Lawrence Hill)

Iveco	7615	7618					
Mercedes-Benz	7837	7844	7845	7846	7847	7848	7849	7850
	7854	7855	7856	7857	7871	7872	7873	7874
	7875	7876	7877	7878	7879			
Dart	1503	1504	1506	1507	1508	1509	1510	1511
	1512	1513	1514	1515	1516	1520	1521	1522
	1523	1524	1525	1526	1527	1528	1529	1530
	1531	1532	1533	1534	1535	1536	1548	1719
Lance	8916	8917	8918	8919	8920	8921	8922	8923
	8924							
Lynx	1600	1646	1647	1648	1649	1650	1651	1652
	1653	1654	1655	1656	1657	1658	1659	1660
	1661	1662						
Olympian	9537	9549	9552	9553	9554	9555	9556	9557
	9559	9560	9561	9562	9563	9565	9567	9661
	9662	9663	9664	9669	9675	9676	9677	9678
	9679	9680	9681	9682	9683	9684	9685	9686
	9687							
Volvo B7TL	9801	9802	9803	9804	9805	9806	9807	9808
	9809	9811	9812	9813	9814	9815	9816	9817
	9818	9819	9821	9822	9823	9824		

Bristol (Hengrove)

Mercedes-Benz	3898	7834	7851	7852	7853	7859	7860	7861
	7862	7863	7864	7865	7866	7867	7868	7869
	7870							
Dart	1537	1538	1547	1549	1550	1551	1552	1553
	1554	1556	1557	1558	1559	1701	1702	1703
	1704	1705	1706	1707	1708	1709	1710	1711
	1712	1713	1718	1720	1721	1722	1723	1724
	1725	1732	1733	1734	1735	1736	1737	1738
Lynx	1614	1615	1616	1617	1618	1625	1632	1633
	1634	1635	1636	1637	1638	1639		
Volvo B6	1801	1810	1811	1812	1813	1814	1815	1816
	1817	1818	1819	1821	1822	1823	1824	1825
	1826	1827	1828	1829	1831	1832	1833	1834

Fourteen Dennis Lance buses with Wright Pathfinder 320 bodywork have been transferred from First London for use on the Temple Meads Rail Link. These carry a variation on the 'Barbie' scheme as illustrated by 8924, ODZ8924 shown here. The space between doors features luggage racks reducing the seating capacity to 34. *David Heath*

Photographed in Penn Street in Bristol is Alexander-bodied Volvo B7L 9815, W815PAE. The Volvo B7 double-deck has replaced the Olympian in the European market, while a low entrance version of the Olympian - known as the Super Olympian is being produced for the Far East market. *Mark Lyons*

Olympian	9631	9632	9633	9634	9635	9636	9637	9638
	9639	9640	9641	9642	9643	9644	9645	9646
	9647	9648	9665	9667	9670	9671	9672	9673
	9674							
Trident	9701	9702	9703	9704	9705	9706	9707	9708

Bristol (Muller Road, Horfield)

Mercedes-Benz	3909	3910	3911	7803	7804	7805	7806	7807
	7808	7809	7810	7811	7812	7813	7814	7815
	7816	7817	7818	7819	7820	7821	7822	7823
	7824	7825	7826	7827	7828	7829	7830	7833
	7838	7839	7840	7841	7842			
Dart	1517	1518	1519	1539	1540	1541	1542	1543
	1544	1545	1546	2326	2327	2328	2329	2330
	2331	2332						
Lynx	1619	1620	1621	1622	1623	1624		
Olympian	9424	9425	9428	9431	9440	9445	9477	9529
	9539	9543	9545	9546	9547	9548	9550	9568
	9606	9607	9608	9609	9610	9611	9612	9613
	9614	9615	9616	9617	9618	9619	9620	9621
	9622	9623	9624	9625	9626	9627	9628	9629
	9630							

FIRST SOUTHERN NATIONAL

Wessex - Southern National

First Southern National Ltd, 4 Hamilton Road, Taunton, TA1 2EH
First Wessex Ltd, Croydon Street, Lawrence Hill, Bristol, BS5 0DY

5	B895YYD	Leyland Tiger TRCTL11/3RH	Plaxton Paramount 3200 II	C48FT	1985	
12	620HOD	Leyland Tiger TRCTL11/3R	Plaxton Paramount 3200 E	C53F	1983	Eastern Counties, 1992
201	L201SHW	Dennis Dart 9.8SDL3035	Plaxton Pointer	B40F	1993	First City Line, 2000
202	L202SHW	Dennis Dart 9.8SDL3035	Plaxton Pointer	B40F	1993	First City Line, 2000
210	L210SHW	Dennis Dart 9.8SDL3035	Plaxton Pointer	B40F	1993	First City Line, 2000
226	N226KAE	Dennis Dart 9.8SDL3054	Plaxton Pointer	B40F	1995	First City Line, 2000
227	N227KAE	Dennis Dart 9.8SDL3054	Plaxton Pointer	B40F	1995	First City Line, 2000
555	ATL555L	Bristol VRT/SL2/6LX	Eastern Coach Works	O43/32F	1973	Western National, 1983
559	ATL559L	Bristol VRT/SL2/6LX	Eastern Coach Works	O43/32F	1973	Western National, 1983
560	MBZ7140	Bristol VRT/SL3/501	Eastern Coach Works	O--/--F	1976	Stephenson, Rochford,1998
574	VOD594S	Bristol VRT/SL3/6LXB	Eastern Coach Works	B43/31F	1978	Western National, 1983

650-657

		Mercedes-Benz 609D		Frank Guy		B20F	1994-95	First Eastern Counties, 2000
650	M372XEX	652	N605GAH	654	N611GAH	656	N622GAH	657	N623GAH
651	M373XEX	653	N609GAH	655	N613GAH				

701-710

		Mercedes-Benz 709D		Carlyle		B29F	1991	
701	H906WYB	703	H908WYB	705	H910WYB	707	H913WYB	709	H915WYB
702	H907WYB	704	H909WYB	706	H912WYB	708	H914WYB	710	H916WYB

719	J969EYD	Mercedes-Benz 709D	Carlyle	B29F	1992
720	J241FYA	Mercedes-Benz 709D	Carlyle	B29F	1992
721	J580FYA	Mercedes-Benz 709D	Carlyle	B29F	1992
722	J601FYA	Mercedes-Benz 709D	Carlyle	B29F	1992
725	M305TSF	Mercedes-Benz 709D	Alexander Sprint	B29F	1994

726-735

		Mercedes-Benz 709D		Alexander Sprint		B29F	1994-95	
726	M804UYA	728	M805UYA	730	M278UYD	732	M281UYD	734	M239VYA
727	M803UYA	729	M802UYA	731	M279UYD	733	M282UYD	735	M240VYA

736	M220PMS	Mercedes-Benz 709D	Alexander Sprint	B29F	1995
737	N46OAE	Mercedes-Benz 709D	Alexander Sprint	B29F	1995

Leyland National 2s joined the Southern National fleet from a variety of sources. Pictured in Yeovil is 2932, RSG815V, which was new to Fife Scottish when part of the Scottish Bus Group. It latterly operated with Stagecoach Red and White.
Richard Godfrey

Pictured on Weymouth sea-front is Carlyle-bodied Mercedes-Benz 720, J241FYA. The vehicle carries promotional colours for the Waterside Holiday Park, the destination of its journey. *Richard Godfrey*

738-742

						Mercedes-Benz 709D	Alexander Sprint	B29F	1996	
738	N556EYB	**739**	N557EYB	**740**	N558EYB	**741**	N559EYB	**742**	N561EYB

743	L26LSG	Mercedes-Benz 709D	Alexander Sprint	B25F	1995	Bryans, Denny, 1995
744	E814XHS	Mercedes-Benz 709D	Alexander AM	B29F	1988	Glyn Williams, Crosskeys, 97
745	L23LSG	Mercedes-Benz 709D	Alexander Sprint	B25F	1995	Henderson, Hamilton, 1997
746	L24LSG	Mercedes-Benz 709D	Alexander Sprint	B25F	1995	Henderson, Hamilton, 1997
747	M14ABC	Mercedes-Benz 709D	Alexander Sprint	B29F	1995	Stonehouse Coaches, 1997
748	M19ABC	Mercedes-Benz 709D	Alexander Sprint	B29F	1995	Stonehouse Coaches, 1997
749	L92LSG	Mercedes-Benz 709D	Alexander Sprint	B25F	1995	Henderson, Hamilton, 1997

751-762

						Mercedes-Benz 811D	Wright NimBus	B33F	1993-94	
751	K751VFJ	**757**	L651CJT	**759**	L329MYC	**761**	L67EPR	**762**	L68EPR
756	L650CJT	**758**	Ł652CJT	**760**	L330MYC				

766	M766FTT	Mercedes-Benz 811D	Marshall C16	B33F	1994	
770	M241VYA	Mercedes-Benz 811D	Wright NimBus	B33F	1995	
771	M242VYA	Mercedes-Benz 811D	Wright NimBus	B33F	1995	
772	M508VYA	Mercedes-Benz 811D	Wright NimBus	B33F	1995	
773	M509VYA	Mercedes-Benz 811D	Wright NimBus	B33F	1995	
774	F154RHK	Mercedes-Benz 811D	Reeve Burgess Beaver	B33F	1989	Jackson, Bicknacre, 1995
775	J185LGE	Mercedes-Benz 811D	Alexander Sprint	B29F	1992	Harte, Greenock, 1997
776	K776AFS	Mercedes-Benz 711D	Alexander Sprint	B31F	1992	

780-785

						Mercedes-Benz 711D	Alexander Sprint	B29F	1996	
780	P442KYC	**782**	P445KYC	**783**	P446KYC	**784**	P447KYC	**785**	P448KYC
781	P443KYC								

786-790

						Mercedes-Benz 711D	Plaxton Beaver	B29F	1997	
786	P179LYB	**787**	P180LYB	**788**	P181LYB	**789**	P182LYB	**790**	P183LYB

The operational boundy between Southern National and Western National's Red Bus sees both companies vehicles in the same towns. Pictured on the north Devon coast of Ilfracombe is Southern National 807, K329KYC, a Dennis Dart with Wright Handybus bodywork preparing to leave for Taunton. The Red Bus Leyland Lynx behind will later return to Barnstaple. *Richard Godfrey*

802	H802GDV	Dennis Dart 9.8SDL3004	Carlyle Dartline	B40F	1991	
806	K328KYC	Dennis Dart 9.8SDL3017	Wright Handybus	BC37F	1993	
807	K329KYC	Dennis Dart 9.8SDL3017	Wright Handybus	BC37F	1993	
808	K330KYC	Dennis Dart 9.8SDL3017	Wright Handybus	BC37F	1993	

817-823

		Dennis Dart SLF		Plaxton Pointer 2		N39F	1998

817	S817KPR	819	S819KPR	821	S821KPR	822	S822KPR	823	S823KPR
818	S818KPR	820	S820KPR						

824	S824WYD	Dennis Dart SLF	East Lancashire Spryte	N35F	1999
825	S825WYD	Dennis Dart SLF	East Lancashire Spryte	N35F	1999
826	T826AFX	Dennis Dart SLF	Plaxton Pointer 2	N39F	1999
827	T827AFX	Dennis Dart SLF	Plaxton Pointer 2	N39F	1999
828	T828AFX	Dennis Dart SLF	Plaxton Pointer 2	N39F	1999
829	T829AFX	Dennis Dart SLF	Plaxton Pointer 2	N39F	1999

830-835

		Dennis Dart SLF		East Lancashire Spryte		N37F	1999

830	T830RYC	832	V832DYD	833	V833DYD	834	V834DYD	835	V835DYD
831	T831RYC								

836-840

		Dennis Lance SLF		Wright Pathfinder 320		N34D	1993	First Cityline, 2001

836	ODZ8911	837	ODZ8912	838	ODZ8913	839	ODZ8914	840	ODZ8915

854-864

		Mercedes-Benz Vario O810		Plaxton Beaver 2		B27F	1998	*857/60/1 are O814

854	R501NPR	857	R504NPR	859	R506NPR	861	R508NPR	863	S863LRU
855	R502NPR	858	R505NPR	860	R507NPR	862	S340WYB	864	S864LRU
856	R503NPR								

934	VDV134S	Bristol VRT/SL3/6LXB	Eastern Coach Works	CO43/31F	1977	Western National, 1983
942	VDV142S	Bristol VRT/SL3/6LXB	Eastern Coach Works	CO43/31F	1978	Devon General, 1983
950	M392KVR	Mercedes-Benz 709D	Alexander Sprint	B27F	1995	Glossopdale, 1997
951	M393KVR	Mercedes-Benz 709D	Alexander Sprint	B27F	1995	Beeline, West Bromwich,97
952	M386KVR	Mercedes-Benz 709D	Alexander Sprint	B27F	1994	Little Red Bus, Smethwick, 97

With the number of Bristol VRs reduced to a dozen, Southern National has undertaken an interesting replacement programme. One of the survivors is 1168, FDV780V which is seen at rest in Taunton bus station, though about to head in the directon of Bridgwater, where the vehicle is allocated. *Mark Bailey*

953	M674RAJ	Mercedes-Benz 709D	Alexander Sprint	B25F	1994	Go-Ahead (OK), 1998
954	M675RAJ	Mercedes-Benz 709D	Alexander Sprint	B25F	1994	Go-Ahead (OK), 1998
958	M381KVR	Mercedes-Benz 709D	Alexander Sprint	B29F	1995	Eastern Counties, 1998
959	M382KVR	Mercedes-Benz 709D	Alexander Sprint	B29F	1995	Essex Buses (T), 1998

960-967

		Mercedes-Benz 709D		Reeve Burgess Beaver		B25F	1990-91	Plymouth Citybus, 1997-98

960	H684BTA	962	J220KTT	964	J205KTT	966	J213KTT	967	J210KTT
961	J208KTT	963	J217KTT	965	H683BTA				

968	N585WND	Mercedes-Benz 709D	Reeve Burgess Beaver	B25F	1995	Western Buses(AA), 1998
969	N584WND	Mercedes-Benz 709D	Reeve Burgess Beaver	B25F	1995	Williamsons, Shrewsbury, 98
970	N586WND	Mercedes-Benz 709D	Reeve Burgess Beaver	B25F	1995	Thompson, South Bank, 1998
971	N583WND	Mercedes-Benz 709D	Reeve Burgess Beaver	B25F	1995	Epsom Coaches, 1998
1111	VDV111S	Bristol VRT/SL3/6LXB	Eastern Coach Works	B43/31F	1978	Western National, 1983
1122	VDV122S	Bristol VRT/SL3/6LXB	Eastern Coach Works	B43/31F	1978	Western National, 1983

1157-1193

		Bristol VRT/SL3/6LXB		Eastern Coach Works		B43/31F	1978	Western National, 1983

1157	AFJ764T	1160	AFJ767T	1163	AFJ770T	1167	FDV779V	1169	FDV781V
1159	AFJ766T	1161	AFJ768T	1166	AFJ773T	1168	FDV780V	1193	FDV837V

1626	F626RTC	Leyland Lynx LX2R11C15Z4R	Leyland Lynx	B49F	1989	First City Line, 2000
1627	F627RTC	Leyland Lynx LX2R11C15Z4R	Leyland Lynx	B49F	1989	First City Line, 2000
1628	F628RTC	Leyland Lynx LX2R11C15Z4R	Leyland Lynx	B49F	1989	First City Line, 2000
1629	F629RTC	Leyland Lynx LX2R11C15Z4R	Leyland Lynx	B49F	1989	First City Line, 2000

1802-1809

		Volvo B6BLE		Wright Crusader 2		N36F	1999	

1802	V802EFB	1804	V804EFB	1806	V806EFB	1808	V808EFB	1809	V809EFB
1803	V803EFB	1805	V805EFB	1807	V807EFB				

1813	A685KDV	Leyland Olympian ONLXB/1R	Eastern Coach Works	B45/32F	1983	Devon General, 1990
1814	G901TWS	Leyland Olympian ONCL10/1RZ	Leyland	B47/31F	1989	First Bristol, 2000
1815	G902TWS	Leyland Olympian ONCL10/1RZ	Leyland	B47/31F	1989	First Bristol, 2000
1816	G903TWS	Leyland Olympian ONCL10/1RZ	Leyland	B47/31F	1989	First Bristol, 2000
1817	G904TWS	Leyland Olympian ONCL10/1RZ	Leyland	B47/31F	1989	First Bristol, 2000

1818-1826 Leyland Olympian ONLXB/1R Roe B47/29F 1984 First Badgerline, 2000

1818	LWS42Y	**1820**	NTC139Y	**1822**	NTC141Y	**1824**	JHU902X	**1826**	JHU904X
1819	LWS43Y	**1821**	NTC140Y	**1823**	A951SAE	**1825**	JHU903X		

2213	A590AHB	Leyland Tiger TRCTL11/3R	Marshall Campaigner	B57F	1983	MoD, 1996 (20KB57)
2214	A696YOX	Leyland Tiger TRCTL11/3R	Marshall Campaigner	B54F	1983	MoD, 1995 (20KB47)
2215	UOB366Y	Leyland Tiger TRCTL11/3R	Marshall Campaigner	B54F	1983	MoD, 1996 (20KB53)
2216	B591FOG	Leyland Tiger TRCTL11/3R	Marshall Campaigner	B57F	1984	MoD, 1996 (20KB61)
2217	A649YOX	Leyland Tiger TRCTL11/3R	Marshall Campaigner	B56F	1983	MoD, 1996 (20KB77)
2218	A624YOX	Leyland Tiger TRCTL11/3R	Marshall Campaigner	B57F	1983	MoD, 1996 (20KB66)
2219	A622YOX	Leyland Tiger TRCTL11/3R	Marshall Campaigner	B57F	1983	MoD, 1996 (20KB53)
2220	LIL5851	Leyland Tiger TRCTL11/3R	Plaxton Paramount 3200 E	C53F	1983	Lancaster, 1993
2221	HHJ372Y	Leyland Tiger TRCTL11/2R	Alexander TE	C53F	1983	Eastern Counties, 1998
2223	A695OHJ	Leyland Tiger TRCTL11/2R	Alexander TE	C53F	1983	SWT, 1998
2224	A691OHJ	Leyland Tiger TRCTL11/2R	Alexander TE	C53F	1983	SWT, 1998
2225	HHJ381Y	Leyland Tiger TRCTL11/2R	Alexander TE	C53F	1983	Essex Buses (T), 1998
2226	HHJ382Y	Leyland Tiger TRCTL11/2R	Alexander TE	C53F	1983	Essex Buses (T), 1998
2227	UFX940	Leyland Tiger TRCTL11/2R	Alexander TE	C53F	1983	Eastern Counties, 1998
2228	595JPU	Volvo B10M-60	Plaxton Expressliner	C46FT	1991	
2229	UFX330	Volvo B10M-60	Plaxton Expressliner	C46FT	1991	
2230	HHJ375Y	Leyland Tiger TRCTL11/3R	Alexander TE	C53F	1983	Eastern Counties, 1999
2231	HHJ376Y	Leyland Tiger TRCTL11/3R	Alexander TE	C53F	1983	Eastern Counties, 1999

2920	VBG114V	Leyland National 2 NL116AL11/1R	B52F	1980	MTL (North),1998
2921	VBG127V	Leyland National 2 NL116AL11/1R	B49F	1980	MTL (North),1998
2923	XLV143W	Leyland National 2 NL116AL11/1R	B53F	1981	MTL (Liverbus),1998
2924	VBG120V	Leyland National 2 NL116AL11/1R	B53F	1980	MTL (North),1998
2925	VBG118V	Leyland National 2 NL116AL11/1R	B53F	1980	HMB, Gateshead,1998
2926	LRB211W	Leyland National 2 NL116AL11/1R	B49F	1981	Border, Burnley,1998
2927	DOC44V	Leyland National 2 NL116AL11/1R	B50F	1980	Border, Burnley,1998
2928	AFM3W	Leyland National 2 NL116AL11/1R	B52F	1981	Arriva North West (M),1998
2929	LRB202W	Leyland National 2 NL116AL11/1R	B52F	1980	Stephenson, Rochford,1998
2931	DMS22V	Leyland National 2 NL116AL11/1R	B52F	1980	Stagecoach Red & White,1998
2932	RSG815V	Leyland National 2 NL116AL11/1R	B52F	1980	Stagecoach Red & White,1998

3306	AFJ726T	Bristol LH6L	Plaxton Supreme III Express	C41F	1979	Western National, 1983
3307	AFJ727T	Bristol LH6L	Plaxton Supreme III Express	C41F	1979	Western National, 1983
6104	T104JBC	Volvo B7R	Plaxton Prima	C49FT	1999	
6105	T105JBC	Volvo B7R	Plaxton Prima	C49FT	1999	
6106	T106JBC	Volvo B7R	Plaxton Prima	C49FT	1999	
6133	M756XET	Volvo B10M-60	Plaxton Expressliner 2	C46FT	1995	
6161	K792OTC	Volvo B10M-60	Plaxton Expressliner 2	C46FT	1993	
6163	K794OTC	Volvo B10M-60	Plaxton Expressliner 2	C46FT	1993	
6169	M92BOU	Volvo B10M-62	Plaxton Expressliner 2	C46FT	1994	
6174	M763CWS	Volvo B10M-62	Plaxton Expressliner 2	C44FT	1994	
6175	M764CWS	Volvo B10M-62	Plaxton Expressliner 2	C44FT	1994	
6176	M765CWS	Volvo B10M-62	Plaxton Expressliner 2	C49FT	1994	
6177	M413DEU	Volvo B10M-62	Plaxton Expressliner 2	C44FT	1995	
6178	M439FHW	Volvo B10M-62	Plaxton Expressliner 2	C49FT	1995	
6179	M440FHW	Volvo B10M-62	Plaxton Expressliner 2	C49FT	1995	
6180	M41FTC	Volvo B10M-62	Plaxton Expressliner 2	C44FT	1995	
6181	P944RWS	Volvo B10M-62	Plaxton Expressliner 2	C46FT	1996	
6182	P945RWS	Volvo B10M-62	Plaxton Expressliner 2	C44FT	1996	
6183	P946RWS	Volvo B10M-62	Plaxton Expressliner 2	C49FT	1996	
6184	R813HWS	Volvo B10M-62	Plaxton Expressliner 2	C49FT	1997	
6185	R814HWS	Volvo B10M-62	Plaxton Expressliner 2	C49FT	1997	
6186	R943LHT	Volvo B10M-62	Plaxton Expressliner 2	C44FT	1998	
6187	T948UEU	Volvo B10M-62	Plaxton Expressliner 2	C44FT	1999	
6188	T64BHY	Volvo B10M-62	Plaxton Expressliner 2	C44FT	1999	
6189	T310AHY	Volvo B10M-62	Plaxton Expressliner 2	C44FT	1996	
6191	X191HFB	Volvo B10M-62	Plaxton Expressliner 2	C48FT	2000	
6192	X192HFB	Volvo B10M-62	Plaxton Expressliner 2	C48FT	2000	
6193	X193HFB	Volvo B10M-62	Plaxton Expressliner 2	C48FT	2000	
6194	X194HFB	Volvo B10M-62	Plaxton Expressliner 2	C48FT	2000	

Southern National preside over the Wessex operation and their major involvement in the National Express network. Seen in Flightline colours is X194HFB an Expressliner 2 delivered in 2000. The Plaxton Expressliner differs in several ways from the Premiére 350 coach version, though outwardly share the same styling.
Paul Stockwell

6201-6212

Dennis Javelin GX 12SDA2153   Plaxton Expressliner 2   C49FT   1995-96

6201	N471KHU	6204	N474KHU	6207	N821KWS	6209	N319NHY	6211	N321NHY
6202	N472KHU	6205	N913KHW	6208	N822KWS	6210	N320NHY	6212	N322NHY
6203	N473KHU	6206	N914KHW						

7003	KDU648	Volvo B10M-61	Van Hool Alizée	C49FT	1983	Taylors Travel, Tintinhull, 1993
7004	RIL1056	Volvo B10M-61	Plaxton Paramount 3200 II	C53F	1985	Taylors Travel, Tintinhull, 1993
7009	TPR354	Leyland Tiger TRCTL11/3R	Plaxton Supreme V	C53F	1982	Taylors Travel, Tintinhull, 1993
7022	RIL1053	Dennis Javelin 12SDA1907	Plaxton Paramount 3200 III	C53F	1989	Beeline, Warminster, 1996
7616	M248NNF	Iveco TurboDaily 59-12	Marshall C31	B25F	1995	Greater Manchester, 1997
7617	M249NNF	Iveco TurboDaily 59-12	Marshall C31	B27F	1995	Greater Manchester, 1997
7618	K929VDV	Iveco TurboDaily 59-12	Mellor	B28F	1993	First Hampshire, 2000
7619	M413RND	Iveco TurboDaily 59-12	Marshall C31	B20F	1995	Greater Manchester, 1997

7831-7907

Mercedes-Benz 709D   Plaxton Beaver   B22F   1994-95   First City Line, 2000

7831	M831ATC	7884	N884HWS	7891	N891HWS	7897	N897HWS	7903	N903HWS
7832	M832ATC	7885	N885HWS	7892	N892HWS	7898	N898HWS	7904	N904HWS
7880	N880HWS	7886	N886HWS	7893	N893HWS	7899	N899HWS	7905	N905HWS
7881	N881HWS	7887	N887HWS	7894	N894HWS	7901	N901HWS	7906	N906HWS
7882	N882HWS	7889	N889HWS	7895	N895HWS	7902	N902HWS	7907	N907HWS
7883	N883HWS	7890	N890HWS	7896	N896HWS				

8013	KFX791	Leyland Tiger TRCTL11/3R	Plaxton Paramount 3200	C53F	1983	Arlington demonstrator, 1983
8015	RIL1069	Leyland Tiger TRCTL11/3ARZM	Plaxton Paramount 3500 III	C45FT	1990	Hill's of Tredegar, 1991
8016	USV821	Leyland Tiger TRCTL11/3R	Plaxton Paramount 3200	C46FT	1984	
8021	IIL2490	Leyland Tiger TRCTL11/2RH	Plaxton Paramount 3200 IIE	C53F	1986	Lancaster, 1993
8025	8683LJ	Dennis Javelin 11SDL1905	Duple 320	C53F	1988	Brighton & Hove, 1997
8026	OJI8786	Dennis Javelin 11SDL1905	Duple 320	C53F	1988	Brighton & Hove, 1997
8342	J142KPX	Iveco Daily 49.10	Marshall C29	B23F	1992	Provincial, 1997
8345	J145KPX	Iveco Daily 49.10	Marshall C29	B23F	1992	Provincial, 1997
8346	J146KPX	Iveco Daily 49.10	Marshall C29	B23F	1992	Provincial, 1997

9001	GIL1684	Volvo B10M-61	Van Hool Alizée	C53F	1988	Allisons, Dunfermline, 1994
9002	TJI3135	Volvo B10M-61	Ikarus Blue Danube	C53F	1988	Bere Regis & District, 1994
9003	TJI3136	Volvo B10M-61	Ikarus Blue Danube	C53F	1988	Bere Regis & District, 1994
9004	TJI3137	Volvo B10M-61	Ikarus Blue Danube	C53F	1988	Bere Regis & District, 1994
9005	TJI3138	Volvo B10M-61	Ikarus Blue Danube	C53F	1988	Bere Regis & District, 1994
9007	TJI3134	Volvo B10M-61	Duple Caribbean	C55F	1984	Bere Regis & District, 1994
9008	USV823	Volvo B10M-61	Duple Dominant IV	C53F	1983	Bere Regis & District, 1994
9045	D659WEY	Bedford YNT	Plaxton Paramount 3200 II	C53F	1986	Nefyn Coaches, 1997
9052	TJI4683	Leyland Tiger TRCTL11/3R	Duple Dominant	C53F	1983	Dorset CC, 1998
9055	XFG27Y	Leyland National 2 NL116AL11/1R		B49F	1983	Brighton & Hove, 1998
9057	J732KBC	Dennis Javelin 11SDL1921	Plaxton Paramount 3200 III	C53F	1982	Jones, Login, 1998,
9058	G802XLO	Volvo B10M-60	Plaxton Paramount 3200 III	C53F	1990	Capital West Drayton, 1998
9059	G803XLO	Volvo B10M-60	Plaxton Paramount 3200 III	C53F	1990	Channel, Bow, 1998
9060	J329LLK	Volvo B10M-60	Plaxton Paramount 3200 III	C53F	1992	Capital West Drayton, 1998

Named vehicles:
6182 *Spirit of Glastonbury*; 6183 *Spirit of Burnham-on-Sea*; 6201 *Spirit of Clevedon*; 6202 *Spirit of Weston-super-Mare*; 6203 *Spirit of Keynsham*; 6204 *Spirit of Kingswood*; 6205 *Spirit of Worle*; 6206 *Spirit of Gordano*; 6207 *Spirit of Portishead*; 6208 *Spirit of Bristol*; 6209 *Spirit of Wells*; 6210 *Spirit of Clifton*; 6211 *Spirit of Eastville*; 6212 *Spirit of Street*;

Previous Registrations:

595JPU	H227CFJ, H228CFJ	N46OAE	TDZ3265
620HOD	A897KCL	OJI8786	E475FWV
8683LJ	E474FWV	RIL1053	F173TRU, RJI8602, F576AEL, 40FER
D659WEY	D933XWP, 610LYB	RIL1056	B904SPR, RFP6
E814XHS	E814XHS, 865GAT	RIL1069	G155JBO, 10HR
GIL1684	E631UNE, LSK813	TJI3134	A600LJT
IIL2490	C90MHG	TJI3135	E221GCG
J185LGE	J259WFS, IIB1618	TJI3136	E222GCG
KDU648	MSU612Y	TJI3137	E223GCG
KFX791	FNM854Y	TJI3138	E224GCG
LIL5851	A620ATV	TJI4683	YPD116Y
M19ABC	M496JRY	TPR354	CYA614X
M802UYA	M805UYA	UFX330	H229CFJ
M804UYA	M802UYA	UFX940	A696OHJ
M805UYA	M804UYA	USV821	A679KDV
MBZ7140	OTO151R	USV823	ENF560Y

Allocations:

Bridgwater (East Quay) - Southern National

Outstation: Minehead

Mercedes-Benz	727	733	744	748	780	968	971	7893
	7894	7895	7896	7897	7898	7899	7901	7902
Dart	830	831						
National	2928							
Tiger	2213	2214	2215	2217	2218	2220		
Bristol VR	1111	1157	1160	1166	1168	1169	1193	

Bridport (Tannery Road) - Southern National

Mercedes-Benz	710	756	766	775	7881	7884
	7885					
Dart	817	818	819			
Tiger	5	8016				
Volvo B10M coach	7003	9058	9059	9060		
Bristol VR	1159	1161	1163			

The South West Bus Handbook

Weymouth is the home of the four Leyland Lynx trasnferred to First Southern National from City Line in 2000. Two of the quartet are seen here with 1628, G628TRC leading 1627. *Richard Godfrey*

Bristol (Easton Road, Lawrence Hill) - Wessex

Dennis Javelin	6201	6202	6203	6204	6205	6206	6207	6208
	6209	6210	6211	6212				
Volvo B10M coach	6131	6163	6169	6174	6175	6176	6177	6178
	6179	6180	6181	6182	6183	6184	6185	6186
	6187	6188	6189	6191	6192	6193	6194	
Volvo B7R	6104	6105	6106					

Martock (Coate Road and Great Western Road) - Southern National (Comfylux Travel)

Tiger	12	2230	2231	7026	8013	9052
Bedford	9045					
Javelin	7022					
Volvo B10M coach	7004	9008				

Taunton (Hamilton Road) - Southern National

Outstation - Minehead

Iveco	7616	7617	7618	7619				
Mercedes-Benz	650	651	652	653	654	655	656	657
	728	734	735	736	737	740	741	742
	743	757	760	761	762	772	773	782
	783	784	786	787	788	789	790	862
	863	864	958	959	969	970	7889	7890
	7891	7892	7903	7904				

Dart	201	802	806	807	808	824	825	832
	833	834	835					
National	2926							
Javelin	8025	8026						
Tiger	2216	2219	2221	2223	2224	2225	2226	2227
	8015	8021						
Volvo B10M coach	2229							
Olympian	1814	1815	1816	1817				

Weymouth (Edward Street) - Southern National

Mercedes-Benz	701	702	705	706	707	708	709	719
	720	721	722	732	759	774	776	854
	855	856	857	858	859	860	861	951
	7880	7882	7883					
Dart	210	820	821	822	823	826	827	828
	829							
Volvo B6	1802	1803	1804	1805	1806	1807	1808	1809
Volvo B10M	2228	6161	9001	9002	9003	9004	9005	9007
National	2927	9055						
Lynx	1626	1627	1628	1629				
Bristol VR	555	559	560	934	942			
Olympian	1819	1820	1821	1822	1823	1824	1825	1826

Yeovil (Reckleford) - Southern National

Mercedes-Benz	725	726	729	730	731	738	739	745
	746	747	749	770	771	785	950	952
	953	954	960	961	962	963	964	965
	966	967	7831	7832	7886	7887	7905	7906
	7907							
Dart	202	226	227					
Tiger	7009							
National	2920	2921	2923	2924	2925	2929	2931	2932
Bristol VR	574	1122	1167					

Unallocated

Iveco	8342	8343	8345	8346	
Lance	836	837	838	839	840
Bristol LH	3316				
Olympian	1818				

Shortly after becoming a constituent part of FirstGroup, Southern Natioanl received several buses cascaded from fellow fleets, including eight Alexander-bodied Leyland Tigers. Representing the type is 2226, HHJ382Y which came from Eastern Counties.
Richard Godfrey

FIRST WESTERN NATIONAL

Western National - Red Bus

First Western National Buses Ltd, Western House, 38 Lemon Street, Truro, TR1 2NS

| 1003 | VDV141S | Bristol VRT/SL3/6LXB | Eastern Coach Works | CO43/31F | 1978 | |
| 1006 | VDV144S | Bristol VRT/SL3/6LXB | Eastern Coach Works | CO43/31F | 1978 | |

| **1007-1011** | | Leyland Atlantean AN68C/1R | Alexander AL | | B45/29D | 1981-82 | First Aberdeen, 2000 |
| 1007 | URS320X | **1008** | NRS320W | **1009** | URS327X | **1010** | URS328X | **1011** | NRS307W |

1012-1017		Leyland Atlantean AN68D/1R	Alexander AL		B45/29D	1983	First Aberdeen, 2001
1012	XSS332Y	**1014**	XSS334Y	**1015**	XSS338Y	**1016**	XSS340Y	**1017**	XSS341Y
1013	XSS333Y								

| 1106 | SFJ106R | Bristol VRT/SL3/6LXB | Eastern Coach Works | B43/31F | 1977 | |

1114-1131		Bristol VRT/SL3/6LXB	Eastern Coach Works	B43/31F	1977-78	
1114	VDV114S	**1118**	VDV118S	**1120w**	VDV120S	**1123**	XDV603S	**1129**	XDV609S
1116	VDV116S	**1119**	VDV119S	**1121**	VDV121S	**1128**	XDV608S	**1131**	XDV601S
1117	VDV117S								

1132-1183		Bristol VRT/SL3/6LXB	Eastern Coach Works	B43/31F	1978-80	
1132	AFJ697T	**1137w**	AFJ702T	**1142**	AFJ744T	**1148**	AFJ750T	**1174**	FDV806V
1133	AFJ698T	**1138**	AFJ703T	**1143**	AFJ745T	**1149**	AFJ751T	**1175**	FDV807V
1134	AFJ699T	**1139**	AFJ704T	**1144w**	AFJ746T	**1153**	AFJ760T	**1176**	FDV808V
1135	AFJ700T	**1140**	AFJ705T	**1145**	AFJ747T	**1154**	AFJ761T	**1182**	FDV814V
1136	AFJ701T	**1141**	AFJ706T	**1147**	AFJ749T	**1155**	AFJ762T	**1183**	FDV815V

| 1187 | BEP968V | Bristol VRT/SL3/501(6LXB) | Eastern Coach Works | B43/31F | 1979 | South Wales, 1989 |

1197-1226		Bristol VRT/SL3/6LXB	Eastern Coach Works	B43/31F	1980-81	
1197	LFJ841W	**1199**	LFJ843W	**1201**	LFJ845W	**1203**	LFJ847W	**1225**	LFJ872W
1198	LFJ842W	**1200**	LFJ844W	**1202**	LFJ846W	**1224**	LFJ871W	**1226**	LFJ873W

| 1227 | EWS747W | Bristol VRT/SL3/680(6LXB) | Eastern Coach Works | BC43/31F | 1981 | Badgerline, 1990 |

The number of Western National buses retaining the blue and red 'flags' along the cantrail is now declining, as are the Bristol VRs. Recently pictured outside the Theatre Royal in Plymouth is 1199, LHJ844W which dates from 1981.
Bill Potter

1228-1237 Bristol VRT/SL3/501(6LXB) Eastern Coach Works B43/31F 1978-79 South Wales, 1990

1228	RTH929S	1230	VTH942T	1232w	WTH945T	1234	WTH950T	1237	BEP966V
1229	TWN936S	1231	WTH943T	1233	WTH946T	1236	WTH961T		

1238-1251 Bristol VRT/SL3/6LXB Eastern Coach Works B43/31F* 1980-81 Thamesway, 1991-92 *1238 is B39/31F

1238	KOO785V	1242	XHK228X	1244	UAR589W	1248	UAR590W	1250	XHK220X
1239	UAR595W	1243	UAR586W	1246	UAR597W	1249	XHK223X	1251	XHK230X
1240	XHK225X								

1252	PHY697S	Bristol VRT/SL3/6LXB	Eastern Coach Works	B39/31F	1977	City Line, 1994
1253	TWS915T	Bristol VRT/SL3/6LXB	Eastern Coach Works	B39/31F	1979	City Line, 1994
1254	AHU516V	Bristol VRT/SL3/6LXB	Eastern Coach Works	B39/31F	1980	City Line, 1994
1256	JWT758V	Bristol VRT/SL3/6LXB	Eastern Coach Works	B43/31F	1979	Yorkshire Rider, 1996
1257	PWY38W	Bristol VRT/SL3/6LXB	Eastern Coach Works	B43/31F	1980	Yorkshire Rider, 1996
1258	STW34W	Bristol VRT/SL3/6LXB	Eastern Coach Works	B39/31F	1981	City Line, 1996
1259	URF668S	Bristol VRT/SL3/501(6LXB)	Eastern Coach Works	B43/31F	1978	Durbins, 1992
1260	PEU518R	Bristol VRT/SL3/6LXB	Eastern Coach Works	B43/31F	1977	Bristol, 1998
1261	RHT503S	Bristol VRT/SL3/6LXB	Eastern Coach Works	B39/31F	1978	Hampshire (P), 1999
1262	NTC573R	Bristol VRT/SL3/6LXB	Eastern Coach Works	B43/31F	1977	Hampshire (P), 1999
1263	VEX288X	Bristol VRT/SL3/6LXB	Eastern Coach Works	B39/31F	1982	First Eastern Counties, 2000
1265	UAR588W	Bristol VRT/SL3/6LXB	Eastern Coach Works	B43/31F	1981	First Cymru, 1999
1301	PTT99R	Bristol VRT/SL3/6LXB	Eastern Coach Works	B43/31F	1977	Western National, 1983
1302	RTH926S	Bristol VRT/SL3/501	Eastern Coach Works	B43/31F	1972	SWT, 1989
1304	XAN431T	Bristol VRT/SL3/6LXB	Eastern Coach Works	B43/34F	1978	Berry's Taunton, 1998
1305	AJH855T	Bristol VRT/SL3/6LXB	Eastern Coach Works	B43/34F	1978	Berry's Taunton, 1998
1306	LFJ860W	Bristol VRT/SL3/6LXB	Eastern Coach Works	B43/31F	1981	Devon General, 1990
1501	X501BFJ	Dennis Trident	East Lancashire Lolyne	N49/30F	2000	
1502	X502BFJ	Dennis Trident	East Lancashire Lolyne	N49/30F	2000	
1503	X503BFJ	Dennis Trident	East Lancashire Lolyne	N49/30F	2000	
1504	X504BFJ	Dennis Trident	East Lancashire Lolyne	N49/30F	2000	

1750-1755 Leyland Olympian ONLXB/1R Eastern Coach Works BC44/32F 1983

1750	A750VAF	1752	A752VAF	1753	A753VAF	1754	A754VAF	1755	A755VAF
1751	A751VAF								

1756	L155UNS	Leyland Olympian ON2R50C13V3	Alexander RL	B47/31F	1993	First Glasgow, 2000
1757	D513HUB	Leyland Olympian ONTL11/1R	Optare	B43/27F	1987	First Yorkshire, 2000
1758	D514HUB	Leyland Olympian ONTL11/1R	Optare	B43/27F	1987	First Yorkshire, 2000
1790	E215BTA	Volvo Citybus B10M-50	Alexander RH	BC47/35F	1988	Bristol (Badgerline), 1997
1791	E216BTA	Volvo Citybus B10M-50	Alexander RH	BC47/35F	1988	Bristol (Badgerline), 1997
1801	K801ORL	Volvo Olympian YN2RV18Z4	Northern Counties Palatine	BC39/30F	1993	
1802	K802ORL	Volvo Olympian YN2RV18Z4	Northern Counties Palatine	BC39/30F	1993	
1803	K803ORL	Volvo Olympian YN2RV18Z4	Northern Counties Palatine	BC39/30F	1993	
1804	K804ORL	Volvo Olympian YN2RV18Z4	Northern Counties Palatine	BC39/30F	1993	
1815	L815CFJ	Volvo Olympian YN2RV18Z4	Northern Counties Palatine	B47/29F	1993	
1816	L816CFJ	Volvo Olympian YN2RV18Z4	Northern Counties Palatine	B47/29F	1993	
1817	L817CFJ	Volvo Olympian YN2RV18Z4	Northern Counties Palatine	B47/29F	1993	
1818	P187TGD	Volvo Olympian YN2RV18V3	Alexander RL	B47/32F	1996	First Leicester, 2001
2101	M101ECV	Volvo B12T	Van Hool Astrobel	C57/14CT	1995	
2102	M102ECV	Volvo B12T	Van Hool Astrobel	C57/14CT	1995	
2103	M103ECV	Volvo B12T	Van Hool Astrobel	C57/14CT	1995	
2207	VOO273	Leyland Tiger TRCTL11/3R	Plaxton Paramount 3200	C57F	1983	Ford's, Gunnislake, 1997
2209	530OHU	Leyland Tiger TRCTL11/3R	Plaxton Paramount 3200	C53F	1983	Badgerline, 1996
2211	WSV408	Leyland Tiger TRCTL11/3R	Plaxton Paramount 3200	C53F	1983	Yorkshire Rider, 1996
2213	HVJ716	Leyland Tiger TRCTL11/3R	Plaxton Paramount 3200	C46FT	1983	Midland Red West, 1997
2214	481FPO	Leyland Tiger TRCTL11/3R	Plaxton Paramount 3200	C53F	1984	M C Travel, Melksham, 1997
2215	FNR923	Leyland Tiger TRCTL11/3RH	Plaxton Paramount 3200 II	C51F	1985	Wealden, Five Oak Green, '96
2216	NER621	Leyland Tiger TRCTL11/3RH	Plaxton Paramount 3200 II	C51F	1985	Wealden, Five Oak Green, '96
2217	B194BAF	Leyland Tiger TRCTL11/3RH	Plaxton Paramount 3200 II	C48FT	1985	
2218	B195BAF	Leyland Tiger TRCTL11/3RH	Plaxton Paramount 3200 II	C48FT	1985	
2219	B196BAF	Leyland Tiger TRCTL11/3RH	Plaxton Paramount 3200 II	C48FT	1985	
2220	B197BAF	Leyland Tiger TRCTL11/3RH	Plaxton Paramount 3200 II	C48FT	1985	
2221	UKT552	Leyland Tiger TRCTL11/3RH	Plaxton Paramount 3200 II	C50FT	1985	Midland Red West, 1997
2223	A206SAE	Leyland Tiger TRCTL11/3R	Plaxton Paramount 3200E	C53F	1983	Bristol (Badgerline), 1997
2224	HHJ373Y	Leyland Tiger TRCTL11/2R	Alexander TE	C53F	1983	Essex Buses (EN), 1998
2226	TJI4838	Leyland Tiger TRCTL11/3ARZA	Plaxton Paramount 3200 II	C53F	1984	Centrewest (B),1998
2227	A665KUM	Leyland Tiger TRCTL11/2R	Duple Dominant	BC47F	1984	Essex Buses (EN), 1998

The South West Bus Handbook

Western National operate a variety of routes on behalf of National Express including Grimsby - Westward Ho!, London - Bideford, Ilfracombe and Westward Ho!, with St. Ives - Nottingham, Bristol - Newquay and Penzance - Edinburgh among those heading north. Pictured in Redruth is 2301, M301BRL, one of the Plaxton Expressliner 2s allocated to these services. *Richard Godfrey*

2247	HFN769	Volvo B10M-61	Plaxton Paramount 3500 III	C48FT	1989	Wallace Arnold, 1992
2248	FNJ905	Volvo B10M-61	Plaxton Paramount 3500 III	C50F	1989	Wallace Arnold, 1992
2252	TJY761	Volvo B10M-60	Plaxton Paramount 3500 III	C53F	1989	Wallace Arnold, 1993
2253	WNN734	Volvo B10M-60	Plaxton Paramount 3500 III	C53F	1990	Wallace Arnold, 1993
2258	H613UWR	Volvo B10M-60	Plaxton Paramount 3500 III	C46FT	1991	Wallace Arnold, 1994
2259	H614UWR	Volvo B10M-60	Plaxton Paramount 3500 III	C48FT	1991	Wallace Arnold, 1994
2260	H615UWR	Volvo B10M-60	Plaxton Paramount 3500 III	C48FT	1991	Wallace Arnold, 1994
2261	FDZ980	Volvo B10M-60	Plaxton Paramount 3500 III	C50F	1990	Wallace Arnold, 1994
2301	M301BRL	Volvo B10M-62	Plaxton Expressliner 2	C46FT	1994	
2302	M302BRL	Volvo B10M-62	Plaxton Expressliner 2	C46FT	1994	
2303	M303BRL	Volvo B10M-62	Plaxton Expressliner 2	C46FT	1994	
2304	R304JAF	Volvo B10M-62	Plaxton Expressliner 2	C44FT	1998	
2305	R305JAF	Volvo B10M-62	Plaxton Expressliner 2	C44FT	1998	
2307	R307JAF	Volvo B10M-62	Plaxton Expressliner 2	C44FT	1998	
2308	R308JAF	Volvo B10M-62	Plaxton Expressliner 2	C44FT	1998	
2309	R309JAF	Volvo B10M-62	Plaxton Expressliner 2	C44FT	1998	
2310	R310JAF	Volvo B10M-62	Plaxton Expressliner 2	C44FT	1998	
2311	S311SCV	Volvo B10M-62	Plaxton Expressliner 2	C44FT	1998	
2312	S312SCV	Volvo B10M-62	Plaxton Expressliner 2	C44FT	1998	
2313	S313SCV	Volvo B10M-62	Plaxton Expressliner 2	C44FT	1998	
2314	S314SRL	Volvo B10M-62	Plaxton Interurban	BC51F	1999	
2315	S315SRL	Volvo B10M-62	Plaxton Interurban	BC57F	1999	
2316	T316KCV	Volvo B10M-62	Plaxton Expressliner 2	C44FT	1999	
2401	J701CWT	Volvo B10M-60	Plaxton Première 350	C48FT	1992	Wallace Arnold, 1995
2402	J703CWT	Volvo B10M-60	Plaxton Première 350	C46FT	1992	Wallace Arnold, 1995
2505	XFF283	Volvo B10M-61	Van Hool Alizée	C50FT	1987	Badgerline, 1995
2506	EWV665	Volvo B10M-61	Van Hool Alizée	C50FT	1987	Badgerline, 1995
2507	RUH346	Volvo B10M-61	Van Hool Alizée	C50FT	1987	Badgerline, 1995
2508	UWB183	Volvo B10M-61	Van Hool Alizée	C50FT	1987	Badgerline, 1991
2511	UHW661	Volvo B10M-61	Van Hool Alizée	C50FT	1987	Badgerline, 1991
2521	P521PRL	Volvo B10M-62	Van Hool Alizée	C44FT	1996	
2522	P522PRL	Volvo B10M-62	Van Hool Alizée	C44FT	1996	

2600-2605 Leyland Lynx LX112TL11R1R Leyland Lynx B51F 1988

2600	E200BOD	2602	E202BOD	2603	E203BOD	2604	E204BOD	2605	E205BOD
2601	E201BOD								

2606	G261LUG	Leyland Lynx LX112L10ZR1R	Leyland Lynx	B51F	1989	Brewers, 1996
2607	F101GRM	Leyland Lynx LX112L10ZR1R	Leyland Lynx	BC48F	1988	First Centrewest (B), 1999

2608-2612 Leyland Lynx LX2R11C15Z4R Leyland Lynx B49F 1989 First City Line, 2001

2608	F604RTC	2609	F605RTC	2610	F606RTC	2611	F607RTC	2612	F608RTC

2613	J375WWK	Leyland Lynx LX2R11C15Z4S	Leyland Lynx 2	B47F	1992	First Cymru, 2001
2801	THX220S	Leyland National 10351A/2R		B44F	1978	Thames Transit, 1991
2802	HTA844N	Leyland National 11351/1R(DAF)		B49F	1975	Western National, 1983
2807	VBG115V	Leyland National 2 NL116L11/1R		B49F	1980	MTL (North) , 1998
2808	RSG325V	Leyland National 2 NL116L11/1R		B52F	1980	Stagecoach Red & White, 1998
2821	G326PEW	Volvo B10M-60		C48FT	1990	Premier Travel, 1993
2822	GIL2967	Volvo B10M-61	Van Hool Alizée	C53F	1988	Allisons, Dunfermline, 1994
2850	N232WFJ	Dennis Javelin GX12SDA2161	Plaxton Expressliner 2	C44FT	1996	
2851	N233WFJ	Dennis Javelin GX12SDA2161	Plaxton Expressliner 2	C44FT	1996	
2852	P234BFJ	Volvo B10M-62	Plaxton Expressliner 2	C50FT	1996	
2853	P235CTA	Dennis Javelin GX12SDA2153	Plaxton Expressliner 2	C44FT	1997	
2854	P236CTA	Dennis Javelin GX12SDA2153	Plaxton Expressliner 2	C44FT	1997	
3544	FDV800V	Leyland Leopard PSU3E/5R(Vo)	Plaxton Supreme IV Express	C49F	1980	
3546	FDV802V	Leyland Leopard PSU3E/5R(Vo)	Plaxton Supreme IV Express	C49F	1980	
4000	H801GDV	Dennis Dart 9.8SDL3000	Carlyle Dartline	B40F	1991	
4001	J803PFJ	Dennis Dart 9.8SDL3012	Wright Handybus	B39F	1992	
4002	K804WTT	Dennis Dart 9.8SDL3017	Wright Handybus	B40F	1993	
4003	K805WTT	Dennis Dart 9.8SDL3017	Wright Handybus	B39F	1993	
4004	M809FTT	Dennis Dart 9.8SDL3040	Marshall C37	B40F	1994	
4005	N810VOD	Dennis Dart SLF	Plaxton Pointer	B36F	1996	
4006	N811VOD	Dennis Dart SLF	Plaxton Pointer	B36F	1996	
4007	P853DTT	Dennis Dart SLF	Plaxton Pointer	B37F	1997	
4008	N22BLU	Dennis Dart 9.8SDL3054	Marshall C37	B40F	1997	Bluebird, Middleton, 1997
4009	N608WND	Dennis Dart 9.8SDL3054	Plaxton Pointer	B41F	1996	Swanbrook, Cheltenham, 1998
4010	N610WND	Dennis Dart 9.8SDL3054	Plaxton Pointer	B40F	1996	Western Buses (AA), 1998
4011	N612WND	Dennis Dart 9.8SDL3054	Plaxton Pointer	B40F	1996	Western Buses (AA), 1998

4401-4406 Dennis Dart 9.8SDL3035 Plaxton Pointer B40F 1994

4401	L401VCV	4403	L403VCV	4404	L404VCV	4405	L405VCV	4406	L406VCV
4402	L402VCV								

4407-4426 Dennis Dart 9.8SDL3054 Plaxton Pointer B38F 1995 4422-6 are BC37F

4407	M407CCV	4411	M411CCV	4415	M415CCV	4419	M419CCV	4423	M423CCV
4408	M408CCV	4412	M412CCV	4416	M416CCV	4420	M420CCV	4424	M424CCV
4409	M409CCV	4413	M413CCV	4417	M417CCV	4421	M421CCV	4425	M425CCV
4410	M410CCV	4414	M414CCV	4418	M418CCV	4422	M422CCV	4426	M426CCV

4427-4440 Dennis Dart SLF Plaxton Pointer NC35F 1996

4427	P427ORL	4430	P430ORL	4433	P433ORL	4436	P436ORL	4439	P439ORL
4428	P428ORL	4431	P431ORL	4434	P434ORL	4437	P437ORL	4440	P440ORL
4429	P429ORL	4432	P432ORL	4435	P435ORL	4438	P438ORL		

4441-4446 Dennis Dart SLF Plaxton Pointer N35F 1997

4441	P441TCV	4443	P443TCV	4444	P444TCV	4445	P445TCV	4446	P446TCV
4442	P442TCV								

4447-4464 Dennis Dart SLF Plaxton Pointer 2 N35F 1997-98

4447	R447CCV	4451	R451CCV	4455	R445CCV	4459	R459CCV	4462	R462CCV
4448	R448CCV	4452	R452CCV	4456	R456CCV	4460	R460CCV	4463	R463CCV
4449	R449CCV	4453	R453CCV	4457	R457CCV	4461	R461CCV	4464	R464CCV
4450	R450CCV	4454	R454CCV	4458	R458CCV				

Some twenty displaced Mercedes-Benz 811Ds from First Centrewest operate for Western National. These feature 28-seat Alexander Sprint bodywork and are all to be found in the Camborne engineering area. Pictured at Truro during May 2001, 6279, F684XMS, sports the pre-'Barbie 2' colours used by Western National. *Richard Godfrey*

4465	N561LHU		Dennis Dart		Plaxton Pointer		B35F	1996	Bristol (Cityline), 1998	
4466	N562LHU		Dennis Dart		Plaxton Pointer		B35F	1996	Bristol (Cityline), 1998	
4467	N563LHU		Dennis Dart		Plaxton Pointer		B35F	1996	Bristol (Cityline), 1998	
4468	N564LHU		Dennis Dart		Plaxton Pointer		B35F	1996	Bristol (Cityline), 1998	

4469-4478

Dennis Dart SLF   Alexander ALX200   N37F   1999-2000

4469	T469JCV	4471	T471JCV	4473	T473YTT	4475	X475SCY	4477	X477SCY
4470	T470JCV	4472	T472YTT	4474	X474SCY	4476	X476SCY	4478	X478SCY

4501	M501CCV	Dennis Dart 9SDL3053	Plaxton Pointer	B35F	1995	
4502	M502CCV	Dennis Dart 9SDL3053	Plaxton Pointer	B35F	1995	
4503	M503CCV	Dennis Dart 9SDL3053	Plaxton Pointer	B35F	1995	

4601-4609

Volvo B6LE   Wright Crusader 2   N37F   2000

4601	W601PAF	4603	W603PAF	4605	W605PAF	4607	W607PAF	4609	W609PAF
4602	W602PAF	4604	W604PAF	4606	W606PAF	4608	W608PAF		

6061	C676ECV	Mercedes-Benz L608D	Reeve Burgess	B20F	1985
6090	C787FRL	Mercedes-Benz L608D	Reeve Burgess	B20F	1985
6104	C801FRL	Mercedes-Benz L608D	Reeve Burgess	B20F	1985
6116	C959GAF	Mercedes-Benz L608D	Reeve Burgess	B20F	1985
6146	C99HGL	Mercedes-Benz L608D	Reeve Burgess	B20F	1986
6152	C105HGL	Mercedes-Benz L608D	Reeve Burgess	B20F	1986
6155	C108HGL	Mercedes-Benz L608D	Reeve Burgess	B20F	1986

6271-6292

Mercedes-Benz 811D   Alexander Sprint   B28F   1988   First Centrewest, 1998

6271	F666XMS	6275	F668XMS	6279	F684XMS	6284	F949BMS	6289	F946BMS
6272	F677XMS	6276	F455TOY	6280	F683XMS	6285	F954BMS	6290	F952BMS
6273	F706XMS	6277	F948BMS	6281	F682XMS	6286	F657XMS	6291	F958BMS
6274	F645XMS	6278	F680XMS	6283	F643XMS	6287	F667XMS	6292	F669XMS

In contrast to the Alexander body styling shown on the previous page, 6357, L357VCV is a similar Mercedes-Benz 811D but with a Plaxton Beaver body. The bus is seen in Plymouth also during May this year.
Richard Godfrey

6301-6326
Mercedes-Benz 811D   Carlyle   B31F*   1990-91   *6301/11 are BC31F

6301	G151GOL	6305	G155GOL	6309	H894LOX	6318	H718HGL	6323	H723HGL
6302	G152GOL	6306	H891LOX	6310	H895LOX	6321	H721HGL	6326	H726HGL
6303	G153GOL	6308	H893LOX	6311	H896LOX	6322	H722HGL		

| 6328 | E808MOU | Mercedes-Benz 811D | Optare StarRider | B33F | 1988 | Badgerline, 1991 |
| 6329 | E812MOU | Mercedes-Benz 811D | Optare StarRider | B33F | 1988 | Badgerline, 1991 |

6331-6343
Mercedes-Benz 811D   Plaxton Beaver   B31F   1992

6331	K331OAF	6334	K334OAF	6337	K337OAF	6340	K340OAF	6342	K342OAF
6332	K332OAF	6335	K335OAF	6338	K338OAF	6341	K341OAF	6343	K343OAF
6333	K333OAF	6336	K336OAF	6339	K339OAF				

6344-6360
Mercedes-Benz 811D   Plaxton Beaver   B31F   1993-94

6344	K344ORL	6348	K348ORL	6352	K352ORL	6355	L355VCV	6358	L358VCV
6345	K345ORL	6349	K349ORL	6353	K353ORL	6356	L356VCV	6359	L359VCV
6346	K346ORL	6350	K350ORL	6354	K354ORL	6357	L357VCV	6360	L360VCV
6347	K347ORL	6351	K351ORL						

| 6370 | J610PTA | Mercedes-Benz 811D | Marshall C16 | B33F | 1992 |

6371-6375
Mercedes-Benz 811D   Wright NimBus   B33F   1993-94

| 6371 | K752XTA | 6372 | K753XTA | 6373 | K754XTA | 6374 | K755XTA | 6375 | L69EPR |

6376	M764FTT	Mercedes-Benz 811D	Marshall C16	B33F	1994	
6377	M765FTT	Mercedes-Benz 811D	Marshall C16	B33F	1994	
6379	M768FTT	Mercedes-Benz 811D	Marshall C16	BC33F	1994	
6380	M769FTT	Mercedes-Benz 811D	Marshall C16	BC33F	1994	
6381	F801RHK	Mercedes-Benz 811D	Reeve Burgess Beaver	B31F	1989	First Capital, 2000
6382	F800RHK	Mercedes-Benz 811D	Reeve Burgess Beaver	B31F	1989	First Capital, 2000
6383	G337XRE	Mercedes-Benz 811D	PMT Ami	B28F	1989	First PMT, 2000
6384	H351HRF	Mercedes-Benz 811D	PMT Ami	B28F	1990	First PMT, 2000

The current cloice of low-floor minibus for FirstGroup fleets is the integral Optare Solo. Available in lengths from 8.5 metres to 9.2 metres, it has entered service across the country. Fifteen joined the Western Natioanl fleet, represented here by 6809, W809PAF, seen in Plymouth. *Mark Bailey*

6385	H353HRF	Mercedes-Benz 811D	PMT Ami	B28F	1990	First PMT, 2000
6386	F802RHK	Mercedes-Benz 811D	Reeve Burgess Beaver	B31F	1989	First Capital, 2000
6500	H324HVT	Mercedes-Benz 811D	Reeve Burgess Beaver	B24F	1990	First PMT, 2000

6520-6528   Mercedes-Benz 709D   Wright NimBus   B29F   1992

6520	J140SJT	6522	J142SJT	6524	J144SJT	6527	J146SJT	6528	J148SJT
6521	J141SJT	6523	J143SJT	6526	J145SJT				

6529	K723WTT	Mercedes-Benz 709D	Wright NimBus	B29F	1993	
6530	L649CJT	Mercedes-Benz 709D	Wright NimBus	B29F	1993	
6531	M901LTT	Mercedes-Benz 609D	Frank Guy	B19F	1995	
6532	M902LTT	Mercedes-Benz 609D	Frank Guy	B19F	1995	
6533	M676RAJ	Mercedes-Benz 709D	Alexander Sprint	B25F	1994	Go-Ahead (Gateshead), 1998
6534	M677RAJ	Mercedes-Benz 609D	Alexander Sprint	B25F	1994	Go-Ahead (Gateshead), 1998
6535	M678RAJ	Mercedes-Benz 609D	Alexander Sprint	B25F	1994	Go-Ahead (Gateshead), 1998

6601-6625   Mercedes-Benz 709D   Plaxton Beaver   B23F*   1993   *6602/20-5 are B25F

6601	K601ORL	6606	K606ORL	6611	K611ORL	6616	K616ORL	6621	K621ORL
6602	K602ORL	6607	K607ORL	6612	K612ORL	6617	K617ORL	6622	K622ORL
6603	K603ORL	6608	K608ORL	6613	K613ORL	6618	K618ORL	6623	K623ORL
6604	K604ORL	6609	K609ORL	6614	K614ORL	6619	K619ORL	6624	K624ORL
6605	K605ORL	6610	K610ORL	6615	K615ORL	6620	K620ORL	6625	K625ORL

6628-6651   Mercedes-Benz 709D   Plaxton Beaver   B23F   1994

6628	L628VCV	6633	L633VCV	6638	L638VCV	6643	L643VCV	6648	L648VCV
6629	L629VCV	6634	L634VCV	6639	L639VCV	6644	L644VCV	6649	L649VCV
6630	L630VCV	6635	L635VCV	6640	L640VCV	6645	L645VCV	6650	L650VCV
6631	L631VCV	6636	L636VCV	6641	L641VCV	6646	L646VCV	6651	L651VCV
6632	L632VCV	6637	L637VCV	6642	L642VCV	6647	L647VCV		

6652	M246VWU	Mercedes-Benz 709D	Plaxton Beaver	B23F	1995	Yorkshire Rider, 1996
6653	M226VWU	Mercedes-Benz 709D	Plaxton Beaver	B23F	1995	Yorkshire Rider (RY), 1996

6654-6658

		Mercedes-Benz 709D	Reeve Burgess Beaver	B25F	1988	First Cymru (SWT), 1998

6654	E283UCY	6655	E284UCY	6656	E285UCY	6657w	E286UCY	6658	E288VEP

6659	N719GRV	Mercedes-Benz 709D	Plaxton Beaver	B27F	1996	Hampshire (P), 1999
6660	F318AWN	Mercedes-Benz 709D	Reeve Burgess Beaver	B25F	1988	
6661	F305AWN	Mercedes-Benz 709D	Reeve Burgess Beaver	B25F	1988	
6662	H346LJN	Mercedes-Benz 709D	Reeve Burgess Beaver	B23F	1992	Essex Buses (EN), 1998
6663	K435XRF	Mercedes-Benz 709D	Plaxton Beaver	B24F	1992	First PMT, 1999
6664	K443XRF	Mercedes-Benz 709D	Plaxton Beaver	B24F	1992	First PMT, 1999
6665	K432XRF	Mercedes-Benz 709D	Plaxton Beaver	B24F	1992	First PMT, 1999
6666	H481JRE	Mercedes-Benz 709D	PMT	B25F	1990	First PMT, 1999
6667	K433XRF	Mercedes-Benz 709D	Plaxton Beaver	B24F	1992	First PMT, 1999
6668	H180JRE	Mercedes-Benz 709D	PMT	B25F	1990	First PMT, 1999
6669	K477XRF	Mercedes-Benz 709D	Plaxton Beaver	B24F	1992	First PMT, 1999
6670	H345LJN	Mercedes-Benz 709D	Reeve Burgess Beaver	B23F	1992	Essex Buses (EN), 1998
6700	R650TDV	Mercedes-Benz Vario O810	Plaxton Beaver 2	B29F	1997	
6701	R851YDV	Mercedes-Benz Vario O810	Plaxton Beaver 2	B29F	1997	
6702	R852TFJ	Mercedes-Benz Vario O810	Plaxton Beaver 2	B27F	1998	
6703	R853TFJ	Mercedes-Benz Vario O810	Plaxton Beaver 2	B27F	1998	

6704-6711

		Mercedes-Benz Vario O810	Plaxton Beaver 2	B29F*	1999	*6704 is B33F, 6706 is B27F

6704	S865NOD	6706	S867NOD	6708	S869NOD	6710	S871NOD	6711	S872NOD
6705	S866NOD	6707	S868NOD	6709	S870NOD				

6801-6815

		Optare Solo M850	Optare	N27F	1999-2000	

6801	V801KAF	6804	W804PAF	6807	W807PAF	6811	W811PAF	6814	W814PAF
6802	V802KAF	6805	W805PAF	6808	W808PAF	6812	W812PAF	6815	W815PAF
6803	V803KAF	6806	W806PAF	6809	W809PAF	6813	W813PAF		

9702	L548CDV	Dennis Dart 8.5SDL	Wright Handybus	B28FL	1993	Operated on behalf of South Devon Council
9712	T789RDV	LDV Convoy	LDV	B18F	1999	On loan
9717	V196LFJ	LDV Convoy	LDV	M12	1999	On loan
9719	N428FOW	Dennis Dart 8.5SDL3054	UVG UrbanStar	B40F	1995	On loan
9720	N762SAV	Dennis Dart 8.5SDL3054	Marshall	B40F	1995	On loan
9721	P644TMV	Setra S250	Setra Special	C48F	1997	Clarkes of London, 2001

Special Event vehicles:

1056	OTA290G	Bristol VRT/SL/6LX	Eastern Coach Works	B39/31F	1969	
1255	VOD125K	Bristol LHS6L	Marshall	B33F	1972	
1300	OCK997K	Bristol VRT/SL2/6LX	Eastern Coach Works	B39/31F	1972	Crosville Cymru, 1987
2019	824KDV	Bristol Lodekka FLF6G	Eastern Coach Works	B38/30F	1963	preservation

Ancillary Vehicles:

2202	894GUO	Leyland Tiger TRCTL11/3R	Plaxton Paramount 3500	C55F	1983	Grampian (Mair's), 1997
3550	JTH44W	Leyland Leopard PSU3F/5R	Plaxton Supreme IV Express	C53F	1982	Brewers, 1994
3551	NTH156X	Leyland Leopard PSU3F/5R	Duple Dominant IV	TV	1982	Brewers, 1994
6054	B41AAF	Mercedes-Benz L608D	G&M	TV	1984	
6099	C796FRL	Mercedes-Benz L608D	Reeve Burgess	Staff	1986	
6177	C377RUY	Mercedes-Benz L608D	Reeve Burgess	Staff	1986	First Midland Red, 2000
9703	RHE987R	Bristol LHS6L	Plaxton Supreme III Express	TV	1977	
9708	UTO835S	Bristol VRT/SL3/501	Eastern Coach Works	Tree	1972	Devon General, 1987
9718	AFJ739T	Bristol LHS6L	Plaxton Supreme III Express	TV	1979	

The South West Bus Handbook

Previous Registrations:

481FPO	B826KRY	NER621	B295KPF
530OHU	A205SAE	NTH156X	MEP969X, YBK132
894GUO	FNM863Y, JCV426, CSO544Y	P644TMV	P300TCC
A206SAE	A206SAE, CSV231	RUH346	D507GHY
EWV665	D506GHY	TJI4838	E322OMG
FDZ980	G521LWU	TJY761	F445DUG
FNJ905	F446DUG	UHW661	D511HHW
FNR923	B291KPF	UKT552	B102JAB
GIL2967	E634UNE, LSK819	UWB183	D508HHW
G326PEW	G326PEW, 920GTA	VOO273	A101JJT
HFN769	F444DUG	WNN734	G541LWU
HVJ716	A658VDA	WSV408	HUA604Y
JTH44W	GTH536W, 948RJO	XFF283	D505GHY

Allocations and special liveries

Barnstaple (Coney Avenue) - First Red Bus

Outstations - Bideford; Bow; Bude; Ilfracombe; Morchard Bishop; Tiverton and Torrington

LDV	9712	9717						
Mercedes-Benz	6370	6371	6372	6373	6374	6375	6376	6377
	6379	6380	6520	6521	6522	6523	6527	6528
	6530	6533	6534	6535	6613	6615	6616	6617
	6618	6619	6624	6625	6652	6653	6654	6655
	6656	6658	6661	6700	6701	6702	6703	6704
	6705	6706	6707	6708	6709	6710	6711	
Solo	6801	6802	6803					
Dart	4000	4001	4002	4003	4004	4005	4006	4008
	4009	4010	4011	4474	4475	4476	4477	4478
	9702							
Lynx	2606	2607	2608	2613				
Volvo B10M	2304	2821						
Setra	9721							
Javelin	2850	2851	2853	2854				
National	2802	2808						
Bristol VR	1175	1229	1265					
Atlantean	1009	1010	1011	1012	1014	1015	1016	1017
Olympian	1815	1816	1817					
Trident	1501	1502	1503	1504				

Camborne (Union Street) - Western National

Outstations: Flambards, Helston; Trecerus Ind Est, Padstow; Long Rock Ind Est, Penzance and Lemon Quay, Truro.

Mercedes-Benz	6271	6272	6273	6274	6275	6276	6277	6278
	6279	6280	6281	6283	6284	6285	6286	6287
	6289	6290	6291	6292	6301	6329	6331	6332
	6333	6334	6335	6336	6337	6338	6339	6340
	6341	6342	6343	6358	6359	6360	6381	6382
	6383	6384	6385	6386	6640	6641	6642	6643
	6644	6645	6646	6647	6662	6663	6664	6666
	6667	6668	6669	6670				
Dart	4401	4410	4412	4413	4414	4415	4416	4417
	4418	4419	4420	4421	4422	4423	4424	4425
	4426	4454	4455	4456	4457	4458	4459	4463
	4464	4469	4470	4471	4472	4473		
Tiger	2213	2217	2218	2219	2220	2226		
Volvo B10M	2247	2252	2301	2302	2303	2305	2307	2308
	2309	2310	2311	2312	2313	2316	2401	2402
	2505	2822	2852					
Volvo B12	2101	2102	2103					
Bristol VR	1003	1123	1128	1131	1135	1136	1145	1147
	1148	1149	1153	1182	1233	1238	1240	1242
	1243	1244	1249	1251	1256	1258	1261	1263
Olympian	1754	1755						

The introduction of low floor double-deck buses into North Devon occurred in 2000 when Red Bus received four Dennis Tridents with East Lancashire Lolyne bodies. These are generally found on the Bideford to Ilfracombe service. Shown here is 1503, X503BFJ. *Richard Godfrey*

Plymouth (Laira Bridge Road) - Western National

Outstations: New Road, Callington; Little Cotton Farm, Dartmouth; Okehampton; Crowndale Road, Tavistock; Wills Road Ind Est, Totnes and Trevol Road, Torpoint.

Mercedes-Benz	6328	6344	6345	6346	6347	6348	6349	6350
	6351	6352	6353	6354	6355	6356	6357	6500
	6524	6526	6529	6601	6602	6603	6604	6605
	6606	6607	6608	6609	6610	6611	6612	6614
	6620	6621	6622	6623	6648	6649	6650	6651
	6659	6660						
Solo	6804	6805	6806	6807	6808	6809	6811	6812
	6813	6814	6815					
Dart	4007	4402	4403	4404	4405	4406	4407	4408
	4409	4411	4433	4434	4435	4436	4437	4438
	4439	4440	4441	4442	4443	4444	4445	4446
	4447	4448	4449	4450	4451	4452	4453	4460
	4461	4462	4465	4466	4467	4468	4501	4502
	4503	9719	9720					
Volvo B6	4601	4602	4603	4604	4605	4606	4607	4608
	4609							
Lynx	2600	2601	2602	2603	2604	2605	2609	2610
	2611	2612						
Leopard	3550							
Tiger	2207	2209	2216	2221	2224	2227		
Volvo B10M	2248	2253	2258	2259	2260	2261	2314	2315
	2506	2507	2507	2511	2521	2522		
Bristol VR	1155	1174	1176	1183	1197	1198	1199	1200
	1201	1202	1203	1227	1228	1239	1248	1252
	1259	1260	1262	1302	1304			
Atlantean	1007	1008	1013					
Olympian	1750	1751	1752	1753	1756	1757	1758	1801
	1802	1803	1804	1818				
Citybus	1790	1791						

Now mostly used on local service, Red Bus 2821, G326PEW is a Plaxton Expressliner based on the syling of the Paramount 3500. When pictured in Taunton in June 2001, it was once again undertaking National Express duties. *Richard Godfrey*

St Austell (Elliot Road) - Western National

Outstations: Bodmin; Camworthy Water; Delabole; Tregonnigie Industrial Estate, Falmouth; Tolcarne Street, Newquay; North Petherwin and Pelynt.

Mercedes-Benz	6090	6146	6152	6155	6302	6303	6308	
	6309	6310	6311	6318	6321	6322	6323	6326
	6531	6532	6628	6629	6630	6631	6632	6633
	6634	6635	6636	6637	6638	6639	6665	
Dart	4427	4428	4429	4430	4431	4432		
Leopard	3544	3546						
Tiger	2211	2214	2215	2223				
Bristol VR	1106	1114	1116	1117	1118	1119	1121	1129
	1132	1133	1134	1138	1139	1140	1141	1142
	1143	1154	1187	1224	1225	1226	1230	1231
	1234	1236	1246	1250	1253	1254	1257	1301
	1306							

Unallocated

Mercedes-Benz	6061	6104	6116	6657			
National	2801	2807					
Bristol VR	1006	1120	1137	1144	1232	1237	1305

FOSSEWAY / FARESAVER

J V Pickford, 10 Bumpers Enterprise Centre, Vincients Road, Chippenham, SN14 6QA

D413TFT	Mercedes-Benz 709D	Reeve Burgess	B25F	1986	Munden, Bristol, 2000
D210OKY	Mercedes-Benz 709D	Reeve Burgess	B23F	1986	Redline, Penwortham, 2000
D131PTT	Ford Transit VE6	Mellor	B16F	1987	Stagecoach Devon, 1999
D647NOD	Ford Transit VE6	Mellor	B16F	1987	Stagecoach Devon, 1999
D656NOD	Ford Transit VE6	Mellor	B16F	1987	Stagecoach Devon, 1997
D796NDV	Ford Transit VE6	Mellor	B16F	1987	Stagecoach Devon, 1998
E210BDV	Ford Transit VE6	Mellor	B16F	1987	Stagecoach Devon, 1998
E806WDV	Ford Transit VE6	Mellor	B16F	1987	Stagecoach Devon, 1998
E45UKL	Mercedes-Benz 609D	Reeve Burgess Beaver	B20F	1987	Arriva Cymru, 2000
E50UKL	Mercedes-Benz 609D	Reeve Burgess Beaver	B20F	1987	Arriva Scotland West, 2000
F378UCP	Mercedes-Benz 609D	Reeve Burgess Beaver	B24F	1988	Whitehead, Hoddlesden, 2001
F125TRU	Mercedes-Benz 709D	Reeve Burgess Beaver	B23F	1988	Arriva The Shires, 2000
F128TRU	Mercedes-Benz 709D	Reeve Burgess Beaver	B23F	1988	Arriva The Shires, 2000
F313PRF	Ford Transit VE6	Dormobile	B20F	1988	The Birmingham Omnibus Co, 1992
TIL2746	Mercedes-Benz 609D	Reeve Burgess Beaver	B20F	1989	A2B Travel, Prenton, 1996
TIL2747	Mercedes-Benz 609D	Reeve Burgess Beaver	B20F	1989	A&S, Leicester, 2001
F132KAO	Mercedes-Benz 609D	Reeve Burgess Beaver	B20F	1989	Devon Services, Crediton, 1996
F328FCY	Mercedes-Benz 814D	Robin Hood	B31F	1989	First Cymru, 1999
PSV244	Mercedes-Benz 811D	Optare StarRider	B33F	1989	Metrobus, 1999
G434ETW	Ford Transit VE6	Dormobile	B16F	1990	White Lion, Tredegar, 1996
G58RGG	Renault-Dodge S56	Reeve Burgess Beaver	B23F	1990	Wilson, Carnwath, 1999
G192NWY	Renault-Dodge S56	Reeve Burgess Beaver	B23F	1990	Wilson, Carnwath, 1999
G193NWY	Renault-Dodge S56	Reeve Burgess Beaver	B23F	1990	Wilson, Carnwath, 1999
G195NWY	Renault-Dodge S56	Reeve Burgess Beaver	B23F	1990	Wilson, Carnwath, 1999
G196NWY	Renault-Dodge S56	Reeve Burgess Beaver	B23F	1990	Wilson, Carnwath, 1999
G197NWY	Renault-Dodge S56	Reeve Burgess Beaver	B23F	1990	Wilson, Carnwath, 1999

By the time Ford's VE6 version of the Transit was produced most large minibus operator had chosen the Mercedes-Benz as their chassis. Transit Holdings purchased the Ford with Mellor bodywork for Bayline and Devon General service. Now operating in Faresaver colours is D796NDV. *Richard Godfrey*

Bath's Pierrepont Street is the loaction for this view of Fosseway TIL2744, a Mercedes-Benz 811D with ...
bodywork and recently re-registered. Its original identity had not been established as we go to press. *Richard*

H523UWE	Mercedes-Benz 709D	Whittaker Europa	B29F	1990	Arriva The Shires, 2000
H882LOX	Mercedes-Benz 811D	Carlyle C17	B28F	1990	Stagecoach Fife Buses, 2000
H204EKO	Mercedes-Benz 709D	Carlyle C19	B25F	1991	Arriva Southern Counties, 2000
H985FTT	Mercedes-Benz 811D	Carlyle C19	BC29F	1991	Stagecoach Bluebird, 2001
H641YWE	Mercedes-Benz 811D	Whittaker Europa	B31F	1991	Arriva The Shires, 2000
H185CNS	Mercedes-Benz 609D	Made-to-Measure	B26F	1991	Arriva Scotland, 2001
L422CPB	Mercedes-Benz 709D	Dormobile Routemaker	B25F	1993	Arriva Cymru, 2001
L423CPB	Mercedes-Benz 709D	Dormobile Routemaker	B25F	1993	Arriva Cymru, 2001
L427CPC	Mercedes-Benz 709D	Dormobile Routemaker	B25F	1993	Arriva Cymru, 2001

Previous Registrations:

G58RGG	G673NUA	TIL2744	?
PIL8283	G840LWR	TIL2746	F133KAO
PSV244	G301CPL	TIL2747	F407MTY

Livery: White and blue

GEOFF WILLETTS

FR Willetts & Co (Yorkley) Ltd, Main Road, Pillowell, Lydney, GL15 4QY

2464FH	Leyland National 11351/1R		B52F	1974	East Yorkshire, 1994
E322UUB	Volvo B10M-61	Plaxton Paramount 3200 III	C53F	1988	Wallace Arnold, 1991
G290XFH	Leyland Tiger TRCL10/3ARZA	Plaxton Paramount 3200 III	C57F	1989	
H937DRJ	Volvo B10M-60	Plaxton Paramount 3200 III	C53F	1991	Shearings, 1995
N993LFH	Ford Transit VE6	Ford	M11	1995	
890CVJ	Setra S250	Setra Special	C53FT	1996	Travellers, Hounslow, 1998
X904ADF	Mercedes-Benz Vario O814	Plaxton Cheetah	C33F	2000	

Previous Registrations:
890CVJ   N200TCC   2464FH   GCY748N

Livery: Mauve, maroon and red

The Geoff Willetts fleet includes a Setra S250 Special, a product from aimed solely at the British and Irish right-hand drive markets. 890CVJ is seen with 50th anniversary lettering. *Robert Edworthy*

GREY CARS

Millmans Coaches Ltd, 6 Daneheath Business Park, Wentworth Road, Heathfield,
Newton Abott, TQ12 6TL

RAN646R	Bristol VRT/SL3/6LXB	Eastern Coach Works	B44/30F	1977	Roselyn Coaches, Par, 1989
KAD355V	Leyland Leopard PSU5C/4R	Plaxton Supreme IV	C57F	1980	Pymouth City Bus, 2000
PWX240X	Volvo B58-61	Plaxton Supreme IV	C57F	1982	Terry Shaw, Barnsley, 1983
YWX401X	Leyland Olympian ONTL11/1R	Northern Counties	B43/28F	1982	Arriva Cymru, 2000
A104OUG	Leyland Olympian ONTL11/1R	Northern Counties	B43/28F	1984	Arriva Cymru, 2000
GIL3113	Volvo B10M-61	Plaxton Paramount 3200 III	C53FT	1985	
PJI2804	Volvo B10M-61	Plaxton Paramount 3200 III	C53F	1985	Frames Rickards, Brentford, 1991
PJI2805	Volvo B10M-61	Plaxton Paramount 3200 III	C53F	1985	Frames Rickards, Brentford, 1991
MIL3010	Volvo B10M-61	Plaxton Paramount 3500 III	C49FT	1987	Park's of Hamilton, 1988
SIL4460	Leyland Tiger TRCTL11/3RZ	Plaxton Paramount 3200 III	C53F	1987	Hedingham, 1999
SIL4466	Leyland Tiger TRCTL11/3RZ	Plaxton Paramount 3200 III	C53F	1987	Hedingham, 1999
E506CTT	Mercedes-Benz 811D	Devon Conversions	C19F	1987	Plymouth Co-op, 1995
MIL2066	Neoplan N122/3	Neoplan Skyliner	C57/18CT	1988	Rothwells Super Travel, 1999
MIL2088	Neoplan N122/3	Neoplan Skyliner	C57/18CT	1988	Airport Coaches Ltd, 1999
PJI2803	Volvo B10M-60	Jonckheere Deauville P599	C51FT	1989	Marbill, Beith, 1991
MIL3012	Volvo B10M-62	Van Hool Alizée	C49FT	1994	Park's of Hamilton, 1996
M582DAF	Toyota Coaster HDB30R	Caetano Optimo III	C21F	1995	First Western National, 1999
SIL4470	Volvo B10M-62	Van Hool Alizée	C51FT	1996	
SIL3066	Dennis Javelin GX	Berkhof Axial 50	C53F	1997	Limebourne, Battersea, 1998
S748XYA	Volvo B10M-62	Van Hool T9 Alizée	C51FT	1998	

Previous Registrations:

E506CTT	E506CTT, MIL3012	MIL3012	LSK483, L629AYS
GIL3113	B230RRU	PJI2803	G842GNV
GIL4604	A306XHE	PJI2804	B534BML
GIL4605	A308XHE	PJI2805	B535BML
		SIL3066	P889FMO
MIL2066	E482YWJ	SIL4460	D584MVR
MIL2088	E473YWJ	SIL4466	D600MVR
MIL3010	D819SGB, 944JTT, D922UOD, PJI2807	SIL4470	N25EYD

Livery: Grey and yellow

**1998 saw the arrival of a Van Hool T9 coach, S748XYA, which is shown here rounding Parliament Square
while on a visit to London. The long-established Grey Cars name has always been associated with south
Devon and was purchased by Millmans Coaches from the previous owners.** *Colin Lloyd*

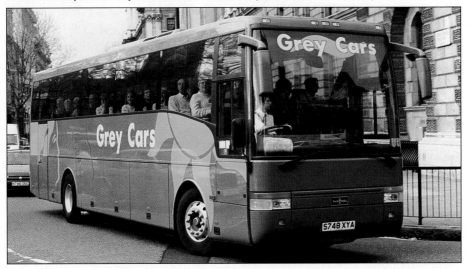

HAMBLYS OF KERNOW

P A & A F Hambly, The Garage, Jubilee Hill, Pelynt, Looe, PL13 2JZ

NFL649R	Bedford YMT	Plaxton Supreme III Express	C53F	1976	Go Whippett, Fenstanton, 1985
BJF889T	Bedford YMT	Plaxton Supreme IV Express	C53F	1978	Ford's Coaches, Gunnislake, 1990
645UCV	Volvo B58-61	Plaxton Supreme IV	C57F	1980	Ford's Coaches, Gunnislake, 1996
GAF167V	Bedford YMT	Duple Dominant II Express	C53F	1980	
539WCV	Volvo B58-61	Plaxton Supreme IV	C53F	1981	Filer, Ilfracombe, 1996
WAF156	Volvo B10M-61	Van Hool Alizée	C48F	1982	Stagecoach Cumberland, 1999
710VCV	Volvo B10M-61	Plaxton Paramount 3500	C53F	1983	Prout, Port Isaac, 1995
YCV500	Volvo B10M-61	Van Hool Alizée	C53F	1985	Taunton Coaches, 1998
H362BDV	Mercedes-Benz 709D	Wadham Stringer Wessex	B25F	1990	Plymouth Citybus, 1998
L329LSC	Mercedes-Benz 709D	Dormobile Routemaker	B29F	1993	HAD, Shotts, 1996
S100PAF	Mercedes-Benz Vario O814	Plaxton Beaver 2	B31F	1998	

Previous Registrations:

539WCV	PFH5W, 29DRH, SFH694W, PJI2417	GAF167V	YCV500
645UCV	CEB135V, WUF955	WAF156	URM141X, LJC800
710VCV	LTR444Y, 800GTR, 710VCV, BYJ967Y	YCV500	B319UNB, XFJ379

Livery: Cream and red

Basking in the sun before heading for the fishing village of Polperro is Hamblys' Mercedes-Benz Vario S100PAF. This 31-seat Plaxton Beaver 2 follows roads previously served by Bedford OBs and Bristol LHSs of similar capacity if not character. *Robert Edworthy*

HOOKWAYS

Hookways - Greenslades - Jennings

G V Hookway, The Garage, Meeth, Okehampton, EX20 3EP

Reg	Chassis	Body	Seating	Year	History
RCV493M	Volvo B58-56	Plaxton Panorama Elite III	C53F	1974	Jennings, Bude, 1998
LUA243V	Volvo B58-61	Plaxton Supreme IV	C51F	1980	Jennings, Bude, 1998
990XYA	Volvo B58-56	Plaxton Supreme IV	C51C	1980	Greenslades, Exeter, 1996
NIW8290	Volvo B58-56	Plaxton Supreme IV	C51C	1981	Greenslades, Exeter, 1996
YNW33X	Leyland Leopard PSU3E/4R	Plaxton Supreme IV	C53F	1982	Lofty's, Bridge Trafford, 1993
OBO631X	Leyland Tiger TRCTL11/2R	Plaxton Supreme V	C51F	1982	Summerdale Cs, Letterston, 1999
KUY443X	Volvo B58-61	Duple Dominant III	C57F	1982	Jennings, Bude, 1998
URU651X	Volvo B10M-61	Plaxton Supreme VI	C51F	1982	Jennings, Bude, 1998
1434HP	Van Hool T815	Van Hool Acron	C49FT	1982	Geen, South Molton, 1989
MIL3727	Volvo B10M-61	Plaxton Paramount 3200	C57F	1983	Jennings, Bude, 1998
6185RU	DAF MB200DKFL600	Plaxton Paramount 3200	C35FL	1983	Reynolds Diplomat, Perivale, 1993
A60AFS	Leyland Tiger TRCTL11/3R	Duple Caribbean	C51F	1983	Whiehead, Rochdale, 1999
3427HP	Setra S211H	Setra	C34FT	1983	Summerfield, Southampton, 1991
223TUO	Mercedes-Benz L608D	Reeve Burgess	C19F	1984	Minibus & Coach, Lancaster, 1988
WXI3860	DAF MB200DKFL600	Duple 320	C51F	1985	Oakfield, Immingham, 1999
B157WRN	Leyland Tiger TRCTL11/3RH	Duple Laser 2	C53F	1985	Reynolds, Watford, 2001
AEF315A	Leyland Tiger TRCTL11/3RZ	Plaxton Paramount 3200	C57F	1986	Inland Travel, Flimwell, 2001
NIL2460	Leyland Tiger TRCTL11/3RZ	Duple 340	C53FT	1986	Young, Ross-on-Wye, 2001
C942DHT	Volvo B10M-61	Duple 320	C57F	1986	Altonian, Alton, 2000
C248OFE	Mercedes-Benz L608D	Reeve Burgess	B20F	1986	Waylands, Beccles, 1996
D510WNV	Fiat 79.14	Caetano Viana	C19F	1986	Berryhurst, Vauxhall, 1989
HIL6253	Leyland Tiger TRCTL11/3RH	Duple 340	C53FT	1987	Sureway Travel, Pemberton, 2001
3692HP	DAF SB2305DHS585	Plaxton Paramount 3500 III	C53F	1987	Go Whippett, Fenstanton, 1992
2603HP	DAF SB2300DHTD685	Plaxton Paramount 3200 III	C57F	1987	Seward, Dalwood, 1999
HIL7541	DAF SB2305DHS585	Duple 340	C51FT	1987	Morris Travel, Pencoed, 1994
789FAY	Volvo B10M-61	Duple 340	C57F	1987	Jennings, Bude, 1998
6740HP	Volvo B10M-61	Plaxton Paramount 3500 III	C53F	1987	Bysia Ffoshelig, 1999
9743HP	Volvo B10M-61	Plaxton Paramount 3200 III	C57F	1987	Jennings, Bude, 1998
3315HP	Volvo B10M-61	Plaxton Paramount 3500 III	C49FT	1987	Jennings, Bude, 1998
E934RWR	Freight Rover Sherpa	Carlyle Citybus 2	B18F	1987	East Midland (Chesterfield), 1995
E672XSW	Freight Rover Sherpa	Leith	M16	1987	Collinson, Longridge, 1994
F554MBC	Toyota Coaster HB31R	Caetano Optimo	C21F	1988	Gosling, Redbourne, 1999
E716CPC	Mercedes-Benz 811D	Robin Hood	BC24F	1988	Altonian, Alton, 2000
PIL6581	Volvo B10M-61	Plaxton Paramount 3200 III	C48FT	1988	Chiltern Queens, Woodcote, 2001
4691HP	LAG G355Z	LAG Panoramic	C49FT	1988	Blue Iris, Nailsea, 1997
6230HP	LAG G355Z	LAG Panoramic	C49FT	1988	Wood Bros, Buckfastleigh, 1993
7105HP	LAG G355Z	LAG Panoramic	C49FT	1988	A Line, Felling, 1998
4846HP	LAG G355Z	LAG Panoramic	C49FT	1988	Mid Wales Motorways, 1998

A picture taken in St Austell shows the winter sun on 9743HP, one of Hookways' Plaxton Paramount-bodied Volvo coaches.
Mark Bailey

Hopley's of Mount Hawke, near Truro, operate a small fleet that includes a Bristol VR and P87SAF, a sixty-seat Volvo B10B with Wright Endurance bodywork. To achieve this number some of the seating is in 3+2 format. The bus is seen in Truro preparing to run Route 304 to Porthtowan. *Richard Godfrey*

GOU908	Volvo B10M-61	Ikarus Blue Danube	C49FT	1989	Thames Transit, 1994
409FRH	Volvo B10M-61	Ikarus Blue Danube	C49FT	1989	Thames Transit, 1994
SJI8117	Volvo B10M-61	Plaxton Paramount 3500 III	C51FT	1989	Buddens, Romsey, 1997
7346HP	Volvo B10M-61	Plaxton Paramount 3500 III	C49FT	1989	Stevens, Bristol, 1999
F921YNV	DAF SB2305DHS585	Jonckheere Deauville P599	C51FT	1989	Fairline, Glasgow, 2001
F714EUG	Toyota Coaster HB31R	Caetano Optimo	C21F	1989	Redhill & Singh, Thornbury, 2000
G604YUT	Toyota Coaster HB31R	Caetano Optimo	C21F	1989	Gale, Hazelmere, 1999
G105APC	Toyota Coaster HB31R	Caetano Optimo	C21F	1990	Chariots, Stanford-le-Hope, 2000
5351HP	LAG G355Z	LAG Panoramic	C49FT	1990	Cumfilux Travel, Hillingdon, 1997
9880HP	Volvo B10M-60	Ikarus Blue Danube	C49FT	1991	Thames Transit, 1994
H660UWR	Volvo B10M-61	Plaxton Paramount 3500 III	C51FT	1991	Hill, Hanwell, 2001
H891JVR	Volvo B10M-61	Plaxton Paramount 3500 III	C51FT	1991	Leon's of Stafford, 2001
H912JVR	Volvo B10M-61	Plaxton Paramount 3500 III	C51FT	1991	Leon's of Stafford, 2001
J42VWO	Volvo B10M-60	Plaxton Paramount 3500 III	C49FT	1992	Ferris, Nantgarw, 2001

Previous Registrations:

223TOU	A710BAO	9880HP	H915FTT
409FRH	F24LBW	AEF315A	C331PEW, B542HAM
789FAY	D36LRL	B157WRN	B157WRN, 927GTA
990XAY	DYW170V	C942DHT	C942DHT, 244SYA
1434HP	XTA752X	E716CPC	E480JLK, WET590, E81LLO, KXI599
2603HP	D490RUS	F921YNV	F921YNV, XIW1184
3315HP	D809SGB	GOU908	F337CHE
3427HP	A202EPA, 156AER, 194AER, A384GPA	H660UWR	H658UWR, H660UWR, GSU382
3692HP	D366CFL	H891JVR	H168ETU, 972SYD
4691HP	E399MVV, GOU908	H912JVR	H169ETU, 588EH
4846HP	F774PFF	HIL6253	D323RNS
5351HP	G487KBD	MIL3727	SGL498Y
6230HP	F631SRP	NIL2460	C974CCV
6740HP	E565UHS, FSU375, E565UHS, DSU772, E857WEP	NIW8290	HYR175W
7105HP	F680BBD, WXI3860	PIL6581	E533PRU
7346HP	H834AHS	SJI8117	F308URU
9743HP	D275MCV	WXI3860	B901KAU, YNR778, B32RJU, NBZ1680, B512HFE,
9878HP	E561RLL		

Livery: Yellow, blue and mauve
Depots: Lansdown Road, Bude; Pinhoe Trading Estate, Exeter and The Garage, Meeth

HOPLEY'S of MOUNT HAWKE

B DR & NA Hopley, Sunic, Rope Walk, Mount Hawke, Truro, TR4 8DW

NNK808P	Bedford YRT	Duple Dominant	B66F	1976	Roselyn Coaches, Par, 1989
KVF248V	Bristol VRT/SL/6LXB	Eastern Coach Works	B43/31F	1980	Stagecoach Red & White, 1999
508AHU	Volvo B10M-56	Plaxton Supreme V Express	C53F	1982	Tillingbourne, Cranleigh, 1994
TSV302	Volvo B10M-61	Jonckheere Jubilee	C49FT	1983	Rover, Horsley, 1998
640UAF	Volvo B10M-60	Jonckheere Deauville P599	C51FT	1992	Vale of Llangollen, 2001
P87SAF	Volvo B10B	Wright Endurance	B60F	1997	
Y922DCY	Mercedes-Benz Sprint 614D	Cymric	C24F	2001	

Previous Registrations:

508AHU	NUH262X		TSV302	ONV653Y
640UAF	J986GLG, VLT149, VLT293, VLT280			

Livery: White, grey and red

JAMES BEVAN

James Bevan (Lydney) Ltd, Bus Station, Hams Road, Lydney, GL15 5PE

A20JAB	Leyland Tiger TRCTL11/3ARZ	Plaxton Paramount 3500 III	C51FT	1988	Thorpe, North Kensington, 1997
E323UUB	Volvo B10M-61	Plaxton Paramount 3500 III	C53F	1988	Wallace Arnold, 1991
F310UBL	Mercedes-Benz 811D	PMT Ami	C29FT	1989	USAF (USAF1326), 1999
K216SUY	Dennis Javelin 10m	Wadham Stringer Vanguard II	BC53F	1992	MoD(), 2001
N663THO	Volvo B10M-62	Plaxton Première 350	C49F	1995	Excelsior, Bournemouth, 1999
R170SUT	Volvo B7R	Plaxton Prima	C53F	1998	
W678DDN	Optare Solo M850	Optare	N30F	2000	

Previous Registrations:

A20JAB	E217RDW		N663THO	XEL254

Livery: Silver

The fleet of James Bevan of Lydney is represented by N663THO, a Volvo B10M with Plaxton Première bodywork. This vehicle features the continental door central to the vehicle now painted in a silver livery with pink and grey relief.
Robert Edworthy

KEITH WEBBER

R K Webber, The Garage, Blisland, Bodmin, PL30 4JE

UAL103L	Leyland Leopard PSU3B/4R	Duple Dominant	C53F	1973	Willis, Bodmin, 1990
GTA807N	Leyland Leopard PSU3B/4R	Plaxton Elite III	C47F	1974	Western National, 1991
GTA811N	Leyland Leopard PSU3B/4R	Plaxton Elite III	C47F	1974	Western National, 1991
LDV176P	Leyland Leopard PSU3C/4R	Plaxton Supreme III	C47F	1976	Western National, 1990
PCW675P	Leyland Leopard PSU3C/4R	Duple Dominant Express	C47F	1976	Prout, Port Isaac, 1994
OJI2834	Volvo B58-56	Plaxton Viewmaster III	C53F	1977	Leamland Travel, Hassocks, 1983
SAD122R	Leyland Leopard PSU3C/4R	Duple Dominant	C53F	1977	Prout, Port Isaac, 1994
SUR284R	Leyland Leopard PSU3C/4R	Plaxton Supreme III	C49F	1977	Prout, Port Isaac, 1994
FAF44V	Volvo B58-56	Duple Dominant II Express	C53F	1980	
EWE759V	Volvo B58-56	Caetano Alpha	C51F	1980	Skill's, Nottingham, 1988
WJS843X	Volvo B58-56	Plaxton Supreme IV	C53F	1982	McNairn, Coatbridge, 1998
LAZ5824	Volvo B10M-61	Duple Goldliner IV	C49FT	1982	Byron's, Skewen, 1996
8212RU	Volvo B10M-61	Jonckheere Jubilee P50	C49FT	1983	Good News Travels, Hull, 1992
TIB8702	Volvo B10M-61	Jonckheere Jubilee	C51F	1983	Redwood, Hemyock, 1993
JIL7792	Volvo B10M-61	Plaxton Paramount 3500	C49F	1983	Westward Coaches, Hayle, 1994
UDZ1287	Volvo B10M-61	LAG Galaxy	C49FT	1984	Lumley, Speke, 1992
PXI1421	Volvo B10M-61	Jonckheere Jubilee	C53F	1984	Coltbus, Dousland, 2000
LIL9397	Volvo B10M-61	Caetano Algarve	C49FT	1985	Happy Days, Woodseaves, 1996
C204HJN	Mercedes-Benz L608D	Reeve Burgess	B20F	1985	Essex Buses, 1997
C405VVN	Mercedes-Benz L608D	Reeve Burgess	B20F	1986	Cygnet, Darton, 1997
D513FAE	Mercedes-Benz L608D	Dormobile	B20F	1986	First Cymru, 1999
D895VAO	Mercedes-Benz 609D	Reeve Burgess	B20F	1987	Gardiner, Spennymoor, 1997
E714LYU	Mercedes-Benz 811D	Optare Starrider	B31F	1988	Bluebird Buses, 1998
F616XMS	Mercedes-Benz 811D	Alexander AM	B28F	1988	Stagecoach Devon, 1998
F641XMS	Mercedes-Benz 811D	Alexander AM	B28F	1988	Stagecoach Devon, 1998
F716FDV	Mercedes-Benz 709D	Reeve Burgess Beaver	BC25F	1988	Stagecoach Devon, 1999
F730FDV	Mercedes-Benz 709D	Reeve Burgess Beaver	BC25F	1988	Stagecoach Devon, 1999
F738FDV	Mercedes-Benz 709D	Reeve Burgess Beaver	BC25F	1988	Stagecoach Devon, 1999
F407KOD	Mercedes-Benz 709D	Reeve Burgess Beaver	BC25F	1988	Stagecoach Devon, 1999
F157AWO	MCW MetroRider MF154/19	MCW	B31F	1989	Tilley, Wainhouse Corner, 2000
G387FSF	Mercedes-Benz 811D	PMT Ami	BC33F	1990	Bolton School, Bolton, 1997
H898LOX	Mercedes-Benz 811D	Carlyle C17	B31F	1991	Hornsby Travel, Ashby, 1998

Previous Registrations:

8212RU	MRP845Y, 9485RH	LIL9397	18XWC, B664SEH, LJI8160, B776SFA
HDZ1287	A980JJU, 8850WU, A372HEC	OJI2834	TGD995R
JIL7792	TMD278Y, GIL5109, NYA162Y	PXI1421	A661UGD
LAZ5824	FHS742X, YDR224, NTH91X, 8405CD, YFJ781X	TIB8702	RAR1M, OO1908, USV800

Livery: Red and orange
Depot: Springfield Meadow, Old Callywith Road, Bodmin

Pictured while undertaking a charter to London Heathrow Airport is Keith Webber Travel JIL7792, a Volvo B10M with Plaxton Paramount 3500 bodywork.
David Heath

LISKEARD & DISTRICT

Liskeard & District Omnibus Company Ltd, 26 Trenouth Close, St Cleer, Liskeard, PL14 5SQ

P106WJO	Peugeot Boxer	TBP	B25F	1996
P107WJO	Peugeot Boxer	TBP	B25F	1996
W921JNF	Dennis Dart SLF	Plaxton Pointer MPD	N29F	2000
W922JNF	Dennis Dart SLF	Plaxton Pointer MPD	N29F	2000
Y263YNB	Dennis Dart SLF	Alexander ALX200	N29F	2001

Livery: White and green
Depot: Clemo Road, Liskeard and Nettings Gate, Davidstow
Named vehicles: P106WJO *Tredinnick*; P107WJO *Trecarne*; W921JNF *St Keyne*; W922JNF *St Cleer*; Y263KNB *St Neot;*

LOVERINGS

Loverings (Combe Martin) Ltd, Broughton Road, Combe Martin,
Ilfracombe, EX34 0AN

F465WFX	Volvo B10M-60	Plaxton Paramount 3200 III	C57F	1989	Independent, Horsforth, 1995
G380VVL	Ford Transit VE6	Translinc	M16	1990	Translinc, Lincoln, 1994
H821AHS	Volvo B10M-60	Plaxton Paramount 3500 III	C53F	1991	Park's of Hamilton, 1992
H822AHS	Volvo B10M-60	Plaxton Paramount 3500 III	C53F	1991	Park's of Hamilton, 1992
H648UWR	Volvo B10M-60	Plaxton Paramount 3500 III	C53F	1991	Wallace Arnold, 1995
J729CWT	Volvo B10M-60	Plaxton Excalibur	C50F	1992	Wallace Arnold, 1996
J732CWT	Volvo B10M-60	Plaxton Excalibur	C50F	1992	Wallace Arnold, 1996
K596VBC	Toyota Coaster HDB30R	Caetano Optimo II	C18F	1993	Viking Bland, Corringham, 1995
L924NWW	Volvo B10M-60	Plaxton Excalibur	C50F	1994	Wallace Arnold, 1998
M134UWY	Volvo B10M-62	Plaxton Première 350	C53F	1995	Wallace Arnold, 2000
N226HWX	Volvo B10M-62	Plaxton Première 350	C53F	1996	Wallace Arnold, 2000

Livery: White; pink and blue

Liskeard and District has recently expanded and gained several routes in the area. Three Mini Pointer Darts formed the inital service fleet with W921JNF seen in Liskeard operating route 281 from Pensilva to Trago Mills.
Mark Bailey

MARCHANTS

Marchants Coaches Ltd, 61 Clarence Street, Cheltenham, GL51 3LB

CRO671K	AEC Reliance 6U3ZR	Plaxton Elite III	BC60F	1972	Edwards, Gloucester, 1983
GDF650L	AEC Reliance 6U3ZR	Plaxton Elite III Express	C53F	1973	
XAK902T	Bristol VRT/SL3/501	Eastern Coach Works	B43/31F	1978	RoadCar, 1996
KTL25V	Bristol VRT/SL3/6LXB	Eastern Coach Works	B43/31F	1979	RoadCar, 1996
KTL26V	Bristol VRT/SL3/6LXB	Eastern Coach Works	B43/31F	1979	RoadCar, 1996
RUA451W	Bristol VRT/SL3/6LXB	Eastern Coach Works	B43/31F	1980	Bennett, Gloucester, 2000
RUA452W	Bristol VRT/SL3/6LXB	Eastern Coach Works	B43/31F	1980	Bennett, Gloucester, 2000
RUA457W	Bristol VRT/SL3/6LXB	Eastern Coach Works	B43/31F	1980	Bennett, Gloucester, 2001
UBC464X	Volvo B10M-61	Plaxton Supreme V	C57F	1981	Nash's, Smethwick, 1989
TSO17X	Leyland Olympian ONLXB/1R	Eastern Coach Works	B43/32F	1982	Pontefract Motorways, 2000
TSO31X	Leyland Olympian ONLXB/1R	Eastern Coach Works	B43/32F	1982	GHA, Corwen, 2000
WDF998X	Volvo B10M-56	Plaxton Supreme V Express	C53F	1982	
WDF999X	Volvo B10M-56	Plaxton Supreme V Express	C53F	1982	
JEY124Y	Volvo B10M-61	Plaxton P'mount 3200 (1990)	C53F	1983	Arvonia, Llanrug, 1990
LIL9843	Neoplan N112/3	Neoplan Skyliner	C57/20CT	1988	Lambert's, Beccles, 1998
E322PMD	Volvo B9M	Plaxton Derwent II	B31C	1988	Capital, West Drayton, 1999
E323PMD	Volvo B9M	Plaxton Derwent II	B31C	1988	Capital, West Drayton, 1999
E324PMD	Volvo B9M	Plaxton Derwent II	B42F	1988	Capital, West Drayton, 1999
E325PMD	Volvo B9M	Plaxton Derwent II	B40F	1988	Capital, West Drayton, 1999
F660RTL	Volvo B10M-60	Plaxton Paramount 3200 III	C53F	1989	Appleby's, 1994
G50ONN	Volvo B10M-60	Plaxton Paramount 3500 III	C53F	1989	Skills, Nottingham, 1997
G51ONN	Volvo B10M-60	Plaxton Paramount 3500 III	C53F	1989	Skills, Nottingham, 1997
G448CDG	Volvo B10M-60	Plaxton Paramount 3500 III	C53F	1990	
G993DDF	Volvo B10M-60	Plaxton Paramount 3500 III	C51FT	1990	
K729GBE	Mercedes-Benz 814D	Autobus Classique	C25F	1993	Classic, Annfield Plain, 1998
L543YUS	Volvo B10M-60	Van Hool Alizée	C47FT	1993	National Holidays, 1998
R431FWT	Volvo B10M-62	Plaxton Excalibur	C48FT	1998	Wallace Arnold, 2000
R432FWT	Volvo B10M-62	Plaxton Excalibur	C48FT	1998	Wallace Arnold, 2000
R452FWT	Volvo B10M-62	Plaxton Première 320	C53F	1998	Wallace Arnold, 2000

Previous Registrations:

F660RTL	F287OFE, 5517RH		L543YUS	XIA257, KSK954
JEY124Y	MSU593Y, VYB704		LIL9843	E214BOD

Livery: Grey and red
Depot: Prestbury Road, Cheltenham

Marchants G993DCF, is one of five Plaxton Paramounts currently operated. The fleet also includes several Bristol double-decks and a selection of Volvo B9 vehicles that spent many years around Heathrow.
David Heath

PETER CAROL

P F Collis, Bamfield House, Bamfield, Whitchurch, Bristol BS14 0XD

ROI8358	MAN 11.180 HOCL-R	Caetano Algarve II	C20FT	1994	
M940JJU	Volvo B12T	Jonckheere Monaco	C30/12CT	1994	
ROI8235	Toyota Coaster HZB50R	Caetano Optimo III	C11FT	1995	
ROI1229	MAN 11.190 HOCL-R	Caetano Algarve II	C15FT	1996	
R262THL	Neoplan N122/3	Neoplan Skyliner	C57/20FT	1997	
ROI6774	MAN 18.370 HOCL-R	Neoplan Transliner	C42FT	1997	
R83RBY	Scania K113CRB	Berkhof Axial 50	C30FT	1998	Shamrock, Pontypridd, 1999
800XPC	Neoplan N316	Neoplan Jetliner	C27FT	1998	
ROI1913	Neoplan N116/3	Neoplan Cityliner	C49FT	1999	Parry, Cheslyn Hay, 2001
S150SET	Neoplan N122/3	Neoplan Skyliner	C57/20DT	1999	
T117AUA	DAF DE33WSSB3000	Van Hool T9 Alizée	C49FT	1999	
T118AUA	DAF DE33WSSB3000	Van Hool T9 Alizée	C49FT	1999	

Previous Registrations:

800XPC	R275THL	ROI6774	R265THL
M940JJU	M940JJU, ROI7435	ROI8235	M944JJU
ROI1229	N790ORY	ROI8358	M487HBC
ROI1913	T774JWA		

Named vehicles: ROI8358 *Demi-Suite*; Plaxton Derwent 2JJU *Astco Suite*; ROI8235 *Wren Suite*.
Livery: Metallic Grey

Peter Carol, named for the founders of the business, specialises in high-quality corporate visits to sporting and entertainment venues. This is often combined with in-board catering and vehicle seating capacities reflect the high level of specification. Neoplan ROI6774 is illustated here. *Robert Edworthy*

PLYMOUTH CITYBUS

Plymouth Citybus Ltd, Milehouse, Plymouth, Devon, PL3 4AA

1-12   Dennis Dart SLF   Plaxton Pointer   N39F   1996

1	N101UTT	4	N104UTT	6	N106UTT	8	N108UTT	10	N110UTT
2	N102UTT	5	N105UTT	7	N107UTT	9	N109UTT	12	N112UTT
3	N103UTT								

13-27   Dennis Dart SLF   Plaxton Pointer 2   N39F   1998-99

13	R113OFJ	16	R116OFJ	19	R119OFJ	22	R122OFJ	25	R125OFJ
14	R114OFJ	17	R117OFJ	20	R120OFJ	23	R123OFJ	26	R126OFJ
15	R115OFJ	18	R118OFJ	21	R121OFJ	24	R124OFJ	27	S127FTA

28-40   Dennis Dart SLF   Plaxton Pointer SPD   N43F   1999

28	T128EFJ	31	T131EFJ	34	T134EFJ	37	T137EFJ	39	T139EFJ
29	T129EFJ	32	T132EFJ	35	T135EFJ	38	T138EFJ	40	T140EFJ
30	T130EFJ	33	T133EFJ	36	T136EFJ				

41-48   Dennis Dart SLF   Plaxton Pointer SPD   N41F   2000-01

| 41 | X141CDV | 43 | X143CFJ | 45 | Y645NYD | 47 | Y647NYD | 48 | Y648NYD |
| 42 | X142CDV | 44 | Y644NYD | 46 | Y646NYD | | | | |

51	M51HOD	Volvo B6-9.9M	Plaxton Pointer	B40F	1994
52	M52HOD	Volvo B6-9.9M	Plaxton Pointer	B40F	1994
53	M53HOD	Volvo B6-9.9M	Plaxton Pointer	B40F	1994

Three batches of the 11.5 metre Super Pointer Dart have been placed in service by Plymouth Citybus. This model was instigated as a joint Henlys (Plaxton) and Mayflower (Dennis) product. Both are now in the Transbus consortium with Pointer production now moved to Falkirk alongside their own ALX200 model. From the Plymouth fleet, 37, T137EFJ, is seen leaving the city. *Richard Godfrey*

The double-deck version of the Volvo Citybus B10M features an overall height greater than the normal high-bridge vehicle, thus restricting the number of operators who favour the model. Plymouth Citybus have acquired the type from the Norfolk operator, Chambers and Trent. Number 185, F602GVO is from the latte and as photographed outside the Asda store in Estover. *Mark Bailey*

55-59

								N41F	2001		
		Dennis Dart SLF			Plaxton Pointer SPD						
55	WA51ACO	56	WA51ACU	57	WA51ACV	58	WA51ACX	59	WA51ACY		

101-110

								B40F	1992		
		Dennis Dart 9.8SDL3017			Plaxton Pointer						
101	K101SFJ	103	K103SFJ	105	K105SFJ	107	K107SFJ	109	K109SFJ		
102	K102SFJ	104	K104SFJ	106	K106SFJ	108	K108SFJ	110	K110SFJ		

112-126

								B40F	1993		
		Dennis Dart 9.8SDL3035			Plaxton Pointer						
112	L112YOD	115	L115YOD	118	L118YOD	121	L121YOD	124	L124YOD		
113	L113YOD	116	L116YOD	119	L119YOD	122	L122YOD	125	L125YOD		
114	L114YOD	117	L117YOD	120	L120YOD	123	L123YOD	126	L126YOD		

127-132

								B40F	1994		
		Dennis Dart 9.8SDL3040			Plaxton Pointer						
127	M127HOD	129	M129HOD	130	M130HOD	131	M131HOD	132	M132HOD		
128	M128HOD										

159	ODV203W	Leyland Atlantean AN68B/1R	East Lancashire	O43/28D	1981	
160	ATK160W	Leyland Atlantean AN68B/1R	East Lancashire	O43/28D	1981	
161	ATK161W	Leyland Atlantean AN68B/1R	East Lancashire	O43/28D	1981	

162-171

								B43/31F	1981		
		Leyland Atlantean AN68C/1R			East Lancashire						
162	TTT162X	164	TTT164X	166	TTT166X	168	TTT168X	170	TTT170X		
163	TTT163X	165	TTT165X	167	TTT167X	169	TTT169X	171	TTT171X		

173	G643CHF	Volvo Citybus B10M-50	East Lancashire	B49/39F	1989	Arriva Southern Counties, 2000
174	G640CHF	Volvo Citybus B10M-50	East Lancashire	B49/39F	1989	Arriva Southern Counties, 2000
175	B175VDV	Volvo Citybus B10M-50	East Lancashire	B42/35F	1984	
176	B176VDV	Volvo Citybus B10M-50	East Lancashire	B42/35F	1984	
177	H177GTT	Volvo Citybus B10M-50	East Lancashire	BC48/30F	1991	
178	H178GTT	Volvo Citybus B10M-50	East Lancashire	BC48/30F	1991	

Plymouth's inital purchase of minibuses saw the Renault-Dodge S56 join the fleet. Though these have now been replaced by Plaxton-bodied Mercedes-Benz 709Ds and even these are being displaced by Darts. Seen at Tamerton Foliot in January 2001, 266, M266HOD, takes a break before returning to the city. *Mark Bailey*

179-190

	Volvo Citybus B10M-50		Alexander RV		B47/37F	1988-89	Trent Buses, 1999-2000
179	G612OTV	182	G621OTV	185	F602GVO	187	F604GVO	189	F606GVO
180	G614OTV	183	F600GVO	186	F603GVO	188	F605GVO	190	F607GVO
181	G615OTV	184	F601GVO						

195	F50ACL	Volvo Citybus B10M-50	Alexander RV	B45/37F	1989	Chambers, Bures, 2000
196	F51ACL	Volvo Citybus B10M-50	Alexander RV	B45/37F	1989	Chambers, Bures, 2000
197	G623OTV	Volvo Citybus B10M-50	Alexander RV	B47/37F	1989	Chambers, Bures, 2000
201	X201CDV	Dennis Dart SLF	Plaxton Pointer MPD	N29F	2000	
202	X202CDV	Dennis Dart SLF	Plaxton Pointer MPD	N29F	2000	
203	X203CDV	Dennis Dart SLF	Plaxton Pointer MPD	N29F	2000	
204	X204CDV	Dennis Dart SLF	Plaxton Pointer MPD	N29F	2000	

241-289

	Mercedes-Benz 709D		Plaxton Beaver		B25F	1992-95	
241	K241SFJ	251	L251YOD	261	M261HOD	271	M271HOD	281	N281PDV
242	K242SFJ	252	L252YOD	262	M262HOD	272	M272HOD	282	N282PDV
243	K243SFJ	253	L253YOD	263	M263HOD	273	M273HOD	283	N283PDV
244	K244SFJ	254	L254YOD	264	M264HOD	274	M274HOD	284	N284PDV
245	K245SFJ	255	L255YOD	265	M265HOD	275	N275PDV	285	N285PDV
246	K246SFJ	256	L256YOD	266	M266HOD	276	N276PDV	286	N286PDV
247	K247SFJ	257	L257YOD	267	M267HOD	277	N277PDV	287	N287PDV
248	L248YOD	258	L258YOD	268	M268HOD	278	N278PDV	288	N288PDV
249	L249YOD	259	L259YOD	269	M269HOD	279	N279PDV	289	N289PDV
250	L250YOD	260	L260YOD	270	M270HOD	280	N280PDV		

The South West Bus Handbook

One of the last journeys of Leyland Atlantean 155, ATK155W, was early in 2001 when pictured in the city. This model, with East Lancashire bodywork has seen extensive sevice during the last two decades though a few exaples now converted to open-top form will remain. *Mark Bailey*

301	K301WTA	Volvo B10M-60	Plaxton Première 350	C51F	1993	
302	L302YOD	Volvo B10M-60	Plaxton Première 350	C51F	1993	
304	M304KOD	Volvo B10M-62	Plaxton Première 350	C49FT	1995	
305	M305KOD	Volvo B10M-62	Plaxton Première 350	C49FT	1995	
307	N307UTT	Volvo B10M-62	Plaxton Première 350	C49FT	1996	
308	P308CTT	Volvo B10M-62	Plaxton Première 350	C49FT	1997	
309	R309STA	Volvo B10M-62	Plaxton Première 350	C49FT	1998	
311	W311SDV	Volvo B10M-62	Plaxton Première 350	C49FT	2000	
312	W312STA	Volvo B10M-62	Plaxton Première 350	C53F	2000	
313	Y313NYD	Volvo B10M-62	Plaxton Paragon	C49FT	2001	
314	Y314NYD	Volvo B10M-62	Plaxton Paragon	C49FT	2001	
340	JSK261	Volvo B10M-60	Plaxton Paramount 3500 III	C53F	1989	Fishwick, Leyland, 1992
341	JSK262	Volvo B10M-60	Plaxton Paramount 3500 III	C53F	1989	Park's of Hamilton, 1992
346	JSK264	Volvo B10M-60	Plaxton Paramount 3500 III	C53F	1990	Park's of Hamilton, 1990
350	JSK265	Volvo B10M-61	Van Hool Alizée	C53F	1984	Park's of Hamilton, 1988
351	MSL352X	Volvo B58-56	Plaxton Supreme IV Express	C53FT	1982	Travel Dundee, 1998

Special event vehicles

89R	CJY299	Leyland Titan PD1	Roe	L27/28R	1946	new to Plymouth Corporation
201R	DDR201C	Leyland Atlantean PDR1/1	Metro-Cammell	B43/34F	1965	new to Plymouth Corporation
358	MCO658	Leyland Titan PD2/12	Metro-Cammell	O30/26R	1956	

Previous Registrations:

JSK261	F973HGE		JSK265	J602UGD, MCO658, UJY932
JSK262	F968HGE		MCO658	MCO658, ADV935A
JSK264	F988HGE		MSL352X	LSP502X, ETS117

Livery: Red, white and grey

POLPERRO TRAM Co

MK, AP, KM, JC and PD Wright, 46-48 Polkyth Road, St Austell, PL25 4LW

JDR661F	Morrison Electricars	Wright, St Austell	M14	1968	milk float conversion, 1994
REO207L	Morrison Electricars	Wright, St Austell	M14	1972	milk float conversion, 1994
BEO731V	Morrison Electricars	Wright, St Austell	M16	1979	milk float conversion, 1994
E334NRL	Bedford Rascal	Wright, St Austell	M8	1988	private owner, 1993

Named vehicles: JDR661F *Maud*; REO207L *Lizzie*; E334NRL *Tinker*
Livery: Red
Depot: Fore Street, Polperro

The most unusual form of bus service in this series is provided by the Polperro Tram Company who use Morrison Electricars - more normally associated with milk floats - to connect the village car park with the harbour. Illustrating this intriguing vehicle is JDR661F. During the summer season this route is closed to normal traffic.
Tony Wilson

PULHAM'S

Pulham & Sons (Coaches) Ltd, Station Road Garage, Bourton-on-the-Water, GL54 2EN

VAD141	Volvo B10M-56	Plaxton Paramount 3200	C53F	1983	Smith's of Tring, 1995
A111EPA	Leyland Tiger TRCTL11/2R	Plaxton Paramount 3200 E	C53F	1983	City of Nottingham, 1997
WDF946	Leyland Tiger TRCTL11/3R	Plaxton Paramount 3200 E	C53F	1984	Pilcher, Strood, 1986
XDG614	Leyland Tiger TRCTL11/3R	Plaxton Paramount 3200 IIE	C53F	1986	
LDD488	Volvo B10M-61	Plaxton Paramount 3500 III	C53F	1988	
UDF936	Volvo B10M-61	Plaxton Paramount 3500 III	C53F	1989	
G680YLP	Ford Transit VE6	Dormobile	M16L	1990	LB Harrow, 1996
HDF661	Volvo B10M-60	Plaxton Paramount 3200 III	C53F	1991	Supreme, Coventry, 1993
PDF567	Volvo B10M-60	Plaxton Paramount 3200 III	C53F	1991	Supreme, Coventry, 1993
FDF965	Volvo B10M-60	Plaxton Paramount 3200 III	C55F	1991	
J914MDG	Volvo B10M-60	Plaxton Paramount 3200 III E	C57F	1991	
VDF365	Leyland Tiger TR2R62C18Z5/8	Plaxton Paramount 3200 III	C53F	1991	Metropolitan Police, 1997
ODF561	Leyland Tiger TRCL10/3ARZA	Plaxton Paramount 3200 III	C53F	1992	Metropolitan Police, 1997
L202MHL	Leyland DAF 400	Ace	M16	1993	private owner, 1998
P9WAC	Volvo B9M	Van Hool Alizée	C38F	1996	Cheyne, Daviot, 1999
WDD194	Volvo B10M-62	Van Hool Alizée	C49FT	1996	
P361UFH	Toyota Coaster HZB51R	Caetano Optimo III	C21F	1996	
P618FTV	Volvo B10M-62	Plaxton Première 350	C53F	1997	Southern Vectis, 2000
R748SDF	Volvo B10M-62	Plaxton Première	C53F	1998	

Previous Registrations:

A111EPA	A111EPA, WDD194	PDF567	H156HAC
FDF965	H345KDF	UDF936	F401UAD
HDF661	H155HAC	VAD141	A22NRO
LDD488	F150RFH	VDF365	J933CYK
		WDD194	N680RDD
ODF561	J935CYK	WDF946	A748JAY
P618FTV	P618FTV, 473CDL	XDG614	C71XDG

Livery: Cream and red

Pulham's use their fleet of Plaxton Paramount 3200 on service work as well as tours and chartes. Pictured on the Cheltenham route is J914NDG which is based on a Volvo chassis.
Robert Edworthy

QUANTOCK MOTOR SERVICES

Rexquote Ltd, 82 Taunton Industrial Estate, Norton Fitzwarren, Taunton, TN

Reg	Chassis	Body	Seating	Year	Previous operator
CYA181J	AEC Reliance 6MU4R	Plaxton Derwent	B53F	1971	H&C, South Petherton
AUF172K	AEC Reliance 6U3ZR	Plaxton Panorama Elite III		1972	
FDG468L	AEC Reliance 6MU4RA	Plaxton Panorama Elite II Exp	C45F	1973	London Country
MUR217L	AEC Reliance 6U3ZR	Plaxton Panorama Elite III		1973	Derek Randall, Acton
NNN9P	AEC Reliance 6U2R	Plaxton Supreme III	C53F	1976	Derby City Transport
NNC853P	AEC Reliance 6U3ZR	Plaxton Supreme III	C49F	1976	London Country
RCV283R	AEC Reliance 6U3ZR	Plaxton Supreme III	C55F	1977	Wheal Briton Bus Services
VMJ967S	AEC Reliance 6U3ZR	Plaxton Supreme III Express	C53F	1977	Bowman, Carlisle
APT834S	AEC Reliance 6U3ZR	Plaxton Supreme III	C53F	1977	Gardiner, Spennymoor
VPH53S	AEC Reliance 6U2R	Duple Dominant II Express	C49F	1978	London Country
TIJ687	AEC Reliance 6U3ZR	Plaxton Supreme III	C53F	1978	Jalna, Church Gresley
BUR438T	AEC Reliance 6U2R	Plaxton Supreme III	C53F	1978	Best, London
ANA5T	AEC Reliance 6U3ZR	Plaxton Supreme III	C53F	1978	Greater Manchester (Godfrey Abbott)
GNK781T	AEC Reliance 6U3ZR	Duple Dominant II	C53F	1979	Olde Luton, Luton
YPL78T	AEC Reliance 6U2R	Duple Dominant II Express	C49F	1979	London Country
YPL92T	AEC Reliance 6U2R	Duple Dominant II Express	C53F	1979	London Country
YPL105T	AEC Reliance 6U2R	Duple Dominant II Express	B53F	1979	London Country
WDK562T	AEC Reliance 6U3ZR	Plaxton Supreme IV	C53F	1979	Yelloway, Rochdale
NUB93V	AEC Reliance 6U3ZR	Plaxton Supreme IV	C53F	1980	Compass, Wakefield
ODV404W	AEC Reliance 6U2R	Duple Dominant II Express	BC53F	1981	Tillingbourne (Metrobus)

Special event vehicles:

Reg	Chassis	Body	Seating	Year	Previous operator
BTF24	Leyland Lion LT7C	Leyland	B34F	1937	Lythem St Annes Corporation
JG9938	Leyland Tiger TS8	Park Royal	C32R	1937	East Kent Road Car
AJA132	Bristol L5G	Burlingham (1950)	B35R	1938	North Western Road Car
HKL819	AEC Regal I 0662	Beadle	OB35F	1946	Maidstone & District
HUO510	AEC Regal I 0662	Weyman	B35F	1948	Devon General OC
ACH441	AEC Regal III 0682	Windover	C32F	1948	Trent Motor Services
JUP233	AEC Regal III 6821A	Burlingham	B35F	1948	Gillet & Baker, Quarrington Hill
JFM575	AEC Regal III	Strachans	B35F	1948	Crosville
JTE546	AEC Regent III 6811A	Park Royal	B33/26R	1949	Morecambe & Heysham
KTF594	AEC Regent III 9621E	Park Royal	O33/26R	1949	Morecambe & Heysham Corporation
JLJ402	Leyland Tiger PS2/3	Burlingham	C31F	1949	Bournemouth Corporation
CFN121	Dennis Lancet III	Park Royal	B35R	1949	East Kent Road Car

Quantock Motor Service has been formed to operate tendered services and budget private hire in North West Somerset. The Origins of this business were in the operation of vintage buses in connection with the North Somerset Railway. This has since developed to traditional sea-side services in Weston-super-Mare and Minehead. Representing the varied fleet is CFN121 a Dennis Lancet. *John Burch*

Seen many miles south of Stockport, whose colours adorn Leyland PD2 HJA965E as it plies local service near Taunton. *John Burch*

LJH665	Dennis Lancet III	Duple A	C35F	1949	Lee, Barnet
GWN432	Dennis Lancet III	Thurgood (1960)	FC37F	1950	Modern Super Coaches, Tottenham
CHL772	Daimler CVD6SD	Willowbrook	B35F	1950	Bullock, Fetherstone
KFM767	Bristol L5G	Eastern Coach Works	B35R	1950	Crosville
KFM893	Bristol L5G	Eastern Coach Works	B35R	1950	Crosville
LFM717	Bristol L5G	Eastern Coach Works	B35R	1950	Crosville Motor Services
LFM734	Bristol LL5G	Eastern Coach Works	B39R	1950	Crosville
FMO949	Bristol LL6B	Eastern Coach Works	B39F	1951	South Midland
DCK219	Leyland Titan PD2/3	East Lancashire	BC27/26R	1951	Ribble Motor Services
LFM302	Leyland Tiger PS1	Weymann	BC35F	1951	Crosville
NLJ271	Leyland Royal Tiger PSU1/13	Burlingham	B42F	1954	Bournemouth Corporation
CHG545	Leyland Tiger PS2/14	East Lancashire	B39F	1954	BCN Joint Transport
JVH378	AEC Regent I 9613E	East Lancashire	B33/28R	1955	Huddersfield JOC
200APB	AEC Reliance MU3RV	Burlingham	B44F	1956	Safeguard
838AFM	Bristol LD6G	Eastern Coach Works	B33/27R	1957	Crosville
ORV991	Leyland Titan PD2/40	Metro Cammell	RV	1957	City of Portsmouth
NDB356	Leyland Tiger Cub PSUC1/13	Crossley	B44F	1958	Stockport Corporation
SHO800	AEC Reliance MU4RA	Duple	C41F	1958	Creamline, Bordon
890ADV	AEC Reliance 2MU3RV	Willowbrook	C41F	1959	Grey Cars
120JRB	Daimler Freeline D650HS	Burlingham Seagull	C37F	1959	Blue Bus, Willington
501BTA	Bristol Lodekka LD6G	Eastern Coach Works	B33/27R	1959	Western National OC
503BTA	Bristol Lodekka LD6G	Eastern Coach Works	B33/27R	1959	Western National OC
LDB756	Leyland Tiger Cub PSUC1/2	Willowbrook	BC43F	1960	North Western Road Car
3655NE	Leyland Tiger Cub PSUC1/12	Park Royal	BC38D	1962	Manchester City Transport
569EFJ	AEC Reliance 2MU4RA	Harrington Cavalier 315	C40F	1962	Devon General (Greenslades)
AFE719A	AEC Reliance 2MU3RV	Harrington	OB40F	1962	Maidstone & District
CYD724C	AEC Reliance 2MU4RA	Harrington Grenader 3110	C41F	1965	H&C, South Petherton
HJA965E	Leyland Titan PD2/40	Neepsend	B36/28R	1967	Stockport Corporation

Livery: Original schemes
Web: www.rexquote.co.uk
Depots: Taunton Industrial Estate, North Fitzwarren, Taunton; Station Road, Bishops Lydeard, Taunton; Langley Green, Wiveliscombe.

REGENCY TOURS

Grasse-Regency Ltd, 48 Nightingale Rise, Portishead, Bristol, BS20 8LN

MEU177P	Leyland Fleetline FE30ALR	MCW	PO44/24D	1976	Chivers, Stratton-on-the-Fosse, 1995
OJD405R	Leyland Fleetline FE30ALR	Park Royal	O44/22D	1977	Kinch, Barrow-on-Soar, 1995
OJD469R	Leyland Fleetline FE30ALR	Park Royal	O44/24D	1977	Kinch, Barrow-on-Soar, 1995

Previous Registrations:

MEU177P   KJD1P

Livery: Yellow and blue

Regency Tours use three Leyland Fleetlines on the Bath tour. Pictured at work is OJD405R with Perk Royal bodywork now converted to open-top form. *Richard Godfrey*

RIVER LINK

Dart Pleasure Craft Ltd, 5 Lower Street, Dartmouth, TQ6 9AJ

UWV604S	Bristol VRT/SL3/6LXB	Eastern Coach Works	CO43/31F	1977	Stagecoach Devon, 2000
UWV614S	Bristol VRT/SL3/6LXB	Eastern Coach Works	CO43/31F	1977	Stagecoach Devon, 2000
V393SVV	Mercedes-Benz Vario O814	Plaxton Beaver 2	B31F	1999	Sevenoaks DC, 2001

Livery: Dark blue and cream
Depot: Baltic Wharf, St Peter's Quay, Totnes

ROSELYN

Roselyn Coaches, Middleway Garage, St Blazey Road, Par, PL24 2JJ

BJV104L	Dailmer Fleetline CRG6LX	Roe	B45/29D	1973	Derby, 1989	
244AJB	AEC Reliance 6U3ZR	Plaxton Supreme III	C57F	1976	Geen, South Molton, 1980	
TMW997S	AEC Reliance 6UZR	Duple Dominant II Express	C49F	1978	MC Travel, Melksham, 1991	
AFH390T	Bedford YMT	Duple Dominant II	C53F	1978	Prout, Port Isaac, 1995	
XAN48T	Bristol VRT/SL3/6LXB	Eastern Coach Works	B43/34F	1978	Berry, Taunton, 1999	
BKH981T	Bristol VRT/SL3/501	Eastern Coach Works	B43/31F	1978	East Yorkshire, 1996	
BKH983T	Bristol VRT/SL3/501	Eastern Coach Works	B43/31F	1978	East Yorkshire, 1996	
BCV91T	Bristol VRT/SL3/6LXB	Eastern Coach Works	B43/31F	1979	Stagecoach South, 1996	
HUD495W	Bristol VRT/SL3/6LXB	Eastern Coach Works	B43/27D	1980	Arriva Cymru, 1998	
HUD501W	Bristol VRT/SL3/6LXB	Eastern Coach Works	B43/27D	1980	Arriva Cymru, 1998	
ATK156W	Leyland Atlantean AB68B/1R	East Lancashire	B45/28D	1980	Plymouth Citybus, 2000	
ATK157W	Leyland Atlantean AB68B/1R	East Lancashire	B45/28D	1980	Plymouth Citybus, 2000	
239AJB	Volvo B58-56	Plaxton Supreme IV Express	C53F	1981		
YOR456	DAF MB200DKTL600	Plaxton Supreme V	C57F	1982	Ford's Coaches, Gunnislake, 1995	
728FDV	Volvo B10M-61	Plaxton Paramount 3500 II	C49FT	1985	Moffatt & Williamson, Gauldry, 1996	
D621SJX	DAF MB200DKVL600	Plaxton Paramount 3500 II	C49FT	1986	Summerdale Cs, Letterston, 1998	
237AJB	Volvo B10M-61	Van Hool Alizée	C53F	1988		
241AJB	Volvo B10M-61	Plaxton Paramount 3500 III	C53F	1988	Bakers, Biddulph, 1995	

Previous Registrations:

237AJB	E44SAF	728FDV	B206WUA, BSK789, B211YSL
239AJB	KAF129W	BCV91T	AET186T
241AJB	9995RU, E803NVT	TMW997S	VPH57S, 701CGA
244AJB	MUN942R	YOR456	LWS116Y, 6130EL, LWS116Y

Livery: Two-tone green and brown

Roselyn Coaches have a collection of Bristol VRs for the fulfilment of school contracts. Two full height versions have moved from East Yorkshire, including BKH981T, shown here. *Robert Edworthy*

SAFEWAY SERVICES

V L Gunn, North Street, South Petherton, TA13 5DA

Reg	Chassis	Body	Seating	Year	Origin
ASV900	Dennis Lance	Reading	C33F	1949	
GIB5970	Leyland Leopard PSU3E/4R	Willowbrook Warrior (1992)	B48F	1977	Border, Burnley, 1992
HFG207T	Leyland Leopard PSU3E/4R	Plaxton Supreme III Express	C53F	1979	Cross Country, Castle Eaton, 1996
FDC417V	Leyland Leopard PSU3E/4R	Plaxton Supreme IV Express	BC53F	1980	Cleveland Transit, 1994
HIL7772	Leyland Leopard PSU3E/4R	Willowbrook Warrior (1991)	B48F	1980	Alexcars, Cirencester, 2000
VYC852W	Leyland Leopard PSU3F/5R	Duple Dominant II Express	C53F	1981	
NPA228W	Leyland Leopard PSU3E/4R	Plaxton Supreme IV Express	C49F	1981	London & Country, 1986
YYA122X	Leyland Leopard PSU3F/5R	Plaxton Supreme IV Express	C53F	1982	
Y	Volvo B10M-61	Duple Laser	C53F	1984	Kingdoms, Tavestock, 2001
A983NYC	Leyland Tiger TRCTL11/2R	Plaxton Paramount 3200 E	C53F	1983	
C744JYA	Leyland Tiger TRCTL11/3RZ	Willowbrook Crusader	C55F	1986	
E565YYA	Leyland Tiger TRCTL11/3RZ	Duple 320	C55F	1988	
F202HSO	Leyland Tiger TRCTL11/3ARZ	Plaxton Paramount 3200 III	C55F	1988	Park's of Hamilton, 1993
G997OKK	Volvo B10M-60	Caetano Algarve II	C53F	1990	Crest Travel, Strathaven, 2000
J601KCU	Dennis Dart 9.8SDL	Wright Handybus	B40F	1991	Go-Coastline, 2001
K835HUM	Volvo B10M-60	Jonckheere Deauville 45	C50F	1993	Burton, Haverhill, 2000

Previous Registrations:

ASV900	ETP184	HIL7772	TPD25V
GIB5970	XCW153R	HHU42V	KUB555V, HHF15
HFG207T	BYJ919T, 423DCD		

Livery: Red and cream

Leyland products remain a dominant feature of Safeway Services. The fleet currently contains two Leyland Leopard coaches which were re-bodied with Willowbrook Warrior bus bodies. One has been in service since 1992 while HIL7772 joined the fleet in 2000. It is seen at Stoke-sub-Hamdon when heading for Yeovil.
Richard Godfrey

SEWARDS

RJ, IA & RM Seward, Glendale, Dalwood, Axminster, EX13 7EJ

SVJ777S	Bedford YLQ	Plaxton Supreme III	C45F	1978	Denslow, Chard, 1998
GIL3129	Bedford YMP	Plaxton Paramount 3200	C35F	1983	JVA, Midsomer Norton, 1999
D759UTA	Leyland Tiger TRCTL11/3RZ	Plaxton Derwent	B54F	1986	MoD (82KF06), 1996
D86VDV	Leyland Tiger TRCTL11/3RZ	Plaxton Derwent	B54F	1987	MoD (82KF11), 1999
E325CTT	Dennis Javelin 12SDA1907	Plaxton Paramount 3200 III	B54F	1987	
G92RGG	Volvo B10M-60	Plaxton Paramount 3500 III	C53F	1990	Bysiau Cwm Taf, Whitland, 1999
G276WFU	Leyland-DAF 200	Leyland-DAF	M8	1990	private owner, 1997
J127DGC	Mercedes-Benz 811D	PMT Ami	BC25F	1992	Crystal Palace FC
K744RBX	Renault Master T35D	Cymric	M16	1992	
K458YPK	Dennis Javelin 12SDA2117	Plaxton Première 320	C53F	1993	LB Lewisham, 2000
L486HKN	Bova FHD 12.340	Bova Futura	C55F	1994	The Kings Ferry, Gillingham, 1999
N335SDV	Bova FLD 12.270	Bova Futura	C57F	1995	
N770VTT	Dennis Javelin 12SDA2155	Berkhof Excellence 1000L	C53F	1996	
N771VTT	MAN 11.190 HOCL-R	Berkhof Excellence 1000	C35F	1996	
P719EOD	Toyota Coaster HZB50R	Caetano Optimo III	C21F	1997	
R608OTA	Dennis Javelin	Caetano Porto	C57F	1998	
R609OTA	MAN 11.220 HOCL-R	Berkhof Axial 30	C35F	1998	
T953RTA	MAN 11.220 HOCL-R	Caetano Algarve II	C35F	1999	
W346VOD	Mercedes-Benz O404-15R	Hispano Vita	C53F	2000	
W347VOD	MAN 13.220 HOCL-R	Berkhof Axial 30	C41F	2000	
X149BTA	Iveco Daily 49-10	G&M	M16	2001	
Y166GTT	Dennis R	Plaxton Paragon	C53F	2001	
Y906GFJ	Mercedes-Benz Vario O815DT	Sitcar Beluga	C27F	2001	

Previous Registrations:

GIL3129	A93GLD	L486HKN	L8KFC

Livery: Cream, green and orange

Christmas in Taunton provides much cheer while Sewards' L737PYC is seen awaiting time. It was one of three Bova Futura coaches the styling known in Holland, where it is made, as the 'pregnant' coach. The latest coach from Bova having a less-curved styling. L737PYC left the Seward fleet shortly before we went to press.
Mark Bailey

The South West Bus Handbook

SHAFTESBURY & DISTRICT

R S Brown, Unit 2 Merbury Motors, Cann Common, Shaftesbury, SP7 0EB

KGJ603D	AEC Routemaster R2RH	Park Royal	B40/32F	1966	Western Scottish, 1992
RIL6390	Bristol LH6L	Plaxton Supreme III Express	C41F	1979	Grey Cars, Newton Abbot, 1999
YAZ6393	AEC Reliance 6UZR	Plaxton Supreme III Express	C53F	1980	Barrys, Weymouth, 1998
YAZ6391	Leyland Tiger TRCTL11/2R	Duple Dominant IV Express	C53F	1983	Dorset CC, 1999
AAL587A	Leyland Tiger TRCTL11/3R	Plaxton Paramount 3200 E	C53F	1983	Continental Cs, South Bank, 1998
YAZ6394	Leyland Tiger TRCTL11/3RH	Alexander TC	C49F	1985	Stagecoach Fife, 2000
POI4905	DAF SB2300DHS585	Berkhof Esprite 340	C57F	1985	Edwards, High Wycombe, 1998
GDZ795	Leyland Tiger TRCTL11/3RH	Duple 320 Express	C51F	1986	Dunn-Line, Nottingham, 2001
YAZ6392	Mercedes-Benz 811D	Optare StarRider	BC29F	1988	Atkinson, Kirkby Malzeard, 1997
RIL9429	Freight Rover Sherpa	Carlyle Citybus 2	B20F	1988	W T Roberts, Colwyn Bay, 2000
G221VDX	Optare MetroRider MR01	Optare	B33F	1989	Houston Ramm, 2001
H913FTT	Volvo B10M-60	Ikarus Blue Danube 350	C49FT	1991	G&A, Caerphilly, 2001

Previous registrations

AAL587A	SDW920Y	YAZ6391	YPD138Y
GDZ795	C249SPC	YAZ6392	E872EHK, MXX481, E872EHK
POI4905	B690BTW, 7947RU	YAZ6393	FCX576W
RIL6390	AFJ734T	YAZ6394	B207FFS, GSU341, B207FFS
RIL9429	E166TWO		

Livery: white, yellow and green
E-mail: rogerroutemaster@aol.com
Depot: Higher Blandford Road, Shaftesbury

Just of the Higher Blandford Road, south of Shafesbury is the home of Shaftesbury and District. The fleet contains a number of interesting buses, mot least the only streached version of a front-doored Routemaster and G221VDX, the very first Optare MetroRider which was exhibited at the 1989 motor show. *Bill Potter*

SOMERBUS

Somerbus Ltd, 64 Brookside, Paulton, Bristol, BS39 7YR

620UKM	Mercedes-Benz Vario O814	Onyx	C21F	1999	
V450FOT	Mercedes-Benz Vario O814	Plaxton Beaver 2	B28F	1999	Tillingbourne, Cranleigh, 2001
704BYL	Optare Solo M850	Optare	N30F	2001	

Special event vehicle:

LHY976	Bristol L5G	Eastern Coach Works	B33D	1949	new to Bristol OC

Previous Registrations:

620UKM	S532GHT		704BYL	from new

Named vehicles: 704BYL *Billy*.
Web: www.somerbus.co.uk
Depot: Stanton Wick, Pensford

The small Somerbus fleet is used to provide town services in Shepton Mallet. The latest arrival is Billy, the name coming ferom the index mark of Optare Solo704BYL. The vehicle is seen by a digital camera when on route 776 in Midsomer Norton on its first day in service in January 2001. *Tim Jennings*

SOUTH GLOUCESTERSHIRE

J G Durbin, Station Road, Patchway, Bristol, BS34 6LP

FFR165S	Bristol VRT/SL3/6LXB	Eastern Coach Works	B43/31F	1978	Eastville, Bristol, 1998
LDS190A	Bristol VRT/SL3/6LXB	Eastern Coach Works	B43/31F	1978	Maidstone & District, 1997
GYE261W	Leyland Titan TNLXB2RR	Leyland	B43/34F	1982	Autocar, Five Oak Green, 2000
OHV766Y	Leyland Titan TNLXB2RR	Leyland	B44/29D	1983	London Central, 2000
OHV798Y	Leyland Titan TNLXB2RR	Leyland	B44/29D	1983	Trustline, Potter Bar, 2000
OFS668Y	Leyland Olympian ONTL11/2R	Eastern Coach Works	B50/31D	1983	Lothian Buses, 2000
ENH634	Volvo B10M-61	Van Hool Alizée HE	C53F	1983	Eastville, Bristol, 1996
A943SYE	Leyland Titan TNLXB2RR	Leyland	B44/26D	1984	London Central, 2000
B883YTC	Leyland Tiger TRCTL11/3LZ	Wadham Stringer Vanguard	BC54F	1985	MoD (), 1999
C681EHU	Leyland Tiger TRCTL11/3LZ	Wadham Stringer Vanguard	BC54F	1985	MoD (37KC45), 1998
C822EHU	Leyland Tiger TRCTL11/3LZ	Wadham Stringer Vanguard	BC54F	1985	MoD (), 1998
C28EHU	Leyland Olympian ONTL11/2R	East Lancashire	C47/31F	1985	First Bristol, 2001
C29EHU	Leyland Olympian ONTL11/2R	East Lancashire	C47/31F	1985	First Bristol, 2001
D840JHW	Leyland Tiger TRCTL11/3LZ	Plaxton Derwent	BC54F	1987	MoD ( ), 1999
ESK812	Volvo B10M-61	Van Hool Alizée HE	C48FT	1987	First Bristol, 2001
PSU527	Volvo B10M-61	Van Hool Alizée HE	C53F	1987	First Bristol, 2001
YYD699	Volvo B10M-60	Plaxton Paramount 3500 III	C51F	1988	Eastville, Bristol, 2000
OIL9262	Leyland Tiger TRCTL11/3ARAZ	Plaxton Paramount 3200 III E	C53F	1988	First Bristol, 2001
OIL9263	Leyland Tiger TRCTL11/3ARAZ	Plaxton Paramount 3200 III E	C53F	1988	First Bristol, 2001
OIL9264	Leyland Tiger TRCTL11/3ARAZ	Plaxton Paramount 3200 III E	C53F	1988	First Bristol, 2001
F538LUF	Leyland Lynx LX112L10ZR1R	Leyland	B47F	1989	Brighton & Hove, 2000
F544LUF	Leyland Lynx LX112L10ZR1R	Leyland	B47F	1989	Brighton & Hove, 2000
F545LUF	Leyland Lynx LX112L10ZR1R	Leyland	B47F	1989	Brighton & Hove, 2000
F546LUF	Leyland Lynx LX112L10ZR1R	Leyland	B47F	1989	Brighton & Hove, 2000
G900TJA	Mercedes-Benz 811D	Mellor	B32F	1990	Arriva Midlands North, 2000

Six former Brighton & Hove Leyland Lynx now operate for South Gloucestershire. Pictured with lettering for route 482 is G993VWV, seen here heading for the Tollgate district of Bristol. *Paul Stockwell*

Three Dennis Javelins formerly used on military service joined the South Gloucestershire fleet in 2000. South Gloucestershire is also the name of the district north of Bristol latterly part of the county known as Avon. These buses feature 70 high-back seating in 3+2 layout with seat belts, a scheme now preferred by several local authorities for school contract work. *David Heath*

G543XWS	Leyland Tiger TRCTL11/3LZM	Plaxton Derwent 2	BC54F	1989	MoD (03KJ35), 2000
G840UDV	Mercedes-Benz 811D	Carlyle C17	B33F	1990	Stagecoach Oxford, 2000
G992VWV	Leyland Lynx LX112L10ZR1R	Leyland	B47F	1990	Brighton & Hove, 2000
G993VWV	Leyland Lynx LX112L10ZR1R	Leyland	B47F	1990	Brighton & Hove, 2000
H544FVN	Leyland Lynx LX2R11C15Z4R	Leyland	B51F	1990	Halton Transport, 2000
H34HBG	Leyland Lynx LX2R11C15Z4R	Leyland	B51F	1991	Halton Transport, 2000
H422GPM	Mercedes-Benz 709D	Phoenix	B27F	1990	Tillingbourne, Cranleigh, 2000
J430PPF	Mercedes-Benz 709D	Dormobile Routemaker	B29F	1991	Tillingbourne, Cranleigh, 2000
J297NNB	Mercedes-Benz 709D	Plaxton Beaver	B27F	1992	Arriva Cymru, 2001
J606WHJ	Mercedes-Benz 709D	Plaxton Beaver	B28F	1991	Arriva London, 2001
J236NNC	Volvo B10M-60	Van Hool Alizée H	C49FT	1992	Shearings, 2001
J237NNC	Volvo B10M-60	Van Hool Alizée H	C49FT	1992	Shearings, 2001
J120SPF	Dennis Lance 11SDA3101	Northern Counties Paladin	B48F	1992	Travel Dundee, 2001
J215OCW	Dennis Lance 11SDA3101	Plaxton Verde	B47F	1992	Travel Dundee, 2001
K326PHT	Dennis Javelin 12SDA2124L	Wadham Stringer Vanguard 2	BC70F	1993	MoD (), 2000
K327PHT	Dennis Javelin 12SDA2124L	Wadham Stringer Vanguard 2	BC70F	1993	MoD (75KK34), 2000
K329PHT	Dennis Javelin 12SDA2124L	Wadham Stringer Vanguard 2	BC70F	1993	MoD (), 2000
K615RNR	Toyota Coaster HDB30R	Caetano Optimo II	C21F	1993	First Badgerline, 2001
M87DEW	Dennis Dart 9.8SDL3054	Marshall C37	B40F	1994	Halton Transport, 2000

Previous Registrations:

ENH634	MSU613Y	OIL9263	F617XWY
ESK812	D502GHY	OIL9264	F620XWY
K695RNR	K695RNR, SSU437	PSU527	D510HHW
LDS190A	JPT906T	YYD699	E576UHS
OIL9262	F615XWY		

Livery: Blue and white

STAGECOACH DEVON

Devon General Ltd, Belgrave Road, Exeter, EX1 2AJ
Bayline Ltd, Regents Close, Torquay, Devon TQ2 5NA

101-118   Mercedes-Benz Vario O814   Alexander ALX100   B29F   1998

101	R101NTA	105	R105NTA	109	R109NTA	113	R113NTA	116	R116NTA
102	R102NTA	107	R107NTA	110	R110NTA	114	R114NTA	117	S117JFJ
103	R103NTA	108	R108NTA	112	R112NTA	115	R115NTA	118	S118JFJ
104	R104NTA								

200	W102PMS	Dennis Dart SLF	Alexander ALX200	N29F	2000

300-314   Iveco TurboDaily 59.12   Mellor Duet   B21D   1994

300	L929CTT	303	L932CTT	306	L935CTT	309	L938CTT	312	L941CTT
301	L930CTT	304	L933CTT	307	L936CTT	310	L939CTT	313	L942CTT
302	L931CTT	305	L934CTT	308	L937CTT	311	L940CTT	314	L943CTT

315-333   Iveco TurboDaily 59.12   WS Wessex II   B21D   1994

315	M638HDV	319	M639HDV	323	M625HDV	327	M630HDV	331	M194HTT
316	M640HDV	320	M629HDV	324	M628HDV	328	M193HTT	332	M191HTT
317	M637HDV	321	M624HDV	325	M626HDV	329	M627HDV	333	M641HDV
318	M636HDV	322	M623HDV	326	M192HTT	330	M622HDV		

335-364   Iveco TurboDaily 59.12   Mellor Duet   B29F   1993

335	K711UTT	342w	K722UTT	347w	K730UTT	353w	K927VDV	358	K925VDV
337	K714UTT	343	K913VDV	348w	K731UTT	354w	K824WFJ	359w	K822WFJ
338	K717UTT	344w	K725UTT	351	K924VDV	356	K821WFJ	363	K816WFJ
339	K719UTT	346w	K727UTT	352	K926VDV	357	K803WFJ	364	K620XOD

365-377   Iveco TurboDaily 59.12   Marshall C31   B29F   1994

365	L193FDV	368	L197FDV	371	L204FDV	374	L210FDV	376	L212FDV
366	L194FDV	369	L201FDV	372	L208FDV	375	L211FDV	377	L214FDV
367	L195FDV	370	L203FDV	373	L209FDV					

Eighteen Mercedes-Benz Varios with Alexander ALX100 bodywork were supplied to Stagecoach Devon shortly after the fleet became part of the Stagecoach group. Pictured on route 55 to Tiverton is 104, R104NTA, an example from the batch.
Mark Bailey

378	N182CMJ	Iveco TurboDaily 59.12	Alexander AM ·	B29F	1996	Midland Red South, 1997
379	N183CMJ	Iveco TurboDaily 59.12	Alexander AM	B29F	1996	Midland Red South, 1998
381	N190GFR	Iveco TurboDaily 59.12	Mellor	B27F	1996	Ribble, 1998
382	N463HRN	Iveco TurboDaily 59.12	Mellor	B27F	1996	Ribble, 1998
383	K171CAV	Iveco TurboDaily 59.12	Marshall C31	B25F	1992	
385	K173CAV	Iveco TurboDaily 59.12	Marshall C31	B25F	1992	
386	L950EOD	Iveco TurboDaily 59-12	Mellor Duet	B26F	1994	Oxford, 1997
387	L946EOD	Iveco TurboDaily 59-12	Mellor Duet	B29F	1994	Oxford, 1997
388	L318BOD	Iveco TurboDaily 59-12	Mellor Duet	B26F	1993	Oxford, 1997
389	L945EOD	Iveco TurboDaily 59-12	Mellor Duet	B26D	1994	Oxford, 1997
390	K718UTT	Iveco TurboDaily 59-12	Mellor Duet	B26F	1993	Oxford, 1997
391	L947EOD	Iveco TurboDaily 59-12	Mellor Duet	B26F	1994	Stagecoach Oxford, 1997
392	L948EOD	Iveco TurboDaily 59-12	Mellor Duet	B26F	1994	Stagecoach Oxford, 1997
393	L949EOD	Iveco TurboDaily 59-12	Mellor Duet	B26F	1994	Stagecoach Oxford, 1997

394-399 — Iveco TurboDaily 59.12 / Mellor / B27F / 1996 / Stagecoach Ribble, 1998

394	L446FFR	396	N189GFR	397	L447FFR	398	N188GFR	399	N464HRN
395	L448FFR								

401-407 — Mercedes-Benz 709D / Alexander Sprint / B25F / 1995 / Stagecoach West & Wales, 2001

401	M701EDD	403	M703EDD	405	M705JDG	406	M706JDG	407	M707JDG
402	M702EDD	404	M704JDG						

444-468 — Mercedes-Benz 709D / Marshall C19 / B21D / 1995

444	M226UTM	449	M231UTM	454	M236UTM	459	M241UTM	464	M246UTM
445	M227UTM	450	M232UTM	455	M237UTM	460	M242UTM	465	M247UTM
446	M228UTM	451	M233UTM	456	M238UTM	461	M243UTM	466	M248UTM
447	M229UTM	452	M234UTM	457	M239UTM	462	M244UTM	467	M249UTM
448	M230UTM	453	M235UTM	458	M240UTM	463	M245UTM	468	M250UTM

470-487 — Mercedes-Benz 709D / Alexander Sprint / B23F / 1996

470	N978NAP	474	N982NAP	478	N509BJA	482	N513BJA	485	N516BJA
471	N979NAP	475	N506BJA	479	N510BJA	483	N514BJA	486	N517BJA
472	N980NAP	476	N507BJA	480	N511BJA	484	N515BJA	487	N518BJA
473	N981NAP	477	N508BJA	481	N512BJA				

488	L685CDD	Mercedes-Benz 709D	Alexander Sprint	B25F	1993	Stagecoach Red & White, 1999
489	M345JBO	Mercedes-Benz 709D	Alexander Sprint	B25F	1994	Stagecoach Red & White, 1999
490	M360JBO	Mercedes-Benz 709D	Alexander Sprint	B25F	1994	Stagecoach Red & White, 1999

491-499 — Mercedes-Benz 709D / Alexander Sprint / B25F / 1994 / Stagecoach Cheltenham, 2000

491	L691CDD	493	L693CDD	495	L695CDD	497	L696CDD	499	M699EDD
492	L692CDD	494	L694CDD	496	L696CDD	498	L696CDD		

601-616 — Iveco Daily 49.10 / Mellor Solo / B17F / 1997 / Stagecoach West, 1998-2001

601	R601KDD	606	R606KDD	609	R609KDD	613	R613KDD	615	R615KDD
602	R602KDD	607	R607KDD	611	R611KDD	614	R614KDD	616	R616KDD
604	R604KDD	608	R608KDD	612	R612KDD				

700	M343NOD	Volvo B6	Alexander Dash	B39F	1994	Citybus, Hong Kong, 2001

701-714 — Volvo B6BLE / Alexander ALX200 / N35F / 1997

701	P701BTA	704	P704BTA	707	P707BTA	710	P710BTA	713	P713BTA
702	P702BTA	705	P705BTA	708	P708BTA	711	P711BTA	714	P714BTA
703	P703BTA	706	P706BTA	709	P709BTA	712	P712BTA		

732-744 — Dennis Dart 9.8SDL3060 / Plaxton Pointer / BC39F / 1995 / Citybus, Hong Kong, 1999

732	N732XDV	735	N735XDV	738	N738XDV	741	N731XDV	743	N743XDV
733	N733XDV	736	N736XDV	739	N739XDV	742	N742XDV	744	N744XDV
734	N734XDV	737	N737XDV	740	N740XDV				

745	L139VRH	Dennis Dart 9SDL3024	Plaxton Pointer	B34F	1993	Stagecoach London, 1999
746	L140VRH	Dennis Dart 9SDL3024	Plaxton Pointer	B34F	1993	Stagecoach London, 1999
747	L141VRH	Dennis Dart 9SDL3024	Plaxton Pointer	B34F	1993	Stagecoach London, 1999
748	N411MBW	Dennis Dart 9.8SDL3054	Plaxton Pointer	B40F	1996	Stagecoach London, 1999
749	N410MBW	Dennis Dart 9.8SDL3054	Plaxton Pointer	B40F	1996	Stagecoach London, 1999

The Plaxton Premiére Interurban was specifically launched to meet the needs of Stagecoach to provide a bus suitable for the longer distance services between towns. In the 1960s this would have been described as a dual purpose bus. Six Volvo examples joined the Devon General fleet in 1996 with Dennis and articulated Volvo buses arriving subsequently. Pictured in Torquay is 803, P803XTA. *Richard Godfrey*

750	N599DWY	Dennis Dart 9.8SDL3054		Plaxton Pointer	B40F	1995	East Devon, Aylesbeare, 1997
751	R751BDV	Dennis Dart SLF		Alexander ALX200	N37F	1997	
752	L547CDV	Dennis Dart 8.5SDL		Wright Handybus	B28FL	1993	Owned by South Devon Council

753-757		Dennis Dart SLF		Alexander ALX200	N37F	1998	Stagecoach Oxford, 1998
753	R807YUD	**754**	R801YUD	**755**	R803YUD	**756**	R804YUD	**757**	R805YUD

758	P758FOD	Dennis Dart SLF	Plaxton Pointer	N37F	1997	Citybus, Hong Kong, 2000
759	P762FOD	Dennis Dart SLF	Plaxton Pointer	N37F	1997	Citybus, Hong Kong, 2000
760	P760FOD	Dennis Dart SLF	Plaxton Pointer	N37F	1997	Citybus, Hong Kong, 2000
769	G32TGW	Dennis Dart 8.5SDL3003	Carlyle Dartline	B28F	1990	Stagecoach Selkent, 1998
770	G33TGW	Dennis Dart 8.5SDL3003	Carlyle Dartline	B30F	1990	Stagecoach Selkent, 1998
771	G28TGW	Dennis Dart 8.5SDL3003	Carlyle Dartline	BC30F	1990	Stagecoach Selkent, 1997
772	G30TGW	Dennis Dart 8.5SDL3003	Carlyle Dartline	BC30F	1990	Stagecoach Selkent, 1997
773	G35TGW	Dennis Dart 8.5SDL3003	Carlyle Dartline	B30F	1990	Stagecoach Selkent, 1997
774	G34TGW	Dennis Dart 8.5SDL3003	Carlyle Dartline	BC28F	1990	Stagecoach Docklands, 1997
775	G37TGW	Dennis Dart 8.5SDL3003	Carlyle Dartline	BC28F	1990	Stagecoach Docklands, 1997
776	G36TGW	Dennis Dart 8.5SDL3003	Carlyle Dartline	B28F	1990	Stagecoach Docklands, 1997
778	NDZ3152	Dennis Dart 8.5SDL3015	Wright Handy-bus	B29F	1993	Stagecoach Selkent, 1998
779	NDZ3153	Dennis Dart 8.5SDL3015	Wright Handy-bus	B29F	1993	Stagecoach Selkent, 1998

780-786		Dennis Dart 8.5SDL3003		Wright Handy-bus	B28F	1992	Stagecoach Selkent, 1998
780	JDZ2360	**782**	JDZ2362	**784**	JDZ2364	**785**	JDZ2365	**786**	JDZ2371
781	JDZ2361	**783**	JDZ2363				

793	XIA857	Leyland National 11351/1R	B48F	1976	Stagecoach South, 1999
794	AAE658V	Leyland National 2 NL116L11/1R	B49F	1980	Stagecoach Cheltenham, 2000
795	AAE665V	Leyland National 2 NL116L11/1R	B49F	1980	Stagecoach Cheltenham, 2000
796	KHH376W	Leyland National 2 NL116L11/1R	B49F	1980	Stagecoach Cheltenham, 2000

801-806		Volvo B10M-62		Plaxton Premiére Interurban	BC51F	1996	
801	P801XTA	**803**	P803XTA	**804**	P804XTA	**805**	P805XTA	**806**	P806XTA
802	P802XTA					

807	R807JDV	Volvo B10M-55	Alexander PS	B49F	1998	
808	R479MCW	Volvo B10M-55	Alexander PS	B49F	1996	Stagecoach North West, 2001
809	CSU978	Volvo B10M-62	Plaxton Premiére 350	C53F	1995	Stagecoach East Kent, 2000
810	R480MCW	Volvo B10M-55	Alexander PS	B49F	1996	Stagecoach North West, 2001
811	R481MCW	Volvo B10M-55	Alexander PS	B49F	1996	Stagecoach North West, 2001
812	R482MCW	Volvo B10M-55	Alexander PS	B49F	1996	Stagecoach North West, 2001
813	N801DNE	Volvo B10M-55	Alexander PS	B49F	1996	Stagecoach North West, 2001
814	N802DNE	Volvo B10M-55	Alexander PS	B49F	1996	Stagecoach North West, 2001
830	M950JBO	Dennis Javelin 11SDL2133	Plaxton Première Interurban	BC47F	1994	Stagecoach Red & White, 1999
831	M105CCD	Dennis Javelin 11SDL2133	Plaxton Première Interurban	BC47F	1995	Stagecoach London, 2001
832	M106CCD	Dennis Javelin 11SDL2133	Plaxton Première Interurban	BC47F	1995	Stagecoach London, 2001
833	M108CCD	Dennis Javelin 11SDL2133	Plaxton Première Interurban	BC47F	1995	Stagecoach London, 2001
851	P563MSX	Volvo B10MA-55	Plaxton Première Interurban	AC71F	1996	Stagecoach Fife, 2001
852	P564MSX	Volvo B10MA-55	Plaxton Première Interurban	AC71F	1996	Stagecoach Fife, 2001
901	R901FDV	Volvo Olympian	Alexander RL	B45/27F	1997	
902	R902JDV	Volvo Olympian	Alexander RL	B51/36F	1998	
903	R903JDV	Volvo Olympian	Alexander RL	B51/36F	1998	
904	R904JDV	Volvo Olympian	Alexander RL	B51/36F	1998	
905	R164HHK	Volvo Olympian	Northern Counties Palatine	B49/30F	1998	Stagecoach London, 2001
906	R816GMU	Volvo Olympian YN2RV18Z4	Northern Counties Palatine	B49/31F	1997	Stagecoach London, 2001
907	R817GMU	Volvo Olympian YN2RV18Z4	Northern Counties Palatine	B49/31F	1997	Stagecoach London, 2001

922-926

		Scania N113DRB	Alexander RH	O47/31F	1991	Stagecoach London, 2000

922	J822HMC	923	J823HMC	924	J824HMC	925	J825HMC	926	J826HMC

927	J827HMC	Scania N113DRB	Alexander RH	B47/31F	1991	Stagecoach London, 2000
928	J828HMC	Scania N113DRB	Alexander RH	B47/31F	1991	Stagecoach London, 2001
929	J829HMC	Scania N113DRB	Alexander RH	B47/31F	1991	Stagecoach London, 2000
935w	VDV135S	Bristol VRT/SL3/6LXB	Eastern Coach Works	CO43/31F	1977	Western National, 1983
951	OHV738Y	Leyland Titan TNLXB2RR	Leyland	B44/27F	1983	East London, 1997
952	OHV729Y	Leyland Titan TNLXB2RR	Leyland	B44/27F	1983	East London, 1997
955	NUW660Y	Leyland Titan TNLXB2RR	Leyland	B44/27F	1982	East London, 1997
956	A67THX	Leyland Titan TNLXB2RR	Leyland	B44/26F	1984	East London, 1997
957	A632THV	Leyland Titan TNLXB2RR	Leyland	B44/26F	1984	East London, 1997
960	A976SYE	Leyland Titan TNLXB2RR	Leyland	B44/29F	1984	East London, 1997
961	EYE229V	Leyland Titan TNLXB2RRSp	Park Royal	B44/26F	1980	Stagecoach South, 1998
962	NUW630Y	Leyland Titan TNLXB2RR	Leyland	B44/27F	1982	East London, 1997
963	NUW585Y	Leyland Titan TNLXB2RR	Leyland	B44/27F	1982	East London, 1997
964	KYV444X	Leyland Titan TNLXB2RR	Leyland	B44/27F	1982	Stagecoach London, 2000
965	KYV462X	Leyland Titan TNLXB2RR	Leyland	B44/27F	1982	Stagecoach London, 2000
966	KYV469X	Leyland Titan TNLXB2RR	Leyland	B44/27F	1982	Stagecoach London, 2000
967	KYV473X	Leyland Titan TNLXB2RR	Leyland	B44/27F	1982	Stagecoach London, 2000

Special event vehicle

992	LRV992	Leyland Titan PD2/12	Metror-Cammel	O33/26R	1956	Thames Transit, 1997

Ancillary vehicles

20	G806YTA	Dodge Commando G13	Wadham Stringer Vanguard	TV	1989	USAF (90B2051), 1999
21	G818YTA	Dodge Commando G13	Wadham Stringer Vanguard	TV	1989	USAF (90B2040), 1999
22	G847LNP	Dodge Commando G13	Wadham Stringer Vanguard	TV	1990	USAF (90B2044), 2000
349	K732UTT	Iveco TurboDaily 59.12	Mellor Duet	TV	1993	

Previous Registrations:

CSU978	M408BFG	N739XDV	GM8269(HK)
G28TGW	G28TGW, 49CLT	N740XDV	GM8240(HK
M343NOD	GJ155(HK)	N742XDV	GM6090(HK)
N731XDV	GM8040(HK)	N743XDV	GM7606(HK)
N732XDV	GM5334(HK)	N744XDV	GM5868(HK)
N733XDV	GM6788(HK)	P758FOD	HB9296(HK)
N734XDV	GM9182(HK)	P760FOD	HC5574(HK)
N735XDV	GM5431(HK)	P762FOD	HB4996(HK)
N736XDV	GM5376(HK)		
N737XDV	GM6331(HK)	XIA857	PKP548R, XIA256
N738XDV	GM7131(HK)		

Named vehicle: 935 Ark Royal

To meet increased loadings on the Exeter to Plymouth service, two articulated Interurban coaches were transferred from Fife. Seen with the new X38 markings in April 2001 is 851, P563MSX. *Mark Bailey*

Allocations:

Exeter (Belgrave Road)

Outstations: Sidmouth, Cullompton, Tiverton and Ottery St Mary.

Iveco	300	301	302	303	304	305	306	307
	308	309	310	311	312	313	314	315
	316	317	318	319	320	321	322	323
	324	325	326	327	328	329	330	331
	332	333	378	379				
Mercedes-Benz	101	102	103	104	105	107	108	109
	110	112	113	114	115	116	117	118
	444	445	446	447	448	449	450	451
	452	453	454	455	456	457	458	459
	460	461	462	463	464	465	466	467
	468	471	473	477	479	481	483	484
	485	486	487	488				
Dart	200	739	740	741	742	743	744	745
	746	747	748	749	750	751	753	758
	759	760	769	770	772	773	776	781
	782	783	784	785	786			
Volvo B6	700							
National	793	794	795	796				
Volvo B10M Interurban	801	802	803	804	805	806	851	852
Volvo B10M coach	809							
Volvo B10M PS	808	810	811	812	813	814		
Javelin suburban	830	831	832	833				
Titan	951	955	956	960	962	963	964	967
Scania	927	928	929					
Olympian	902	903	904	905	906	907		

Following the delivery of larger single-deck buses to Stagecoach's Citybus operation in Hong Kong, low-floor Dennis Darts with Plaxton Pointer bodywork have returned to England for further service. These buses featured air conditioning for use on the island, that is retained by the batch on repatriation. Seen carrying the special livery for Exeter Park and Ride is 760, P760FOD. *Mark Bailey*

Exmouth (Imperial Road)

Mercedes-Benz	470	472	474	475	476	478	480	482
	489							
Dennis Dart	754	755	756	757	778	779	780	
Volvo B10M bus	807							
Titan	957	961						

Torquay (Regent Close)

Iveco	335	337	338	339	343	351	352	356
	357	358	359	363	364	365	366	367
	368	369	370	371	372	373	374	375
	376	377	381	382	383	385	386	388
	389	390	391	392	393	396	397	398
	399							
Mercedes-Benz	401	402	403	404	405	406	407	490
	491	492	493	494	495	496	497	498
	499							
Dart	732	733	734	735	736	737	738	
Volvo B6	701	702	703	704	705	706	707	708
	709	710	711	712	713	714		
Scania	922	923	924	925	926			
Titan	952	965	966					
Olympian	901							

Unallocated:-

Iveco	340	341	342	344	345	346	347	348
	360	386	387	388	394	601	602	604
	606	607	608	609	610	611	612	613
	614	615	616					
Dart	752	771	774	775				
Bristol VR(OT)	935							
Titan	953	955	992(PD2)					

STAGECOACH WEST & WALES

Cheltenham & Gloucester Omnibus Company Ltd;
Cheltenham District Traction Company Ltd; Swindon & District Bus Company Ltd
3/4 Bath Street, Cheltenham, GL50 1YE

Cheltenham, the Cotswolds, Gloucester, Swindon and Wye and Dean fleet:
The full Stagecoach West fleet is detailed in the annual Staagecoach Bus Handbook.

101-105
Leyland Olympian ONLXB/2RZ   Alexander RL   B51/36F   1990

101	G101AAD	102	G102AAD	103	G103AAD	104	G104AAD	105	G105AAD

112-124
Leyland Olympian ONLXB/1R   Roe   B47/29F   1982-83   113 Yorkshire Rider, 1987

112	JHU899X	115	LWS33Y	118	LWS36Y	121	LWS39Y	123	LWS41Y
113	UWW7X	116	LWS34Y	119	LWS37Y	122	LWS40Y	124	NTC132Y
114	JHU912X	117	LWS35Y	120	LWS38Y				

No.	Reg	Chassis	Body			
125	R203DHB	Volvo Olympian	Alexander RL	B47/32F	1998	Stagecoach Red & White, 1999
126	R204DHB	Volvo Olympian	Alexander RL	B47/32F	1998	Stagecoach Red & White, 1999
127	R205DHB	Volvo Olympian	Alexander RL	B47/32F	1998	Stagecoach Red & White, 1999
128	A648THV	Leyland Titan TNLXB2RR	Leyland	B44/27F	1984	Stagecoach London, 1999
129	A854SUL	Leyland Titan TNLXB2RR	Leyland	B44/27F	1984	Stagecoach London, 2000
130	C610LFT	Leyland Olympian ONLXB/1R	Alexander RH	B45/31F	1985	Stagecoach Busways, 1999
131	C659LFT	Leyland Olympian ONLXB/1R	Alexander RH	B45/31F	1985	Stagecoach Busways, 1999
132	C650LFT	Leyland Olympian ONLXB/1R	Alexander RH	B45/31F	1985	Stagecoach Busways, 1999
133	C624LFT	Leyland Olympian ONLXB/1R	Alexander RH	B45/31F	1985	Stagecoach Busways, 1999
134	C641LFT	Leyland Olympian ONLXB/1R	Alexander RH	B45/31F	1985	Stagecoach Busways, 2000
137	C647LFT	Leyland Olympian ONLXB/1R	Alexander RH	B45/31F	1985	Stagecoach Busways, 2000
138	MHS4P	Leyland Olympian ONLXB/1RV	Alexander RL	BC43/27F	1986	Stagecoach Bluebird, 2001
139	MHS5P	Leyland Olympian ONLXB/1RV	Alexander RL	BC43/27F	1986	Stagecoach Bluebird, 2001
141	R206DHB	Volvo Olympian	Alexander RL	B47/32F	1998	Stagecoach Red & White, 2000
142	R207DHB	Volvo Olympian	Alexander RL	B47/32F	1998	Stagecoach Red & White, 2000
143	R208DHB	Volvo Olympian	Alexander RL	B47/32F	1998	Stagecoach Red & White, 2000
310	VEU231T	Leyland National 11351A/1R(DAF)		B52F	1977	
314	YFB972V	Leyland National 11351A/1R(DAF)		B52F	1979	

The former Stagecoach Cheltenham & Gloucester fleet forms the English part of the West and Wales company. As the fleet is currently numbered separately just the part for this region is included here - the other part being included in the annual Stagecoach Bus Handbook. Pictured at Crowthorne is 412, P319EFL which was transferred from Cambus in 2000.
Tim Hall

The supply of low-floor buses for Swindon depot saw the introduction of Easyrider branding. Pictured at Swindon Market is 912, P912SMR, a Dennis Dart. During the summer 2001 the early Volvo B6s were being taken out of service for transfer to other fleets in the UK. *Richard Godfrey*

401-409

									BC48F	1995	Volvo B10M-55	Alexander PS

401	N401LDF	403	N403LDF	405	N405LDF	407	N407LDF	409	N409LDF
402	N402LDF	404	N404LDF	406	N406LDF	408	N408LDF		

410	P317EFL	Volvo B10M-55	Alexander PS	B49F	1996	Stagecoach Cambus, 2000
411	P318EFL	Volvo B10M-55	Alexander PS	B49F	1996	Stagecoach Cambus, 2000
412	P319EFL	Volvo B10M-55	Alexander PS	B49F	1996	Stagecoach Cambus, 2000

417-428

Volvo B10M-55 Alexander PS B49F 1996 Stagecoach Manchester, 1999

417	N817DNE	420	P820GNC	423	P823FVU	425	P825FVU	427	P827FVU
418	N818DNE	421	P821FVU	424	P824FVU	426	P826FVU	428	P828FVU
419	P819GNC	422	P822FVU						

501-513

Dennis Dart SLF 11.3m Plaxton Pointer SPD N41F 2000

501	W501VDD	504	W504VDD	507	X507ADF	510	X510ADF	512	X512ADF
502	X502ADF	505	W505VDD	508	W508VDD	511	X511ADF	513	X513ADF
503	X503ADF	506	X506ADF	509	W509VDD				

550-554

Volvo B10M-62 Plaxton Expressliner 2 C49FT 1997

550	R550JDF	551	R551JDF	552	R552JDF	553	R553JDF	554	R554JDF

561	N91RVK	Volvo B10M-62	Plaxton Expressliner 2	C44FT	1996	Stagecoach North East, 2001
562	P92URG	Volvo B10M-62	Plaxton Expressliner 2	C44FT	1996	Stagecoach North East, 2001

708-717

Mercedes-Benz 709D Alexander Sprint B25F 1995

708	M708JDG	710	M710JDG	712	M712FMR	714	M714FMR	716	N716KAM
709	M709JDG	711	M711FMR	713	M713FMR	715	M715FMR	717	N717KAM

718-735   Mercedes-Benz 709D   Alexander Sprint   B25F*   1996   *731-5 are BC25F

718	N718RDD	722	N722RDD	726	N726RDD	730	N730RDD	733	N733RDD
719	N719RDD	723	N723RDD	727	N727RDD	731	N731RDD	734	N734RDD
720	N720RDD	724	N724RDD	728	N728RDD	732	N732RDD	735	N735RDD
721	N721RDD	725	N725RDD	729	N729RDD				

736	N644VSS	Mercedes-Benz 709D	Alexander Sprint	B25F	1996	Stagecoach Cambus, 1999
737	N618VSS	Mercedes-Benz 709D	Alexander Sprint	B25F	1996	Stagecoach Cambus, 1999
738	N643VSS	Mercedes-Benz 709D	Alexander Sprint	B25F	1996	Stagecoach Cambus, 1999
803	L803XDG	Mercedes-Benz 811D	Marshall C16	B33F	1993	
804	L804XDG	Mercedes-Benz 811D	Marshall C16	B33F	1993	
805	L805XDG	Mercedes-Benz 811D	Marshall C16	B33F	1993	
806	L806XDG	Mercedes-Benz 811D	Marshall C16	B33F	1993	
807	L330CHB	Mercedes-Benz 811D	Marshall C16	B33F	1993	Red & White, 1994
808	K308YKG	Mercedes-Benz 811D	Wright NimBus	B33F	1992	Red & White, 1995
809	J413PRW	Mercedes-Benz 811D	Wright NimBus	B31F	1991	Midland Red South, 1997
811	J417PRW	Mercedes-Benz 811D	Wright NimBus	B31F	1991	Stagecoach Midland Red, 1998
812	J412PRW	Mercedes-Benz 811D	Wright NimBus	B31F	1991	Stagecoach Midland Red, 1998
813	J411PRW	Mercedes-Benz 811D	Wright NimBus	B31F	1991	Stagecoach Midland Red, 1998
814	J304UKG	Mercedes-Benz 811D	Wright NimBus	B33F	1992	Stagecoach Red & White, 2000
816	K311YKG	Mercedes-Benz 811D	Wright NimBus	B33F	1992	Stagecoach Red & White, 2000
819	J409PRW	Mercedes-Benz 811D	Wright NimBus	BC33F	1991	Stagecoach Red & White, 2000

831-845   Volvo B6-9.9M   Alexander Dash   B40F   1994

831	L831CDG	834	L834CDG	837	L837CDG	840	L840CDG	843	M843EMW
832	L832CDG	835	L835CDG	838	L838CDG	841	L841CDG	844	M844EMW
833	L833CDG	836	L836CDG	839	L839CDG	842	L842CDG	845	M845EMW

846	L248CCK	Volvo B6-9.9m	Alexander Dash	BC40F	1993	Ribble, 1995
847	M847HDF	Volvo B6-9.9m	Alexander Dash	B40F	1994	
848	L709FWO	Volvo B6-9.9m	Alexander Dash	B40F	1994	Red & White, 1995
849	L710FWO	Volvo B6-9.9m	Alexander Dash	B40F	1994	Red & White, 1995
850	L711FWO	Volvo B6-9.9m	Alexander Dash	B40F	1994	Red & White, 1995
851	L712FWO	Volvo B6-9.9m	Alexander Dash	B40F	1994	Red & White, 1995
901	P901SMR	Dennis Dart	Alexander Dash	B40F	1997	
902	P902SMR	Dennis Dart	Alexander Dash	B40F	1997	
903	P903SMR	Dennis Dart	Alexander Dash	B40F	1997	

904-914   Dennis Dart SLF   Alexander ALX200   N36F   1996-97

904	P904SMR	907	P907SMR	909	P909SMR	911	P911SMR	913	P913SMR
905	P905SMR	908	P908SMR	910	P910SMR	912	P912SMR	914	P914SMR
906	P906SMR							

915	R915GMW	Dennis Dart SLF	Alexander ALX200	N37F	1997
916	R916GMW	Dennis Dart SLF	Alexander ALX200	N37F	1997
917	R917GMW	Dennis Dart SLF	Alexander ALX200	N37F	1997
918	R918GMW	Dennis Dart SLF	Alexander ALX200	N37F	1997

919-923   Dennis Dart 9.8SDL3054   Alexander Dash   B36F   1995   Stagecoach London, 1998

919	N318NMC	920	N319NMC	921	N320NMC	922	N313NMC	923	N317NMC

924-930   Dennis Dart SLF   Alexander ALX200   N37F   1998

924	S924PDD	926	S926PDD	928	S928PDD	929	S929PDD	930	S930PDD
925	S925PDD	927	S927PDD					

931-935   Dennis Dart SLF   Alexander ALX200   N37F   1998   Oxford, 1998

931	R808YUD	932	R809YUD	933	R810YUD	934	R811YUD	935	R812YUD

936	M85DEW	Dennis Dart 9.8SDL3054	Marshall C37	B40F	1994	Stagecoach Manchester, 1999
937	M86DEW	Dennis Dart 9.8SDL3054	Marshall C37	B40F	1994	Stagecoach Manchester, 1999

Recently transferred from Stagecoach Bluebird is 138, MHS5P, a Leyland Olympian with Alexander RL bodywork and, unusually, a voith gearbox. It is pictured at Swindon bus station wearing the new corporate livery. *Tim Hall*

938-962 Dennis Dart SLF Alexander ALX200 N37F 1999

938	V938DFH	943	V943DFH	948	V948DDG	953	V953DDG	958	V958DDG
939	V939DFH	944	V944DFH	949	V949DDG	954	V954DDG	959	V959DDG
940	V940DFH	945	V945DFH	950	V950DDG	955	V955DDG	960	V960DDG
941	V941DFH	946	V946DFH	951	V951DDG	956	V956DDG	961	V961DFH
942	V942DFH	947	V947DFH	952	V952DDG	957	V957DDG	962	V962DFH

963	R601SWO	Dennis Dart SLF	Alexander ALX200	N37F	1998	Stagecoach Red & White, 2000
964	R602SWO	Dennis Dart SLF	Alexander ALX200	N37F	1998	Stagecoach Red & White, 2000
965	R603SWO	Dennis Dart SLF	Alexander ALX200	N37F	1998	Stagecoach Red & White, 2000

966-978 Dennis Dart SLF Alexander ALX200 N37F 2001

966	X966AFH	969	X969AFH	973	X973AFH	975	X975AFH	977	X977AFH
967	X967AFH	971	X971AFH	974	X974AFH	976	X976AFH	978	X978AFH
968	X968AFH	972	X972AFH						

1108	B108WUV	Leyland Titan TNLXB2RR	Leyland		B44/29F	1984	Stagecoach Devon, 1998
1112	B112WUV	Leyland Titan TNLXB2RR	Leyland		B44/29F	1984	Stagecoach London, 1999
1118	B118WUV	Leyland Titan TNLXB2RR	Leyland		B44/29F	1984	Stagecoach London, 1999
1403	H403MRW	Mercedes-Benz 811D	Wright NimBus		B31F	1991	Midland Red South, 1998
1407	H407PRW	Mercedes-Benz 811D	Wright NimBus		BC31F	1991	Midland Red South, 1998
1416	J416PRW	Mercedes-Benz 811D	Wright NimBus		B33F	1991	Midland Red South, 1998
1636	NUW636Y	Leyland Titan TNLXB2RR	Leyland		B44/27F	1982	Stagecoach London, 1998
1669	NUW669Y	Leyland Titan TNLXB2RR	Leyland		B44/27F	1982	Stagecoach London, 1998
1691	OHV691Y	Leyland Titan TNLXB2RR	Leyland		B44/27F	1983	Stagecoach London, 1998
1801	K801OMW	Mercedes-Benz 811D	Wright NimBus		B33F	1993	
1838	A838SUL	Leyland Titan TNLXB2RR	Leyland		B44/29F	1983	Stagecoach London, 1999
1845	A845SUL	Leyland Titan TNLXB2RR	Leyland		B44/29F	1983	Stagecoach London, 1999

The first batch of buses to be delivered in the new corporate colours were low-floor Dennis Darts for Gloucester services. Seen in the city is 972, X972AFH, illustrating the correct lettering used in the scheme. Interestingly, the central part of the circle motif is the colour of the background. *Robert Edworthy*

Ancillary vehicles

1078	M78HHB	Volvo B6-9M	Plaxton Pointer	TV	1994	Red & White (Rhondda), 1998
1173	M73HHB	Volvo B6-9M	Plaxton Pointer	TV	1994	Stagecoach Red & White, 1999
DT7	5110HU	Dodge Commando G13	Wadham Stringer Vanguard	TV	1987	MoD, 2000 (?, E789CHS)
DT8	HIL6075	Dodge Commando G13	Wadham Stringer Vanguard	TV	1989	USAF, 2000 (90B2068)
DT10	HIL8410	Dodge Commando G13	Wadham Stringer Vanguard	TV	1986	MoD, 2000 (81KF02)
DT11	D891DWP	Dodge Commando G13	Wadham Stringer Vanguard	TV	1987	MoD, 2000 (93KF07)
DT12	EJV32Y	Dennis Falcon H SDA411	Wadham Stringer Vanguard	TV	1983	Stagecoach East Midlands, 2001

Previous registrations:

MHS4P	C464SSO	MHS5P	C465SSO

Allocations:-

Cheltenham (Lansdown Ind Est, Gloucester Road) - *Stagecoach in Cheltenham*

Outstation: Bourton-on-the-Water

Mercedes-Benz	708	709	712	715	717	718	728	729
	730	731	732					
Dart	501	502	503	504	505	506	507	508
	509	510	511	512	513	926	927	928
	929	930	938	939	940	953	954	955
	956	957	958	959	961	962		
Volvo B6	842	848	850	851				
Volvo B10M coach	550	551	552	553	554	561	562	
Titan	1112							
Olympian	131	132	133	134				

Cinderford (Valley Road) - *Stagecoach in the Wye and Dean*

Mercedes-Benz	816	819	1407
Volvo B6	841	846	847
National	310		
Titan	1108		
Olympian	125	126	127

Cirencester (Love Lane) - *Stagecoach in the Cotswolds*

Mercedes-Benz	809	812		
Volvo B10	401	402	403	404
Titan	129			

Gloucester (London Road) - *Stagecoach in Gloucester*

Mercedes-Benz	710	711	714	716	719	723	724	726
	727	733	734	1416	1801			
Volvo B6	833	837	838	843	844			
Dart	925	938	941	944	945	946	947	948
	949	950	951	952	960	963	964	965
	966	967	968	969	970	971	972	973
	974	975	976	977				
National	314							
Volvo PS	418	419	420					
Titan	1118	1636	1691	1845				
Olympian	114	115	119	120	122	130	137	

Ross-on-Wye - *Stagecoach in the Wye and Dean*

Mercedes-Benz	811	813	814
Volvo B6	839	840	845
Volvo PS	417		
Olympian	141	142	143

Stroud (London Road) - *Stagecoach in the Cotswolds*

Mercedes-Benz	720	721	722	725	735	736	737	803
	804	805	806	807	808	1403		
Dart	901	902	903	936	937			
Volvo B10M bus	424	425	426	427	428			
Olympian	101	102	103	104	105	118	123	

Swindon (Eastcott Road) - *Stagecoach in Swindon*

Outstation: Chippenham

Dart	904	905	906	907	908	909	910	911
	912	913	914	915	916	917	918	919
	920	921	922	923	924	931	942	943
Volvo B10M bus	405	406	407	408	409	410	411	412
	421	422	423					
Titan	128	1669	1838					
Olympian	112	113	116	117	121	124		

Unallocated

Mercedes-Benz	713					
Volvo B6	831	832	834	835	836	849
Olympian	138	139				

SWANBROOK

Swanbrook Coaches Ltd, Thomas House, St Margaret's Road, Cheltenham, GL50 4DZ

WYV47T	Leyland Titan TNLXB2RR	Park Royal	B44/26D	1979	Kinch, Barrow-on-Soar, 1995
BYX186V	MCW Metrobus DR101/9	MCW	B43/28D	1979	London United, 1998
JIL8210	MCW Metrobus DR102/20	MCW	B42/31F	1981	Bullock, Cheadle, 1999
KJW301W	MCW Metrobus DR102/22	MCW	B43/30F	1981	Arriva Midlands North, 1999
KJW320W	MCW Metrobus DR102/22	MCW	B43/30F	1981	Arriva Midlands North, 1999
A900SUL	MCW Metrobus DR101/16	MCW	B43/32F	1984	London General, 2000
A926SUL	MCW Metrobus DR101/16	MCW	B43/32F	1984	London General, 2000
A958SYF	MCW Metrobus DR101/17	MCW	B43/28D	1984	London United, 1998
A703THV	MCW Metrobus DR101/18	MCW	B43/28D	1984	London United, 1998
B120UUD	Leyland Tiger TRCTL11/3RH	Plaxton Paramount 3500 IIE	C51F	1985	Oxford Bus Company, 1996 ˙
B121UUD	Leyland Tiger TRCTL11/3RH	Plaxton Paramount 3500 IIE	C51F	1985	Oxford Bus Company, 1996
C142SPB	Leyland Tiger TRCTL11/3RH	Berkhof Everest 370	C53F	1986	Coombs, Weston-super-Mare, 1999
D122EFH	Bedford YMT	Plaxton Derwent	B55F	1987	
D123EFH	Bedford YMT	Plaxton Derwent	B55F	1987	
E300BWL	Mercedes-Benz 709D	Reeve Burgess Beaver	B25F	1988	Owen, Nefyn, 1997
E303BWL	Mercedes-Benz 709D	Reeve Burgess Beaver	B25F	1988	Owen, Nefyn, 1997
F258CEY	Iveco Daily 49-10	Robin Hood City Nippy	B25F	1988	Brijan, Bishops Waltham, 2000
F71LAL	Mercedes-Benz 811D	Alexander Sprint	B31F	1989	Windle Travel, St Helens, 2000
G103TND	Mercedes-Benz 811D	Carlyle C16	B31F	1989	Arriva North West, 1998
G134CLF	DAF SB220LC590	Hispano	B45D	1990	Jones, Llanfaethll, 2000
H683NEF	Iveco Daily 49-10	Dormobile Routemaker	B25F	1991	Dinorwic Power Station, 2000
UJI1761	Volvo B10M-60	Plaxton Paramount 3500 III	C51F	1991	Oxford Bus Company, 2000
UJI1762	Volvo B10M-60	Plaxton Paramount 3500 III	C51F	1991	Oxford Bus Company, 2000
UJI1763	Volvo B10M-60	Plaxton Paramount 3500 III	C53F	1991	Oxford Bus Company, 2000
J291NNB	Mercedes-Benz 811D	Carlyle C16	B29F	1989	Arriva North West, 1998

Two Optare Excel buses from Blackpool are now operated by Swanbrook where they joined three examples purchased new to operate the Cheltenham park and ride service. Pictured on route 12B is N205LCK.
Robert Edworthy

Swanbrook use a silver livery on which stylish lettering in red orange and white are applied in a manner appropriate to each vehicle style. Pictured at the Oxford end of the route from Gloucester, is UJI1762, one of three Volvo B10Ms with Plaxton Paramount 3500 bodywork that were new to Shearings. *David Heath*

N202LCK	Optare Excel L1070	Optare	N36F	1996	Blackpool Buses, 2001
N205LCK	Optare Excel L1070	Optare	N36F	1996	Blackpool Buses, 2001
R100PAR	Optare Excel L1150	Optare	N40F	1997	
R200PAR	Optare Excel L1150	Optare	N40F	1997	
R300PAR	Optare Excel L1150	Optare	N40F	1997	
R12SBK	Dennis Dart SLF	UVG UrbanStar	N40F	1997	
T12SBK	Dennis Dart SLF	Marshall Capital	N37F	1999	

Previous Registrations:

F71LAL	F71LAL, WNF26	UJI1761	H957DRJ
G134CLF	TIB391D(Singapore) G476CLE,	UJI1762	H960DRJ
JIL8210	JBO79W	UJI1763	H958DRJ
R12SBK	R162KFH		

Livery: White, red and blue (older coaches); grey/silver, red, orange and yellow (newer coaches); yellow, orange and red
Depot: Pheasant Lane, Golden Valley, Staverton

SWIFTLINK

Eurotaxis (Bristol) Ltd, 16 Highfields Close, Harry Stoke, Bristol, BS34 8YA

RBO507Y	Leyland Olympian ONLXB/1R	East Lancashire	B43/31F	1983	Crown, Bristol, 1999
A513VKG	Leyland Olympian ONLXB/1R	East Lancashire	B43/31F	1984	Crown, Bristol, 1999
D580JNA	Mercedes-Benz L307D	Reeve Burgess	M8	1986	Manchester MA, Manchester, 1998
	Leyland Tiger TRCTL11/3RZ	Plaxton Derwent 2	BC54F	1987	MoD (87KF49), 1999
E631LSF	Mercedes-Benz L507D	Devon Conversions	M16	1987	Ferguson, East Whitburn, 1998
E460CGM	Mercedes-Benz 609D	Robin Hood	B20F	1987	The Bee Line, 1997
E954YGA	Mercedes-Benz 609D	Robin Hood	C24F	1987	private owner, 1996
E660XND	Mercedes-Benz 507D	Cunliffe	M15L	1988	Manchester Social Services, 1997
F132OYO	Renault Commando G10	Wadham Stringer Vanguard	B30FL	1988	Patterson, Birmingham, 1997
F425JFT	Mercedes-Benz L507D	Cunliffe	M16L	1989	Manchester MB, 1998
F278LND	Mercedes-Benz L307D	Northern Counties	M12L	1989	?, Oldham, 1998
G	Leyland Tiger TRCTL11/3RZM	Plaxton Derwent 2	BC54F	1989	MoD (03KJ40), 1999
G	Leyland Tiger TRCTL11/3RZM	Plaxton Derwent 2	BC54F	1989	MoD (03KJ47), 1999
G258UFB	Mercedes-Benz 408D	Devon Conversions	M16	1989	
G817YPU	Sanos 315-21	Sanos Charisma	C53F	1989	Abbeyways-Hanson, Halifax, 1998
G629XWS	Leyland Tiger TRCTL11/3LZM	Plaxton Derwent 2	BC54F	1989	MoD (03KJ33), 1997
G783XWS	Leyland Tiger TRCTL11/3ARZM	Plaxton Derwent 2	BC54F	1990	MoD (), 1998
G828XWS	Leyland Tiger TRCTL11/3ARZM	Plaxton Derwent 2	BC54F	1990	MoD (), 1998
G747SAV	Mercedes-Benz 308D	Devon Conversions	M12	1990	
H338FLH	Mercedes-Benz 308D	Pilcher Greene	M10L	1991	South London Dial-a-Ride, 1998
H606GLT	Mercedes-Benz 308D	Pilcher Greene	M6L	1991	South London Dial-a-Ride, 1998
H82PTG	Mercedes-Benz 811D	Optare StarRider	B33F	1991	City Nippy, 1997
K998WNC	Mercedes-Benz 410D	Made-to-Measure	M16	1992	
K271BRJ	Dennis Javelin 10SDA2120	Wadham Stringer Vanguard II	BC40F	1993	Bennett, Hayes End, 2000
L703JSC	Mercedes-Benz 410D	Devon Conversions	M16L	1994	Ferguson, East Whitburn, 2000
L340NMV	Mercedes-Benz 308D	Pilcher Greene	M8	1994	Holiday Inn, Gatwick, 1997
L3RDC	Mercedes-Benz 814D	Autobus Classique	C33F	1994	Reynolds Diplomat, Bushey, 1998

Swiftlink operates a large fleet of minibuses on a variety of local authority services and special needs transport as well as commercial contracts throughout the City of Bristol. A number of former MoD Tigers are also employed on school duties. Pictured in the depot is G111OGA
Robert Edworthy

M48GRY Mercedes-Benz 811D carries Mellor body work fitted with high-back seating. It is seen near its base in south west Bristol. *Robert Edworthy*

M778PDC	Mercedes-Benz 609D	Autobus Classique	B23F	1994	?, 1999
M45GRY	Mercedes-Benz 811D	Mellor	BC33F	1994	
M46GRY	Mercedes-Benz 811D	Mellor	BC33F	1994	
M47GRY	Mercedes-Benz 811D	Mellor	BC33F	1994	
M48GRY	Mercedes-Benz 811D	Mellor	BC33F	1994	
M675TNA	Mercedes-Benz 709D	Mellor	B27F	1995	
M676TNA	Mercedes-Benz 709D	Mellor	B26F	1995	
M301TSF	Mercedes-Benz 308D	Aitken	M8L	1995	Ferguson, East Whitburn, 2000
N541BFY	Mercedes-Benz 409D	Concept	M15	1995	
N542BFY	Mercedes-Benz 409D	Concept	M15	1995	
N543BFY	Mercedes-Benz 409D	Concept	M15	1995	
N990AEF	Mercedes-Benz 814L	Buscraft	C31F	1995	Fairley, Tudhoe, 2001
N482BFY	Mercedes-Benz 208D	Olympus	M11	1995	?, 1999
N472JCA	Renault Trafic	Renault	M4L	1995	?, 2001
P314GTO	Renault Trafic	Renault	M8L	1996	?, 2001
P317GTO	Renault Trafic	Renault	M8	1996	?, 2001
P183RSC	Mercedes-Benz Sprinter 614D	Aitken	C24F	1997	Haggis B'packers, Edinburgh, 1999
P473MNA	Mercedes-Benz Vita 312D	Mercedes-Benz	M12	1997	Sky Park, Manchester, 2000
P474MNA	Mercedes-Benz Vita 312D	Mercedes-Benz	M12	1997	Sky Park, Manchester, 2000
R991HNS	Mercedes-Benz Vita 208D	Mercedes-Benz	M11	1998	
R625GFS	Mercedes-Benz Vita 208D	Mercedes-Benz	M11	1998	
R35WDA	Mercedes-Benz 814D	Autobus Classique	C33F	1998	BT, 1998
S233FGD	Mercedes-Benz Sprinter 614D	Crest	C24F	1998	Haggis B'packers, Edinburgh, 1999
S234FGD	Mercedes-Benz Sprinter 614D	Crest	C24F	1998	Haggis B'packers, Edinburgh, 1999

Previous Registrations:
K271BRJ   15KL46

Livery: Red and yellow
Web:
Depots: Emmachris Way, Filton and Wellington Road, St Phillips, Bristol

TALLY HO!

J H, D E & S J Wellington and L Horswill, Station Yard, Kingsbridge, TQ7 1ES

KJD410P	Bristol LH6L	Eastern Coach Works	B43F	1976	London Buses, 1986
KJD413P	Bristol LH6L	Eastern Coach Works	B43F	1976	London Transport, 1982
KJD414P	Bristol LH6L	Eastern Coach Works	B43F	1976	London Buses, 1986
KJD419P	Bristol LH6L	Eastern Coach Works	B39F	1976	Centrewest, 1992
KJD420P	Bristol LH6L	Eastern Coach Works	B43F	1976	London Transport, 1982
KJD422P	Bristol LH6L	Eastern Coach Works	B39F	1976	London Buses, 1986
KJD431P	Bristol LH6L	Eastern Coach Works	B39F	1976	Oxon Travel, Bicester, 1995
OJD45R	Bristol LH6L	Eastern Coach Works	B39F	1976	Tyne & Wear Omnibus, 1990
OJD51R	Bristol LH6L	Eastern Coach Works	B43F	1976	London Transport, 1982
OJD54R	Bristol LH6L	Eastern Coach Works	B43F	1976	Carters Bus Services, Ipswich, 1999
OJD56R	Bristol LH6L	Eastern Coach Works	B43F	1976	Tyne & Wear Omnibus, 1990
OJD58R	Bristol LH6L	Eastern Coach Works	B43F	1976	London Transport, 1982
OJD59R	Bristol LH6L	Eastern Coach Works	B43F	1976	London Transport, 1982
OJD77R	Bristol LH6L	Eastern Coach Works	BC43F	1976	London Transport, 1982
OJD83R	Bristol LH6L	Eastern Coach Works	B39F	1976	Magpie Travel, High Wycombe, 1994
OJD84R	Bristol LH6L	Eastern Coach Works	B39F	1977	Shaftesbury & District, 1999
RAW19R	Bedford YMT	Duple Dominant II	C53F	1977	Willis, Stibb Cross, 2000
VJT458S	Bedford YLQ	Plaxton Supreme III	C45F	1978	Stevensl, Modbury, 1999
YYO685	Ford R1114	Plaxton Supreme III	C53F	1978	Lehane, Sturry, 1997
AIW257	DAF MB200DKL600	Plaxton Supreme IV	C55F	1978	Stevens, Modbury, 1999
AJD19T	Bedford YMT	Plaxton Supreme IV	C53F	1979	Stevens, Modbury, 1999
DCZ2307	Volvo B58-61	Plaxton Supreme IV	C53F	1979	Dorington & Totnes DC, 1999
HIL4966	Ford R1114	Plaxton Supreme IV	C53F	1979	Wm Heath, Stibbs Cross, 2000
KIW6512	Ford R1114	Plaxton Supreme IV	C53F	1980	Chalkwell, Sittingbourne, 1996
HFX411V	Ford R1114	Plaxton Supreme IV	C53F	1980	Taunton Coaches, 1998
KPP619V	Ford R1014	Duple Dominant II	C35F	1980	Hills Services, Stibb Cross, 2000
WDR598	Volvo B58-56	Unicar	C55F	1980	Brennan, Bradford, 1984
JCV433W	Bedford YMT	Plaxton Supreme IV	C53F	1981	Stevens, Modbury, 1999
PJT524W	Ford R1114	Plaxton Supreme IV	C53F	1981	Powell's of Lapford, 1997
VIB5239	Ford R1114	Plaxton Supreme IV	C53F	1981	Chalkwell, Sittingbourne, 1996
RAW777X	Ford R1114	Plaxton Supreme VI Express	C53F	1982	Claversham Coaches, Yatton, 1996
CNH176X	Leyland Leopard PSU3F/4R	Eastern Coach Works B51	C49F	1981	Timeline, 1995
CNH177X	Leyland Leopard PSU3F/4R	Eastern Coach Works B51	C49F	1981	Timeline, 1995
TTY696Y	Ford R1114	Duple Dominant II	C53F	1983	Hills Services, Stibb Cross, 20001
YSU923	Ford R1115	Plaxton Paramount 3200	C53F	1983	Harrington's, Coventry, 1996
312KTT	Ford R1115	Plaxton Paramount 3200	C53F	1983	Harrington's, Coventry, 1996
A561OTA	Dodge S46	Dormobile	B20F	1984	Arrow Cars, Kingsbridge, 1990
HIL2897	DAF SB2300DHTD585	Plaxton Paramount 3200	C53F	1984	Stevens, Modbury, 1999
B630DDW	Bedford YNT	Plaxton Paramount 3200	C53F	1985	Oakley Coaches, 2000
D184LTA	Renault-Dodge S56	Reeve Burgess	B23F	1986	Western National, 1995
E201WMB	Mercedes-Benz 609D	Whittaker Europa	C21F	1987	Stevensl, Modbury, 1999

Purchased by Tally Ho! to link Kingsbridge with Salcombe, RIL3899 is an Optare Vecta. This model is based on the MAN 11.190 chassis. A low-floor version of thechassis will be introduced into the UK during the Autumn of 2001 with early eamples being bodied by Alexander and East Lancashire.
Mark Bailey

Tally Ho! Now operate the largest collections of Bristol LHs, all of which were new to London Transport. Pictured while parked at Modbury is OJD77R and , as can be seen in this view, the vehicle is fitted with high-back seating. *Mark Bailey*

E39SBO	Dennis Javelin 11SDA1906	Duple 320	C53F	1988	Bebb, Llantwit Fardre, 1989
E40SBO	Dennis Javelin 11SDA1906	Duple 320	C53F	1988	Bebb, Llantwit Fardre, 1989
E210XWG	Renault-Dodge S56	Reeve Burgess Beaver	B25F	1988	B&S, Newton Abbott, 1998
ALZ3248	Renault-Dodge S56	Reeve Burgess Beaver	B25F	1988	Mainline, 1997
G105DPB	Renault-Dodge S56	Northern Counties	B25F	1989	Metrobus, Orpington, 1998
MAZ6792	Volvo B10M-60	Plaxton Expressliner	C51FT	1990	Dorset Travel Services, 1997
LAZ5826	Volvo B10M-60	Plaxton Expressliner	C49FT	1990	Dorset Travel Services, 1997
RAZ8598	Volvo B10M-60	Plaxton Expressliner	C49FT	1990	Dorset Travel Services, 1997
SAZ2511	Volvo B10M-60	Plaxton Expressliner	C51FT	1990	Dorset Travel Services, 1997
RIL3899	MAN 11.190 HOCL-R	Optare Vecta	B49F	1992	Seamarks, Luton, 1999
J96UBL	Dennis Javelin GX	Berkhof Excellence	C53F	1992	Pearce Coaches, Hounslow, 2001
J97UBL	Dennis Javelin GX	Berkhof Excellence	C53F	1992	Pearce Coaches, Hounslow, 2001
SIL4465	Dennis Javelin 12SDA2117	Berkhof Excellence	C51FT	1993	Arriva North West, 2000
M583WLV	Dennis Dart 9.8SDL3054	Marshall C37	B40F	1994	Halton Buses, 2001
M584WLV	Dennis Dart 9.8SDL3054	Marshall C37	B40F	1994	Halton Buses, 2001

Previous Registrations:

312KTT	TUK665Y, HBZ2459	MAZ6792	G342FFX
AIW257	XVW453S, MIA626	RAZ8598	G343FFX
ALZ3248	E212XWG	RIL3899	J367BNW
DCZ2307	CNA827T	SAZ2511	G328PEW
HIL2897	A351RUA	SIL4465	K200SLT, K792YFV
HIL4966	FNR8V	VIB5239	PNW315W
KIW6512	SMB264V	WDR598	ACP54V
LAZ5826	G329PEW	YSU923	BLJ717Y, HBZ4299

Livery: Blue and white
Web: www.tallyhocoaches.com
Depots: East Way, Lee Mill Industrial Estate, Ivybridge; Union Road, Kingsbridge and Station Yard Industrial Estate, Kingsbridge

TAW & TORRIDGE

Taw & Torridge Coaches Ltd,Merton Garage, Merton, Okehampton, EX20 3ED

PFX572K	Bedford YRQ	Plaxton Elite	C45F	1971	Rendell, Parkstone, 1978
MHO101L	Bedford YRT	Duple Dominant	C53F	1973	Kingdom's, Tiverton, 1981
ODV287P	Volvo B58-56	Duple Dominant	C53F	1975	Newquay Motors, 1986
ODV283P	Volvo B58-61	Duple Dominant	C57F	1976	Newquay Motors, 1986
NOK43	Volvo B58-61	Plaxon Supreme III	C57F	1976	Park's of Hamilton,
VAB893R	Bristol LHS6L	Plaxton Supreme III	C53F	1976	Coombe Hill Cs, Salisbury, 1989
OGL262R	Bedford YMT	Duple Dominant Express	C53F	1977	Jennings, Bude, 1985
YTT178S	Bedford YMT	Plaxton Supreme III	C40FT	1978	Gouldbourn, Royton, 1988
JCW517S	Volvo B58-56	Plaxton Supreme III	C53F	1978	Abbott, Blackpool, 2001
AFJ740T	Bristol LH6L	Plaxton Supreme III Express	C43F	1979	Grey Cars, Exeter, 1992
AFJ742T	Bristol LH6L	Plaxton Supreme III Express	C43F	1979	Bordon International, 1992
DMJ374T	Bedford YMT	Duple Dominant II	C53F	1979	Tanners, Sibford Gower, 1983
JMJ134V	Ford R1114	Duple Dominant II	C53F	1980	Tarka Travel, Bideford, 1989
FIB2118	Fiat 60F10	Harwin	C20F	1980	Tilley's, Wainhouse Corner, 1991
RLN230W	Bristol LHS6L	Plaxton Supreme V	C31F	1980	British Airways, Heathrow, 1996
PJI4713	Bristol LHS6L	Plaxton Supreme V	C33F	1981	British Airways, Heathrow, 1996
509HUO	Volvo B58-61	Van Hool Aragon	C49FT	1981	Lowland, 1993
TIW7681	Bedford YMQ	Plaxton Supreme IV	C35F	1981	Bromyard Bus Company, 1999
6986RU	Van Hool T815	Van Hool Alizée	C49FT	1982	Tourist, Figheldean, 1989
FIL7303	MAN SR280	MAN	C47FT	1982	Shanks, Galashiels, 1993
B400RHN	Ford Transit 190	Carlyle	C16F	1985	Western National, 1995
C104TFP	Bova FHD12.280	Bova Futura	C49FT	1985	Robinson, Stewkeley, 1997
C546BHY	Ford Transit 190	Dormobile	B16F	1986	Badgerline, 1994
C550BHY	Ford Transit 190	Dormobile	B16F	1986	Badgerline, 1994
D137LTA	Renault-Dodge S56	Reeve Burgess	B25F	1986	Plymouth Citybus, 1994

Pictured while on lay-over in Exeter bus station is Bristol LHS6L RLN230W which was new to British Airways who used the type for crew transport. The vehicle was being used on service 645 to Merton when pictured in August. The operator is named after two local rivers that enter the Bristol Channel at Barnstaple and Bideford respectivly. *Mark Bailey*

An integral Van Hool T815 is seen taking a break in the M4 services in the colours of Taw & Torridge. Registered 775HOD, it is one of a pair in the fleet and when imported into Britain carries either the Alicron or Alizée names although both are integral models similar to the Alizée. *David Heath*

676GDV	Hestair Duple SDA1512	Duple 425	C55FT	1987	Forest, East Ham, 1994
E278RNW	Ford Transit VE6	Evans	M8	1988	Kim's Coach Hire, Morriston, 1995
E518KNV	Scania K112CRB	Jonckheere Jubilee P50	C49FT	1988	Hayward, Horndean, 1998
7646RU	Scania K112CRB	Jonckheere Jubilee P50	C51FT	1988	Dreamline, Blackburn, 1991
775HOD	Van Hool T815	Van Hool Alizée	C49FT	1991	Pettigrew, Kirkoswald, 1993
J130LVM	Leyland-DAF 400	Deansgate	M16	1991	Tally Ho!, Kingsbridge, 2001
L257UCV	Volvo B10M-60	Plaxton Expressliner 2	C46FT	1993	First Western National, 1999
N855XMO	Dennis Javelin 12SDA2159	Berkhof Excellence 1000	C53F	1996	Dunn-Line, Nottingham, 1999
N869XMO	Dennis Javelin 12SDA2159	Berkhof Excellence 1000	C53F	1996	Dunn-Line, Nottingham, 1999
N870XMO	Dennis Javelin 12SDA2159	Berkhof Excellence 1000	C53F	1996	Dunn-Line, Nottingham, 1999
N871XMO	Dennis Javelin 12SDA2159	Berkhof Excellence 1000	C53F	1996	Dunn-Line, Nottingham, 1999
N873XMO	Dennis Javelin 12SDA2159	Berkhof Excellence 1000	C53F	1996	Dunn-Line, Nottingham, 1999
R10TAW	Dennis Javelin GX	Neoplan Transliner	C49FT	1998	

Previous Registrations:

509HUO	RHS2W		
676GDV	D760TTA	FIL7303	KMR7X, 5497D, OON749X
775HOD	G254VML	NOK43	NGB5P
6986RU	NOX740X	ODV283P	KDR487P, 509HUO
7646RU	E699NNH	ODV287P	KTT316P, 676GDV
C104TFP	C104TFP, 4542VU	PJI4713	RLN231W
FIB2118	CPO899W	TIW7681	NPC387W, TIW7681, 81CW271(EI)
		YTT178S	XLJ426S, 11AFC, 407JWO

Livery: Red, green and white; white (Majestic Holidays)
Depots: Grange Lane Depot, Merton; Merton Garage, Merton

THAMESDOWN

Thamesdown Transport Ltd, Corporation Street, Swindon, Wiltshire, SN1 1DU

59-63				Dennis Dominator DDA174		Northern Counties		B43/31F	1984		
59	A59WMW	**61**	A61WMW	**63**	A63WMW						

65	B65GHR	Dennis Dominator DDA909	Northern Counties	BC43/31F	1985
66	B66GHR	Dennis Dominator DDA909	Northern Counties	BC43/31F	1985
67	B67GHR	Dennis Dominator DDA909	Northern Counties	BC43/31F	1985
68	B68GHR	Dennis Dominator DDA909	Northern Counties	BC43/31F	1985

69-73				Dennis Dominator DDA1033		East Lancashire		B45/31F	1990		
69	H969XHR	**70**	H970XHR	**71**	H971XHR	**72**	H972XHR	**73**	H973XHR		

74-79				Dennis Dominator DDA1026		East Lancashire		B45/30F	1989	Arriva Southern Counties, 1998-99	
74	F602RPG	**76**	F604RPG	**77**	F606RPG	**78**	F608RPG	**79**	F605RPG		
75	F603RPG										

101-110				Dennis Dart 8.5SDL3010		Plaxton Pointer		B33F	1993		
101	K101OMW	**103**	K103OMW	**105**	K105OMW	**107**	K107OMW	**109**	K109OMW		
102	K102OMW	**104**	K104OMW	**106**	K106OMW	**108**	K108OMW	**110**	K110OMW		

111-119				Dennis Dart 9.8SDL3040		Plaxton Pointer		B40F	1994		
111	M711BMR	**113**	M113BMR	**115**	M115BMR	**117**	M117BMR	**119**	M119BMR		
112	M112BMR	**114**	M114BMR	**116**	M116BMR	**118**	M118BMR				

120-128				Dennis Dart 9.8SDL3054		Plaxton Pointer		B40F	1995		
120	XMW120	**122**	N122JHR	**124**	N124JHR	**126**	N126LMW	**128**	N128LMW		
121	N121JHR	**123**	N123JHR	**125**	N125LMW	**127**	N127LMW				

129	XBZ7729	Dennis Dart 9.8SDL3054	Plaxton Pointer	B40F	1995	Isle of Man RS, 2000
130	XBZ7730	Dennis Dart 9.8SDL3054	Plaxton Pointer	B40F	1995	Isle of Man RS, 2000
131	XBZ7731	Dennis Dart 9.8SDL3054	Plaxton Pointer	B40F	1994	Isle of Man RS, 2000
132	XBZ7732	Dennis Dart 9.8SDL3054	Plaxton Pointer	B40F	1994	Isle of Man RS, 2000
141	R314NGM	Dennis Dart SLF	Plaxton Pointer 2	N37F	1997	The King's Ferry, Gillingham, 2000
142	R315NGM	Dennis Dart SLF	Plaxton Pointer 2	N37F	1997	The King's Ferry, Gillingham, 2000
143	R317NGM	Dennis Dart SLF	Plaxton Pointer 2	N37F	1997	The King's Ferry, Gillingham, 2000

The Dennis Dominator continues to provide service to Thamesdown with further buses joining the fleet in 1999. Pictured in the town centre is 69, H969XHR which carries an East Lancashire body.
David Heath

The countyside around Swinton is seen in this view of Thamesdown 106, K106OMW, seen here passing through Hinton Parva on a return journey on one of a number of inter-urban services. Thamesdown apply names to all of their buses, Goldfinch being visible over the entrance in this case. *Richard Godfrey*

151-158

								Dennis Dart SLF	Plaxton Pointer	B41F	1996

151	P151SMW	153	P153SMW	155	P155SMW	157	P157SMW	158	P158SMW
152	P152SMW	154	P154SMW	156	P156SMW				

159	P159VHR	Dennis Dart SLF	Plaxton Pointer 2	N41F	1997
160	P160VHR	Dennis Dart SLF	Plaxton Pointer 2	N41F	1997
161	P161VHR	Dennis Dart SLF	Plaxton Pointer 2	N41F	1997
162	S162BMR	Dennis Dart SLF	Plaxton Pointer 2	N38F	1998
163	T163RMR	Dennis Dart SLF	Plaxton Pointer 2	N40F	1999
164	T164RMR	Dennis Dart SLF	Plaxton Pointer 2	N40F	1999
165	T165RMR	Dennis Dart SLF	Plaxton Pointer 2	N40F	1999
175	KMW175P	Daimler Fleetline CRG6LX	Eastern Coach Works	O43/31F	1976
180	S838VAG	Dennis Dart SLF	Plaxton Pointer SPD	N45F	1998	Plaxton demonstrator, 2000

181-191

								Dennis Dart SLF	Plaxton Pointer SPD	N45F	1998-2000	*184-6 are N41F

181	S181BMR	184	S184BMR	186	S186BMR	188	V188EAM	190	V190EAM
182	S182BMR	185	S185BMR	187	V187EAM	189	V189EAM	191	V191EAM
183	S183BMR								

192-197

								Dennis Dart SLF	Plaxton Pointer 2	N41F	2001

192	Y192YMR	194	Y194YMR	195	Y195YMR	196	Y196YMR	197	Y197YMR
193	Y193YMR								

199-205

								Leyland Fleetline FE30AGR	Eastern Coach Works	B43/31F	1978-80

199	UMR199T	201	BMR201V	203	BMR203V	204	BMR204V	205	BMR205V
200	UMR200T	202	BMR202V						

216	BVR59T	Leyland Fleetline FE30AGR	Northern Counties	B43/32F	1978	GM Buses, 1989
217	BVR89T	Leyland Fleetline FE30AGR	Northern Counties	B43/32F	1978	GM Buses, 1989
218	TWH698T	Leyland Fleetline FE30AGR	Northern Counties	B43/32F	1979	GM Buses, 1989
219	TWH699T	Leyland Fleetline FE30AGR	Northern Counties	B43/32F	1979	GM Buses, 1989
221	ANA21T	Leyland Fleetline FE30AGR	Northern Counties	B43/32F	1978	GMS, Stockport, 1996
222	BVR98T	Leyland Fleetline FE30AGR	Northern Counties	B43/32F	1978	GMS, Stockport, 1996

262-266

		Leyland Fleetline FE30AGR	Alexander	B43/31F	1980	Yellow Buses, 2000

262	GRU162V	263	GRU163V	264	GRU164V	265	GRU165V	266	GRU166V

316	DCZ2316	Leyland Tiger TRCTL11/3R	Plaxton Paramount 3200	C57F	1985	British Airways, 1986
317	DCZ2317	Leyland Tiger TRCTL11/2R	Plaxton Paramount 3200 Express	C53F	1984	London Country NE, 1989
318	DCZ2318	Leyland Tiger TRCTL11/2R	Plaxton Paramount 3200 Express	C53F	1983	Southend, 1995
319	DCZ2319	Leyland Tiger TRCTL11/2R	Plaxton Paramount 3200 Express	C53F	1984	Southend, 1995
322	J22PJT	Volvo B10M-60	Jonckheere Deauville P599	C53F	1992	Kingston Coaches, 1998
334	M934FHR	Volvo B10M-62	Jonckheere Deauville P599	C51FT	1995	Kingston Coaches, 1998
335	M935FHR	Volvo B10M-62	Jonckheere Deauville P599	C51FT	1995	Kingston Coaches, 1998
345	PIL5345	Volvo B10M-60	Plaxton Paramount 3200 III	C57F	1990	Excelsior, Bournemouth, 1995
346	PIL5346	Volvo B10M-60	Plaxton Paramount 3200 III	C57F	1990	Excelsior, Bournemouth, 1995

Ancilliary vehicles:

383	OHR183R	Leyland Fleetline FE30AGR	Eastern Coach Works	O-F	1977	Mobile workshop and tree-lopper

Previous Registrations

DCZ2316	B416CMC	PIL5346	G505EFX, A12EXC, G372GJT, TIW2372
DCZ2317	A127EPA	XBZ7729	MAN14A, M410XTC
DCZ2318	A103EPA	XBZ7730	MAN15D, M409XTC
DCZ2319	A126EPA	XBZ7731	CMN76X, M505XTC
PIL5345	G506EFX, A6EXC, G357GJT	XBZ7732	CMN78X, M506XTC

Named vehicles:- 65 *City of Truro*; 66 *King George V*; 68 *Western Enterprise*; 69 *Western Pathfinder*; 70 *Western Explorer*, 71 *Western Pioneer*, 72 *Western Crusader*; 73 *Western Venturer*; 74, *Western Stalwart*; 75 *Western Talisman*; 76 *Western Harrier*, 77 *Western Invader*; 78 *Western Campaigner*; 79 *Western Thunderer*, 101 *Blackbird*; 102 *Bull Finch*; 103 *Chaffinch*; 104 *Cormorant*; 105 *Flamingo*; 106 *Goldfinch*; 107 *Jackdaw*; 108 *Kingfisher*; 109 *Nightingale*; 110 *Peacock*; 111 *Dog Star*; 112 *Lode Star*; 113 *Morning Star*; 114 *Polar Star*; 115 *Red Star*; 116 *Rising Star*; 117 *Royal Star*, 118 *Shooting Star*, 119 *Western Star*; 120 *North Star*; 121 *Evening Star*; 122 *Knight of the Garter*; 123 *Knight of the Thistle*; 124 *Knight of St Patrick*; 125 *Knight of the Bath*; 126 *Knight of St John*; 127 *Knight of the Golden Fleece*; 128 *Knight of the Grand Cross*; 129 *County of Gloucester*; 130 *County of Oxford*; 131 *County of Berks*; 132 *County of Wilts*; 141 *Sir Daniel Gooch*; 142 *Armstrong*; 143 *William Dean*; 144 *G J Churchward*; 151 *Saint Ambrose*; 152 *Saint Andrew*; 153 *Saint Augustine*; 154 *Saint Bartholomew*, 155 *Saint Benedict*; 156 *Saint Bernard*; 157 *Saint Cuthbert*; 158 *Saint David*; 159 *Saint Agatha*; 160 *Saint Catherine*; 161 *St Helena*; 162 *Saint Dunstan*; 163 *Saint Gabriel*; 164 *Saint George*; 165 *Saint Nicholas*; 175 *Isambard Kingdom Brunel*; 180 *Caerphilly Castle*; 181 *Eclipse*; 182 *Vanguard*; 183 *Formidable*; 184 *Albion*; 185 *Avenger*; 186 *Benow*; 187 *Caradoc*; 188 *Centaur*, 189 *Champion*; 190 *Cockade*; 191 *Daring*; 192 *Despatch*; 193 *Diadem*; 194 *Dragon*; 195 *Druid*; 196 *Glory*; 197 *Magnificent*.

Livery: Blue and white

TILLEY'S

P A & L A Tilley, New Garage, Wainhouse Corner, Bude, EX23 0JG

TIL1263	Volvo Ailsa B55-10	Marshall	B44/35F	1982	Arriva Derby, 1982
TIL1260	Bova EL26/581	Bova Europa	C51F	1982	Cross Keys, Newingreen, 1990
TIL1257	DAF MB200DKFL600	Plaxton Paramount 3500	C53F	1985	Slack, Matlock, 1998
TIL1256	Van Hool T809	Van Hool Alizée	C32FT	1986	JJ Kavanagh, Urlingford (EI), 1998
TIL1258	DAF SB2305DHS585	Duple 340	C53FT	1988	Capital, West Drayton, 1995
TIL1259	Dennis Javelin 11SDA1906	Duple 320	C53F	1988	Vince, Burghclere, 1999
R997RHL	Mercedes-Benz Vario O817	SC Coachcraft	C31F	1998	Escort Coaches, Enfield, 2000
TIL1253	Mercedes-Benz 811D	Robin Hood	C29F	1989	R&I Tours, Harlesden, 1996
TIL1254	Mercedes-Benz 811D	Robin Hood	C29F	1989	R&I Tours, Harlesden, 1996
TIL1255	Mercedes-Benz 814L	North West Coach Sales	C31F	1990	Rowberry, Naunton, 1996
TIL1262	Mercedes-Benz 711D	Mellor	BC27F	1995	
TIL1261	Optare Solo M850	Optare	N30F	2000	

Previous Registrations:

TIL1253	F85GGC	TIL1258	E24ETN, MIL1064
TIL1254	F89GGC	TIL1259	F869TLJ
TIL1255	G122SMA, VJI1156	TIL1260	VWX358X, FSU358
TIL1256	C344TRT, PIL8380	TIL1261	W676DDN
TIL1257	B953KNU, PSV592, PIL8381	TIL1262	M729UWJ
		TIL1263	STV123X

Livery: White, cream and maroon or red

Duple 340 MIL1064 represents the Tilley's fleet, most of which now carries a TIL index number. The fleet aslo contains some interesting oddities, a rare Marshall-bodied Ailsa, a short Van Hool integral and two unusual Mercedes midibuses, an O817 and an 814L. *Richard Godfrey*

TRATHENS

Trathens Travel Services Ltd, Walkham Park, Burrington Way, Plymouth, PL5 3LS

Part of Park's Motor Group

SR	LSK825	Volvo B10M-61	Van Hool Astral	C12/6CT	1984	Deeble, Darley Ford, 1995
SR	290WE	Volvo B10M-53	Van Hool Astral	C10/6CT	1984	Express Travel, Perth, 1993
CL	FXU355	Neoplan N122/3	Neoplan Skyliner	C57/16CT	1992	
SR	LSK613	Volvo B12T	Van Hool Astrobel	C10/6CT	1993	
CL	M863TYC	Volvo B12T	Van Hool Astrobel	C57/14CT	1994	
NX	M864TYC	Volvo B12T	Van Hool Astrobel	C57/14CT	1994	
CL	M865TYC	Volvo B12T	Van Hool Astrobel	C57/14CT	1994	
SR	LSK614	Volvo B12T	Jonckheere Monaco	C10/6CT	1994	Park's of Hamilton, 1996
SR	LSK615	Volvo B12T	Jonckheere Monaco	C10/6CT	1994	Park's of Hamilton, 1996
SR	LSK812	Volvo B12T	Van Hool Astrobel	C10/6CT	1994	Park's of Hamilton, 1996
SR	LSK814	Volvo B12T	Van Hool Astrobel	C10/6CT	1994	Park's of Hamilton, 1996
NX	N315BYA	Volvo B12T	Van Hool Astrobel	C57/14CT	1995	
SR	N317BYA	Volvo B12T	Van Hool Astrobel	C57/14CT	1995	
NX	N318BYA	Volvo B12T	Van Hool Astrobel	C57/14CT	1995	
NX	N319BYA	Volvo B12T	Van Hool Astrobel	C57/14CT	1995	
SR	LSK611	Volvo B12T	Van Hool Astrobel	C10/6CT	1995	Park's of Hamilton, 1996
SR	LSK612	Volvo B12T	Van Hool Astrobel	C10/6CT	1995	Park's of Hamilton, 1996
NX	N754CYA	Volvo B12T	Van Hool Astrobel	C57/14CT	1996	
NX	N755CYA	Volvo B12T	Van Hool Astrobel	C57/14CT	1996	
NX	N708CYC	Volvo B12T	Van Hool Astrobel	C57/14CT	1996	
NX	P926KYC	Volvo B12T	Van Hool Astrobel	C57/14CT	1997	
NX	P927KYC	Volvo B12T	Van Hool Astrobel	C57/14CT	1997	
SR	TSU603	Van Hool TD824	Van Hool Astromega	C14/8CT	1997	Deeble, Darley Ford, 1995
NX	R261OFJ	Volvo B12T	Van Hool Astrobel	C57/14CT	1998	

Most of the National Express double-deck operations are undertaken by Trathens using a fleet of Astrobel coaches. This model is built in Belgium on the Volvo B12T tri-axle chassis. Pictured rounding Hyde Park corner is N315BYA which was heading north on the daily working to the Lancashire port of Fleetwood. Part of the National Express fleet is expected to be replaced before the end of 2001.

The Trathens fleet includes luxury coaches in their charter *Star Riders* livery that serve a growing market for executives, pop-starts and polititien parties to travel in comfort and with the latest communications and technology. All this fleet are double-deck, with 290WE, illustrated here. *R Anderson*

NX	R262OFJ	Volvo B12T	Van Hool Astrobel	C57/14CT	1998	
NX	R263OFJ	Volvo B12T	Van Hool Astrobel	C57/14CT	1998	
NX	R264OFJ	Volvo B12T	Van Hool Astrobel	C57/14CT	1998	
NX	S104JGB	Volvo B10M-62	Plaxton Expressliner 2	C44FT	1998	Park's of Hamilton, 1999
NX	S105JGB	Volvo B10M-62	Plaxton Expressliner 2	C44FT	1998	Park's of Hamilton, 1999
NX	KSK984	Volvo B10M-62	Jonckheere Mistral 50	C49FT	1999	Park's of Hamilton, 2001
NX	T871RGA	Volvo B10M-62	Plaxton Expressliner 2	C46FT	1999	
NX	T872RGA	Volvo B10M-62	Plaxton Expressliner 2	C46FT	1999	
NX	T867RGA	Volvo B10M-62	Plaxton Expressliner 2	C44FT	1999	Parks of Hamilton, 2000
NX	T868RGA	Volvo B10M-62	Plaxton Expressliner 2	C44FT	1999	Parks of Hamilton, 2000
NX	T869RGA	Volvo B10M-62	Plaxton Expressliner 2	C44FT	1999	Parks of Hamilton, 2000
NX	T870RGA	Volvo B10M-62	Plaxton Expressliner 2	C44FT	1999	Parks of Hamilton, 2000

Ancillary vehicle

| CL | GPT224S | Volvo B58-61 | Plaxton Supreme III | TV | 1977 | Burgin, Darnall, 1999 |

Previous Registrations:

290WE	B418CGG		LSK811	LSK831
FXU355	J449NTT		LSK812	LSK832
GPT224S	OJY577S, 891HUM		LSK825	B320HSC, FXU355
LSK613	L977KDT		TSU603	R406FSH

Livery: White (private hire and National Express); Grey/multi ("Stariders" - band bus specification).
Notes: CL Club Liner (private Hire); NX National Express and SR Starider.

TRURONIAN

Truronian Ltd, 24 Lemon Street, Truro, Cornwall TR1 2LS

FHE806L	Bristol VRT/SL2/6LX	Eastern Coach Works	B43/34F	1973	RoadCar, 1991
NNK809P	Bedford YRT	Willowbrook 007	B63F	1976	Roselyn, 1994
SNN158R	Bristol VRT/SL3/6LXB	Eastern Coach Works	B43/31F	1977	Tally Ho! Kingsbridge, 1996
AAP668T	Bristol VRT/SL3/6LXB	Eastern Coach Works	B43/31F	1979	Stagecoach South, 1997
AFJ753T	Bristol VRT/SL3/6LXB	Eastern Coach Works	B43/31F	1979	City Tour, Bath, 1996
AFJ771T	Bristol VRT/SL3/6LXB	Eastern Coach Works	B43/31F	1979	Tally Ho! Kingsbridge, 1996
BKE851T	Bristol VRT/SL3/6LXB	Eastern Coach Works	B43/31F	1979	Tally Ho! Kingsbridge, 1996
BKE857T	Bristol VRT/SL3/6LXB	Eastern Coach Works	B43/31F	1979	Arriva Southern Counties, 1998
FKM876V	Bristol VRT/SL3/6LXB	Eastern Coach Works	B43/31F	1979	Maidstone & District, 1997
SGR790V	Bristol VRT/SL3/6LXB	Eastern Coach Works	B43/31F	1980	Hopley, 2000
EAP985V	Bristol VRT/SL3/6LXB	Eastern Coach Works	B43/31F	1980	Weladon Beeline, 1998
PRC849X	Bristol VRT/SL3/6LXB	Eastern Coach Works	B43/31F	1981	Trent, 1991
PRC856X	Bristol VRT/SL3/6LXB	Eastern Coach Works	B43/31F	1981	Trent, 1991
NCV942X	Bedford YNT	Plaxton Supreme VI Express	C53F	1982	Williams, St Agnes, 1993
TPL762X	Leyland Tiger TRBL11/2R	Plaxton Supreme V Express	C53F	1982	Vale of Manchester, 1997
XBF976	Leyland Tiger TRCTL11/2R	Plaxton Viewmaster IV Exp	C53F	1982	Powell Bus, Wickersley, 1997
PAF189X	Leyland Tiger TRCTL11/3R	Duple Dominant III	C51F	1982	J&S Powell, Wickersley, 1997
C812BYY	Leyland Olympian ONLXB/1RH	Eastern Coach Works	B42/30F	1986	Arriva London, 2001
C819BYY	Leyland Olympian ONLXB/1RH	Eastern Coach Works	B42/30F	1986	Arriva London, 2001
C23CHM	Leyland Olympian ONLXB/1RH	Eastern Coach Works	B42/30F	1986	Arriva London, 2001
C74CHM	Leyland Olympian ONLXB/1RH	Eastern Coach Works	B42/30F	1986	Arriva London, 2001
C83CHM	Leyland Olympian ONLXB/1RH	Eastern Coach Works	B42/30F	1986	Arriva London, 2001
C87CHM	Leyland Olympian ONLXB/1RH	Eastern Coach Works	B42/30F	1986	Arriva London, 2001
E872PGL	Mercedes-Benz 609D	Reeve Burgess Beaver	C19F	1987	
F314VCV	Mercedes-Benz 609D	Reeve Burgess Beaver	B19F	1988	
F315VCV	Mercedes-Benz 609D	Reeve Burgess Beaver	DP25F	1988	
H920XYN	Renault Commando G10	Wadham Stringer Vanguard	B32FL	1990	Crystals, Dartford, 1996
H932XYN	Renault Commando G10	Wadham Stringer Vanguard	B32FL	1990	LB Hackney, 1998
L995VAF	Ford Transit VE6	Ford	M14	1994	
L338WAF	Volvo B10M-62	Caetano Algarve 2	C49FT	1994	
L339WAF	Volvo B10M-62	Caetano Algarve 2	C49FT	1994	
L725WCV	Mercedes-Benz 811D	Plaxton Beaver	B31F	1994	
L726WCV	Mercedes-Benz 811D	Plaxton Beaver	B31F	1994	
M372CRL	Volvo B10M-62	Plaxton Première 320	C46FT	1995	
M373CRL	Volvo B10M-62	Plaxton Première 320	C46FT	1995	
N212KBJ	Mercedes-Benz 711D	Autobus Clasique	BC24F	1995	Galloway, Mendelsham, 2000
N166KAF	Dennis Dart 9.8SDL3054	Plaxton Pointer	B37F	1996	
N167KAF	Dennis Dart 9.8SDL3054	Plaxton Pointer	B37F	1996	
N168KAF	Dennis Dart 9.8SDL3054	Plaxton Pointer	B37F	1996	
N169KAF	Dennis Dart 9.8SDL3054	Plaxton Pointer	B37F	1996	
N170KAF	Mercedes-Benz 711D	Plaxton Beaver	C25F	1996	

w

Redruth rail station is the location for this view of Truronian's Dennis Dart T34JCV. This bus operates with extra luggage area provision as 'The Helston Branch Line', connecting to trains at Redruth.
Richard Godfrey

Truronian have two Dennis Darts in the livery of the newly-opened Eden Project. They operate the connecting service from Newquay as *The Eden Branch Line*. Shown here is Y2EDN which had just arrived ar Newquay on a fast run from St Austell during Easter week 2001. *David Donati*

P452SCV	Dennis Dart SLF	Plaxton Pointer	B34F	1997
P453SCV	Dennis Dart SLF	Plaxton Pointer	B34F	1997
P454SCV	Dennis Dart SLF	Plaxton Pointer	B34F	1997
P455SCV	Dennis Dart SLF	Plaxton Pointer	B34F	1997
R1TRU	Volvo B10M-62	Van Hool T9 Alizée	C49FT	1998
S549SCV	Dennis Dart SLF	Plaxton Pointer MPD	N29F	1998
T32JCV	Dennis Dart SLF	Plaxton Pointer 2	NC32F	1999
T34JCV	Dennis Dart SLF	Plaxton Pointer 2	NC32F	1999
T35JCV	Dennis Dart SLF	Plaxton Pointer 2	NC32F	1999
T12TRU	Dennis Dart SLF	Plaxton Pointer 2	N29F	1999
T2TRU	Volvo B10M-62	Plaxton ?	C49FT	1999
W3TRU	Volvo B10M-62	Plaxton ?	C49FT	2000
W4TRU	Mercedes-Benz Vario O814	Plaxton Cheetah	C27F	2000
Y1EDN	Dennis Dart SLF	Plaxton Pointer 2	N37F	2001
Y2EDN	Dennis Dart SLF	Plaxton Pointer 2	N37F	2001
Y5TRU	Volvo B10M-62	Plaxton Panther	C49FT	2001

Previous Registrations:

PAF189X	NTG18X, 8921WF, 260ERY
XBF976	GCA123X, 3810VT, XAY875X, WSV490, LES991X

Livery: Silver and red; yellow (school bus) or red (buses); green (Eden/Helson Branchline) Y1/2EDN, T34/5JCV
Web: www.truronian.co.uk
Depots: Flambards, Helston & Newham Industrial Estate, Truro

TURNERS

Turners Coachways (Bristol) Ltd, 59 Days Road, St Phillips, Bristol, BS2 0QS

BFX570T	Bristol VRT/SL3/6LXB	Eastern Coach Works	B43/31F	1979	Cambus (Viscount), 1997
D78JHY	Leyland Tiger TRCTL11/3LZ	Plaxton Derwent 2	BC70F	1986	MoD (82KF21), 1998
D202JHY	Leyland Tiger TRCTL11/3LZ	Plaxton Derwent 2	BC70F	1987	MoD (82KF29), 1998
E691NOU	Leyland Tiger TRCTL11/3LZ	Plaxton Derwent 2	BC56F	1987	MoD (87KF17), 1998
E787NOU	Leyland Tiger TRCTL11/3LZ	Plaxton Derwent 2	BC70F	1987	MoD (87KF33), 1998
G826XWS	Leyland Tiger TRCTL11/3LZ	Plaxton Derwent 2	BC56F	1989	MoD (03KJ28), 1998
G829XWS	Leyland Tiger TRCTL11/3LZ	Plaxton Derwent 2	BC56F	1989	MoD (03KJ23), 1998
OYY3	Volvo B10M-60	Van Hool Alizée	C57F	1990	North Mymms, Potters Bar, 1993
K5CJT	Toyota Coaster HDB30R	Caetano Optimo II	C21F	1992	
K6CJT	Volvo B10M-60	Van Hool Alizée	C57F	1993	
K7CJT	Volvo B10M-60	Van Hool Alizée	C57F	1993	
L8CJT	Volvo B10M-60	Van Hool Alizée	C49FT	1994	
L9CJT	Volvo B10M-60	Van Hool Alizée	C49FT	1994	
M10CJT	Volvo B10M-62	Jonckheere Deauville 45	C53F	1995	Park's of Hamilton, 1996
M11CJT	Volvo B10M-62	Jonckheere Deauville 45	C49FT	1995	Park's of Hamilton, 1996
M12CJT	Volvo B10M-62	Jonckheere Deauville 45	C53F	1995	Park's of Hamilton, 1996
M13CJT	Volvo B10M-62	Jonckheere Deauville 45	C45FT	1995	Park's of Hamilton, 1996
M20CJT	Volvo B12T	Jonckheere Monaco	C57/15CT	1995	Excelsior, Bournemouth, 1998
M40CJT	Volvo B12T	Jonckheere Monaco	C57/15CT	1995	Excelsior, Bournemouth, 1998
N895VEG	Mercedes-Benz 811D	Marshall C16	B33F	1996	Richmond, Barley, 2000
N14CJT	Toyota Coaster HZB50R	Caetano Optimo III	C21F	1996	
MIL8583	Volvo B10M-62	Plaxton Excalibur	C49FT	1996	Tillingbourne, Cranleigh, 2001
P15CJT	Volvo B10M-62	Plaxton Première 320	C57F	1997	
P16CJT	Volvo B10M-62	Plaxton Première 320	C57F	1997	
R2CJT	Volvo B10M-62	Jonckheere Mistral	C49FT	1997	
R3CJT	Volvo B10M-62	Jonckheere Mistral	C49FT	1997	
R18CJT	Volvo B10M-62	Plaxton Première 320	C57F	1998	
R19CJT	Volvo B10M-62	Plaxton Première 320	C57F	1998	
R30CJT	Mercedes-Benz O1120L	Ferqui Solera	C35F	1998	
S853PKH	Mercedes-Benz Vario O814	Plaxton Beaver 2	B31F	1998	Plaxton demonstrator, 2000
S50CJT	Volvo B10M-62	Berkhof Axial 50	C49FT	1998	
S60CJT	Volvo B10M-62	Berkhof Axial 50	C49FT	1998	
X70CJT	Volvo B10M-62	Jonckheere Mistral 50	C49FT	2000	
X80CJT	Volvo B10M-62	Jonckheere Mistral 50	C49FT	2000	

Previous Registrations:

M10CJT	LSK825, M983HHS	M20CJT	XEL4
M11CJT	LSK821, M984HHS	M40CJT	XEL14, M459MRU
M12CJT	KSK977, M985HHS	MIL8583	A5XEL, N997THO
M13CJT	KSK985, M987HHS	OYY3	G879ARO

Livery: Silver and blue

Turners Ambassadeur Service's Berkhof Axial 50 S60CJT is one of a pair on Volvo B10M chassis. It was providing National Express duplication when pictured. From 2001 Berkhof coachwork will generally be available on Volvo chassis only in the UK through the Loughborough dealership.
Paul Stockwell

WAKES

Wakes - Hulberts

South West Coaches Ltd, Southgate Road, Wincanton, BA9 9EB

OFA2P	Leyland Leopard PSU3/3R	Plaxton Supreme III(1976)	C53F	1965	Regent, Whitstable, 1985
ETL545T	Bedford YLQ	Plaxton Supreme IV	BC45F	1978	Delaine, Bourne, 1987
LYA315V	Bedford YMT	Duple Dominant II Express	B53F	1979	
NYC398V	Bedford YMT	Duple Dominant II Express	BC53F	1980	
WSV323	Leyland Leopard PSU5C/4R	Plaxton P'mount 3200 III(1992)	C57F	1980	Ebdon's, Sidcup, 1983
XYC248W	Bedford YMT	Duple Dominant II Express	BC53F	1980	
XYC249W	Bedford YMT	Duple Dominant II Express	BC53F	1980	
XBJ860	Bedford YMQ	Plaxton Supreme IV	C35F	1981	
UYD950W	Bedford YMT	Duple Dominant	B57F	1981	Osmond, Curry Rivel, 1988
WYD103W	Leyland Leopard PSU3F/5R	Duple Dominant IV	C53F	1981	
WYD104W	Leyland Leopard PSU3F/5R	Duple Dominant IV	C53F	1981	
OPS550X	Bedford YMQ	Duple Dominant IV	BC35F	1981	Mills, Balta Sand, 1986
PWJ497X	Bedford YMT	Duple Dominant	B55F	1982	Priory of Gosport, 1988
BYD795X	Leyland Leopard PSU3F/5R	Duple Dominant IV Express	BC53F	1982	
LUI2528	Leyland Tiger TRCTL11/2R	Plaxton Paramount 3200	C53F	1983	Lodge's, High Easter, 1989
KYA284Y	Leyland Tiger TRCTL11/3R	Plaxton Paramount 3200	C57F	1983	
JIL8319	Leyland Tiger TRCTL11/2R	Plaxton Paramount 3200E	BC53F	1983	Torr's Coaches, Gedling, 1995
LIL2167	Leyland Tiger TRCTL11/2R	Plaxton Paramount 3200E	BC53F	1983	Torr's Coaches, Gedling, 1995
EGV695Y	Leyland Tiger TRCTL11/2R	Plaxton Paramount 3200E	BC53F	1983	Leiston Motor Hire, 1996
WSV868	Leyland Tiger TRCTL11/3R	East Lancashire EL2000 (1995)	B59F	1983	Northern Bus, Anston, 1994
A799REO	Leyland Tiger TRCTL11/3R	Marshall Campaigner	B56F	1983	Holmeswood Coaches, 1994
LUI2527	Leyland Tiger TRCTL11/3R	Plaxton Paramount 3200	C57F	1984	Armchair, Brentford, 1986
A109EPA	Leyland Tiger TRCTL11/2R	Plaxton Paramount 3200 E	BC53F	1984	The Bee Line, 1996
A130EPA	Leyland Tiger TRCTL11/2R	Plaxton Paramount 3200 E	BC53F	1984	Scarlet Coaches, Minehead, 1995
A256VYC	Leyland Tiger TRCTL11/3R	Wadham Stringer Vanguard	B59F	1984	MoD (), 1999
RIL1475	Leyland Tiger TRCTL11/3R	Plaxton Paramount 3200 II	BC53F	1984	Edward Bros, Tiers Cross, 1999
B155AYD	Leyland Tiger TRCTL11/3RZ	Plaxton Paramount 3200 II Exp	C57F	1985	
D649NYC	Volkswagen LT28	Devon Conversion	M13	1987	Hulberts Coaches, Yeovil, 2000
D65RMW	Ford Transit VE6	Chassis Developments	M12	1987	Hulberts Coaches, Yeovil, 2000
D929PYB	Volkswagen LT28	Devon Conversion	M8	1987	Hulberts Coaches, Yeovil, 2000
E758XYB	Volkswagen LT28	Devon Conversion	M8	1988	Hulberts Coaches, Yeovil, 2000
E845YYA	Volkswagen LT28	Devon Conversion	M8	1988	Hulberts Coaches, Yeovil, 2000
E416YYB	Volkswagen LT28	Devon Conversion	M8	1988	Hulberts Coaches, Yeovil, 2000
F997KCU	Mercedes-Benz 609D	Devon Conversion	BC23F	1988	Hulberts Coaches, Yeovil, 2000
F734USF	Mercedes-Benz 609D	Alexander Sprint	BC24F	1988	Hulberts Coaches, Yeovil, 2000
ANZ4374	Dennis Javelin 8.5SDL1903	Plaxton Paramount 3200 III	C35F	1989	Hulberts Coaches, Yeovil, 2000
GLZ7465	Volvo B10M-61	Plaxton Paramount 3200 III	C53F	1989	Hulberts Coaches, Yeovil, 2000
F387FYC	Ford Transit VE8	Ford	M7L	1989	Hulberts Coaches, Yeovil, 2000

Yeovil is the location for this view of East Lancashire-bodied Leyland Tiger WSV868. The body was fitted in 1995 displacing an ECW coach body.
Richard Godfrey

Taking a break in Plymouth, F555FYD in the Wakes fleet is a Volvo B10M with the lower Plaxton Paramount 3200 body. South West Coaches Ltd was formed to acquire the Wakes of Sparkford business from its revious owners and it also absorbed the Yeovil-based Hulbertson & Sons fleet of minibuses. *Mark Bailey*

F329GYA	Volkswagen LT28	Devon	M8	1989	Hulberts Coaches, Yeovil, 2000
F693GYD	Volkswagen LT28	Devon	M14	1989	Hulberts Coaches, Yeovil, 2000
F134JHO	Ford Transit VE6	Ford	M14	1989	Stoford Van Hire, 1992
F578SHT	Ford Transit VE6	Ford	M14	1989	Stoford Van Hire, 1992
F449XFX	Ford Transit VE6	Bristol Street Motors	M12	1989	Hulberts Coaches, Yeovil, 2000
F450XFX	Ford Transit VE6	Bristol Street Motors	M12	1989	Hulberts Coaches, Yeovil, 2000
G883OYC	Volkswagen LT28	Volkswagen	M14	1990	?, 19
TIL9865	Volvo B10M-60	Plaxton Paramount 3500 III	C53F	1990	
G518EFX	Volvo B10M-60	Plaxton Paramount 3200 III	C57F	1990	Excelsior, Bournemouth, 1993
LUI2529	Mercedes-Benz 811D	LHE Commuter	B29F	1990	Arriva North Midlands, 2001
G444NYC	Ford Transit VE6	Ford	M14	1990	Stoford Van Hire, 1992
H484BND	Ford Transit VE6	Made-to-Measure	M16	1990	Hulberts Coaches, Yeovil, 2000
H538ETT	Ford Transit VE6	Ford	M14	1991	Stoford Van Hire, 1992
H170SAB	Ford Transit VE6	Ford	M8	1991	Hulberts Coaches, Yeovil, 2000
ANZ4372	DAF SB3000DKV601	Van Hool Alizeé DH	C51FT	1992	Aztecbird, Guiseley, 2001
L210OYC	Mercedes-Benz 410D	Deansgate	M16	1994	Hulberts Coaches, Yeovil, 2000
L211OYC	Mercedes-Benz 410D	Deansgate	M16	1994	Hulberts Coaches, Yeovil, 2000
L687PYD	Volkswagen LT35D	Devon conversion	B14F	1994	Vincemt Group, 2001
L688PYD	Volkswagen LT35D	Devon conversion	B14F	1994	Vincemt Group, 2001
ANZ4373	Volvo B10M-62	Plaxton Première 320	C53F	1995	Excelsior, Bournemouth, 1997
M101SWG	Ford Transit VE6	Ford	M8	1995	van, 1999
M102SWG	Ford Transit VE6	Ford	M8	1995	van, 1999
M103SWG	Ford Transit VE6	Ford	M8	1995	van, 1999
M104SWG	Ford Transit VE6	Ford	M8	1995.	van, 1999
R652TYA	Mercedes-Benz 412D	G&M	M16	1997	
V852DYB	Mercedes-Benz Vario O814	Onyx	C24F	1999	

Previous Registrations:

A799REO	20KB46	LUI2529	G166YRE
ANZ4372	J823KHD	OFA2P	ECH7C
ANZ4373	A17EXC, M375MRU	RIL1475	B268KPF, WJB490
ANZ4374	F990FYB	TIL9865	G183OYC
EGV695Y	EVH240Y, 448HWT	UIL1335	G520EFX, G518EFX
GLZ7465	F555FYD	WSV323	LVS421V
JIL8319	GNW121Y	WSV868	BDF205Y
LIL2167	GNW122Y	XBJ860	UUR341W
LUI2527	A831PPP	XYC248W	SYD1W
LUI2528	FNM862Y	XYC249W	SYD2W

Livery: Beige, navy and red; **Depot:** Southgate Road, Wincanton and Victoria Avenue, Yeovil

WEAVERBUS

Weaverbus - Dorset Linkrider

RG & JE Weaver, 1 Hazeldown Avenue, Weymouth, DT3 6HT

G515VYE	Dennis Dart 8.5SDL3003	Duple Dartline	BC28F	1990	London United, 2000

Livery: Green

WESSEX BUS

G A Douglass, 439 Radipole Lane, Weymouth, DT4 0QF

B424NJF	Ford Transit 190	Rootes	B16F	1985	Bluebird, Weymouth, 2001
D463CKV	Freight Rover Sherpa	Rootes	B16F	1986	Charlton, Weymouth, 2001
D202KWT	Freight Rover Sherpa	Dormobile	B16F	1986	Charlton, Weymouth, 2001
E654DGW	Freight Rover Sherpa	Crystals	M16	1986	Charlton, Weymouth, 2001
E28MCE	Ford Transit VE6	Ford	M8	1987	
E167URJ	Peugeot-Talbot Express	Made-to-Measure	M12L	1987	
E204EPB	Iveco Daily 49-10	Robin Hood City Nippy	B25F	1987	Charlton, Weymouth, 2001
F949CUA	Freight Rover Sherpa	Carlyle Citybus 2	B20F	1988	Charlton, Weymouth, 2001
J112LKO	Iveco Daily 49-10	Carlyle Dailybus 2	B25F	1991	Brian Issac, Morriston, 2001
K712FNO	Iveco TurboDaily 59-12	Dormobile Routemaker	B25F	1993	Arriva The Shires, 2001

Previous registrations
K712FNO   K811JKH

Livery: Dark pink and white

Wessex Bus' Freight Rover F949CUA is pictured on the promanade in Weymouth. This vehicle carries the Citybus 2 body constructed by Carlyle at their now closed Birmingham unit. The designs for the larger buses were sold to Marshall though this production of this model ceased. *Richard Godfrey*

WESTERN GREYHOUND

Western Greyhound Ltd, 14 East Street, Newquay, TR7 1BH

1	VOD596S	Bristol VRT/SL3/6LXB	Eastern Coach Works	B43/31F	1978	Stagecoach Cheltenham, 2000
2	JWV252W	Bristol VRT/SL3/6LXB	Eastern Coach Works	B43/31F	1981	Brighton & Hove, 2000
6	TAH276W	Bristol VRT/SL3/6LXB	Eastern Coach Works	B43/31F	1981	First Eastern Counties, 2001
8	EDT918V	Bristol VRT/SL3/6LXB	Eastern Coach Works	B43/31F	1980	Bugler, Bristol, 2001
9	VVV959W	Bristol VRT/SL3/6LXB	Eastern Coach Works	B43/31F	1981	Brighton & Hove, 2000
50	RDF500R	Leyland Leopard PSU3C/4R	Plaxton Supreme III Express	C53F	1976	Tippett, St Columb Minor, 1999
65	WHW465T	Leyland Leopard PSU5C/4R	Plaxton Supreme III	C57F	1978	Coyne, Redruth, 2000
82	LUA282V	Leyland Leopard PSU5D/4R	Plaxton Supreme IV	C53F	1980	Gill, Wadebridge, 1998
119	TFO319	Leyland Tiger TRCTL11/3R	Plaxton Paramount 3500	C53F	1983	Bygone Tours, Smarden, 1998
137	WSV537	Leyland Tiger TRCTL11/3R	Plaxton Paramount 3500	C57F	1983	Gill, Wadebridge, 1998
214	N514BSR	Mercedes-Benz 410D	G&M	BC16F	1999	
301	E301BWL	Mercedes-Benz 709D	Reeve Burgess Beaver	BC25F	1988	Carmel Coaches, Northlew, 1999
498	UWR498	Mercedes-Benz 811D	Reeve Burgess Beaver	B33F	1989	Arriva The Shires, 2000
501	S501SRL	Mercedes-Benz Vario O814	Plaxton Beaver 2	B27F	1999	
502	S502SRL	Mercedes-Benz Vario O814	Plaxton Beaver 2	BC27F	1999	
503	S503SRL	Mercedes-Benz Vario O814	Plaxton Beaver 2	BC27F	1999	
509	R809HWS	Mercedes-Benz Vario O814	Plaxton Beaver 2	B33F	1998	Andybus, Tetbury, 2001
510	R810HWS	Mercedes-Benz Vario O814	Plaxton Beaver 2	B33F	1998	Andybus, Tetbury, 2001
530	S30ARJ	Mercedes-Benz Vario O814	Plaxton Beaver 2	B33F	1998	Andybus, Tetbury, 2001
534	S34BMR	Mercedes-Benz Vario O814	Plaxton Beaver 2	B33F	1998	Andybus, Tetbury, 2001
568	R668DNS	Mercedes-Benz Vario O614	Adamson	C24F	1997	Reay, Fletchertown, 1999
665	XOD665	Volvo B58-56	Plaxton Supreme IV	C53F	1980	Plymouth Citybus, 2001
674	674SHY	Volvo B58-56	Plaxton Supreme IV	C53F	1980	Plymouth Citybus, 2001
907	DSU107	Volvo B10M-61	Van Hool Alizée	C49FT	1992	Shearings, 1999
933	ULL933	Volvo B10M-61	Van Hool Alizée	C49FT	1992	Shearings, 1999

Previous registrations:

674SHY	DSR478V	TFO319	THL291Y, 1056AR, LBH460Y, JIL5289
DSU107	J232NNC	ULL933	J234NNC
F126TRU	F126TRU, JIL4005, 6962WF	UWR498	G896TGG
RDF500R	RDF500R, 674SHY	WSV537	WWA279Y, RBA480
SJI4783	B846BLG	XOD665	DSR476V

Livery: Pink and white
Web: westerngreyhound.com
Depot: St Austell Street, Summercourt.

Mercedes-Benz minibuses provide the backbone to the service needs of Western Greyhound, while the Bristol VRs is used on schools and contract work. Pictured in St Columb Major when working service 594 is S501SRL. The services plies between Truro and Wadebridge. *Mark Bailey*

F T WILLIAMS TRAVEL

F T Williams, Dolcoath Industrial Park, Dolcoath Road, Camborne, TR14 8RA

739JUA	Volvo B58-61	Jonckheere Bermuda	C49F	1981	Saffords, Little Gransden, 1989
SVL175W	Bristol VRT/SL3/6LXB	Eastern Coach Works	B45/28F	1981	Swiftlink, Harry Stoke, 1997
XPG295Y	DAF MB200DKTL600	Plaxton Supreme V	C57F	1982	Garrett, Newton Abbot, 1992
9996WX	Volvo B10M-61	Van Hool Alizée	C50FT	1983	Park's of Hamilton, 1993
A749UYL	Leyland Cub CU335	Wadham Stringer Vanguard	B23FL	1984	LB Islington, 1994
A766UYL	Leyland Cub CU335	Wadham Stringer Vanguard	B23FL	1984	Poynter, Wye, 1996
B269TLJ	Mercedes-Benz L608D	Reeve Burgess	C19F	1985	Cheney, Banbury, 1994
B710EOF	Volvo B10M-53	Jonckheere Jubilee P90	C54/13CT	1985	Travellers Choice, Carnforth, 2001
511HCV	Volvo B10M-61	Plaxton Paramount 3500 II	C53F	1985	St Buryan Garage, St Buryan,
C105AFX	Volvo B10M-61	Plaxton Paramount 3200 II	C53F	1986	Safeguard, Guildford, 1997
MJI6251	Scania K112TR	Plaxton Panorama 4000 II	C53/20CT	1986	Alex Head, Lutton, 2001
E920EAY	Volvo B10M-61	Plaxton Paramount 3500 III	C53F	1987	Stevens, Colchester, 1997
PJI5014	Volvo B10M-61	Van Hool Alizée	C50FT	1987	Eastville, Bristol, 1999
XSU910	Volvo B10M-61	Jonckheere Jubilee	C49FT	1988	Viscount Central, Burnley, 1999
F659VDF	Freight Rover Sherpa	Crystals	M16	1989	Cheney, Banbury, 1994
F246OFP	Toyota Coaster HB31R	Caetano Optimo	C21F	1989	Jennings, Bude, 1998
G33UWL	Ford Transit VE6	Ford	M12	1990	Cheney, Banbury, 1994
G764BGL	Peugeot Talbot Express	Dormobile	M14L	1990	Cornwall CC, 1996
G823MNH	Volvo B10M-60	Jonckheere Jubilee	C53F	1990	
RIL3706	Volvo B10M-60	Jonckheere Deauville	C51FT	1990	Knowles, Paignton, 2000
H165DJU	Volvo B10M-60	Duple 340	C53FT	1990	Jennings, Bude, 1998
H794FAF	Dennis Javelin 11SDA1923	Wadham Stringer Vanguard II	BC40FL	1990	Cornwall Disabled Association, 2000
H521HWL	Leyland-DAF 200	Leyland-DAF	M8	1991	Cheney, Banbury, 1994
H823GAF	Peugeot Talbot Express	Dormobile	M14L	1991	Cornwall CC, 1996
J953SBU	Dennis Dart 9.8SDL3012	Northern Counties Paladin	BC31D	1992	D&J Travel, Silvertown, 1997
K919WNR	Volvo B10M-60	Jonckheere Deauville	C51FT	1993	
L872WCV	Peugeot Talbot Express	Devon Conversions	M8	1994	Cornwall CC, 2000
M498ACV	Peugeot Talbot Express	Devon Conversions	M2L	1994	Cornwall CC, 2000

Previous Registrations:

511HCV	C483HAK	MJI6251	C351DWR
739JUA	XNV149W	PJI5014	D616MVR
9996WX	TCV137Y	RIL3706	G141MNH, RIL3707
B710EOF	B710EOF, LSU939	XSU910	

Livery: Various

F T Williams' Dennis Javelin H794FAF, with Wadham Stringer Vanguard II bodywork is seen outside the depot in Camborne.
Mark Bailey

WILTS & DORSET

Wilts & Dorset - Damory - Lever's Coaches - Bell's Coaches - Kingston

Wilts & Dorset Bus Co Ltd, Towngate House, Parkstone Road, Poole, BH15 2PR

2222-2241 — Optare Metrorider MR15 — Optare — B31F — 1995-96 — Trent Buses, 2000

2222	N322WCH	2227	P227CTV	2231	P231CTV	2235	P235CTV	2239	P239CTV
2224	N224VRC	2228	P228CTV	2232	P232CTV	2236	P236CTV	2240	P240CTV
2225	N225VRC	2229	P229CTV	2233	P233CTV	2237	P237CTV	2241	P241CTV
2226	N226VRC	2230	P230CTV	2234	P234CTV	2238	P238CTV		

2514-2533 — Optare MetroRider MR05 — Optare — B31F — 1992-93

2514	J514RPR	2518	K518UJT	2522	K522UJT	2526	K526UJT	2530	K530UJT
2515	J515RPR	2519	K519UJT	2523	K523UJT	2527	K527UJT	2531	K531UJT
2516	K516UJT	2520	K520UJT	2524	K524UJT	2528	K528UJT	2532	K532UJT
2517	K517UJT	2521	K521UJT	2525	K525UJT	2529	K529UJT	2533	K533UJT

2534-2547 — Optare MetroRider MR15 — Optare — B31F — 1995-96

2534	M534JLJ	2537	M537JLJ	2540	M540LEL	2543	N543UFX	2546	N546UFX
2535	M535JLJ	2538	M538LEL	2541	M541LEL	2544	N544UFX	2547	N547UFX
2536	M536JLJ	2539	M539LEL	2542	N542UFX	2545	N545UFX		

2601-2632 — Optare Solo M850 — Optare — N30F — 1998

2601	R601NFX	2608	R608NFX	2615	R615NFX	2621	R621NFX	2627	S627JRU
2602	R602NFX	2609	R609NFX	2616	R616NFX	2622	R622NFX	2628	S628JRU
2603	R603NFX	2610	R610NFX	2617	R617NFX	2623	S623JRU	2629	S629JRU
2604	R604NFX	2611	R611NFX	2618	R618NFX	2624	S624JRU	2630	S630JRU
2605	R905NFX	2612	R612NFX	2619	R619NFX	2625	S625JRU	2631	S631JRU
2606	R606NFX	2613	R613NFX	2620	R620NFX	2626	S626JRU	2632	S632JRU
2607	R607NFX	2614	R614NFX						

Wilts & Dorset have found that Optare products fully meet their needs and operate all of their major models. The current low-floor minibus being supplied across the country and to the Stagecoach Firstgroup and Arriva groups, is the Solo. Wilts & Dorset now have 88 including 2642, T642AJT, shown here.
Mark Lyons

The Optare Solo replaced the MetroRider on the production line. This popular minibus was conceived by MCW before that builder ceased production and sold the design to Optare. In 2000, Wilts and Dorset acquired a Optare-built batch from Trent, to replace MCWs. Number 2236, P236CTV is pictured at Warminster. *Tim Hall*

2633-2688   Optare Solo M850   Optare   N30F   1999-2000

2633	T633AJT	2644	T644AJT	2656	V656DFX	2667	V667DFX	2678	V678FEL
2634	T634AJT	2645	T645AJT	2657	V657DFX	2668	V668DFX	2679	V679FEL
2635	T635AJT	2646	T646AJT	2658	V658DFX	2669	V669DFX	2680	V680FEL
2636	T636AJT	2647	T647AJT	2659	V659DFX	2670	V670DFX	2681	V681FEL
2637	T637AJT	2648	T648AJT	2660	V660DFX	2671	V671FEL	2682	V682FEL
2638	T638AJT	2649	T649AJT	2661	V661DFX	2672	V672FEL	2683	V683FEL
2639	T639AJT	2651	V651DFX	2662	V662DFX	2673	V673FEL	2684	V684FEL
2640	T640AJT	2652	V653DFX	2663	V663DFX	2674	V674FEL	2685	V685FEL
2641	T641AJT	2653	V652DFX	2664	V664DFX	2675	V675FEL	2686	V686FEL
2642	T642AJT	2654	V654DFX	2665	V665DFX	2676	V676FEL	2687	X687XJT
2643	T643AJT	2655	V655DFX	2666	V966DFX	2677	V677FEL	2688	X688XJT

3101-3147   DAF DB250WB505*   Optare Spectra   B48/29F*   1993-95   *3136-9 are B45/28F
*3136-47 are type DB250RS200505

3101	K101VLJ	3111	L711ALJ	3120	L120ALJ	3130	L130ELJ	3139	M139KRU
3103	K103VLJ	3112	L112ALJ	3122	L122ELJ	3131	L131ELJ	3140	M140KRU
3104	K104VLJ	3113	L113ALJ	3123	L123ELJ	3132	M132HPR	3141	M141KRU
3105	K105VLJ	3114	L114ALJ	3124	L124ELJ	3133	M133HPR	3142	M142KRU
3106	K106VLJ	3115	L115ALJ			3134	M134HPR	3143	M143KRU
3107	K107VLJ	3116	L116ALJ	3126	L126ELJ	3135	M135HPR	3144	M144KRU
3108	K108VLJ	3117	L117ALJ	3127	L127ELJ	3136	M136KRU	3145	M145KRU
3109	K109VLJ	3118	L118ALJ	3128	L128ELJ	3137	M137KRU	3146	M146KRU
3110	K110VLJ	3119	L119ALJ	3129	L129ELJ	3138	M138KRU	3147	M947KRU

The number of DAF double-deck buses built has been low in comparison to Dennis and Volvo products, though they form the base for the Optare Spectra. When Wall's of Manchester ceased service work in 1997, Wilts & Dorset acquired several of their buses which feature Northern Counties bodywork on similar DAF chassis. Five have been converted for open-top work in Bournemouth, where 3149, M18WAL is pictured.
Tim Hall

3148	M17WAL	DAF DB250RS505	Northern Counties Palatine	B47/30F	1995	Wall's of Manchester, 1998
3149	M18WAL	DAF DB250RS505	Northern Counties Palatine	CO47/30F	1995	Wall's of Manchester, 1998
3150	M19WAL	DAF DB250RS505	Northern Counties Palatine	CO47/30F	1995	Wall's of Manchester, 1998
3151	M20WAL	DAF DB250RS505	Northern Counties Palatine	CO47/30F	1995	Wall's of Manchester, 1998
3152	N13WAL	DAF DB250RS505	Northern Counties Palatine	CO47/30F	1995	Wall's of Manchester, 1998
3153	N14WAL	DAF DB250RS505	Northern Counties Palatine	B47/30F	1995	Wall's of Manchester, 1998
3157	M645RCP	DAF DB250RS505	Northern Counties Palatine	CO47/30F	1995	A Bus, Brislington, 1998

3154-3166   DAF DE02RSDB250   Optare Spectra   N50/28F   1998-2000

3154	R154NPR	3158	T158ALJ	3161	W161RFX	3163	W163RFX	3165	W165RFX
3155	R155NPR	3159	T159ALJ	3162	W162RFX	3164	W164RFX	3166	W166RFX
3156	R156NPR	3160	T160ALJ						

3167-3175   DAF DE02RSDB250   Optare Spectra   N50/27F   2001

3167	Y167FEL	3169	Y169FEL	3171	Y171FEL	3173	Y173FEL	3175	Y175FEL
3168	Y168FEL	3170	Y199FEL	3172	Y172FEL	3174	Y174FEL		

3207	PIL5207	Leyland Tiger TRCTL11/3RH	Duple Laser 2	C53F	1984
3208	B208REL	Leyland Tiger TRCTL11/3RH	Duple Laser 2	C53F	1984
3209	B209REL	Leyland Tiger TRCTL11/3RH	Duple Laser 2	C53F	1984
3210	XIB3910	Leyland Tiger TRCTL11/3RH	Duple Laser 2	C53F	1984
3211	L211CRU	Bova FHD12.270	Bova Futura Club	C49FT	1993
3212	L212CRU	Bova FHD12.270	Bova Futura Club	C49FT	1993
3213	L213CRU	Bova FHD12.270	Bova Futura Club	C49FT	1993
3214	R214NFX	DAF DE33WSSB3000	Plaxton Premiére 320	C53F	1998
3215	R215NFX	DAF DE33WSSB3000	Plaxton Premiére 320	C53F	1998
3216	T216REL	DAF DE33WSSB3000	Plaxton Prima	C53F	1999
3217	T217REL	DAF DE33WSSB3000	Plaxton Prima	C53F	1999
3218	T218REL	DAF DE33WSSB3000	Plaxton Prima	C53F	1999

Damory is one of the four Wilts & Dorset subsidiaries that operate country bus and school contracts alongside private hire in the rural areas of Dorset and Wiltshire. Pictured at Milton Abbas is Leyland Lynx 5054, E65WDT, which is based at Balndford Forum. *Richard Godfrey*

3278	B278KPF	Leyland Tiger TRCTL11/3R	Plaxton Paramount 3200E	C53F	1985	Damory Coaches, 1994
3298	SIB4903	Leyland Tiger TRCTL11/3R	Plaxton Paramount 3200 II	C53F	1985	Thamesdown (Kingston), 1998
3299	SMY635X	Leyland Tiger TRCTL11/3R	Plaxton Supreme V	C50F	1982	Johnson Bros, Hodthorpe, 1993
3351	OEL232P	Bristol VRT/SL3/501	Eastern Coach Works	O43/31F	1976	Hants & Dorset, 1983

3501-3506

		DAF SB220LC550		Optare Delta		B48F	1993	
3501	L501AJT	3503	L503AJT	3504	L504AJT	3505	L505AJT	3506	L506AJT
3502	L502AJT							

3507	N10WAL	DAF DE02LTSB220	Ikarus CitiBus	B49F	1995	Wall's of Manchester, 1998
3509	N15WAL	DAF DE02LTSB220	Ikarus CitiBus	B49F	1995	Wall's of Manchester, 1998
3510	N16WAL	DAF DE02LTSB220	Ikarus CitiBus	B49F	1995	Wall's of Manchester, 1998

3601-3609

		Optare Excel L1180		Optare		N43F	2000	
3601	W601PLJ	3603	W603PLJ	3605	X605XFX	3607	X607XFX	3609	X609WLJ
3602	W602PLJ	3604	W604PLJ	3606	X606XFX	3608	X608XFX	

3906	A989XAF	Leyland Olympian ONLXB/1R	Eastern Coach Works	CO45/30F	1984	Red Bus, 1986
3907	A990XAF	Leyland Olympian ONLXB/1R	Eastern Coach Works	CO45/30F	1984	Red Bus, 1986
4334	JJT446N	Bristol VRT/SL3/6LXB	Eastern Coach Works	B43/31F	1975	Hants & Dorset, 1983

4367-4456

		Bristol VRT/SL3/6LXB		Eastern Coach Works		B43/31F	1977-78	Hants & Dorset, 1983
4383	URU690S	4422	ELJ214V	4427	ELJ219V	4432	GEL682V	4451	KRU851W
4404	BFX572T	4423	ELJ215V	4428	ELJ220V	4437	GEL687V	4453	KRU853W
4407	BFX575T	4424	ELJ216V	4429	GEL679V	4448	KRU848W	4454	KRU854W
4412	BFX665T	4425	ELJ217V	4430	GEL680V	4449	KRU849W	4455	KRU855W
4417	UDL674S	4426	ELJ218V	4431	GEL681V	4450	KRU850W	4456	KRU856W

The South West Bus Handbook

Principally used on the Bristol to Salisbury service, 3215, R215NFX was pictured while on a private hire to London. One of a pair of DAF SB3000 with Plaxton Premiére 320 bodywork it shows the smart application of the Wilts & Dorset colours to this model. *David Heath*

4901-4905

							Leyland Olympian ONLXB/1R	Eastern Coach Works		B45/32F	1984	
4901	A901JPR	**4902**	A902JPR	**4903**	A903JPR	**4904**	A904JPR	**4905**	A905JPR			

4908	UWW12X	Leyland Olympian ONLXB/1R	Roe	CO47/29F 1982	West Yorkshire PTE, 1987
4909	UWW17X	Leyland Olympian ONLXB/1R	Roe	CO47/29F 1982	West Yorkshire PTE, 1987
4911	CUB70Y	Leyland Olympian ONLXB/1R	Roe	CO47/29F 1983	West Yorkshire PTE, 1987
4912	EWY80Y	Leyland Olympian ONLXB/1R	Roe	CO47/29F 1984	West Yorkshire PTE, 1987
4920	A160FPG	Leyland Olympian ONTL11/1R	Roe	B43/29F 1984	County, 1990
4921	A173VFM	Leyland Olympian ONLXB/1R	Eastern Coach Works	B45/32F 1984	Crosville Cymru, 1990
4922	A174VFM	Leyland Olympian ONLXB/1R	Eastern Coach Works	B45/32F 1984	Crosville Cymru, 1990
4923	A175VFM	Leyland Olympian ONLXB/1R	Eastern Coach Works	B45/32F 1984	Crosville Cymru, 1990

Damory Coaches

5005	B203REL	Leyland Tiger TRCTL11/3RH	Duple Laser 2	C51F 1984	
5011	VUV246	DAF DE33WSSB3000	Plaxton Premiére 350	C51FT 1996	Armchair, Brentford, 1999
5012	LIL3748	DAF DE33WSSB3000	Plaxton Premiére 350	C53F 1996	
5013	M574RCP	DAF SB3000WS601	Van Hool Alizée	C55F 1994	North Kent Express, 2001
5014	M746RCP	DAF DE33WSSB3000	Van Hool Alizée	C55F 1994	North Kent Express, 2001
5021	C877CYX	Volvo B10M-61	Plaxton Paramount 3200 II	C53F 1986	Happy Days, Woodseaves, 1997
5022	D880FYL	Volvo B10M-61	Plaxton Paramount 3200 III	C53F 1986	Happy Days, Woodseaves, 1997
5023	UEL489	Volvo B10M-60	Plaxton Premiére 320	C53F 1993	Thamesdown, 1999
5024	LIL2665	Volvo B10M-60	Jonckheere Deauville 45L	C51FT 1990	Southampton, 1992
5031	M15WAL	DAF SB220LC550	Ikarus CitiBus	B48F 1994	Wall's of Manchester, 1997
5051	D165HML	Leyland Lynx LX112TL11FR1	Leyland Lynx	B49F 1987	Safeguard, Guildford, 1996
5052	E51MMT	Leyland Lynx LX112TL11FR1S	Leyland Lynx	B49F 1987	Safeguard, Guildford, 1996
5053	E64WDT	Leyland Lynx LX112TL11ZR1R	Leyland Lynx	B49F 1987	Rhondda, 1996
5054	E65WDT	Leyland Lynx LX112TL11ZR1R	Leyland Lynx	B49F 1987	Rhondda, 1996
5055	D112NDW	Leyland Lynx LX112TL11FR1S	Leyland Lynx	B51F 1987	Filers, Ilfracombe, 1998
5056	E297OMG	Leyland Lynx LX112TL11ZR1R	Leyland Lynx	B49F 1998	Safeguard, Guildford, 1996
5057	E298OMG	Leyland Lynx LX112TL11ZR1R	Leyland Lynx	B49F 1998	Safeguard, Guildford, 1996

5063	URU691S	Bristol VRT/SL3/6LXB	Eastern Coach Works	B43/31F	1978	Hants & Dorset, 1983
5066	URU673S	Bristol VRT/SL3/6LXB	Eastern Coach Works	B43/31F	1977	Hants & Dorset, 1983
5068	GEL683V	Bristol VRT/SL3/6LXB	Eastern Coach Works	B43/31F	1978	Hants & Dorset, 1983
5069	GEL685V	Bristol VRT/SL3/6LXB	Eastern Coach Works	B43/31F	1978	Hants & Dorset, 1983
5070	GEL686V	Bristol VRT/SL3/6LXB	Eastern Coach Works	B43/31F	1978	Hants & Dorset, 1983
5071	BFX664T	Bristol VRT/SL3/6LXB	Eastern Coach Works	B43/31F	1978	Hants & Dorset, 1983
5072	BFX666T	Bristol VRT/SL3/6LXB	Eastern Coach Works	B43/31F	1978	Hants & Dorset, 1983
5125	R710YFL	LDV Convoy	LDV	M16	1997	private owner, 1998
5126	R815UOK	LDV Convoy	LDV	M16	1997	private owner, 1998
5127	N626BDU	LDV 400	LDV	M8	1996	Adams Morey, Ringwood, 1999
5131	J501RPR	Optare MetroRider MR05	Optare	B31F	1992	
5132	J502RPR	Optare MetroRider MR05	Optare	B31F	1992	
5133	J503RPR	Optare MetroRider MR05	Optare	B31F	1992	
5134	J504RPR	Optare MetroRider MR05	Optare	B31F	1992	
5135	J505RPR	Optare MetroRider MR05	Optare	B31F	1992	
5136	J506RPR	Optare MetroRider MR05	Optare	B31F	1992	
5137	J507RPR	Optare MetroRider MR05	Optare	B31F	1992	
5138	J508RPR	Optare MetroRider MR05	Optare	B31F	1992	
5139	J513RPR	Optare MetroRider MR05	Optare	B31F	1992	
5164	L546WDE	LDV 200	LDV	M8	1993	Adams Morey, Ringwood, 1996
5166	N614HRV	LDV 200	LDV	M8	1996	MoD (FD64AA), 1997
5168	P319DOP	LDV Pilot	LDV	M8	1996	
5173	F919TRP	Ford Granada	Ford	M4	1990	

Tourist Coaches

6003	OJI1875	Leyland Tiger TRCTL11/3RZ	Plaxton Paramount 3200 III	C53F	1988	Hatts Coaches, Foxham, 1997
6015	HJI2615	DAF MB230LTF615	Van Hool Alizée HE	C53F	1993	Wootten, Northampton, 2000
6016	HSV342	DAF DE33WSSB3000	Van Hool Alizée HE	C49FT	1996	Couplands & Cronin, Wyre, 1999
6017	TJI9462	DAF MB230LTRF615	Van Hool Alizée HE	C57F	1993	First Lowland, 2001
6036	RJI6155	Volvo B10M-61	Plaxton Paramount 3200 III	C53F	1986	Staffordian, Stafford, 1997
6037	USV115	Volvo B10M-60	Plaxton Paramount 3500 III	C53F	1989	Fishwick, Leyland, 1994
6040	UJI2507	Volvo B10M-61	Plaxton Paramount 3200 III	C53F	1990	Excelsior, Bournemouth, 1995
6043	NXI5358	Volvo B10M-60	Plaxton Paramount 3200 III	C57F	1990	Thamesdown, 1998
6051	SJI8751	Dennis Javelin 8.5SDA1915	Plaxton Paramount 3200 III	C33F	1989	Kingston, Salisbury, 1991
6111	J509RPR	Optare MetroRider MR05	Optare	BC31F	1992	
6112	J510RPR	Optare MetroRider MR05	Optare	B31F	1992	
6113	J511RPR	Optare MetroRider MR05	Optare	B31F	1992	
6114	J512RPR	Optare MetroRider MR05	Optare	B31F	1992	
6121	VJI3968	Toyota Coaster HB31R	Caetano Optimo	C18F	1989	Chalk, Salisbury, 1991
6134	L739NHE	Ford Transit VE6	Advanced Vehicle	M12	1994	Pilling, Sowerby Bridge, 1997
6164	M817ARV	LDV 200	LDV	M8	1995	Adams, Morey, 1995
6166	P693UAE	LDV Pilot	LDV	M8	1997	Churchfields, Salisbury, 1998
6167	R37GDE	LDV Pilot	Lonsdale	M8	1998	Couplands & Cronin, Wyre, 1998
6213	701GOO	DAF DE33WSSB3000	Plaxton Premiére 350	C51FT	1996	Carplan & Craine, Rossall, 1999
6214	MJI7514	DAF MB230LTRH615	Van Hool Alizée	C51FT	1993	First Lowland, 2000
6235	LSV749	Volvo B10M-60	Plaxton Premiére 350	C49F	1993	Spirit of London, Bedfont, 1996
6241	SIB5373	Volvo B10M-60	Plaxton Paramount 3200 III	C57F	1990	Thamesdown, 1998
6242	PJI7002	Volvo B10M-60	Plaxton Paramount 3200 III	C57F	1990	Excelsior, Bournemouth, 1995
6318	YMW843	DAF DE33WSSB3000	Van Hool Alizée	C53F	1997	Berkley, Hemel Hempstead, 2001
6322	L396YAM	Toyota Coaster HZB50R	Caetano Optimo	C21F	1994	Bell, Winterslow, 1999
6323	N411WJL	Mercedes-Benz 711D	Autobus Classique Nouvelle	C24F	1995	Bell, Winterslow, 1999
6345	K750RHR	Volvo B10M-60	Plaxton Paramount 3500 III	C53F	1993	Bell, Winterslow, 1999
6346	XAM152	Volvo B10M-60	Plaxton Paramount 3500	C53F	1993	Bell, Winterslow, 1999
6347	XAA299	Volvo B10M-62	Plaxton Premiére 320	C53F	1996	Bell, Winterslow, 1999
6352	T35RJL	Mercedes-Benz O1120L	Ferqui Solera	C35F	1999	Atlantic, Heywood, 2001

The Tourist Coaches operation is based at Figheldean, north of Annesbury and uses a livery of cream and orange. Its vehicles are numbered in the 6xxx series. Showing the livery is Leyland Tiger 6003, OJI1875, with Plaxton Paramount 3200 bodywork. *Robert Edworthy*

Levers Coaches

7001	B477UNB	Volvo B10M-61	Van Hool Alizée	C53F	1985	Shearings, 1990
7002	E313OMG	Volvo B10M-61	Plaxton Paramount 3200 III	C57F	1988	Limebourne, Battersea, 1994
7003	F441DUG	Volvo B10M-61	Plaxton Paramount 3500 III	C53F	1989	Direct, Birmingham, 1994
7004	G94RGG	Volvo B10M-60	Plaxton Paramount 3500 III	C49F	1990	Park's of Hamilton, 1995
7005	B909SPR	Volvo B10M-60	Plaxton Paramount 3500 II	C53F	1985	
7012	F205EWN	DAF SB2305DHS585	Caetano Algarve	C53F	1989	D Coaches, Morriston, 1996
7013	F206EWN	DAF SB2305DHS585	Caetano Algarve	C53F	1989	D Coaches, Morriston, 1996
7014	SIL7914	DAF MB230LTF615	Van Hool Alizée	C49FT	1995	Wilson, Bonnyrigg, 2000
7015	381VHX	DAF DE33WSSB3000	Van Hool Alizée	C49FT	1996	Wood, Barnsley, 2000
7016	L526EHD	DAF MB230LTRH615	Van Hool Alizée	C51F	1994	Hallmark, Luton, 2001
7031	F40KRO	Dennis Lancet SDA523	Wadham Stringer Vanguard II	BC40DLT	1988	Bedfordshire CC, 1997
7041	RNY313Y	Leyland Tiger TRCTL11/2R	Plaxton Paramount 3200 E	C49F	1983	Enterprise, Chatteris, 1997
7043	XXI8502	Leyland Tiger TRCTL11/3R	Plaxton Paramount 3200	C53F	1985	Thamesdown (Kingston), 1998
7101	G609THR	Mercedes-Benz 811D	Reeve Burgess Beaver	C25F	1990	
7111	C86AHW	Mercedes-Benz L608D	Reeve Burgess	C19F	1985	Bere Regis & District, 1996
7112	E239LRV	Mercedes-Benz 709D	Robin Hood	C19F	1988	
7124	P24DOR	LDV Convoy	LDV	M16	1996	

Ancillary vehicles

9085	B201REL	Leyland Tiger TRCTL11/3RH	Duple Laser 2	C51F	1984	

Previous Registrations:

381VHX	N89FWU		
701GOO	N61FWU	SIB5373	G508EFX, A8EXC, G373GJT
B201REL	B201REL, 701GOO	SIL7914	K547RJX
B202REL	B202REL,VUV246	SJI8751	F910UPR, XIB3910
B909SPR	B909SPR, XAM152	TJI9462	K535RJX
HJI2615	K529RJX	UEL489	K728JWX
HSV342	N68FWU	UJI2507	G510EFX, A10EXC, G392GJT
LIL2665	B216NDG, HIL6075, B178SFH	USV115	G56RGG
LIL3748	N983FWT	VJI3968	F659YLJ
LSV749	K855BUR, HSV342	VUV246	N45FWU
MJI7514	K537RJX	XAA299	A11XEL, N225THO
NXI5358	G509EFX, A9EXC, G358GJT	XAM152	K727JWX
OIL5207	B207REL	XIB3910	B210REL
OJI1875	E678UNE	XSL228A	866NHT
PJI7002	G507EFX, A7EXC, G391GJT	XXI8502	B126PEL
RJI6155	D879FYL	YPD124Y	YPD124Y, UJI2507
SIB4903	C194WJT	YMW843	P890PWW

Liveries: Red, white and black (Wilts & Dorset); white, turquoise and maroon (Damory); cream and orange (Tourist); white (National Express); green and cream (Guide Friday); cream and red (Kingston Coaches); white and blue (Levers Coaches)

Allocations:

Blandford (Salisbury Road) - Wilts & Dorset

Outstation - Shaftesbury

MetroRider	2225	2226	2227	2240	2241	2538
Solo	2686					
Bristol VR	4384					
DAF Spectra	3113	3114	3133	3134	3145	

Blandford (Sunrise Business Park) - Damory Coaches

MetroRider	5131	5132	5135	5138	5139	
DAF/Ikarus	5031					
Lynx	5051	5052	5053	5054	5055	5057
Bristol VR	5063	5066	5068	5072		

Blandford (Clump Farm, Blandford Heights Ind Est) - Damory Coaches

Outstation: Verwood, Shaftesbury

Sherpa/LDV	5125	5126	5164	5166
MetroRider	5136			
Tiger	5005			
DAF	5011	5012	5013	5014
Volvo	5023	5024		
Cars	5173			
Bristol VR	5071			

Fovant (Swallowcliffe) - Levers

LDV	7124				
Mercedes-Benz	7101	7111	7112		
Dennis	6051	7031			
DAF	7011	7012	7013	7014	7015	7016
Tiger	7041	7043			
Volvo	7001	7002	7003	7004	7005

Figheldean - Tourist

Outstations - Salisbury, Sherfield English, Upavon Winterslow.

LDV	6164	6166	6167	
MetroRider	6111	6112	6113	6114
Toyota/Optimo	6121			
Dennis	6051			
DAF	6015	6016	6017	
Tiger	6003			
Volvo	6036	6037	6040	6043

Lymington (Station Road) - Wilts & Dorset

Outstations - Hythe, Lyndhurst

MetroRider	2222	2224	2518	2519	2520	2528	2539	2540
	2541							
Solo	2633	2634	2635	2681	2682	2683	2684	2685
Bristol VR	4453	4455	4456					
Spectra	3103	3111	3112	3126	3127	3128	3141	3147
	3162	3163	3164	3167	3168			

Poole (Kingsland Road) - Wilts & Dorset - Damory Coaches

Sherpa	5127							
MetroRider	2533	2542	2546	2547	5134	5137		
Solo	2601	2602	2603	2604	2605	2606	2607	2608
	2609	2610	2611	2612	2613	2636	2637	2638
	2639	2640	2641	2642	2643	2644	2645	2646
	2647	2648	2649	2651	2652	2653	2654	2655
	2656	2657	2658	2659	2660	2661	2662	2663
	2664	2665	2666	2667	2668	2669	2670	2673
	2674	2675	2676	2687	2688			
Excel	3601	3602	3603	3604				
Delta	3501	3502	3503					
DAF	3507	3509	3510					
Volvo	5021							
Lynx	5056							
Bristol VR	4404	4407	4422	4423	4426	4427	4429	4437
	4449	4450	4451	5069	5070			
Olympian	4908	4912	4920					
DAF/Palatine	3149							
Spectra	3101	3118	3122	3123	3124	3142	3143	3144
	3146	3165	3166	3169	3170	3171		

Ringwood (West Street) - Wilts & Dorset

MetroRider	2516	2517	2521	2522	2529	2530	
Solo	2614	2615	2616	2677	2678	2679	2680
Bristol VR	4424	4425	4454				
Spectra	3104	3115	3116	3117	3135	3161	3172	3173
	3174						

Salisbury (Castle Street) - Wilts & Dorset -

Outstations - Amesbury, Bowerchalke, Devizes, Downton, Hindon, Pewsey, Porton Down, Romsey, Ringwood, Shaftesbury, Warminster.

MetroRider	2228	2229	2230	2231	2232	2233	2234	2235
	2236	2237	2238	2239	2514	2515	2523	2524
	2525	2526	2527	2532	2534	2535	2536	2537
	2543	2544	2545					
Solo	2617	2618	2619	2620	2621	2622	2623	2624
	2625	2626	2627	2628	2629	2630	2631	2632
	2671	2672						
Excel	3605	3606	3607	3608	3609			
Tiger	3207	3208	3210	3278	3298	3299		
Bova	3211	3212	3213					
Delta	3504	3505	3506					
Bristol VR	4334	4428	4430	4431	4432	4448		
Olympian	4901	4902	4903	4904	4905	4921	4922	4923
Spectra	3105	3106	3107	3108	3109	3110	3111	3119
	3120	3129	3130	3131	3132	3136	3137	3138
	3139	3154	3155	3156	3158	3159	3160	3175
DAF/Palatine	3215	3216	3217	3218				

Salisbury (Castle Street) - Bell's Coaches - Kingston Coaches

Transit	6134						
Mercedes-Benz	6323	6352					
Toyota	6322						
DAF	6213	6214	6318				
Volvo	6235	6241	6242	6345	6346	6347	6350

Swanage (Kings Road West) - Wilts & Dorset

MetroRider	2531					
Bristol VR	4412					
Olympian	3906	3907	4909	3911		
Spectra	3140					
DAF/Palatine	3148	3150	3151	3152	3155	3157

Withdrawn & unallocated

Freight Rover/LDV	5122	5163					
Fiat	6132						
MetroRider	2223	2338	2341	2347	2356	2375	2385	5103
	5104	5109	5115	6101	6102	6103		
Solo	2650						
Leopard	6011	9079					
Tiger	3205	3206	5004	5006	5007	5008	6001	7042
DAF	3508	6012	7011				
Volvo	6032	6033	6034	6238			
Bristol VR	4332	3351	4367	4368	4403		
Olympian	3910	4913	4914	4927			
Spectra	3121	3125					

YELLOW BUSES

Yellow Buses - Dorset Travel - Yellow Coaches - Whippett Coaches

Bournemouth Transport Ltd, Mallard Road, Bournemouth, BH8 4PN

101	RUF970M	Leyland Leopard PSU3B/4R	Willowbrook Warrier	B49F	1973	Stagecoach South, 1999
102	OUF863W	Leyland Leopard PSU3F/4R	Willowbrook Warrier	B48F	1981	Brighton & Hove, 1999
103	RFC13T	Leyland Leopard PSU3E/4R	Willowbrook Warrier	B48F	1979	Brighton & Hove, 1999
104	JNJ718V	Leyland Leopard PSU3E/4R	Willowbrook Warrier	BC60F	1979	Stagecoach South, 1999
105	WPD27Y	Leyland Leopard PSU3G/4R	Willowbrook Warrier	B48F	1982	Brighton & Hove, 1999
106	PIB5145	Leyland Leopard PSU3E/4R	Willowbrook Warrier	B48F	1978	Brighton & Hove, 1999
108	RFC14T	Leyland Leopard PSU3E/4R	Willowbrook Warrier	B48F	1979	Brighton & Hove, 1999
109	JYJ269N	Leyland Leopard PSU3B/4R	Willowbrook Warrier	B53F	1975	Stagecoach South, 1999

132-137 — Daimler Fleetline CRL6-30, Alexander AL, CO43/31F 1976

132	NFX132P	**134**	NFX134P	**135**	NFX135P	**136**	NFX136P	**137**	NFX137P
133	NFX133P								

138	VJT138S	Leyland Fleetline FE30ALR	Alexander AL	CO43/31F	1978
139	VJT139S	Leyland Fleetline FE30ALR	Alexander AL	CO43/31F	1978
140	VJT140S	Leyland Fleetline FE30ALR	Alexander AL	CO43/31F	1978
154	CRU154V	Leyland Fleetline FE30ALR	Alexander AL	B43/31F	1979
160	CRU160V	Leyland Fleetline FE30ALR	Alexander AL	B43/31F	1979

167-176 — Leyland Fleetline FE30AGR, Alexander AL, B43/31F 1980-81

167	GRU167V	**169**	MFX169W	**171**	MFX171W	**173**	MFX173W	**175**	MFX175W
168	GRU168V	**170**	MFX170W	**172**	MFX172W	**174**	MFX174W	**176**	MFX176W

193-199 — Leyland Olympian ONLXB/1R, Marshall, B47/31F 1982

193	TJT193X	**195**	TJT195X	**197**	TJT197X	**198**	TJT198X	**199**	TJT199X
194	TJT194X	**196**	TJT196X						

200-204 — Volvo Citybus B10M-50, East Lancashire, BC43/33F 1986

200	D200ELJ	**201**	C201YPR	**202**	D202ELJ	**203**	D203ELJ	**204**	D204ELJ

205-214 — Volvo Citybus B10M-50, Alexander RH, B47/33F 1988-89

205	E205GCG	**207**	E207GCG	**209**	E209GCG	**211**	F211WRU	**213**	F213WRU
206	E206GCG	**208**	E208GCG	**210**	F210WRU	**212**	F212WRU	**214**	F214WRU

251-269 — Dennis Dominator DDA1033, East Lancashire, B47/33F 1990-92

251	H251JJT	**255**	H255JJT	**259**	H259MFX	**264**	H264MFX	**267**	J267SPR
252	H252JJT	**256**	H256JJT	**261**	H261MFX	**265**	H265MFX	**268**	J268SPR
253	H253JJT	**257**	H257JJT	**262**	H262MFX	**266**	J266SPR	**269**	J269SPR
254	H254JJT	**258**	H258MFX	**263**	H263MFX				

270-278 — Dennis Trident 2-axle, East Lancashire Lolyne, N51/33F 1999

270	T270BPR	**272**	T272BPR	**274**	T274BPR	**276**	T276BPR	**278**	T278BPR
271	T271BPR	**273**	T273BPR	**275**	T275BPR	**277**	T277BPR		

315	X315WFX	Mercedes-Benz 614D	Crest	C24F	2000
319	R319NRU	Volvo B10M-62	Berkhof Axial 50	C49FT	1998
320	T320AFX	Volvo B10M-62	Berkhof Axial 50	C49FT	1999
321	P321ARU	Volvo B10M-62	Berkhof Axial 50	C49FT	1997
322	P322ARU	Volvo B10M-62	Berkhof Axial 50	C49FT	1997
323	P323ARU	Volvo B10M-62	Berkhof Axial 50	C49FT	1997
324	W324UEL	Volvo B10M-62	Berkhof Axial 50	C49FT	1999
326	R326NRU	Volvo B10M-62	Van Hool T9 Alizée	C49FT	1998
327	R327NRU	Volvo B10M-62	Van Hool T9 Alizée	C49FT	1998
329	R329NRU	Volvo B10M-62	Van Hool T9 Alizée	C49FT	1998
330	T330AFX	Volvo B10M-62	Van Hool T9 Alizée	C49FT	1999
331	T331AFX	Volvo B10M-62	Van Hool T9 Alizée	C49FT	1999

334	W334UEL	Volvo B10M-62	Berkhof Axial 50	C49FT	1999	
335	T335AFX	Volvo B10M-62	Berkhof Axial 50	C49FT	1999	
336	Y336CJT	Volvo B10M-62	Berkhof Axial 50	C49FT	2001	
338	R338NRU	Volvo B10M-62	Berkhof Axial 50	C49FT	1998	
339	R339NRU	Volvo B10M-62	Berkhof Axial 50	C49FT	1998	
340	R340MPR	Scania L94	Irizar Intercentury 12.32	C55FT	1997	
341	R341LPR	Scania K113CRB	Irizar Century 12.35	C34FT	1997	
343	N3YCL	Scania K113CRB	Irizar Century 12.35	C41FT	1996	
345	RIB8745	Scania K93CRB	Van Hool Alizée	C55F	1992	Brittains, Northampton, 1996
350	R350LPR	Scania L94	Van Hool Alizée T9	C55FT	1997	
351	R351LPR	Scania L94	Van Hool Alizée T9	C55FT	1997	
352	P352ARU	Scania K113TRB	Van Hool Alizée	C49FT	1997	
353	P353ARU	Scania K113TRB	Van Hool Alizée	C49FT	1997	
354	R354NRU	Volvo B10M-62	Van Hool T9 Alizée	C49FT	1998	
355	R355NRU	Volvo B10M-62	Van Hool T9 Alizée	C49FT	1998	

356-360

	Scania K113CRB		Van Hool Alizée	C49FT	1995

356	M356LFX	357	M357LFX	358	M358LFX	359	M359LFX	360	M360LFX

367	N367TJT	Scania K113CRB	Van Hool Alizée	C44FT	1996	
368	N368TJT	Scania K113CRB	Van Hool Alizée	C44FT	1996	
369	N369TJT	Scania K113CRB	Van Hool Alizée	C44FT	1996	
370	N370TJT	Scania K113CRB	Van Hool Alizée	C44FT	1996	
381	W381UEL	Scania L94IB	Van Hool T9 Alizée	C49FT	2000	
382	W382UEL	Scania L94IB	Van Hool T9 Alizée	C49FT	2000	
383	W383UEL	Scania L94IB	Van Hool T9 Alizée	C49FT	2000	
384	W384UEL	Scania L94IB	Van Hool T9 Alizée	C49FT	2000	
390	R998FNW	DAF DE33WSSB3000	Ikarus Blue Danube	C51FT	1998	Whippet Cs, Bournemouth, 2000
391	P892FMO	Dennis Javelin GX	Berkhof Axial 50	C53F	1997	Whippet Cs, Bournemouth, 2000
392	RAZ5279	DAF MB230LB615	Plaxton Paramount 3500 III	C49FT	1989	Whippet Cs, Bournemouth, 2000
393	SIB6442	Bedford YMT	Plaxton Supreme IV	C40FT	1980	Whippet Cs, Bournemouth, 2000
394	SHP696R	Bedford YMT	Plaxton Supreme	C53F	1977	Whippet Cs, Bournemouth, 2000
395	H570DOW	Leyland DAF 400	Phoenix	BC16F	1991	Whippet Cs, Bournemouth, 2000
398	R531CPW	LDV Convoy	LDV	M16	1998	
399	R37DPW	LDV Convoy	LDV	M16	1998	

401-406

	Dennis Lance 11SDA3107		East Lancashire	B48F	1993

401	L401BFX	403	L403BFX	404	L404BFX	405	L405BFX	406	L406BFX
402	L402BFX								

In 1993 Yellow Buses, the trading name of Bournemouth Transport, purchased a batch of Dennis Lance buses with East Lancashire bodywork. One of the batch, 403, L403BFX, is shown here.
Robert Edworthy

411-418

		Volvo B7TL		East Lancashire Vyking		N45/31F	2001		
411	Y411CFX	413	Y413CFX	415	Y415CFX	417	Y417CFX	418	Y418CFX
412	Y412CFX	414	Y414CFX	416	Y416CFX				

451-462

		Dennis Dart 9.8SDL3054		East Lancashire		B40F	1995		
451	M451LLJ	454	M454LLJ	457	M457LLJ	459	M459LLJ	461	M461LLJ
452	M452LLJ	455	M455LLJ	458	M458LLJ	460	M460LLJ	462	M462LLJ
453	M453LLJ	456	M456LLJ						

463-472

		Dennis Dart 9.8SDL3054		East Lancashire		B40F	1996		
463	N463TPR	465	N465TPR	467	N467TPR	469	N469TPR	471	N471TPR
464	N464TPR	466	N466TPR	468	N468TPR	470	N470TPR	472	N472TPR

473	P473BLJ	Dennis Dart SLF	East Lancashire Spryte	N32F	1997
474	P474BLJ	Dennis Dart SLF	East Lancashire Spryte	N32F	1997

475-482

		Dennis Dart SLF		East Lancashire Spryte		N37F	1998		
475	R475NPR	477	R477NPR	479	R479NPR	481	R481NPR	482	R482NPR
476	R476NPR	478	R478NPR	480	R480NPR				

Vintage Yellow Buses

112	DLJ112L	Daimler Fleetline CRL6	Alexander AL	B43/31F	1973	
143	AJT143T	Leyland Fleetline FE30ALR	Alexander AL	B43/31F	1978	
245	ADV299A	Leyland Atlantean PDR1/1	Metro-Cammell	CO44/31F	1961	Leisurelink, Newhaven, 1996
248	928GTA	Leyland Atlantean PDR1/1	Metro-Cammell	CO44/31F	1961	Leisurelink, Newhaven, 1996

Ancilliary vehicle

107	MUD27W	Leyland Leopard PSU3F/4R	Willowbrook Warrier	TV	1981	Brighton & Hove, 1999

Previous Registrations:

ADV299A	925GTA	RAZ5278	E935KBK
H570DOW	H570DOW, RAZ5278	RAZ5279	F855RJX, 509DBL, F203DRN
JNJ718V	OMA506V, TCS157, CSU992	RIB8745	J235XKY
JYJ269N	HWY718N, CSU934, CSU978	RUF970M	OKG158M, XSU682
OUF863W	PWY278W, XSU612	SIB6442	NFP113W
PIB5145	UTD204T		

Livery: Yellow and blue; yellow and maroon (Vintage Yellow Buses); white (National Express) 331-4/6-40/52-70; white (Eurolines) 321-3.

East Lancashire has provided buses for Bournemouth for many years and the bodybuilder was again chosen to supply a recent batch of eight low-floor Volvo B7 double-decks. Showing the Vyking body style is 416, Y416CFX, pictured in Christchurch while heading for Somerford.
David Heath

Vehicle index

Reg	Operator	Reg	Operator	Reg	Operator	Reg	Operator	Reg	Operator
8RDV	Dawlish Cs	6220WY	Beeline	A685KDV	First Southern Nat	AFJ698T	First Western Nat	B195BAF	First Western Nat
86JBF	Castleways	6230HP	Hookways	A691OHJ	First Southern Nat	AFJ699T	First Western Nat	B196BAF	First Western Nat
116XYD	Dukes Travel	6986RU	Taw & Torridge	A693TPO	Bluebird Cs	AFJ700T	First Western Nat	B197BAF	First Western Nat
120JRB	Quantock	7105HP	Hookways	A695OHJ	First Southern Nat	AFJ701T	First Western Nat	B201REL	Wilts & Dorset
200APB	Quantock	7346HP	Hookways	A696YOX	First Southern Nat	AFJ702T	First Western Nat	B202REL	Wilts & Dorset
222FCH	Curran	7646RU	Taw & Torridge	A703THV	Swanbrook	AFJ703T	First Western Nat	B203REL	Wilts & Dorset
223TUO	Hookways	7740KO	Bakers Dolphin	A740THV	Bath Bus Company	AFJ704T	First Western Nat	B204REL	Wilts & Dorset
228FHT	DAC Coaches	8212RU	Keith Webber	A749UYL	F T Williams	AFJ705T	First Western Nat	B205REL	Wilts & Dorset
237AJB	Roselyn Coaches	8683LJ	First Southern Nat	A750VAF	First Western Nat	AFJ706T	First Western Nat	B206REL	Wilts & Dorset
239AJB	Roselyn Coaches	9743HP	Hookways	A751VAF	First Western Nat	AFJ726T	First Southern Nat	B207REL	Wilts & Dorset
241AJB	Roselyn Coaches	9743HP	Hookways	A752VAF	First Western Nat	AFJ727T	First Southern Nat	B208REL	Wilts & Dorset
244AJB	Roselyn Coaches	9880HP	Hookways	A753VAF	First Western Nat	AFJ739T	First Western Nat	B209REL	Wilts & Dorset
280OHT	Buglers	9996WX	F T Williams	A754VAF	First Western Nat	AFJ740T	Taw & Torridge	B210REL	Wilts & Dorset
290WE	Trathens	A1XEL	Excelsior	A755VAF	First Western Nat	AFJ742T	Taw & Torridge	B269TLJ	F T Williams
312KTT	Tally Ho!	A2EXC	Excelsior	A756VAF	First Badgerline	AFJ744T	First Western Nat	B278KPF	Wilts & Dorset
315MWL	Bakers Dolphin	A2XEL	Excelsior	A757VAF	First Badgerline	AFJ745T	First Western Nat	B289KPF	Coombs
317LDV	Bluebird Cs	A3EXC	Excelsior	A766UYL	F T Williams	AFJ746T	First Western Nat	B400RHN	Taw & Torridge
340MYA	Bakers Dolphin	A3XEL	Excelsior	A799REO	Wakes	AFJ747T	First Western Nat	B424NJF	Wessex Bus
381VHX	Wilts & Dorset	A4EXC	Excelsior	A809THW	First Badgerline	AFJ749T	First Western Nat	B477UNB	Wilts & Dorset
409FRH	Hookways	A4XEL	Excelsior	A810THW	First Badgerline	AFJ750T	First Western Nat	B591FOG	First Southern Nat
426VNU	Buglers	A5XEL	Excelsior	A811THW	First Badgerline	AFJ751T	First Western Nat	B630DDW	Tally Ho!
481FPO	First Western Nat	A6ECS	Ebley	A812THW	First Badgerline	AFJ753T	Truronian	B658XYB	Wakes
4846HP	Hookways	A6EXC	Excelsior	A813THW	First Badgerline	AFJ760T	First Western Nat	B710EOF	F T Williams
501BTA	Quantock	A6XEL	Excelsior	A814THW	First Badgerline	AFJ761T	First Western Nat	B823YTC	A Bus
503BTA	Quantock	A7EXC	Excelsior	A831PPP	Wakes	AFJ762T	First Western Nat	B883YTC	South Gloucestershire
508AHU	Hopley's	A7XCL	Excelsior	A838SUL	Stagecoach West	AFJ764T	First Southern Nat	B895YYD	First Southern Nat
509HUO	Taw & Torridge	A7XEL	Excelsior	A845SUL	Stagecoach West	AFJ766T	First Western Nat	B909SPR	Wilts & Dorset
511HCV	F T Williams	A8XCL	Excelsior	A854SUL	Stagecoach West	AFJ767T	First Western Nat	B910SPR	Berry's
513SRL	Curran	A8XEL	Excelsior	A900SUL	Swanbrook	AFJ768T	First Western Nat	BAZ7386	Boomerang Bus Co
539WCV	Hambleys	A9ECS	Ebley	A901JPR	Wilts & Dorset	AFJ770T	First Southern Nat	BBZ6818	Bath Bus Company
569EFJ	Quantock	A9XCL	Excelsior	A902JPR	Wilts & Dorset	AFJ771T	Truronian	BBZ8027	Bath Bus Company
586PHU	Buglers	A9XEL	Excelsior	A903JPR	Wilts & Dorset	AFJ773T	First Southern Nat	BBZ8051	Bath Bus Company
595JPU	First Southern Nat	A10EXC	Excelsior	A904JPR	Wilts & Dorset	AFM3W	First Western Nat	BCL213T	Bath Bus Company
620HOD	First Southern Nat	A11HOU	Eastville	A905JPR	Wilts & Dorset	AHU516V	First Western Nat	BCV91T	Roselyn Coaches
620UKM	Somerbus	A13XEL	Excelsior	A926SUL	Swanbrook	AHW198V	A Bus	BEO731V	Polerro Tram Co
640UAF	Hopley's	A14EXC	Excelsior	A931SUL	Bath Bus Company	AHW199V	Citytours	BEP966V	First Western Nat
645UCV	Hambleys	A16EXC	Excelsior	A940SUL	Bath Bus Company	AIW257	Tally Ho!	BEP968V	First Western Nat
654JHU	Bluebird Cs	A17EFA	Applegates	A943SYE	South Gloucestershire	AJA132	Quantock	BFR958Y	Applegates
6740HP	Hookways	A17EXC	Excelsior	A945SAE	First Cityline	AJD19T	Tally Ho!	BFX570T	Turners
674SHY	Western Greyhound	A18EFA	Applegates	A946SAE	First Cityline	AJH854T	Berry's	BFX572T	Wilts & Dorset
676GBD	Dukes Travel	A18EXC	Excelsior	A947SAE	First Cityline	AJH855T	First Western Nat	BFX575T	Wilts & Dorset
676GDV	Taw & Torridge	A19EFA	Applegates	A947SUL	Bath Bus Company	AJT143T	Yellow Buses	BFX664T	Wilts & Dorset
701GOO	Wilts & Dorset	A19EXC	Excelsior	A948SAE	First Cityline	ALZ3248	Tally Ho!	BFX665T	Wilts & Dorset
704BYL	Somerbus	A19XEL	Excelsior	A949SAE	First Cityline	ANA5T	Quantock	BFX666T	Wilts & Dorset
710VCV	Hambleys	A20EFA	Applegates	A950SAE	First Cityline	ANA21T	Thamesdown	BJF889T	Hambleys
728FDV	Roselyn Coaches	A20EXC	Excelsior	A951SAE	First Southern Nat	ANA24T	Thamesdown	BJV104L	Roselyn Coaches
739JUA	F T Williams	A20JAB	James Bevan	A952SAE	First Cityline	ANA32T	Thamesdown	BKE851T	Truronian
751CRT	Caradon	A20XEL	Excelsior	A953SAE	First Cityline	ANA41T	Thamesdown	BKE857T	Truronian
775HOD	Taw & Torridge	A59WMM	Thamesdown	A954SAE	First Cityline	ANA565Y	Citytours	BKH981T	Roselyn Coaches
783DYE	Bath Bus Company	A60AFS	Hookways	A955THW	First Cityline	ANZ3607	Beeline	BKH983T	Roselyn Coaches
789FAY	Hookways	A61WMW	Thamesdown	A956THW	First Cityline	ANZ4373	Wakes	BMR201V	Thamesdown
791WHT	Bakers Dolphin	A63WMW	Thamesdown	A957THW	First Cityline	ANZ4374	Wakes	BMR202V	Thamesdown
800XPC	Peter Carol	A67THX	Stagecoach Devon	A958SYF	Swanbrook	APT834S	Quantock	BMR203V	Thamesdown
824KDV	First Western Nat	A104OUG	Grey Cars	A959THW	First Cityline	ASV900	Safeway	BMR204V	Thamesdown
832JYA	Beeline	A105EBC	First Cityline	A960THW	First Cityline	ATK156W	Roselyn Coaches	BMR205V	Thamesdown
838AFM	Quantock	A109EPA	Wakes	A961THW	First Cityline	ATK157W	Roselyn Coaches	BNZ4922	Beeline
865GAT	First Badgerline	A111EPA	Pullham's	A962THW	First Cityline	ATK160W	Plymouth Citybus	BPF131Y	Eastville
890ADV	Quantock	A130EPA	Wakes	A963THW	First Cityline	ATK161W	Plymouth Citybus	BTF24	Quantock
890CVJ	Geoff Willetts	A144DPE	Wilts & Dorset	A964THW	First Badgerline	ATL555L	First Southern Nat	BUI4646	Ebley
894GUO	First Western Nat	A158EPA	Coombs	A965THW	First Southern Nat	ATL559L	First Southern Nat	BUR438T	Quantock
924CRT	Caradon	A160FPG	Wilts & Dorset	A966THW	First Badgerline	AUF172K	Quantock	BVA787V	Caradon
928GTA	Yellow Buses	A168PAE	Dawlish Cs	A967THW	First Cityline	AYA912S	Berry's	BVR59T	Thamesdown
958VKM	Bakers Dolphin	A169PAE	Dawlish Cs	A968THW	First Badgerline	B6GBD	Dukes Travel	BVR83T	Thamesdown
969EHW	A Bus	A173VFM	Wilts & Dorset	A968THW	First Cityline	B7BEN	Bennetts	BVR89T	Thamesdown
971CYB	Curran	A174VFM	Wilts & Dorset	A976SYE	Stagecoach Devon	B21AUS	Ebley	BVR98T	Thamesdown
972EHW	A Bus	A175VFM	Wilts & Dorset	A983NYC	Safeway	B41AAF	First Western Nat	BYD795X	Wakes
990XYA	Hookways	A191MNE	Bluebird Cs	A989XAF	Wilts & Dorset	B65GHR	Thamesdown	BYX186V	Swanbrook
1434HP	Hookways	A206SAE	First Western Nat	A990XAF	Wilts & Dorset	B66GHR	Thamesdown	**C23CHM**	Truronian
2464FH	Geoff Willetts	A256VYC	Wakes	AAE658V	Stagecoach Devon	B67GHR	Thamesdown	C28EHU	South Gloucestershire
2603HP	Hookways	A513VKG	Swiftlink	AAE665V	Stagecoach Devon	B68GHR	Thamesdown	C29EHU	South Gloucestershire
3315HP	Hookways	A523YSD	Ebley	AAL520A	Boomerang Bus Co	B87WUV	Axe Valley	C30EUH	Eastville
3427HP	Hookways	A531MVU	Duchy Travel	AAL587A	Shaftesbury & Dist	B108WUV	Stagecoach West	**C74CHM**	Truronian
3655NE	Quantock	A561OTA	Tally Ho!	AAP648T	Curran	B112WUV	Stagecoach West	**C83CHM**	Truronian
3692HP	Hookways	A590AHB	First Southern Nat	AAP668T	Truronian	B118WUV	Stagecoach West	C86AHW	Wilts & Dorset
4529WF	Boomerang Bus Co	A600XGL	Curran	ACH441	Quantock	B120UUD	Swanbrook	**C87CHM**	Truronian
4691HP	Hookways	A622YOX	First Southern Nat	ADV299A	Yellow Buses	B121UUD	Swanbrook	C99HGL	First Western Nat
5110HU	Stagecoach West	A624YOX	First Southern Nat	AEF315A	Hookways	B155AYD	Wakes	C104TFP	Taw & Torridge
530OHU	First Western Nat	A632THV	Stagecoach Devon	AFE719A	Quantock	B157WRN	Hookways	C105AFX	F T Williams
5351HP	Hookways	A648THV	Stagecoach West	AFH186T	Ebley	B175VDV	Plymouth Citybus	C105HGL	First Western Nat
5904WF	Boomerang Bus Co	A649YOX	First Southern Nat	AFH390T	Roselyn Coaches	B176VDV	Plymouth Citybus	C108HGL	First Western Nat
6185RU	Hookways	A665KUM	First Western Nat	AFJ697T	First Western Nat	B194BAF	First Western Nat	C113JCS	Andy James

Reg	Operator	Reg	Operator	Reg	Operator	Reg	Operator	Reg	Operator
C142SPB	Swanbrook	D60NOF	Coombs	D910HOU	Alexcars	E453WJK	Ebley	F77MFJ	Dawlish Cs
C158TLF	First Badgerline	D65RMW	Wakes	D914HOU	Alexcars	E460CGM	Swiftlink	F92XBV	Caradon
C159TLF	First Badgerline	D75YRF	Belle Vue	D929PYB	Wakes	E461CGM	Bath Bus Company	F93XBV	Caradon
C165VRE	Alexcars	D78JHY	Turners	D930LYC	DAC Coaches	E471CGM	Bath Bus Company	F94XBV	Caradon
C201YPR	Yellow Buses	D86VDV	Seawards	DAD256T	Caradon	E477CGM	Bath Bus Company	F95XBV	Caradon
C204HJN	Keith Webber	D98CFA	Alexcars	DCK219	Quantock	E478AFJ	Cottrell's	F101GRM	First Western Nat
C208FFJ	Belle Vue	D100GHY	First Badgerline	DCZ2307	Tally Ho!	E486ONX	Alexcars	F125TRU	Fosseway
C248OFE	Hookways	D101GHY	First Badgerline	DCZ2316	Thamesdown	E506CTT	Grey Cars	F126TRU	Western Greyhound
C256CFG	First Cityline	D102CFA	Alexcars	DCZ2317	Thamesdown	E518KNV	Taw & Torridge	F128TRU	Fosseway
C307VMX	Filer's	D102GHY	First Badgerline	DCZ2318	Thamesdown	E565YYA	Safeway	F132KAO	Fosseway
C308FYA	Berry's	D103GHY	First Badgerline	DCZ2319	Thamesdown	E631LSF	Swiftlink	F132OYO	Swiftlink
C355ALJ	Beard	D104GHY	First Badgerline	DDR201C	Plymouth Citybus	E654DGW	Wessex Bus	F134JHO	Wakes
C377RUY	First Western Nat	D105GHY	First Badgerline	DEG952V	Wilts & Dorset	E660XND	Swiftlink	F141KDV	Filer's
C405VVN	Keith Webber	D106GHY	First Badgerline	DLJ112L	Yellow Buses	E664JAD	Wilts & Dorset	F154RHK	First Southern Nat
C432VGX	Bakers Dolphin	D107GHY	First Badgerline	DMJ374T	Taw & Torridge	E668JAD	Wilts & Dorset	F157AWO	Keith Webber
C468BHY	First Badgerline	D108GHY	First Badgerline	DMS22V	First Southern Nat	E670JDG	Wilts & Dorset	F157DBO	Bluebird Cs
C473BHY	First Cityline	D109GHY	First Badgerline	DOC44V	First Southern Nat	E672XSW	Hookways	F167UDG	Beard
C500BFB	Alexcars	D110GHY	First Badgerline	DSD950V	Caradon	E691NOU	Turners	F183UFH	Cottrell's
C526FFJ	DAC Coaches	D111GHY	First Badgerline	DSD953V	Caradon	E694UND	First Badgerline	F202HSO	Safeway
C546BHY	Taw & Torridge	D112GHY	First Badgerline	DSU107	Western Greyhound	E714LYU	Keith Webber	F205EWN	Wilts & Dorset
C550BHY	Taw & Torridge	D112NDW	Wilts & Dorset	DVK489W	Axe Valley	E716CPC	Hookways	F206EWN	Wilts & Dorset
C561BHY	Alexcars	D113GHY	First Badgerline	E28MCE	Wessex Bus	E752YDY	First Badgerline	F210WRU	Yellow Buses
C610LFT	Stagecoach West	D122EFH	Swanbrook	E39SBO	Tally Ho!	E758XYB	Wakes	F211WRU	Yellow Buses
C624LFT	Stagecoach West	D123EFH	Swanbrook	E40SBO	Tally Ho!	E768HJF	Bluebird Cs	F212LOD	Belle Vue
C631BEX	Belle Vue	D128HML	Filer's	E45UKL	Fosseway	E782RAF	DAC Coaches	F212WRU	Yellow Buses
C641LFT	Stagecoach West	D131PTT	Fosseway	E50UKL	Fosseway	E787NOU	Turners	F213WRU	Yellow Buses
C647LFT	Stagecoach West	D134LTA	Axe Valley	E51MMT	Wilts & Dorset	E801MOU	First Badgerline	F214WRU	Yellow Buses
C650LFT	Stagecoach West	D137LTA	Taw & Torridge	E64WDT	Wilts & Dorset	E802MOU	First Badgerline	F246OFP	F T Williams
C659LFT	Stagecoach West	D144LTA	Axe Valley	E65WDT	Wilts & Dorset	E804MOU	First Cityline	F258CEY	Swanbrook
C671FFJ	Alexcars	D160UDA	Cottrell's	E124RAX	Wessex Bus	E805MOU	First Cityline	F276WAF	Dawlish Cs
C672FFJ	Alexcars	D165HML	Wilts & Dorset	E167URJ	Wessex Bus	E806MOU	First Cityline	F278LND	Swiftlink
C676ECV	First Western Nat	D184LTA	Tally Ho!	E181BTT	Dawlish Cs	E806WDV	Fosseway	F293AWW	Dukes Travel
C680KDS	Bluebird Cs	D200ELJ	Yellow Buses	E200BOD	First Western Nat	E808MOU	First Western Nat	F305AWN	First Western Nat
C681EHU	South Gloucestershire	D202ELJ	Yellow Buses	E201BOD	First Western Nat	E809MOU	First Badgerline	F309RMH	Cottrell's
C681KDS	Filer's	D202JHY	Turners	E201WMB	Tally Ho!	E810MOU	First Badgerline	F310UBL	James Bevan
C694FFJ	Alexcars	D202KWT	Wessex Bus	E202BDV	First Cityline	E811MOU	First Badgerline	F313PRF	Fosseway
C695FFJ	Alexcars	D203ELJ	Yellow Buses	E202BOD	First Western Nat	E812MOU	First Western Nat	F314VCV	Truronian
C705FFJ	Alexcars	D204ELJ	Yellow Buses	E202HRY	Alexcars	E813MOU	First Badgerline	F315VCV	Truronian
C744JYA	Safeway	D210OKY	Fosseway	E203BOD	First Western Nat	E814MOU	First Badgerline	F318AWN	First Western Nat
C745FFJ	Alexcars	D241OOJ	Caradon	E203HRY	Alexcars	E814XHS	First Southern Nat	F318EWF	Bennetts
C746FFJ	Alexcars	D260HFX	Berry's	E204BDV	First Cityline	E816MOU	First Cityline	F328FCY	Fosseway
C752FFJ	Alexcars	D283XCX	A Bus	E204BOD	First Western Nat	E817MOU	First Cityline	F329GYA	Wakes
C759FFJ	Alexcars	D309PEJ	Caradon	E204EPB	Wessex Bus	E819MOU	First Badgerline	F378UCP	Fosseway
C787FRL	First Western Nat	D327TRN	Coombs	E204YGC	Andy James	E845YYA	Wakes	F387FYC	Wakes
C796FRL	First Western Nat	D401TMW	Coombs	E205BOD	First Western Nat	E872PGL	Truronian	F404CKU	Filer's
C801FRL	First Western Nat	D413TFT	Fosseway	E205GCG	Yellow Buses	E920EAY	F T Williams	F407KOD	Keith Webber
C812BYY	**Truronian**	D463CKV	Wessex Bus	E206GCG	Yellow Buses	E920HAR	Duchy Travel	F425JFT	Swiftlink
C819BYY	**Truronian**	D500GHY	First Badgerline	E207GCG	Yellow Buses	E934RWR	Hookways	F432OBK	Buglers
C822EHU	South Gloucestershire	D501GHY	First Badgerline	E208GCG	Yellow Buses	E944LAE	First Badgerline	F441DUG	Wilts & Dorset
C833CVX	Alexcars	D503GHY	First Badgerline	E209GCG	Yellow Buses	E954YGA	Swiftlink	F444ENB	Duchy Travel
C849CSN	Caradon	D510WNV	Hookways	E210BDV	Fosseway	EAP985V	Truronian	F449XFX	Wakes
C877CYX	Wilts & Dorset	D513FAE	Keith Webber	E210XWG	Tally Ho!	EEH902Y	Bennetts	F450XFX	Wakes
C911DVF	Belle Vue	D513HUB	First Western Nat	E211JDD	A Bus	EGV695Y	Wakes	F455TOY	First Western Nat
C942DHT	Hookways	D514HUB	First Western Nat	E215BTA	First Western Nat	EKU75V	First Badgerline	F465WFX	Loverings
C959GAF	First Western Nat	D574SUS	DAC Coaches	E216BTA	First Western Nat	ELJ214V	Wilts & Dorset	F476EOD	DAC Coaches
CCZ3164	Alexcars	D575PKW	Wilts & Dorset	E217BTA	First Badgerline	ELJ215V	Wilts & Dorset	F476WFX	Berry's
CCZ3165	Alexcars	D580JNA	Swiftlink	E222BDV	Duchy Travel	ELJ216V	Wilts & Dorset	F484MTA	Dartline
CCZ8927	Alexcars	D586EWS	Belle Vue	E239LRV	Wilts & Dorset	ELJ217V	Wilts & Dorset	F487WPR	Carmel Coaches
CEL919T	Bluebird Cs	D621SJX	Roselyn Coaches	E272XYA	Berry's	ELJ218V	Wilts & Dorset	F512LTT	Dawlish Cs
CFN121	Quantock	D647NOD	Fosseway	E278RNW	Taw & Torridge	ELJ219V	Wilts & Dorset	F538LUF	South Gloucestershire
CHG545	Quantock	D649NYC	Wakes	E283UCY	First Western Nat	ELJ220V	Wilts & Dorset	F544LUF	South Gloucestershire
CHL772	Quantock	D656NOD	Fosseway	E284UCY	First Western Nat	ENF573Y	DAC Coaches	F545LUF	South Gloucestershire
CJY299	Plymouth Citybus	D659WEY	First Southern Nat	E285UCY	First Western Nat	ENH634	South Gloucestershire	F546LUF	South Gloucestershire
CLJ413Y	Caradon	D700GHY	First Badgerline	E286UCY	First Western Nat	ERB548T	Bakers Dolphin	F554MBC	Hookways
CNH176X	Tally Ho!	D701GHY	First Badgerline	E288VEP	First Western Nat	ERU392V	Yellow Buses	F555FYD	Wakes
CNH177X	Tally Ho!	D702GHY	First Badgerline	E296OMG	Dawlish Cs	ESC847S	Duchy Travel	F564HPP	Dawlish Cs
CRO671K	Marchants	D703GHY	First Badgerline	E297OMG	Wilts & Dorset	ESK812	South Gloucestershire	F578SHT	Wakes
CRU154V	Yellow Buses	D704GHY	First Badgerline	E298OMG	Wilts & Dorset	ETL545T	Wakes	F590OHT	Alexcars
CRU160V	Yellow Buses	D705GHY	First Badgerline	E300BWL	Swanbrook	EWE759V	Keith Webber	F600GVO	Plymouth Citybus
CRW520T	Wilts & Dorset	D706GHY	First Badgerline	E301BWL	Western Greyhound	EWR77Y	First Cityline	F600RTC	First Cityline
CSU926	Dartline	D707GHY	First Badgerline	E303BWL	Swanbrook	EWS739W	A Bus	F601GVO	Plymouth Citybus
CSU978	Stagecoach Devon	D708GHY	First Badgerline	E313OMG	Wilts & Dorset	EWS741W	A Bus	F602GVO	Plymouth Citybus
CUB24Y	First Cityline	D709GHY	First Badgerline	E318UUB	Beard	EWS742W	A Bus	F602RPG	Thamesdown
CUB25Y	First Cityline	D710GHY	First Badgerline	E322PMD	Marchants	EWS747W	First Western Nat	F603GVO	Plymouth Citybus
CUB28Y	First Cityline	D711GHY	First Badgerline	E322UUB	Geoff Willetts	EWV665	First Western Nat	F603RPG	Thamesdown
CUB31Y	First Cityline	D726VAM	Andy James	E323PMD	Marchants	EWW212T	Dawlish Cs	F604GVO	Plymouth Citybus
CUB40Y	First Cityline	D749LYD	Wakes	E323UUB	James Bevan	EWY80Y	Wilts & Dorset	F604RPG	Thamesdown
CUB45Y	First Cityline	D759PTU	Alexcars	E324PMD	Marchants	EYE229V	Stagecoach Devon	F604RTC	First Western Nat
CUB67Y	Wilts & Dorset	D759UTA	Seawards	E325CTT	Seawards	F32HGG	Filer's	F605GVO	Plymouth Citybus
CUB70Y	Wilts & Dorset	D796NDV	Fosseway	E325PMD	Marchants	F40KRO	Wilts & Dorset	F605RPG	Thamesdown
CYA181J	Quantock	D603NBO	Cotirell's	E334NRL	Polerro Tram Co	F50ACL	Plymouth Citybus	F605RTC	First Western Nat
CYD722C	Quantock	D640JHW	South Gloucestershire	E352GAA	Wilts & Dorset	F51ACL	Plymouth Citybus	F606GVO	Plymouth Citybus
D21CTR	Coombs	D879FYL	Wilts & Dorset	E358KPO	Axe Valley	F66SMC	Cottrell's	F606RPG	Thamesdown
D22CTR	Coombs	D880FYL	Wilts & Dorset	E402TVC	Caradon	F71FKK	Duchy Travel	F606RTC	Plymouth Citybus
D23CTR	Coombs	D891DWP	Stagecoach West	E416YYB	Wakes	F71LAL	Swanbrook	F607GVO	Plymouth Citybus
D33FYH	Ebley	D895VAO	Keith Webber	E446AFT	Western Greyhound	F72EKK	Duchy Travel	F607JSS	Bennetts

F607RTC	First Western Nat	FDV802V	First Western Nat	G543XWS	South Gloucestershire	GTX751W	Eastville	H648UWR	Loverings
F608RPG	Thamesdown	FDV806V	First Western Nat	G604YUT	Hookways	GWN432	Quantock	H648YHT	First Cityline
F608RTC	First Western Nat	FDV807V	First Western Nat	G609THR	Wilts & Dorset	GYE261W	South Gloucestershire	H649YHT	First Cityline
F609RTC	First Badgerline	FDV808V	First Western Nat	G612OTV	Plymouth Citybus	GYE277W	Applegates	H650YHT	First Cityline
F610RTC	First Badgerline	FDV814V	First Western Nat	G614OTV	Plymouth Citybus	H4GBD	Dukes Travel	H651UWR	Cottrell's
F611RTC	First Badgerline	FDV815V	First Western Nat	G615OTV	Plymouth Citybus	H5GBD	Dukes Travel	H651YHT	First Cityline
F612RTC	First Badgerline	FDV837V	First Southern Nat	G621OTV	Plymouth Citybus	H7GBD	Dukes Travel	H652DOD	Duchy Travel
F613RTC	First Badgerline	FDZ980	First Western Nat	G623OTV	Plymouth Citybus	H9GBD	Dukes Travel	H652YHT	First Cityline
F614RTC	First Cityline	FFR165S	South Gloucestershire	G629XWS	Swiftlink	H24GRE	Ebley	H653YHT	First Cityline
F615RTC	First Cityline	FHE806L	Truronian	G640CHF	Plymouth Citybus	H34HBG	South Gloucestershire	H654YHT	First Cityline
F616RTC	First Cityline	FIB2118	Taw & Torridge	G643CHF	Plymouth Citybus	H82PTG	Swiftlink	H655YHT	First Cityline
F616XMS	Keith Webber	FIL7303	Taw & Torridge	G680YLP	Pullham's	H132CDB	Alexcars	H656YHT	First Cityline
F617RTC	First Cityline	FKM876V	Truronian	G693NUB	Coombs	H141UUA	Dukes Travel	H657YHT	First Cityline
F618RTC	First Cityline	FMO949	Quantock	G699NUB	Coombs	H156UUA	Dukes Travel	H658YHT	First Cityline
F619RTC	First Cityline	FNJ905	First Western Nat	G747SAV	Swiftlink	H158UUA	Dukes Travel	H659YHT	First Cityline
F621RTC	First Cityline	FNM862Y	Wakes	G764BGL	F T Williams	H165DJU	F T Williams	H660UWR	Hookways
F621RTC	First Cityline	FNR923	First Western Nat	G783XWS	Swiftlink	H170SAB	Wakes	H660YHT	First Cityline
F622RTC	First Cityline	FSU803	Dukes Travel	G800PTT	Dartline	H175UUA	Dukes Travel	H661YHT	First Cityline
F623RTC	First Cityline	FTO550V	Caradon	G802XLO	First Southern Nat	H176DVM	Duchy Travel	H662YHT	First Cityline
F624RTC	First Cityline	FTO552V	Bakers Dolphin	G803XLO	First Southern Nat	H177GTT	Plymouth Citybus	H683BTA	First Southern Nat
F625RTC	First Cityline	FXU355	Trathens	G806YTA	Stagecoach Devon	H178GTT	Plymouth Citybus	H683NEF	Swanbrook
F626RTC	First Southern Nat	G28TGW	Stagecoach Devon	G817YPU	Swiftlink	H180JRE	First Western Nat	H684BTA	First Southern Nat
F627RTC	First Southern Nat	G30TGW	Stagecoach Devon	G818YTA	Stagecoach Devon	H185CNS	Fosseway	H6GBD	Dukes Travel
F628RTC	First Southern Nat	G32TGW	Stagecoach Devon	G823MNH	F T Williams	H204EKO	Fosseway	H718HGL	First Western Nat
F629RTC	First Southern Nat	G33TGW	Stagecoach Devon	G826XWS	Turners	H251JJT	Yellow Buses	H721HGL	First Western Nat
F630RTC	First Badgerline	G33UWL	F T Williams	G828XWS	Swiftlink	H252JJT	Yellow Buses	H722HGL	First Western Nat
F631RTC	First Badgerline	G34TGW	Stagecoach Devon	G829XWS	Turners	H253JJT	Yellow Buses	H723HGL	First Western Nat
F632RTC	First Cityline	G35TGW	Stagecoach Devon	G837UDV	Duchy Travel	H254JJT	Yellow Buses	H726HGL	First Western Nat
F641XMS	Keith Webber	G36TGW	Stagecoach Devon	G840UDV	South Gloucestershire	H255JJT	Yellow Buses	H794FAF	F T Williams
F643XMS	First Western Nat	G37TGW	Stagecoach Devon	G847LNP	Stagecoach Devon	H256JJT	Yellow Buses	H801GDV	First Western Nat
F645XMS	First Western Nat	G44TGW	Boomerang Bus Co	G883OYC	Wakes	H257JJT	Yellow Buses	H802GDV	First Southern Nat
F657XMS	First Western Nat	G50ONN	Marchants	G900TJA	South Gloucestershire	H258MFX	Yellow Buses	H821AHS	Loverings
F659VDF	F T Williams	G51ONN	Marchants	G901TWS	First Southern Nat	H259MFX	Yellow Buses	H822AHS	Loverings
F660RTL	Marchants	G58RGG	Fosseway	G902TWS	First Southern Nat	H261MFX	Yellow Buses	H823GAF	F T Williams
F666XMS	First Western Nat	G66JVV	Andy James	G903TWS	First Southern Nat	H262MFX	Yellow Buses	H882LOX	Fosseway
F667XMS	First Western Nat	G82BHP	Castleways	G904TWS	First Southern Nat	H263MFX	Yellow Buses	H891JVR	Hookways
F668XMS	First Western Nat	G92RGG	Seawards	G905TWS	First Badgerline	H264MFX	Yellow Buses	H891LOX	First Western Nat
F669XMS	First Western Nat	G94RGG	Wilts & Dorset	G906TWS	First Badgerline	H265MFX	Yellow Buses	H893LOX	First Western Nat
F677XMS	First Western Nat	G100VNM	Boomerang Bus Co	G907TWS	First Badgerline	H324HVT	First Western Nat	H894LOX	First Western Nat
F680CYC	Carmel Coaches	G101AAD	Stagecoach West	G908TWS	First Badgerline	H338FLH	Swiftlink	H895LOX	First Western Nat
F680XMS	First Western Nat	G102AAD	Stagecoach West	G909TWS	First Badgerline	H345LJN	First Western Nat	H896LOX	First Western Nat
F682XMS	First Western Nat	G103AAD	Stagecoach West	G910TWS	First Badgerline	H346LJN	First Western Nat	H898LOX	Keith Webber
F683XMS	First Western Nat	G103TND	Swanbrook	G955EUH	Bluebird Cs	H351HRF	First Western Nat	H906WYB	First Southern Nat
F684XMS	First Western Nat	G104AAD	Stagecoach West	G958VBC	Dartline	H353HRF	First Western Nat	H907WYB	First Southern Nat
F693GYD	Wakes	G105AAD	Stagecoach West	G992VWV	South Gloucestershire	H362BDV	Hambleys	H908WYB	First Southern Nat
F706XMS	First Western Nat	G105APC	Hookways	G993DDF	Marchants	H370DOW	Yellow Buses	H909WYB	First Southern Nat
F714EUG	Hookways	G105DPB	Tally Ho!	G993VWV	South Gloucestershire	H380XHG	Citytours	H910WYB	First Southern Nat
F715RDG	Beard	G113PGT	Duchy Travel	G997OKK	Safeway	H397JJH	Trathens	H912JVR	Hookways
F716FDV	Keith Webber	G127TJA	Alexcars	G998OKK	Dartline	H403MRW	Stagecoach West	H912WYB	First Southern Nat
F730FDV	Keith Webber	G134CLF	Swanbrook	GAF69V	Dartline	H407PRW	Stagecoach West	H913FTT	Shaftesbury & Dist
F734USF	Wakes	G151GOL	First Western Nat	GAF167V	Hambleys	H422GPM	South Gloucestershire	H913WYB	First Western Nat
F737HFJ	Belle Vue	G152GOL	First Western Nat	GBU2V	Cottrell's	H437BVU	DAC Coaches	H914WYB	First Southern Nat
F738FDV	Keith Webber	G153GOL	First Western Nat	GBU6V	Cottrell's	H481JRE	First Western Nat	H915WYB	First Southern Nat
F751FDV	Alexcars	G155GOL	First Western Nat	GBU7V	Cottrell's	H484BND	Wakes	H916WYB	First Southern Nat
F751PPU	Filer's	G165NAG	DAC Coaches	GBU8V	Axe Valley	H521HWL	F T Williams	H920BPN	Dawlish Cs
F753FDV	Alexcars	G192NWY	Fosseway	GDF650L	Marchants	H523UWE	Fosseway	H920XYN	Truronian
F800RHK	First Western Nat	G193NWY	Fosseway	GDZ795	Shaftesbury & Dist	H538ETT	Wakes	H932DRJ	Cottrell's
F801CNY	Wilts & Dorset	G195NWY	Fosseway	GEL679V	Wilts & Dorset	H544FVN	South Gloucestershire	H932XYN	Truronian
F801RHK	First Western Nat	G196NWY	Fosseway	GEL680V	Wilts & Dorset	H606GLT	Swiftlink	H937DRJ	Geoff Willetts
F802RHK	First Western Nat	G197NWY	Fosseway	GEL681V	Wilts & Dorset	H610YTC	First Badgerline	H969XHR	Thamesdown
F850TCW	First Badgerline	G218SWL	Carmel Coaches	GEL682V	Wilts & Dorset	H611YTC	First Badgerline	H970XHR	Thamesdown
F871UAC	Alexcars	G221VDX	Shaftesbury & Dist	GEL683V	Wilts & Dorset	H612YTC	First Badgerline	H971XHR	Thamesdown
F891TOY	Andy James	G229EOA	First Badgerline	GEL685V	Wilts & Dorset	H613UWR	First Western Nat	H972XHR	Thamesdown
F905FHE	Alexcars	G230EOA	Alexcars	GEL686V	Wilts & Dorset	H613YTC	First Badgerline	H973XHR	Thamesdown
F906FHE	Alexcars	G238VYJ	Dartline	GEL687V	Wilts & Dorset	H614UWR	First Western Nat	H985FTT	Fosseway
F921YNV	Hookways	G247CLE	Bennetts	GFB146W	Wilts & Dorset	H614YTC	First Badgerline	H987FTT	Duchy Travel
F946BMS	First Western Nat	G258UFB	Swiftlink	GHT127	First Badgerline	H615UWR	First Western Nat	H989FTT	Duchy Travel
F948BMS	First Western Nat	G261LUG	First Western Nat	GHV504N	Caradon	H615YTC	First Badgerline	HAZ2963	Buglers
F949BMS	First Western Nat	G264GKG	Belle Vue	GIB5970	Safeway	H616YTC	First Badgerline	HDF661	Pullham's
F949CUA	Wessex Bus	G265GKG	Duchy Travel	GIL1683	Dawlish Cs	H621AEE	Belle Vue	HFG207T	Safeway
F951HTT	Dartline	G276WFU	Seawards	GIL1684	First Southern Nat	H633YHT	First Cityline	HFN769	First Western Nat
F952BMS	First Western Nat	G290XFH	Geoff Willetts	GIL2967	First Western Nat	H634YHT	First Cityline	HFX411V	Tally Ho!
F954BMS	First Western Nat	G293CLE	Bennetts	GIL3113	Grey Cars	H636YHT	First Cityline	HHJ372Y	First Southern Nat
F958BMS	First Western Nat	G326PEW	First Western Nat	GIL3129	Seawards	H637YHT	First Cityline	HHJ373Y	First Western Nat
F982EDS	Bath Bus Company	G337XRE	First Western Nat	GNK781T	Quantock	H638YHT	First Cityline	HHJ376Y	First Western Nat
F997KCU	Wakes	G340KWE	Applegates	GOU908	Hookways	H639YHT	First Cityline	HHJ379Y	First Western Nat
FAD708T	Castleways	G380VVL	Loverings	GRU162V	Thamesdown	H640YHT	First Cityline	HHJ381Y	First Western Nat
FAF44V	Keith Webber	G382RCW	Bennetts	GRU163V	Thamesdown	H641YHT	First Badgerline	HHJ382Y	First Western Nat
FDC417V	Safeway	G387FSF	Keith Webber	GRU164V	Thamesdown	H641YWE	Fosseway	HHU146V	Bakers Dolphin
FDF965	Pullham's	G434ETW	Fosseway	GRU165V	Thamesdown	H642GRO	Coombs	HHU31V	Bakers Dolphin
FDG468L	Quantock	G444NYC	Wakes	GRU166V	Thamesdown	H642YHT	First Badgerline	HHW920L	A Bus
FDV779V	First Southern Nat	G448CDG	Marchants	GRU167V	Yellow Buses	H643YHT	First Badgerline	HIL2146	Bluebird Cs
FDV780V	First Southern Nat	G451XJH	Ebley	GRU168V	Yellow Buses	H644YHT	First Badgerline	HIL2379	Caradon
FDV781V	First Southern Nat	G485KBD	Applegates	GSU344	Caradon	H645YHT	First Badgerline	HIL2897	Tally Ho!
FDV793V	Coombs	G515VYE	Weaverbus	GTA807N	Keith Webber	H646YHT	First Cityline	HIL3451	Citytours
FDV800V	First Western Nat	G518EFX	Wakes	GTA811N	Keith Webber	H647YHT	First Cityline	HIL3471	Buglers

K821WFJ	Stagecoach Devon
K822WFJ	Stagecoach Devon
K824WFJ	Stagecoach Devon
K835HUM	Safeway
K867NEU	First Badgerline
K868NEU	First Badgerline
K869NEU	First Badgerline
K870NEU	First Badgerline
K871NEU	First Badgerline
K872NEU	First Badgerline
K873NEU	First Badgerline
K874NEU	First Badgerline
K875NEU	First Badgerline
K876NEU	First Badgerline
K913VDV	Stagecoach Devon
K919WNR	F T Williams
K922UFX	Dawlish Cs
K922VDV	First Badgerline
K924VDV	Stagecoach Devon
K925VDV	Stagecoach Devon
K926VDV	Stagecoach Devon
K927VDV	Stagecoach Devon
K929VDV	First Southern Nat
K989TOD	Alexcars
K998WNC	
KAD355V	Grey Cars
KAU573V	Bakers Dolphin
KAZ4504	Coombs
KAZ4505	Coombs
KDU648	First Southern Nat
KEP829X	Axe Valley
KFM767	Quantock
KFM893	Quantock
KFX791	First Southern Nat
KGJ603D	Shaftesbury & Dist
KHH376W	Stagecoach Devon
KIW4489	Dartline
KIW6512	Tally Ho!
KIW8606	Duchy Travel
KJD410P	Tally Ho!
KJD413P	Tally Ho!
KJD414P	Tally Ho!
KJD419P	Tally Ho!
KJD420P	Tally Ho!
KJD422P	Tally Ho!
KJD431P	Tally Ho!
KJW301W	Swanbrook
KJW320W	Swanbrook
KKW525W	First Badgerline
KMW175P	Thamesdown
KOO785V	First Western Nat
KOO791V	A Bus
KOO792V	A Bus
KOO793V	A Bus
KPP619V	Tally Ho!
KRU848W	Wilts & Dorset
KRU849W	Wilts & Dorset
KRU850W	Wilts & Dorset
KRU851W	Wilts & Dorset
KRU853W	Wilts & Dorset
KRU854W	Wilts & Dorset
KRU855W	Wilts & Dorset
KRU856W	Wilts & Dorset
KSK984	Trathens
KTF594	Quantock
KTL25V	Marchants
KTL26V	Marchants
KUY443X	Hookways
KVF248V	Hopley's
KYA284Y	Wakes
KYV444X	Stagecoach Devon
KYV462X	Stagecoach Devon
KYV469X	Stagecoach Devon
KYV473X	Stagecoach Devon
L3RDC	Swiftlink
L8CJT	Turners
L9CJT	Turners
L23LSG	First Southern Nat
L24LSG	First Southern Nat
L26LSG	First Southern Nat
L67EPR	First Southern Nat
L68EPR	First Southern Nat
L69EPR	First Western Nat
L92LSG	First Southern Nat
L110UHF	Coombs
L112ALJ	Wilts & Dorset
L112YOD	Plymouth Citybus
L113ALJ	Wilts & Dorset
L113YOD	Plymouth Citybus
L114ALJ	Wilts & Dorset
L114YOD	Plymouth Citybus
L115ALJ	Wilts & Dorset
L115YOD	Plymouth Citybus
L116ALJ	Wilts & Dorset
L116NYB	Berry's
L116YOD	Plymouth Citybus
L117ALJ	Wilts & Dorset
L117YOD	Plymouth Citybus
L118ALJ	Wilts & Dorset
L118YOD	Plymouth Citybus
L119ALJ	Wilts & Dorset
L119YOD	Plymouth Citybus
L120ALJ	Wilts & Dorset
L120YOD	Plymouth Citybus
L121YOD	Plymouth Citybus
L122ELJ	Wilts & Dorset
L122TFB	First Badgerline
L122YOD	Plymouth Citybus
L123ELJ	Wilts & Dorset
L123TFB	First Badgerline
L123YOD	Plymouth Citybus
L124ELJ	Wilts & Dorset
L124TFB	First Badgerline
L124YOD	Plymouth Citybus
L125TFB	First Badgerline
L125YOD	Plymouth Citybus
L126ELJ	Wilts & Dorset
L126TFB	First Badgerline
L126YOD	Plymouth Citybus
L127ELJ	Wilts & Dorset
L127TFB	First Badgerline
L128ELJ	Wilts & Dorset
L128TFB	First Badgerline
L129ELJ	Wilts & Dorset
L129TFB	First Badgerline
L130ELJ	Wilts & Dorset
L130TFB	First Badgerline
L131ELJ	Wilts & Dorset
L131TFB	First Badgerline
L132TFB	First Badgerline
L133TFB	First Badgerline
L134TFB	First Badgerline
L135TFB	First Badgerline
L136TFB	First Badgerline
L139VRH	Stagecoach Devon
L140VRH	Stagecoach Devon
L141VRH	Stagecoach Devon
L155UNS	First Western Nat
L179KHG	Dukes Travel
L182PMX	Dawlish Cs
L193FDV	Stagecoach Devon
L194FDV	Stagecoach Devon
L195FDV	Stagecoach Devon
L197FDV	Stagecoach Devon
L201FDV	Stagecoach Devon
L201SHW	First Southern Nat
L202MHL	Pullham's
L202SHW	First Southern Nat
L203FDV	Stagecoach Devon
L203SHW	First Badgerline
L204FDV	Stagecoach Devon
L204SHW	First Badgerline
L205SHW	First Badgerline
L206SHW	First Badgerline
L207SHW	First Badgerline
L208FDV	Stagecoach Devon
L208SHW	First Badgerline
L209FDV	Stagecoach Devon
L209SHW	First Badgerline
L210FDV	Stagecoach Devon
L210OYC	Wakes
L210SHW	First Southern Nat
L211CRU	Wilts & Dorset
L211FDV	Stagecoach Devon
L211OYC	Wakes
L211VHU	First Badgerline
L212CRU	Wilts & Dorset
L212FDV	Stagecoach Devon
L212VHU	First Badgerline
L213CRU	Wilts & Dorset
L213VHU	First Badgerline
L214FDV	Stagecoach Devon
L214VHU	First Badgerline
L215VHU	First Badgerline
L216VHU	First Badgerline
L217VHU	First Badgerline
L218VHU	First Badgerline
L219VHU	First Badgerline
L220VHU	First Badgerline
L221AAB	First Badgerline
L221VHU	First Badgerline
L223AAB	First Badgerline
L223VHU	First Badgerline
L224AAB	First Badgerline
L224VHU	First Badgerline
L225AAB	First Badgerline
L225BUT	Carmel Coaches
L225VHU	First Badgerline
L226AAB	First Badgerline
L227AAB	First Badgerline
L228AAB	First Badgerline
L229AAB	First Badgerline
L230AAB	First Badgerline
L238OYC	Berry's
L248CCK	Stagecoach West
L248YOD	Plymouth Citybus
L249YOD	Plymouth Citybus
L250YOD	Plymouth Citybus
L251YOD	Plymouth Citybus
L252YOD	Plymouth Citybus
L253YOD	Plymouth Citybus
L254YOD	Plymouth Citybus
L255YOD	Plymouth Citybus
L256YOD	Plymouth Citybus
L257UCV	Taw & Torridge
L257YOD	Plymouth Citybus
L258YOD	Plymouth Citybus
L259YOD	Plymouth Citybus
L260YOD	Plymouth Citybus
L302YOD	Plymouth Citybus
L318BOD	Stagecoach Devon
L322AAB	First Badgerline
L329LSC	Hambleys
L329MYC	First Southern Nat
L330CHB	Stagecoach West
L330MYC	First Southern Nat
L336DTG	Filer's
L338WAF	Truronian
L339WAF	Truronian
L340NMV	Swiftlink
L345ATA	Dartline
L355VCV	First Western Nat
L356VCV	First Western Nat
L357VCV	First Western Nat
L358VCV	First Western Nat
L359VCV	First Western Nat
L360VCV	First Western Nat
L390UHU	First Badgerline
L396YAM	Wilts & Dorset
L401BFX	Yellow Buses
L401VCV	First Western Nat
L402BFX	Yellow Buses
L402VCV	First Western Nat
L403BFX	Yellow Buses
L403VCV	First Western Nat
L404BFX	Yellow Buses
L404VCV	First Western Nat
L405BFX	Yellow Buses
L405VCV	First Western Nat
L406BFX	Yellow Buses
L406VCV	First Western Nat
L422CPB	Fosseway
L422WHR	Dartline
L423CPB	Fosseway
L427CPC	Fosseway
L434XRF	First Badgerline
L441XRF	First Badgerline
L442XRF	First Badgerline
L446FFR	Stagecoach Devon
L447FFR	Stagecoach Devon
L448FFR	Stagecoach Devon
L455LVT	First Badgerline
L463RDN	Bennetts
L486HKN	Seawards
L494HRE	First Badgerline
L495HRE	First Badgerline
L501AJT	Wilts & Dorset
L502AJT	Wilts & Dorset
L503AJT	Wilts & Dorset
L503VHU	First Cityline
L504AJT	Wilts & Dorset
L504VHU	First Cityline
L505AJT	Wilts & Dorset
L505VHU	First Badgerline
L506AJT	Wilts & Dorset
L506VHU	First Cityline
L507VHU	First Cityline
L508VHU	First Cityline
L519EHD	Bennetts
L526EHD	Wilts & Dorset
L543YUS	Marchants
L546WDE	Wilts & Dorset
L547CDV	Stagecoach Devon
L548CDV	First Western Nat
L554LVT	First Badgerline
L556LVT	First Badgerline
L557LVT	First Badgerline
L628VCV	First Western Nat
L629VCV	First Western Nat
L630VCV	First Western Nat
L631SEU	First Cityline
L631VCV	First Western Nat
L632SEU	First Cityline
L632VCV	First Western Nat
L633SEU	First Cityline
L633VCV	First Western Nat
L634SEU	First Cityline
L634VCV	First Western Nat
L635SEU	First Cityline
L635VCV	First Western Nat
L636SEU	First Cityline
L636VCV	First Western Nat
L637SEU	First Cityline
L637VCV	First Western Nat
L638SEU	First Cityline
L638VCV	First Western Nat
L639SEU	First Cityline
L639VCV	First Western Nat
L640SEU	First Cityline
L640VCV	First Western Nat
L641SEU	First Cityline
L641VCV	First Western Nat
L642SEU	First Cityline
L642VCV	First Western Nat
L643SEU	First Cityline
L643VCV	First Western Nat
L644SEU	First Cityline
L644VCV	First Western Nat
L645SEU	First Cityline
L645VCV	First Western Nat
L646SEU	First Cityline
L646VCV	First Western Nat
L647SEU	First Cityline
L647VCV	First Western Nat
L648SEU	First Cityline
L648VCV	First Western Nat
L649CJT	First Western Nat
L649SEU	First Badgerline
L649VCV	First Western Nat
L650CJT	First Southern Nat
L650SEU	First Badgerline
L650VCV	First Western Nat
L651CJT	First Southern Nat
L651SEU	First Badgerline
L651VCV	First Western Nat
L652CJT	First Southern Nat
L652SEU	First Badgerline
L653SEU	First Badgerline
L654SEU	First Badgerline
L685CDD	Stagecoach Devon
L691CDD	Stagecoach Devon
L691WHY	Coombs
L692CDD	Stagecoach Devon
L692WHY	Coombs
L693CDD	Stagecoach Devon
L694CDD	Stagecoach Devon
L694JEC	Beeline
L695CDD	Stagecoach Devon
L696CDD	Stagecoach Devon
L696CDD	Stagecoach Devon
L696CDD	Stagecoach Devon
L703JSC	Swiftlink
L709FWO	Stagecoach West
L710FWO	Stagecoach West
L711ALJ	Wilts & Dorset
L711FWO	Stagecoach West
L712FWO	Stagecoach West
L725WCV	Truronian
L726WCV	Truronian
L739NHE	Wilts & Dorset
L796DTT	Dawlish Cs
L801SAE	First Badgerline
L801SAE	First Cityline
L802SAE	First Badgerline
L802SAE	First Cityline
L803SAE	First Cityline
L803XDG	Stagecoach West
L804SAE	First Cityline
L804XDG	Stagecoach West
L805SAE	First Cityline
L805XDG	Stagecoach West
L806XDG	Stagecoach West
L808SAE	First Cityline
L809SAE	First Cityline
L810SAE	First Cityline
L811SAE	First Cityline
L812SAE	First Cityline
L813SAE	First Cityline
L814SAE	First Cityline
L815CFJ	First Western Nat
L815SAE	First Cityline
L816CFJ	First Western Nat
L816SAE	First Cityline
L817CFJ	First Western Nat
L817SAE	First Cityline
L818SAE	First Cityline
L819SAE	First Cityline
L820SAE	First Cityline
L821SAE	First Cityline
L822SAE	First Cityline
L823SAE	First Cityline
L824SAE	First Cityline
L825SAE	First Cityline
L826SAE	First Cityline
L827WHY	First Cityline
L828WHY	First Cityline
L829WHY	First Cityline
L830WHY	First Cityline
L831CDG	Stagecoach West
L832CDG	Stagecoach West
L833CDG	Stagecoach West
L834CDG	Stagecoach West
L835CDG	Stagecoach West
L836CDG	Stagecoach West
L837CDG	Stagecoach West
L838CDG	Stagecoach West
L839CDG	Stagecoach West
L840CDG	Stagecoach West
L841CDG	Stagecoach West
L842CDG	Stagecoach West
L858COD	Dartline
L860NYC	Coombs
L872WCV	F T Williams
L877TFB	First Badgerline
L878VHT	First Badgerline
L879VHT	First Badgerline
L880VHT	First Badgerline
L881VHT	First Badgerline
L883VHT	First Badgerline
L884VHT	First Badgerline
L885VHT	First Badgerline
L886VHT	First Badgerline
L887VHT	First Badgerline
L889VHT	First Badgerline
L890VHT	First Badgerline
L891VHT	First Badgerline
L892VHT	First Badgerline
L893VHT	First Badgerline
L894VHT	First Badgerline
L895VHT	First Badgerline
L896VHT	First Badgerline
L897VHT	First Badgerline
L898VHT	First Cityline
L899VHT	First Badgerline
L901VHT	First Badgerline
L902VHT	First Badgerline
L903VHT	First Badgerline
L904VHT	First Badgerline
L905VHT	First Badgerline
L906VHT	First Badgerline

Reg	Operator	Reg	Operator	Reg	Operator	Reg	Operator	Reg	Operator
HIL4966	Tally Ho!	J504RPR	Wilts & Dorset	JHU899X	Stagecoach West	K246SFJ	Plymouth Citybus	K611LAE	First Cityline
HIL6075	Stagecoach West	J505RPR	Wilts & Dorset	JHU900X	First Badgerline	K247SFJ	Plymouth Citybus	K611ORL	First Western Nat
HIL6253	Hookways	J506RPR	Wilts & Dorset	JHU901X	First Badgerline	K271BRJ	Swiftlink	K612LAE	First Cityline
HIL7541	Hookways	J507RPR	Wilts & Dorset	JHU902X	First Southern Nat	K29OEU	First Badgerline	K612ORL	First Western Nat
HIL7772	Safeway	J508RPR	Wilts & Dorset	JHU903X	First Southern Nat	K301WTA	Plymouth Citybus	K613LAE	First Cityline
HIL8410	Stagecoach West	J509RPR	Wilts & Dorset	JHU904X	First Southern Nat	K302FYG	Bennetts	K613ORL	First Western Nat
HJA965E	Quantock	J510RPR	Wilts & Dorset	JHU905X	First Badgerline	K308YKG	Stagecoach West	K614LAE	First Cityline
HJB470W	Wills & Dorset	J511RPR	Wilts & Dorset	JHU906X	First Badgerline	K311YKG	Stagecoach West	K614ORL	First Western Nat
HJI2615	Wills & Dorset	J512RPR	Wilts & Dorset	JHU907X	First Badgerline	K321AUX	Beard	K615LAE	First Cityline
HKL819	Quantock	J513RPR	Wilts & Dorset	JHU908X	First Badgerline	K326PHT	South Gloucestershire	K615ORL	First Western Nat
HPL422V	Bakers Dolphin	J514RPR	Wilts & Dorset	JHU909X	First Badgerline	K327PHT	South Gloucestershire	K615RNR	South Gloucestershire
HRO987V	First Badgerline	J515RPR	Wilts & Dorset	JHU910X	First Badgerline	K328KYC	First Southern Nat	K616LAE	First Cityline
HSV342	Wills & Dorset	J518LRY	Bennetts	JHU911X	First Badgerline	K329KYC	First Southern Nat	K616ORL	First Western Nat
HTA844N	First Western Nat	J580FYA	First Southern Nat	JHU912X	Stagecoach West	K329PHT	South Gloucestershire	K617LAE	First Cityline
HUD495W	Roselyn Coaches	J601FYA	First Southern Nat	JHU913X	First Badgerline	K330KYC	First Southern Nat	K617ORL	First Western Nat
HUD501W	Roselyn Coaches	J601KCU	Safeway	JHU914X	First Badgerline	K310OAF	First Western Nat	K618LAE	First Cityline
HUO510	Quantock	J601WHJ	Bath Bus Company	JHW107P	First Badgerline	K331RCN	Axe Valley	K618ORL	First Western Nat
HVJ716	First Western Nat	J606WHJ	South Gloucestershire	JHW108P	First Badgerline	K332OAF	First Western Nat	K619LAE	First Cityline
IIB8903	Ebley	J608WHJ	Bath Bus Company	JHW109P	First Badgerline	K332RCN	Axe Valley	K619ORL	First Western Nat
IIL1353	Beeline	J610PTA	First Western Nat	JIL6902	Citytours	K332YDW	Filer's	K620LAE	First Cityline
IUI4360	Bakers Dolphin	J611WHJ	Bath Bus Company	JIL7792	Keith Webber	K333OAF	First Western Nat	K620ORL	First Western Nat
J2EST	Carmel Coaches	J688MFE	Castleways	JIL8210	Swanbrook	K334OAF	First Western Nat	K621LAE	First Cityline
J21GCX	Bennetts	J689MFE	Castleways	JIL8319	Wakes	K335OAF	First Western Nat	K621XOD	Stagecoach Devon
J22PJT	Thamesdown	J701CWT	First Western Nat	JJI5614	Duchy Travel	K336OAF	First Western Nat	K622LAE	First Cityline
J42VWO	Hookways	J703CWT	First Western Nat	JLJ402	Quantock	K337OAF	First Western Nat	K622ORL	First Western Nat
J86LLA	Dartline	J729CWT	Loverings	JMJ134V	Taw & Torridge	K338OAF	First Western Nat	K623LAE	First Cityline
J96UBL	Tally Ho!	J732CWT	Loverings	JSK261	Plymouth Citybus	K339EJV	Filer's	K623ORL	First Western Nat
J97UBL	Tally Ho!	J732KBC	First Southern Nat	JSK262	Plymouth Citybus	K339OAF	First Western Nat	K624LAE	First Cityline
J120SPF	South Gloucestershire	J803PFJ	First Western Nat	JSK264	Plymouth Citybus	K340OAF	First Western Nat	K624ORL	First Western Nat
J127DGC	Seawards	J813KHD	Beard	JSK265	Plymouth Citybus	K341OAF	First Western Nat	K625LAE	First Cityline
J130LVM	Taw & Torridge	J819EYC	Berry's	JSV983	Caradon	K342OAF	First Western Nat	K625ORL	First Western Nat
J140SJT	First Western Nat	J822HMC	Stagecoach Devon	JTE546	Quantock	K343OAF	First Western Nat	K626LAE	First Cityline
J141SJT	First Western Nat	J823HMC	Stagecoach Devon	JTH44W	First Western Nat	K344ORL	First Western Nat	K627LAE	First Cityline
J142KPX	First Southern Nat	J824HMC	Stagecoach Devon	JUI3073	Beeline	K345ORL	First Western Nat	K628LAE	First Cityline
J142SJT	First Western Nat	J824MOD	Dartline	JUP233	Quantock	K346ORL	First Western Nat	K629LAE	First Cityline
J143SJT	First Western Nat	J825HMC	Stagecoach Devon	JVH378	Quantock	K347ORL	First Western Nat	K630LAE	First Cityline
J144SJT	First Western Nat	J825MOD	Dartline	JWE244W	Caradon	K348ORL	First Western Nat	K690UFV	First Badgerline
J145KPX	First Southern Nat	J826HMC	Stagecoach Devon	JWT758V	First Western Nat	K349ORL	First Western Nat	K691UFV	First Badgerline
J145SJT	First Western Nat	J827HMC	Stagecoach Devon	JWV252W	Bath Bus Company	K350ORL	First Badgerline	K692UFV	First Badgerline
J146KPX	First Southern Nat	J828HMC	Stagecoach Devon	JWV252W	Western Greyhound	K351ORL	First Badgerline	K693UFV	First Badgerline
J146SJT	First Western Nat	J829HMC	Stagecoach Devon	JYA941N	Berry's	K352ORL	First Western Nat	K694UFV	First Badgerline
J148SJT	First Western Nat	J850FTC	First Badgerline	JYD877Y	Filer's	K353ORL	Filer's	K711UTT	Stagecoach Devon
J177MCW	Dukes Travel	J850OBV	First Badgerline	JYJ269N	Yellow Buses	K354ORL	First Western Nat	K712FNO	Wessex Bus
J185LGE	First Southern Nat	J851FTC	First Badgerline	K2BCC	Bennetts	K424WUT	Bennetts	K712RNR	Bennetts
J205KTT	First Southern Nat	J852FTC	First Badgerline	K5CJT	Turners	K427HWY	Dawlish Cs	K714UTT	Stagecoach Devon
J208KTT	First Southern Nat	J853FTC	First Badgerline	K6CJT	Turners	K432XRF	First Western Nat	K717UTT	Stagecoach Devon
J210KTT	First Southern Nat	J854FTC	First Badgerline	K7CJT	Turners	K433XRF	First Western Nat	K718UTT	Stagecoach Devon
J213KTT	First Southern Nat	J855FTC	First Badgerline	K34VFV	Bennetts	K435XRF	First Western Nat	K719UTT	Stagecoach Devon
J215OCW	South Gloucestershire	J857FTC	First Badgerline	K39XUK	Wilts & Dorset	K443XRF	First Western Nat	K720UTT	Stagecoach Devon
J217KTT	First Southern Nat	J858FTC	First Badgerline	K101OMW	Thamesdown	K458YPK	Seawards	K721HYA	Coombs
J220KTT	First Southern Nat	J859FTC	First Badgerline	K101SFJ	Plymouth Citybus	K477XRF	First Western Nat	K721UTT	Stagecoach Devon
J228JJR	Andy James	J860HWS	First Badgerline	K101VLJ	Wilts & Dorset	K516UJT	Wilts & Dorset	K722HYA	Coombs
J229JJR	Ebley	J861HWS	First Badgerline	K102OMW	Thamesdown	K517UJT	Wilts & Dorset	K722UTT	Stagecoach Devon
J230JJR	Ebley	J862HWS	First Badgerline	K102SFJ	Plymouth Citybus	K518UJT	Wilts & Dorset	K723WTT	First Western Nat
J236NNC	South Gloucestershire	J863HWS	First Badgerline	K103OMW	Thamesdown	K519UJT	Wilts & Dorset	K725UTT	Stagecoach Devon
J237NNC	South Gloucestershire	J864HWS	First Badgerline	K103SFJ	Plymouth Citybus	K520UJT	Wilts & Dorset	K726UTT	Stagecoach Devon
J241FYA	First Southern Nat	J865HWS	First Badgerline	K103VLJ	Wilts & Dorset	K521UJT	Wilts & Dorset	K727UTT	Stagecoach Devon
J243MFP	Citytours	J866HWS	First Badgerline	K104OMW	Thamesdown	K522UJT	Wilts & Dorset	K729GBE	Marchants
J266SPR	Yellow Buses	J870FGX	Dartline	K104SFJ	Plymouth Citybus	K523UJT	Wilts & Dorset	K730UTT	Stagecoach Devon
J267SPR	Yellow Buses	J877LRG	Carmel Coaches	K104VLJ	Wilts & Dorset	K524UJT	Wilts & Dorset	K731UTT	Stagecoach Devon
J268SPR	Yellow Buses	J914MDG	Pullham's	K105OMW	Thamesdown	K525UJT	Wilts & Dorset	K732UTT	Stagecoach Devon
J269SPR	Yellow Buses	J953SBU	F T Williams	K105SFJ	Plymouth Citybus	K526UJT	Wilts & Dorset	K744RBX	Seawards
J271TTX	Coombs	J969EYD	First Southern Nat	K105VLJ	Wilts & Dorset	K527UJT	Wilts & Dorset	K750RHR	Wilts & Dorset
J272NNC	Coombs	JAM145E	Thamesdown	K106OMW	Thamesdown	K528UJT	Wilts & Dorset	K751VFJ	First Southern Nat
J275NNC	Coombs	JCV433W	Tally Ho!	K106SFJ	Plymouth Citybus	K529UJT	Wilts & Dorset	K752XTA	First Southern Nat
J278NNC	Coombs	JCW517S	Taw & Torridge	K106VLJ	Wilts & Dorset	K530UJT	Wilts & Dorset	K753XTA	First Southern Nat
J291NNB	Swanbrook	JDR661F	Polerro Tram Co	K107OMW	Thamesdown	K531UJT	Wilts & Dorset	K754XTA	First Southern Nat
J297NNB	South Gloucestershire	JDZ2326	First Cityline	K107SFJ	Plymouth Citybus	K532UJT	Wilts & Dorset	K755XTA	First Southern Nat
J302BVO	Dukes Travel	JDZ2327	First Cityline	K107VLJ	Wilts & Dorset	K533UJT	Wilts & Dorset	K75XCW	Dukes Travel
J303BVO	Dukes Travel	JDZ2328	First Cityline	K108OMW	Thamesdown	K596VBC	Loverings	K775UTT	Dartline
J304BVO	Dukes Travel	JDZ2329	First Cityline	K108SFJ	Plymouth Citybus	K597EKU	Duchy Travel	K776AFS	First Western Nat
J304UKG	Stagecoach West	JDZ2330	First Cityline	K109OMW	Thamesdown	K601ORL	First Western Nat	K792OTC	First Southern Nat
J305BVO	Dukes Travel	JDZ2331	First Cityline	K109SFJ	Plymouth Citybus	K602ORL	First Western Nat	K794OTC	First Southern Nat
J329LLK	First Southern Nat	JDZ2332	First Cityline	K109VLJ	Wilts & Dorset	K603ORL	First Western Nat	K801OMW	Stagecoach West
J362BNW	Castleways	JDZ2360	Stagecoach Devon	K110OMW	Thamesdown	K604ORL	First Western Nat	K801ORL	First Western Nat
J375WWK	First Western Nat	JDZ2361	Stagecoach Devon	K110SFJ	Plymouth Citybus	K605ORL	First Western Nat	K802ORL	First Western Nat
J409PRW	Stagecoach West	JDZ2362	Stagecoach Devon	K110VLJ	Wilts & Dorset	K606LAE	First Cityline	K803ORL	First Western Nat
J411PRW	Stagecoach West	JDZ2363	Stagecoach Devon	K171CAV	Stagecoach Devon	K606ORL	First Western Nat	K803WFJ	Stagecoach Devon
J412PRW	Stagecoach West	JDZ2364	Stagecoach Devon	K173CAV	Stagecoach Devon	K607LAE	First Cityline	K804ORL	First Western Nat
J413PRW	Stagecoach West	JDZ2365	Stagecoach Devon	K216SUY	James Bevan	K607ORL	First Western Nat	K804WTT	First Western Nat
J416PRW	Stagecoach West	JDZ2371	Stagecoach Devon	K241SFJ	Plymouth Citybus	K608LAE	First Cityline	K805WFJ	Stagecoach Devon
J417PRW	Stagecoach West	JEO587X	First Western Nat	K242SFJ	Plymouth Citybus	K608ORL	First Western Nat	K805WTT	First Western Nat
J430PPF	South Gloucestershire	JEY124Y	Marchants	K243SFJ	Plymouth Citybus	K609LAE	First Cityline	K806WFJ	Stagecoach Devon
J501RPR	Wilts & Dorset	JFJ875	Carmel Coaches	K244SFJ	Plymouth Citybus	K609ORL	First Western Nat	K807EET	Carmel Coaches
J502RPR	Wilts & Dorset	JFM575	Quantock	K245SFJ	Plymouth Citybus	K610LAE	First Cityline	K816WFJ	Stagecoach Devon
J503RPR	Wilts & Dorset	JG9938	Quantock			K610ORL	First Western Nat		

L907VHT	First Badgerline	LNU582W	Bakers Dolphin	M119BMR	Thamesdown	M274HOD	Plymouth Citybus	M515DHU	First Cityline
L908VHT	First Badgerline	LOD495	Carmel Coaches	M127HOD	Plymouth Citybus	M278UYD	First Southern Nat	M516DHU	First Cityline
L909VHT	First Cityline	LRB202W	First Southern Nat	M128HOD	Plymouth Citybus	M279UYD	First Southern Nat	M517DHU	First Cityline
L910VHT	First Cityline	LRB211W	First Southern Nat	M129HOD	Plymouth Citybus	M281UYD	First Southern Nat	M518DHU	First Cityline
L911VHT	First Cityline	LRV992	Stagecoach Devon	M12BUS	Dawlish Cs	M282UYD	First Southern Nat	M519DHU	First Cityline
L913UGA	Andy James	LSJ872W	Ebley	M130HOD	Plymouth Citybus	M290FAE	First Badgerline	M520FFB	First Cityline
L917NWW	Bakers Dolphin	LSK527	Carmel Coaches	M131HOD	Plymouth Citybus	M291FAE	First Badgerline	M521FFB	First Cityline
L920NWW	Berry's	LSK611	Trathens	M132HOD	Plymouth Citybus	M292FAE	First Badgerline	M522FFB	First Cityline
L920UGA	Andy James	LSK612	Trathens	M132HPR	Wilts & Dorset	M293FAE	First Badgerline	M523FFB	First Cityline
L924NWW	Loverings	LSK613	Trathens	M133HPR	Wilts & Dorset	M301BRL	First Western Nat	M524FFB	First Cityline
L929CTT	Stagecoach Devon	LSK614	Trathens	M134HPR	Wilts & Dorset	M301TSF	Swiftlink	M525FFB	First Cityline
L929UGA	Andy James	LSK615	Trathens	M134UWY	Loverings	M302BRL	First Western Nat	M526FFB	First Cityline
L930CTT	Stagecoach Devon	LSK812	Trathens	M135HPR	Wilts & Dorset	M303BRL	First Western Nat	M527FFB	First Cityline
L931CTT	Stagecoach Devon	LSK814	Trathens	M136KRU	Wilts & Dorset	M304KOD	Plymouth Citybus	M528FFB	First Cityline
L932CTT	Stagecoach Devon	LSK825	Trathens	M137FAE	First Badgerline	M305KOD	Plymouth Citybus	M529FFB	First Cityline
L933CTT	Stagecoach Devon	LSU788	First Badgerline	M137KRU	Wilts & Dorset	M305TSF	First Southern Nat	M530FFB	First Cityline
L934CTT	Stagecoach Devon	LSV749	Wilts & Dorset	M138FAE	First Badgerline	M343NOD	Stagecoach Devon	M531FFB	First Cityline
L935CTT	Stagecoach Devon	LTY551X	Bakers Dolphin	M138KRU	Wilts & Dorset	M345JBO	Stagecoach Devon	M532FFB	First Cityline
L936CTT	Stagecoach Devon	LTY552X	Bakers Dolphin	M139KRU	Wilts & Dorset	M356LFX	Yellow Buses	M533FFB	First Cityline
L937CTT	Stagecoach Devon	LTY553X	Bakers Dolphin	M139LNP	Castleways	M357LFX	Yellow Buses	M534FFB	First Cityline
L938CTT	Stagecoach Devon	LUA243V	Hookways	M140FAE	First Badgerline	M358LFX	Yellow Buses	M534JLJ	Wilts & Dorset
L939CTT	Stagecoach Devon	LUA282V	Western Greyhound	M140KRU	Wilts & Dorset	M359LFX	Yellow Buses	M535FFB	First Cityline
L940CTT	Stagecoach Devon	LUA287V	Bluebird Cs	M141FAE	First Badgerline	M360JBO	Stagecoach Devon	M535JLJ	Wilts & Dorset
L941CTT	Stagecoach Devon	LWS32Y	First Badgerline	M141KRU	Wilts & Dorset	M360LFX	Yellow Buses	M536FFB	First Cityline
L942CTT	Stagecoach Devon	LWS33Y	Stagecoach West	M142FAE	First Badgerline	M372CRL	Truronian	M536JLJ	Wilts & Dorset
L943CTT	Stagecoach Devon	LWS34Y	Stagecoach West	M142KRU	Wilts & Dorset	M372XEX	First Southern Nat	M537FFB	First Cityline
L945EOD	Stagecoach Devon	LWS35Y	Stagecoach West	M143KRU	Wilts & Dorset	M373CRL	Truronian	M537JLJ	Wilts & Dorset
L946EOD	Stagecoach Devon	LWS36Y	Stagecoach West	M144KRU	Wilts & Dorset	M373XEX	First Southern Nat	M538FFB	First Cityline
L947EOD	Stagecoach Devon	LWS37Y	Stagecoach West	M145KRU	Wilts & Dorset	M381KVR	First Southern Nat	M538LEL	Wilts & Dorset
L948EOD	Stagecoach Devon	LWS38Y	Stagecoach West	M146KRU	Wilts & Dorset	M382KVR	First Southern Nat	M539LEL	Wilts & Dorset
L949EOD	Stagecoach Devon	LWS39Y	Stagecoach West	M151KDD	Castleways	M386KVR	First Southern Nat	M53HOD	Plymouth Citybus
L950EOD	Stagecoach Devon	LWS40Y	Stagecoach West	M158KOD	Dartline	M392KVR	First Southern Nat	M540LEL	Wilts & Dorset
L995VAF	Truronian	LWS41Y	Stagecoach West	M191HTT	Stagecoach Devon	M393KVR	First Southern Nat	M541LEL	Wilts & Dorset
LAK304W	Duchy Travel	LWS42Y	First Southern Nat	M192HTT	Stagecoach Devon	M407CCV	First Western Nat	M572TYB	Coombs
LAK310W	Duchy Travel	LWS43Y	First Southern Nat	M193HTT	Stagecoach Devon	M408CCV	First Western Nat	M573TYB	Coombs
LAZ5824	Keith Webber	LWS44Y	First Cityline	M194HTT	Stagecoach Devon	M409CCV	First Western Nat	M574RCP	Wilts & Dorset
LAZ5826	Tally Ho!	LWS45Y	First Cityline	M19ABC	First Southern Nat	M410CCV	First Western Nat	M582DAF	Grey Cars
LBZ2571	Dartline	LYA315V	Wakes	M201TYB	Berry's	M411CCV	First Western Nat	M582KTG	Carmel Coaches
LDB756	Quantock	M9FUG	Cottrell's	M220PMS	First Southern Nat	M411RND	First Cityline	M583WLV	Tally Ho!
LDD488	Pullham's	M10CJT	Turners	M226UTM	Stagecoach Devon	M412CCV	First Western Nat	M584WLV	Tally Ho!
LDS190A	South Gloucestershire	M11CJT	Turners	M226VWU	First Western Nat	M413CCV	First Western Nat	M587KTT	Dawlish Cs
LDV176P	Keith Webber	M12CJT	Turners	M227UTM	Stagecoach Devon	M413DEU	First Southern Nat	M606RCP	First Badgerline
LEU256P	First Badgerline	M13CJT	Turners	M228UTM	Stagecoach Devon	M413RND	First Southern Nat	M622HDV	Stagecoach Devon
LEU269P	First Badgerline	M14ABC	First Southern Nat	M229UTM	Stagecoach Devon	M414CCV	First Western Nat	M623HDV	Stagecoach Devon
LFH719V	Castleways	M15WAL	Wilts & Dorset	M230UTM	Stagecoach Devon	M414RND	First Cityline	M624HDV	Stagecoach Devon
LFH720V	Castleways	M17WAL	Wilts & Dorset	M231UTM	Stagecoach Devon	M415CCV	First Western Nat	M625HDV	Stagecoach Devon
LFJ841W	First Western Nat	M18WAL	Wilts & Dorset	M232UTM	Stagecoach Devon	M416CCV	First Western Nat	M626HDV	Stagecoach Devon
LFJ842W	First Western Nat	M19WAL	Wilts & Dorset	M233UTM	Stagecoach Devon	M417CCV	First Western Nat	M627HDV	Stagecoach Devon
LFJ843W	First Western Nat	M20CJT	Turners	M234UTM	Stagecoach Devon	M418CCV	First Western Nat	M628HDV	Stagecoach Devon
LFJ844W	First Western Nat	M20WAL	Wilts & Dorset	M235UTM	Stagecoach Devon	M419CCV	First Western Nat	M629HDV	Stagecoach Devon
LFJ845W	First Western Nat	M38KAX	DAC Coaches	M236UTM	Stagecoach Devon	M419VYD	Eastville	M630HDV	Stagecoach Devon
LFJ846W	First Western Nat	M40CJT	Turners	M237UTM	Stagecoach Devon	M420CCV	First Western Nat	M636HDV	Stagecoach Devon
LFJ847W	First Western Nat	M41FTC	First Southern Nat	M238UTM	Stagecoach Devon	M421CCV	First Western Nat	M637HDV	Stagecoach Devon
LFJ860W	First Western Nat	M41KAX	DAC Coaches	M239UTM	Stagecoach Devon	M421VYD	Dawlish Cs	M638HDV	Stagecoach Devon
LFJ871W	First Western Nat	M45BEG	First Badgerline	M239VYA	First Southern Nat	M422CCV	First Western Nat	M639HDV	Stagecoach Devon
LFJ872W	First Western Nat	M45GRY	Swiftlink	M240UTM	Stagecoach Devon	M423CCV	First Western Nat	M640HDV	Stagecoach Devon
LFJ873W	First Western Nat	M46BEG	First Badgerline	M240VYA	First Southern Nat	M424CCV	First Western Nat	M641HDV	Stagecoach Devon
LFM302	Quantock	M46GRY	Swiftlink	M241UTM	Stagecoach Devon	M425CCV	First Western Nat	M646HFJ	Dartline
LFM717	Quantock	M47GRY	Swiftlink	M241VYA	First Southern Nat	M426CCV	First Western Nat	M674RAJ	First Southern Nat
LFM734	Quantock	M48BEG	First Badgerline	M242UTM	Stagecoach Devon	M439FHW	First Southern Nat	M675RAJ	First Southern Nat
LHT730P	Eastville	M48GRY	Swiftlink	M242VYA	First Southern Nat	M440FHW	First Southern Nat	M675TNA	Swiftlink
LHY976	Somerbus	M51HOD	Plymouth Citybus	M243UTM	Stagecoach Devon	M451LLJ	Yellow Buses	M676RAJ	First Western Nat
LIL2167	Wakes	M52HOD	Plymouth Citybus	M244UTM	Stagecoach Devon	M452LLJ	Yellow Buses	M676TNA	Swiftlink
LIL2665	Wilts & Dorset	M73HHB	Stagecoach West	M245UTM	Stagecoach Devon	M453LLJ	Yellow Buses	M677RAJ	First Western Nat
LIL2665	Wilts & Dorset	M78HHB	Stagecoach West	M246UTM	Stagecoach Devon	M454LLJ	Yellow Buses	M678RAJ	First Western Nat
LIL3066	Boomerang Bus Co	M85DEW	Stagecoach West	M246VWU	First Western Nat	M455LLJ	Yellow Buses	M699EDD	Stagecoach Devon
LIL5851	First Southern Nat	M86DEW	Stagecoach West	M247UTM	Stagecoach Devon	M456LLJ	Yellow Buses	M701EDD	Stagecoach Devon
LIL6536	Duchy Travel	M87DEW	South Gloucestershire	M248NNF	First Southern Nat	M457LLJ	Yellow Buses	M702EDD	Stagecoach Devon
LIL6537	Dartline	M92BOU	First Southern Nat	M248UTM	Stagecoach Devon	M458LLJ	Yellow Buses	M703EDD	Stagecoach Devon
LIL6538	Dartline	M101ECV	First Western Nat	M249NNF	First Southern Nat	M459LLJ	Yellow Buses	M704JDG	Stagecoach Devon
LIL7802	Dartline	M101SWG	Wakes	M249UTM	Stagecoach Devon	M460LLJ	Yellow Buses	M705JDG	Stagecoach Devon
LIL8052	Dartline	M102ECV	First Western Nat	M250UTM	Stagecoach Devon	M461LLJ	Yellow Buses	M706JDG	Stagecoach Devon
LIL8557	Dartline	M102SWG	Wakes	M252LFJ	Dawlish Cs	M462LLJ	Yellow Buses	M707JDG	Stagecoach Devon
LIL8823	Dartline	M103ECV	First Western Nat	M261HOD	Plymouth Citybus	M498ACV	F T Williams	M708JDG	Stagecoach West
LIL8876	Dartline	M103SWG	Wakes	M262HOD	Plymouth Citybus	M501CCV	First Western Nat	M709JDG	Stagecoach West
LIL9017	Dartline	M104SWG	Wakes	M263HOD	Plymouth Citybus	M502CCV	First Western Nat	M710JDG	Stagecoach West
LIL9267	Boomerang Bus Co	M105CCD	Stagecoach Devon	M264HOD	Plymouth Citybus	M503CCV	First Western Nat	M711BMR	Thamesdown
LIL9268	Boomerang Bus Co	M106CCD	Stagecoach Devon	M265HOD	Plymouth Citybus	M505XFY	Carmel Coaches	M711FMR	Stagecoach West
LIL9270	Boomerang Bus Co	M108CCD	Stagecoach Devon	M266HOD	Plymouth Citybus	M508VYA	First Southern Nat	M712FMR	Stagecoach West
LIL9271	Boomerang Bus Co	M112BMR	Thamesdown	M267HOD	Plymouth Citybus	M509DHU	First Cityline	M713FMR	Stagecoach West
LIL9397	Keith Webber	M113BMR	Thamesdown	M268HOD	Plymouth Citybus	M509VYA	First Southern Nat	M714FMR	Stagecoach West
LIL9843	Marchants	M114BMR	Thamesdown	M269HOD	Plymouth Citybus	M510DHU	First Cityline	M715FMR	Stagecoach West
LIL9990	Dartline	M115BMR	Thamesdown	M270HOD	Plymouth Citybus	M511DHU	First Cityline	M740RCP	Bluebird Cs
LJH665	Quantock	M116BMR	Thamesdown	M271HOD	Plymouth Citybus	M512DHU	First Cityline	M741RCP	Bluebird Cs
LNU578W	Bakers Dolphin	M117BMR	Thamesdown	M272HOD	Plymouth Citybus	M513DHU	First Cityline	M745ARP	Coombs
LNU579W	Bakers Dolphin	M118BMR	Thamesdown	M273HOD	Plymouth Citybus	M514DHU	First Cityline	M746RCP	Wilts & Dorset

Reg	Operator	Reg	Operator	Reg	Operator	Reg	Operator	Reg	Operator
M756XET	First Southern Nat	MFX169W	Yellow Buses	N212KBJ	Truronian	N409LDF	Stagecoach West	N605GAH	First Southern Nat
M763CWS	First Southern Nat	MFX170W	Yellow Buses	N224VRC	Wilts & Dorset	N410MBW	Stagecoach Devon	N608WND	First Western Nat
M764CWS	First Southern Nat	MFX171W	Yellow Buses	N225VRC	Wilts & Dorset	N410WJL	Coombs	N609GAH	First Southern Nat
M764FTT	First Western Nat	MFX172W	Yellow Buses	N226HWX	Loverings	N411MBW	Stagecoach Devon	N610WND	First Western Nat
M765CWS	First Southern Nat	MFX173W	Yellow Buses	N226KAE	First Southern Nat	N411WJL	Wilts & Dorset	N611GAH	First Southern Nat
M765FTT	First Western Nat	MFX174W	Yellow Buses	N226VRC	Wilts & Dorset	N428FOW	First Western Nat	N612WND	First Western Nat
M766FTT	First Western Nat	MFX175W	Yellow Buses	N227KAE	First Southern Nat	N460KMW	Beeline	N613GAH	First Western Nat
M768FTT	First Western Nat	MFX176W	Yellow Buses	N228KAE	First Badgerline	N463HRN	Stagecoach Devon	N614HRV	Wills & Dorset
M769FTT	First Western Nat	MGL953P	Applegates	N229KAE	First Badgerline	N463TPR	Yellow Buses	N618VSS	Stagecoach West
M778PDC	Swiftlink	MHO101L	Taw & Torridge	N230KAE	First Badgerline	N464HRN	Stagecoach Devon	N622GAH	First Southern Nat
M802UYA	First Southern Nat	MHS4P	Stagecoach West	N231KAE	First Badgerline	N464TPR	Yellow Buses	N623GAH	First Southern Nat
M803UYA	First Southern Nat	MHS5P	Stagecoach West	N231YCT	Dawlish Cs	N465TPR	Yellow Buses	N626BDU	Wilts & Dorset
M804UYA	First Southern Nat	MIJ9795	Duchy Travel	N232KAE	First Badgerline	N466TPR	Yellow Buses	N643VSS	Stagecoach West
M805UYA	First Southern Nat	MIL2066	Grey Cars	N232WFJ	First Western Nat	N467TPR	Yellow Buses	N644VSS	Stagecoach West
M809FTT	First Western Nat	MIL2088	Grey Cars	N233KAE	First Badgerline	N468TPR	Yellow Buses	N663THO	James Bevan
M809RCP	Bennetts	MIL3010	Grey Cars	N233WFJ	First Western Nat	N469TPR	Yellow Buses	N708CYC	Trathens
M817ARV	Wilts & Dorset	MIL3012	Grey Cars	N234KAE	First Badgerline	N470TPR	Yellow Buses	N716KAM	Stagecoach West
M829HNS	Duchy Travel	MIL3292	Duchy Travel	N235KAE	First Badgerline	N471KHU	First Southern Nat	N717KAM	Stagecoach West
M831ATC	First Southern Nat	MIL3727	Hookways	N236KAE	First Badgerline	N471TPR	Yellow Buses	N718RDD	Stagecoach West
M832ATC	First Southern Nat	MIL8583	Turners	N237KAE	First Badgerline	N472JCA	Swiftlink	N719GRV	First Western Nat
M833ATC	First Cityline	MIL9750	Filer's	N238KAE	First Badgerline	N472KHU	First Southern Nat	N719RDD	Stagecoach West
M834ATC	First Cityline	MIL9751	Filer's	N239KAE	First Badgerline	N472TPR	Yellow Buses	N720RDD	Stagecoach West
M835ATC	First Badgerline	MJI6251	F T Williams	N240KAE	First Badgerline	N473KHU	First Southern Nat	N721RDD	Stagecoach West
M836ATC	First Badgerline	MJI7514	Wilts & Dorset	N241KAE	First Badgerline	N474KHU	First Southern Nat	N722RDD	Stagecoach West
M837ATC	First Cityline	MOU739R	Duchy Travel	N242KAE	First Badgerline	N482BFY	Swiftlink	N723RDD	Stagecoach West
M838ATC	First Cityline	MOU747R	A Bus	N243LHT	First Badgerline	N506BJA	Stagecoach Devon	N724RDD	Stagecoach West
M839ATC	First Cityline	MSL352X	Plymouth Citybus	N244LHT	First Badgerline	N507BJA	Stagecoach Devon	N725RDD	Stagecoach West
M840ATC	First Cityline	MUD27W	Yellow Buses	N245LHT	First Badgerline	N508BJA	Stagecoach Devon	N726RDD	Stagecoach West
M841ATC	First Cityline	MUR217L	Quantock	N246LHT	First Badgerline	N509BJA	Stagecoach Devon	N727RDD	Stagecoach West
M842ATC	First Cityline	N1FOR	Dartline	N247LHT	First Badgerline	N510BJA	Stagecoach Devon	N728RDD	Stagecoach West
M843ATC	First Badgerline	N3ARJ	Andy James	N248LHT	First Badgerline	N511BJA	Stagecoach Devon	N729RDD	Stagecoach West
M843EMW	Stagecoach West	N3YCL	Yellow Buses	N249LHT	First Badgerline	N512BJA	Stagecoach Devon	N730RDD	Stagecoach West
M844ATC	First Cityline	N7FTG	Excelsior	N250LHT	First Badgerline	N513BJA	Stagecoach Devon	N731RDD	Stagecoach West
M844EMW	Stagecoach West	N8FTG	Excelsior	N270KAM	Beeline	N514BJA	Stagecoach Devon	N731XDV	Stagecoach Devon
M845ATC	First Cityline	N9FTG	Excelsior	N271KAM	Beeline	N514BSR	Western Greyhound	N732RDD	Stagecoach West
M845CWS	Buglers	N10WAL	Wilts & Dorset	N272KAM	Beeline	N515BJA	Stagecoach Devon	N732XDV	Stagecoach Devon
M845EMW	Stagecoach West	N13WAL	Wilts & Dorset	N273KAM	Beeline	N516BJA	Stagecoach Devon	N733RDD	Stagecoach West
M846ATC	First Cityline	N14CJT	Turners	N274KAM	Beeline	N517BJA	Stagecoach Devon	N733XDV	Stagecoach Devon
M847ATC	First Cityline	N14WAL	Wilts & Dorset	N275KAM	Beeline	N518BJA	Stagecoach Devon	N734RDD	Stagecoach West
M847HDF	Stagecoach West	N15WAL	Wilts & Dorset	N275PDV	Plymouth Citybus	N539HAE	First Cityline	N734XDV	Stagecoach Devon
M848ATC	First Cityline	N16WAL	Wilts & Dorset	N276KAM	Beeline	N540HAE	First Cityline	N735RDD	Stagecoach West
M849ATC	First Cityline	N22BLU	First Western Nat	N276PDV	Plymouth Citybus	N541BFY	Swiftlink	N735XDV	Stagecoach Devon
M850ATC	First Cityline	N24EYB	Eastville	N277KAM	Beeline	N541CYA	Coombs	N736XDV	Stagecoach Devon
M851ATC	First Cityline	N28FWU	First Badgerline	N278PDV	Plymouth Citybus	N541HAE	First Cityline	N737XDV	Stagecoach Devon
M852ATC	First Cityline	N29FWU	First Badgerline	N279PDV	Plymouth Citybus	N542BFY	Swiftlink	N738XDV	Stagecoach Devon
M853ATC	First Cityline	N34FWU	First Badgerline	N280PDV	Plymouth Citybus	N542HAE	First Cityline	N739XDV	Stagecoach Devon
M854ATC	First Cityline	N40TCC	Dartline	N281PDV	Plymouth Citybus	N542UFX	Wilts & Dorset	N740XDV	Stagecoach Devon
M855ATC	First Cityline	N46OAE	First Southern Nat	N282PDV	Plymouth Citybus	N543BFY	Swiftlink	N742XDV	Stagecoach Devon
M856ATC	First Cityline	N91RVK	Stagecoach West	N283PDV	Plymouth Citybus	N543HAE	First Cityline	N743XDV	Stagecoach Devon
M857ATC	First Cityline	N101UTT	Plymouth Citybus	N284PDV	Plymouth Citybus	N543UFX	Wilts & Dorset	N744XDV	Stagecoach Devon
M857XHY	First Badgerline	N102UTT	Plymouth Citybus	N285PDV	Plymouth Citybus	N544HAE	First Cityline	N751DAK	Filer's
M858ATC	First Badgerline	N103UTT	Plymouth Citybus	N286PDV	Plymouth Citybus	N544UFX	Wilts & Dorset	N754CYA	Trathens
M859ATC	First Cityline	N104UTT	Plymouth Citybus	N287PDV	Plymouth Citybus	N545HAE	First Cityline	N755CYA	Trathens
M860ATC	First Cityline	N105UTT	Plymouth Citybus	N288PDV	Plymouth Citybus	N545UFX	Wilts & Dorset	N758CYA	Berry's
M861ATC	First Cityline	N106UTT	Plymouth Citybus	N289PDV	Plymouth Citybus	N546HAE	First Cityline	N762SAV	First Western Nat
M861TYC	Eastville	N107UTT	Plymouth Citybus	N307UTT	Plymouth Citybus	N546UFX	Wilts & Dorset	N770VTT	Seawards
M862ATC	First Cityline	N108UTT	Plymouth Citybus	N313NMC	Stagecoach West	N547HAE	First Cityline	N771VTT	Seawards
M862TYC	Eastville	N109UTT	Plymouth Citybus	N315BYA	Trathens	N547UFX	Wilts & Dorset	N801DNE	Stagecoach Devon
M863ATC	First Cityline	N110UTT	Plymouth Citybus	N316BYA	Trathens	N548HAE	First Cityline	N802DNE	Stagecoach Devon
M863TYC	Trathens	N112UTT	Plymouth Citybus	N316BYA	Trathens	N549LHU	First Cityline	N810VOD	First Western Nat
M864ATC	First Cityline	N121JHR	Thamesdown	N317BYA	Trathens	N550LHU	First Cityline	N811VOD	First Western Nat
M864TYC	Trathens	N122JHR	Thamesdown	N317NMC	Stagecoach West	N551LHU	First Cityline	N817DNE	Stagecoach West
M865ATC	First Cityline	N123DNV	Beeline	N318BYA	Trathens	N552LHU	First Cityline	N818DNE	Stagecoach West
M865TYC	Trathens	N123JHR	Thamesdown	N318NMC	Stagecoach West	N553LHU	First Cityline	N821KWS	First Southern Nat
M866ATC	First Cityline	N124JHR	Thamesdown	N319BYA	Trathens	N554LHU	First Cityline	N822KWS	First Southern Nat
M867ATC	First Cityline	N125LMW	Thamesdown	N319NHY	First Southern Nat	N556EYB	First Southern Nat	N855XMO	Taw & Torridge
M868ATC	First Cityline	N126LMW	Thamesdown	N319NMC	Stagecoach West	N556LHU	First Cityline	N859XMO	Bluebird Cs
M869ATC	First Cityline	N127LMW	Thamesdown	N320BYA	Berry's	N557EYB	First Southern Nat	N869XMO	Taw & Torridge
M870ATC	First Cityline	N128LMW	Thamesdown	N320NHY	First Southern Nat	N557LHU	First Cityline	N870XMO	Taw & Torridge
M871ATC	First Cityline	N166KAF	Truronian	N320NMC	Stagecoach West	N558EYB	First Southern Nat	N871XMO	Taw & Torridge
M872ATC	First Cityline	N167KAF	Truronian	N321NHY	First Southern Nat	N558LHU	First Cityline	N873XMO	Taw & Torridge
M873ATC	First Cityline	N168KAF	Truronian	N322NHY	First Southern Nat	N559EYB	First Southern Nat	N875HWS	First Cityline
M874ATC	First Cityline	N169KAF	Truronian	N322WCH	Wilts & Dorset	N559LHU	First Cityline	N876HWS	First Cityline
M882BEU	First Badgerline	N170KAF	Truronian	N335SDV	Seawards	N561EYB	First Southern Nat	N877HWS	First Cityline
M901LTT	First Southern Nat	N182CMJ	Stagecoach West	N367TJT	Yellow Buses	N561LHU	First Western Nat	N878HWS	First Cityline
M902LTT	First Western Nat	N183CMJ	Stagecoach Devon	N368TJT	Yellow Buses	N562LHU	First Western Nat	N879HWS	First Cityline
M934FHR	Thamesdown	N188GFR	Stagecoach Devon	N369TJT	Yellow Buses	N563LHU	First Western Nat	N880HWS	First Southern Nat
M935FHR	Thamesdown	N189GFR	Stagecoach Devon	N370TJT	Yellow Buses	N564LHU	First Western Nat	N881HWS	First Southern Nat
M940JJU	Peter Carol	N190GFR	Stagecoach Devon	N401LDF	Stagecoach West	N574CEH	First Badgerline	N882HWS	First Southern Nat
M947KRU	Wilts & Dorset	N199DYB	Berry's	N402LDF	Stagecoach West	N583WND	First Southern Nat	N883HWS	First Southern Nat
M950JBO	Stagecoach Devon	N201DYB	Dawlish Cs	N403LDF	Stagecoach West	N584WND	First Southern Nat	N884HWS	First Southern Nat
M968USC	First Badgerline	N201LCK	Dukes Travel	N404LDF	Stagecoach West	N585WND	First Southern Nat	N885HWS	First Southern Nat
MAZ6792	Tally Ho!	N202DYB	Dawlish Cs	N405LDF	Stagecoach West	N586WND	First Southern Nat	N886HWS	First Southern Nat
MBZ7140	First Southern Nat	N202LCK	Swanbrook	N406LDF	Stagecoach West	N599DWY	Stagecoach Devon	N887HWS	First Southern Nat
MCO658	Plymouth Citybus	N205LCK	Swanbrook	N407LDF	Stagecoach West	N604ADC	Beeline	N889HWS	First Southern Nat
MEU177P	Regency Tours	N206LCK	Dukes Travel	N408LDF	Stagecoach West	N605DOR	Coombs	N890HWS	First Southern Nat

N891HWS	First Southern Nat
N892HWS	First Southern Nat
N893HWS	First Southern Nat
N894HWS	First Southern Nat
N895HWS	First Southern Nat
N895VEG	Turners
N896HWS	First Southern Nat
N897HWS	First Southern Nat
N898HWS	First Southern Nat
N899HWS	First Southern Nat
N901HWS	First Southern Nat
N902HWS	First Southern Nat
N903HWS	First Southern Nat
N904HWS	First Southern Nat
N905HWS	First Southern Nat
N906HWS	First Southern Nat
N907HWS	First Southern Nat
N913KHW	First Southern Nat
N914KHW	First Southern Nat
N967BYC	Coombs
N970BYC	Coombs
N978NAP	Stagecoach Devon
N979NAP	Stagecoach Devon
N980NAP	Stagecoach Devon
N981NAP	Stagecoach Devon
N982NAP	Stagecoach Devon
N988KUS	DAC Coaches
N990AEF	Swiftlink
N993LFH	Geoff Willetts
NCV942X	Truronian
NDB356	Quantock
NDE147Y	Cottrell's
NDZ3152	Stagecoach Devon
NDZ3153	Stagecoach Devon
NER621	First Western Nat
NFB113R	A Bus
NFB115R	Bath Bus Company
NFL649R	Hambleys
NFX132P	Yellow Buses
NFX133P	Yellow Buses
NFX134P	Yellow Buses
NFX135P	Yellow Buses
NFX136P	Yellow Buses
NFX137P	Yellow Buses
NIL1387	Beeline
NIL2460	Hookways
NIL4981	Bakers Dolphin
NIL4982	Bakers Dolphin
NIL4983	Bakers Dolphin
NIL4984	Bakers Dolphin
NIL4985	Bakers Dolphin
NIL4986	Bakers Dolphin
NIL5381	Bakers Dolphin
NIL5382	Bakers Dolphin
NIL5651	DAC Coaches
NIL5652	DAC Coaches
NIL9886	Beeline
NIW8290	Hookways
NIW8794	Curnan
NLJ271	Quantock
NMW329X	Axe Valley
NNC853P	Quantock
NNK808P	Hopley's
NNK809P	Truronian
NNN9P	Quantock
NOK43	Taw & Torridge
NPA228W	Safeway
NRS307W	First Western Nat
NRS320W	First Western Nat
NTC129Y	First Badgerline
NTC130Y	First Badgerline
NTC131Y	First Badgerline
NTC132Y	Stagecoach West
NTC133Y	First Badgerline
NTC134Y	First Badgerline
NTC135Y	First Badgerline
NTC136Y	First Cityline
NTC137Y	First Badgerline
NTC138Y	First Cityline
NTC139Y	First Southern Nat
NTC140Y	First Southern Nat
NTC141Y	First Southern Nat
NTC142Y	First Cityline
NTC573R	First Western Nat
NTH156X	First Western Nat
NUB93V	Quantock

NUD106L	Citytours
NUW585Y	Stagecoach Devon
NUW630Y	Stagecoach Devon
NUW636Y	Stagecoach West
NUW660Y	Stagecoach Devon
NUW669Y	Stagecoach West
NWW163K	Caradon
NXI5358	Wilts & Dorset
NXI608	Citytours
NYC398V	Wakes
OAE954M	A Bus
OBO631X	Hookways
OCK997K	First Western Nat
ODF561	Pullham's
ODV203W	Plymouth Citybus
ODV283P	Taw & Torridge
ODV287P	Taw & Torridge
ODV404W	Quantock
ODZ8911	First Southern Nat
ODZ8912	First Southern Nat
ODZ8913	First Southern Nat
ODZ8914	First Southern Nat
ODZ8915	First Southern Nat
ODZ8916	First Cityline
ODZ8917	First Cityline
ODZ8918	First Cityline
ODZ8919	First Cityline
ODZ8920	First Cityline
ODZ8921	First Cityline
ODZ8922	First Cityline
ODZ8923	First Cityline
ODZ8924	First Cityline
OEL232P	Wilts & Dorset
OFA2P	Wakes
OFS668Y	South Gloucestershire
OFS701Y	Bennetts
OFS702Y	Bennetts
OGL262R	Taw & Torridge
OHR183R	Thamesdown
OHR184R	A Bus
OHV691Y	Stagecoach West
OHV707Y	Applegates
OHV729Y	Stagecoach Devon
OHV738Y	Stagecoach Devon
OHV766Y	South Gloucestershire
OHV768Y	Applegates
OHV798Y	South Gloucestershire
OIL9262	South Gloucestershire
OIL9263	South Gloucestershire
OIL9264	South Gloucestershire
OJD45R	Tally Ho!
OJD51R	Tally Ho!
OJD54R	Tally Ho!
OJD56R	Tally Ho!
OJD58R	Tally Ho!
OJD59R	Tally Ho!
OJD77R	Tally Ho!
OJD83R	Tally Ho!
OJD84R	Tally Ho!
OJD405R	Regency Tours
OJD469R	Regency Tours
OJI1875	Wilts & Dorset
OJI2834	Keith Webber
OJI8786	First Southern Nat
OPS550X	Wakes
ORV991	Quantock
OTA290G	First Western Nat
OUF359W	Bakers Dolphin
OUF863W	Yellow Buses
OYY3	Turners
P4BBC	Bluebird Cs
P9WAC	Pullham's
P15CJT	Turners
P16CJT	Turners
P87JYC	Coombs
P87SAF	Hopley's
P89JYC	Coombs
P92URG	Stagecoach West
P106WJO	Liskeard & District
P107WJO	Liskeard & District
P137XFW	Curnan
P151SMW	Thamesdown
P152SMW	Thamesdown
P153SMW	Thamesdown
P154SMW	Thamesdown

P155SMW	Thamesdown
P156SMW	Thamesdown
P157SMW	Thamesdown
P158SMW	Thamesdown
P159VHR	Thamesdown
P160VHR	Thamesdown
P161VHR	Thamesdown
P179LYB	First Southern Nat
P180LYB	First Southern Nat
P181LYB	First Southern Nat
P182LYB	First Southern Nat
P183LYB	First Southern Nat
P183RSC	Swiftlink
P187TGD	First Western Nat
P200TCC	Castleways
P227CTV	Wilts & Dorset
P228CTV	Wilts & Dorset
P229CTV	Wilts & Dorset
P230CTV	Wilts & Dorset
P231CTV	Wilts & Dorset
P232CTV	Wilts & Dorset
P233CTV	Wilts & Dorset
P234BFJ	First Western Nat
P234CTV	Wilts & Dorset
P235CTA	First Western Nat
P235CTV	Wilts & Dorset
P236CTA	First Western Nat
P236CTV	Wilts & Dorset
P237CTV	Wilts & Dorset
P238CTV	Wilts & Dorset
P239CTV	Wilts & Dorset
P240CTV	Wilts & Dorset
P241CTV	Wilts & Dorset
P251PAE	First Badgerline
P252PAE	First Badgerline
P253PAE	First Badgerline
P254PAE	First Badgerline
P255PAE	First Badgerline
P256PAE	First Badgerline
P257PAE	First Badgerline
P258PAE	First Badgerline
P259PAE	First Badgerline
P260PAE	First Badgerline
P261PAE	First Badgerline
P262PAE	First Badgerline
P263PAE	First Badgerline
P264PAE	First Badgerline
P308CTT	Plymouth Citybus
P314GTO	Swiftlink
P317EFL	Stagecoach West
P317GTO	Swiftlink
P318EFL	Stagecoach West
P319DOP	Wilts & Dorset
P319EFL	Stagecoach West
P321ARU	Yellow Buses
P322ARU	Yellow Buses
P323ARU	Yellow Buses
P352ARU	Yellow Buses
P353ARU	Yellow Buses
P361UFH	Pullham's
P427ORL	First Western Nat
P428ORL	First Western Nat
P429JDT	Dartline
P429ORL	First Western Nat
P430ORL	First Western Nat
P431ORL	First Western Nat
P432ORL	First Western Nat
P433ORL	First Western Nat
P434ORL	First Western Nat
P435ORL	First Western Nat
P436ORL	First Western Nat
P437ORL	First Western Nat
P438ORL	First Western Nat
P439ORL	First Western Nat
P440ORL	First Western Nat
P441TCV	First Western Nat
P442KYC	First Southern Nat
P442TCV	First Western Nat
P443KYC	First Southern Nat
P443TCV	First Western Nat
P444TCV	First Western Nat
P445KYC	First Southern Nat
P445TCV	First Western Nat
P446KYC	First Southern Nat
P446TCV	First Western Nat
P447KYC	First Southern Nat

P448KYC	First Southern Nat
P452SCV	Truronian
P453SCV	Truronian
P454SCV	Truronian
P455SCV	Truronian
P473BLJ	Yellow Buses
P473MNA	Swiftlink
P474BLJ	Yellow Buses
P474MNA	Swiftlink
P521PRL	First Western Nat
P522PRL	First Western Nat
P536YEU	Buglers
P563MSX	Stagecoach Devon
P564MSX	Stagecoach Devon
P618FTV	Pullham's
P644TMV	First Western Nat
P655UFB	First Badgerline
P656UFB	First Badgerline
P657UFB	First Badgerline
P658UFB	First Badgerline
P659UFB	First Badgerline
P660UFB	First Badgerline
P689VHU	Beeline
P693UAE	Wilts & Dorset
P701BTA	Stagecoach Devon
P702BTA	Stagecoach Devon
P703BTA	Stagecoach Devon
P704BTA	Stagecoach Devon
P705BTA	Stagecoach Devon
P706BTA	Stagecoach Devon
P707BTA	Stagecoach Devon
P708BTA	Stagecoach Devon
P709BTA	Stagecoach Devon
P710BTA	Stagecoach Devon
P711BTA	Stagecoach Devon
P712BTA	Stagecoach Devon
P713BTA	Stagecoach Devon
P714BTA	Stagecoach Devon
P719EOD	Seawards
P725JYA	Bakers Dolphin
P726JYA	Bakers Dolphin
P727JYA	Berry's
P741HND	Bath Bus Company
P742HND	Bath Bus Company
P748HND	Bath Bus Company
P758FOD	Stagecoach Devon
P760FOD	Stagecoach Devon
P762FOD	Stagecoach Devon
P801XTA	Stagecoach Devon
P802XTA	Stagecoach Devon
P803XTA	Stagecoach Devon
P804XTA	Stagecoach Devon
P805XTA	Stagecoach Devon
P806XTA	Stagecoach Devon
P819GNC	Stagecoach West
P820GNC	Stagecoach West
P821FVU	Stagecoach West
P822FVU	Stagecoach West
P823FVU	Stagecoach West
P824FVU	Stagecoach West
P825FVU	Stagecoach West
P826FVU	Stagecoach West
P827FVU	Stagecoach West
P828FVU	Stagecoach West
P828KTP	First Badgerline
P829KTP	First Badgerline
P853DTT	First Western Nat
P892FMO	Yellow Buses
P901SMR	Stagecoach West
P902SMR	Stagecoach West
P903SMR	Stagecoach West
P904SMR	Stagecoach West
P905SMR	Stagecoach West
P906SMR	Stagecoach West
P907SMR	Stagecoach West
P908SMR	Stagecoach West
P909SMR	Stagecoach West
P910SMR	Stagecoach West
P911SMR	Stagecoach West
P912SMR	Stagecoach West
P913SMR	Stagecoach West
P914SMR	Stagecoach West
P926KYC	Trathens
P927KYC	Trathens
P928KYC	Dawlish Cs
P929KYC	Dawlish Cs

P934KYC	Dartline
P944RWS	First Southern Nat
P945RWS	First Southern Nat
P946RWS	First Southern Nat
P985OTP	A Bus
PAF189X	Truronian
PBZ9154	Belle Vue
PCW675P	Keith Webber
PDF567	Pullham's
PEU518R	First Western Nat
PFX572K	Taw & Torridge
PGP201L	Duchy Travel
PHT114Y	Bakers Dolphin
PHT885Y	Applegates
PHY697S	First Western Nat
PHY698S	Buglers
PIB2470	Berry's
PIB3360	Berry's
PIB4019	Berry's
PIB5145	Yellow Buses
PIB5767	Berry's
PIL5345	Thamesdown
PIL5346	Thamesdown
PIL6501	Carmel Coaches
PIL6581	Hookways
PJI2803	Grey Cars
PJI2804	Grey Cars
PJI2805	Grey Cars
PJI4713	Taw & Torridge
PJI5013	Eastville
PJI5014	F T Williams
PJI5016	Eastville
PJI7002	Wilts & Dorset
PJT524W	Tally Ho!
POI4905	Shaftesbury & Dist
PPH471R	A Bus
PRC849X	Truronian
PRC856X	Truronian
PSO178W	Boomerang Bus Co
PSU527	South Gloucestershire
PSV244	Fosseway
PTT99R	First Western Nat
PWJ497X	Wakes
PWX240X	Grey Cars
PWY38W	First Western Nat
PWY41W	Western Greyhound
PXI1421	Keith Webber
PYA646P	Berry's
R1TRU	Truronian
R2CJT	Turners
R3CJT	Turners
R9BBC	Bluebird Cs
R10TAW	Taw & Torridge
R12SBK	Swanbrook
R18CJT	Turners
R19CJT	Turners
R30ARJ	Andy James
R30CJT	Turners
R35WDA	Swiftlink
R37DPW	Yellow Buses
R37GDE	Wilts & Dorset
R57JSG	Andy James
R83RBY	Peter Carol
R100PAR	Swanbrook
R101NTA	Stagecoach Devon
R102NTA	Stagecoach Devon
R103NTA	Stagecoach Devon
R104NTA	Stagecoach Devon
R105NTA	Stagecoach Devon
R107NTA	Stagecoach Devon
R108NTA	Stagecoach Devon
R109NTA	Stagecoach Devon
R110NTA	Stagecoach Devon
R112NTA	Stagecoach Devon
R113NTA	Stagecoach Devon
R113OFJ	Plymouth Citybus
R114NTA	Stagecoach Devon
R114OFJ	Plymouth Citybus
R115NTA	Stagecoach Devon
R115OFJ	Plymouth Citybus
R116NTA	Stagecoach Devon
R116OFJ	Plymouth Citybus
R117OFJ	Plymouth Citybus
R118OFJ	Plymouth Citybus
R119OFJ	Plymouth Citybus
R120OFJ	Plymouth Citybus

R121OFJ	Plymouth Citybus	R463CCV	First Western Nat	R708BAE	First Cityline	REO207L	Polerro Tram Co	S632JRU	Wilts & Dorset
R122OFJ	Plymouth Citybus	R464CCV	First Western Nat	R709BAE	First Cityline	RFC13T	Yellow Buses	S659ETT	Bluebird Cs
R123OFJ	Plymouth Citybus	R475NPR	Yellow Buses	R710BAE	First Cityline	RHE987R	First Western Nat	S665AAE	First Cityline
R124OFJ	Plymouth Citybus	R476NPR	Yellow Buses	R710YFL	Wilts & Dorset	RHT503S	First Western Nat	S667AAE	First Cityline
R125OFJ	Plymouth Citybus	R477CKN	Applegates	R711BAE	First Cityline	RIB8745	Yellow Buses	S668AAE	First Cityline
R126OFJ	Plymouth Citybus	R477NPR	Yellow Buses	R712BAE	First Cityline	RIL1053	First Southern Nat	S669AAE	First Cityline
R154NPR	Wilts & Dorset	R478NPR	Yellow Buses	R713BAE	First Cityline	RIL1056	First Southern Nat	S670AAE	First Cityline
R155NPR	Wilts & Dorset	R479MCW	Stagecoach Devon	R714BAE	First Badgerline	RIL1069	First Southern Nat	S671AAE	First Cityline
R156NPR	Wilts & Dorset	R479NPR	Yellow Buses	R715BAE	First Badgerline	RIL1203	Beeline	S671ETT	Dartline
R164HHK	Stagecoach Devon	R480MCW	Stagecoach Devon	R716BAE	First Badgerline	RIL2102	Citytours	S672AAE	First Cityline
R170SUT	James Bevan	R480NPR	Yellow Buses	R717BAE	First Badgerline	RIL2103	Citytours	S673AAE	First Cityline
R199WYD	Berry's	R481MCW	Stagecoach Devon	R718BAE	First Cityline	RIL3706	F T Williams	S674AAE	First Cityline
R200PAR	Swanbrook	R481NPR	Yellow Buses	R719RAD	First Cityline	RIL3899	Tally Ho!	S675AAE	First Cityline
R202WYD	Berry's	R482MCW	Stagecoach Devon	R748SDF	Pulham's	RIL5088	Curnan	S676AAE	First Cityline
R203DHB	Stagecoach West	R482NPR	Yellow Buses	R751BDV	Stagecoach Devon	RIL6390	Shaftesbury & Dist	S677AAE	First Cityline
R204DHB	Stagecoach West	R500BEN	Bennetts	R767HOY	Beeline	RIL9429	Shaftesbury & Dist	S678AAE	First Cityline
R205DHB	Stagecoach West	R501NPR	First Southern Nat	R778MFH	Bakers Dolphin	RIL9772	Boomerang Bus Co	S679AAE	First Cityline
R206DHB	Stagecoach West	R502NPR	First Southern Nat	R801YUD	Stagecoach Devon	RIL9773	Boomerang Bus Co	S680AAE	First Cityline
R207DHB	Stagecoach West	R503NPR	First Southern Nat	R803YUD	Stagecoach Devon	RIL9774	Boomerang Bus Co	S681AAE	First Cityline
R208DHB	Stagecoach West	R504NPR	First Southern Nat	R804YUD	Stagecoach Devon	RIL9776	Boomerang Bus Co	S682AAE	First Cityline
R208WYD	Dawlish Cs	R505NPR	First Southern Nat	R805YUD	Stagecoach Devon	RIL9865	Beard	S683AAE	First Cityline
R209WYD	Dawlish Cs	R506NPR	First Southern Nat	R807HWS	Andy James	RJI5716	Bakers Dolphin	S684AAE	First Cityline
R214NFX	Wilts & Dorset	R507NPR	First Southern Nat	R807JDV	Stagecoach Devon	RJI8602	Beeline	S685AAE	First Cityline
R215NFX	Wilts & Dorset	R508NPR	First Southern Nat	R807YUD	Stagecoach Devon	RJI8606	Filer's	S686AAE	First Cityline
R221MSA	First Badgerline	R531CPW	Yellow Buses	R808HWS	Andy James	RJI8611	Carmel Coaches	S687AAE	First Cityline
R222AJP	A Bus	R550JDF	Stagecoach West	R808YUD	Stagecoach West	RLN230W	Taw & Torridge	S688AAE	First Badgerline
R222MSA	First Badgerline	R551JDF	Stagecoach West	R809HWS	Western Greyhound	RNY313Y	Wilts & Dorset	S689AAE	First Badgerline
R252SDT	Andy James	R552JDF	Stagecoach West	R809YUD	Stagecoach West	ROI1229	Peter Carol	S690AAE	First Badgerline
R261OFJ	Trathens	R553JDF	Stagecoach West	R810HWS	Western Greyhound	ROI1913	Peter Carol	S691AAE	First Badgerline
R262OFJ	Trathens	R554JDF	Stagecoach West	R810YUD	Stagecoach West	ROI6774	Peter Carol	S720AFB	First Cityline
R262THL	Peter Carol	R600BEN	Bennetts	R811YUD	Stagecoach West	ROI8235	Peter Carol	S721AFB	First Cityline
R263OFJ	Trathens	R601KDD	Stagecoach Devon	R812YUD	Stagecoach West	ROI8358	Peter Carol	S722AFB	First Cityline
R264OFJ	Trathens	R601NFX	Wilts & Dorset	R813HWS	First Southern Nat	RSG325V	First Western Nat	S723AFB	First Cityline
R275LDE	Citytours	R601SWO	Stagecoach West	R814HWS	First Southern Nat	RSG815V	First Southern Nat	S724AFB	First Cityline
R297AYB	First Badgerline	R602KDD	Stagecoach Devon	R815UOK	Wilts & Dorset	RTH926S	First Western Nat	S725AFB	First Cityline
R298AYB	First Badgerline	R602NFX	Wilts & Dorset	R816GMU	Stagecoach Devon	RTH929S	First Western Nat	S748XYA	Grey Cars
R299AYB	First Badgerline	R602SWO	Stagecoach West	R817GMU	Stagecoach Devon	RTH931S	First Badgerline	S750RNE	Dukes Travel
R300PAR	Swanbrook	R603KDD	Stagecoach Devon	R851YDV	First Western Nat	RUA451W	Marchants	S817KPR	First Southern Nat
R304JAF	First Western Nat	R603NFX	Wilts & Dorset	R852TFJ	First Western Nat	RUA452W	Marchants	S818KPR	First Southern Nat
R305JAF	First Western Nat	R603SWO	Stagecoach West	R853TFJ	First Western Nat	RUA457W	Marchants	S819KPR	First Southern Nat
R307JAF	First Western Nat	R604KDD	Stagecoach Devon	R901BOU	First Badgerline	RUA458W	Bennetts	S820KPR	First Southern Nat
R308JAF	First Western Nat	R604NFX	Wilts & Dorset	R901FDV	Stagecoach Devon	RUE300W	DAC Coaches	S821KPR	First Southern Nat
R309JAF	First Western Nat	R605NFX	Wilts & Dorset	R902BOU	First Badgerline	RUF970M	Yellow Buses	S822KPR	First Southern Nat
R309STA	Plymouth Citybus	R606KDD	Stagecoach Devon	R902JDV	Stagecoach Devon	RUH346	First Western Nat	S823KPR	First Southern Nat
R310JAF	First Western Nat	R606NFX	Wilts & Dorset	R903BOU	First Badgerline	S18RED	Carmel Coaches	S824WYD	First Southern Nat
R314NGM	Thamesdown	R607KDD	Stagecoach Devon	R903JDV	Stagecoach Devon	S30ARJ	Western Greyhound	S825WYD	First Southern Nat
R315NGM	Thamesdown	R608KDD	Stagecoach Devon	R904BOU	First Badgerline	S34BMR	Western Greyhound	S838VAG	Thamesdown
R317NGM	Thamesdown	R608NFX	Wilts & Dorset	R904JDV	Stagecoach Devon	S50CJT	Turners	S853PKH	Turners
R319NGM	Thamesdown	R608OTA	Seawards	R905BOU	First Badgerline	S60CJT	Turners	S863LRU	First Southern Nat
R319NRU	Yellow Buses	R609KDD	Stagecoach Devon	R906BOU	First Badgerline	S100PAF	Hambleys	S864LRU	First Southern Nat
R326NRU	Yellow Buses	R609NFX	Wilts & Dorset	R907BOU	First Badgerline	S104JGB	Trathens	S865NOD	First Western Nat
R327NRU	Yellow Buses	R609OTA	Seawards	R907NFX	Wilts & Dorset	S105JGB	Trathens	S866NOD	First Western Nat
R329NRU	Yellow Buses	R611KDD	Stagecoach Devon	R908BOU	First Badgerline	S111AJP	A Bus	S867NOD	First Western Nat
R338NRU	Yellow Buses	R611NFX	Wilts & Dorset	R909BOU	First Badgerline	S117JFJ	Stagecoach Devon	S868NOD	First Western Nat
R339NRU	Yellow Buses	R612KDD	Stagecoach Devon	R910BOU	First Badgerline	S118JFJ	Stagecoach Devon	S869NOD	First Western Nat
R340MPR	Yellow Buses	R612NFX	Wilts & Dorset	R910NFX	Wilts & Dorset	S127FTA	Plymouth Citybus	S870NOD	First Western Nat
R341LPR	Yellow Buses	R613KDD	Stagecoach Devon	R912BOU	First Badgerline	S139ATA	Filer's	S871NOD	First Western Nat
R350LPR	Yellow Buses	R613NFX	Wilts & Dorset	R913BOU	First Badgerline	S150SET	Peter Carol	S872NOD	First Western Nat
R351LPR	Yellow Buses	R614KDD	Stagecoach Devon	R913ULA	Dawlish Cs	S162BMR	Thamesdown	S923KOD	Dartline
R354NRU	Yellow Buses	R614NFX	Wilts & Dorset	R914BOU	First Badgerline	S181BMR	Thamesdown	S924KOD	Dartline
R355NRU	Yellow Buses	R615KDD	Stagecoach Devon	R915BOU	First Badgerline	S182BMR	Thamesdown	S924PDD	Stagecoach West
R372XYD	Bakers Dolphin	R615NFX	Wilts & Dorset	R915GMW	Stagecoach West	S183BMR	Thamesdown	S925KOD	Dartline
R373XYD	Bakers Dolphin	R616KDD	Stagecoach Devon	R916BOU	First Badgerline	S184BMR	Thamesdown	S925PDD	Stagecoach West
R380XYD	Berry's	R616NFX	Wilts & Dorset	R916GMW	Stagecoach West	S185BMR	Thamesdown	S926KOD	Dartline
R400BEN	Bennetts	R617NFX	Wilts & Dorset	R917BOU	First Badgerline	S186BMR	Thamesdown	S926PDD	Stagecoach West
R431FWT	Marchants	R618NFX	Wilts & Dorset	R917GMW	Stagecoach West	S233FGD	Swiftlink	S927PDD	Stagecoach West
R432FWT	Marchants	R619NFX	Wilts & Dorset	R918BOU	First Badgerline	S234FGD	Swiftlink	S928PDD	Stagecoach West
R445CCV	First Western Nat	R620NFX	Wilts & Dorset	R918GMW	Stagecoach West	S311SCV	First Western Nat	S929PDD	Stagecoach West
R447CCV	First Western Nat	R621NFX	Wilts & Dorset	R919BOU	First Badgerline	S312SCV	First Western Nat	S930PDD	Stagecoach West
R448CCV	First Western Nat	R622NFX	Wilts & Dorset	R920COU	First Badgerline	S313SCV	First Western Nat	S944WYB	Dartline
R449CCV	First Western Nat	R625GFS	Swiftlink	R920ULA	Dawlish Cs	S314SRL	First Western Nat	SAD122R	Keith Webber
R450CCV	First Western Nat	R632VYB	Bakers Dolphin	R943LHT	First Southern Nat	S315SRL	First Western Nat	SAZ2511	Tally Ho!
R451CCV	First Western Nat	R650TDV	First Western Nat	R964MDV	Dartline	S340WYB	First Southern Nat	SFJ106R	First Western Nat
R452CCV	First Western Nat	R652TYA	Wakes	R991HNS	Swiftlink	S501SRL	Western Greyhound	SGR790V	Truronian
R452FWT	Marchants	R661NHY	First Cityline	R997RHL	Tilley's	S502SRL	Western Greyhound	SHO800	Quantock
R453CCV	First Western Nat	R662NHY	First Cityline	R998FNW	Yellow Buses	S503SRL	Western Greyhound	SHP696R	Yellow Buses
R454CCV	First Western Nat	R663NHY	First Cityline	RAN646R	Grey Cars	S549SCV	Truronian	SIB4903	Wilts & Dorset
R455YDT	Curnan	R664NHY	First Cityline	RAW19R	Tally Ho!	S623JRU	Wilts & Dorset	SIB5373	Wilts & Dorset
R456CCV	First Western Nat	R668DNS	Western Greyhound	RAW777X	Tally Ho!	S624JRU	Wilts & Dorset	SIB6442	Yellow Buses
R457CCV	First Western Nat	R701BAE	First Cityline	RAZ5279	Yellow Buses	S625JRU	Wilts & Dorset	SIB8357	Buglers
R458CCV	First Western Nat	R702BAE	First Cityline	RAZ8598	Tally Ho!	S626JRU	Wilts & Dorset	SIB9309	Berry's
R459CCV	First Western Nat	R703BAE	First Cityline	RBO506Y	A Bus	S627JRU	Wilts & Dorset	SIB9313	Berry's
R460CCV	First Western Nat	R704BAE	First Cityline	RBO507Y	Swiftlink	S628JRU	Wilts & Dorset	SIL3066	Grey Cars
R460VOP	First Badgerline	R705BAE	First Cityline	RBO508Y	A Bus	S629JRU	Wilts & Dorset	SIL4460	Grey Cars
R461CCV	First Western Nat	R706BAE	First Cityline	RCV283R	Quantock	S630JRU	Wilts & Dorset	SIL4465	Tally Ho!
R462CCV	First Western Nat	R707BAE	First Cityline	RCV493M	Hookways	S631JRU	Wilts & Dorset	SIL4466	Grey Cars

Reg	Operator	Reg	Operator	Reg	Operator	Reg	Operator	Reg	Operator
SIL4470	Grey Cars	T641AJT	Wilts & Dorset	TNJ998S	Citytours	V2EFA	Applegates	V947DFH	Stagecoach West
SIL6715	Bakers Dolphin	T642AJT	Wilts & Dorset	TPD112X	Eastville	V10SAF	Currian	V948DDG	Stagecoach West
SIL6716	Bakers Dolphin	T643AJT	Wilts & Dorset	TPD120X	Eastville	V54MOD	DAC Coaches	V949DDG	Stagecoach West
SIL7914	Wilts & Dorset	T644AJT	Wilts & Dorset	TPD125X	Eastville	V116GWP	Beeline	V950DDG	Stagecoach West
SIW1909	Wilts & Dorset	T645AJT	Wilts & Dorset	TPL762X	Truronian	V187EAM	Thamesdown	V951DDG	Stagecoach West
SJI4783	Western Greyhound	T646AJT	Wilts & Dorset	TPR354	First Southern Nat	V188EAM	Thamesdown	V952DDG	Stagecoach West
SJI8117	Hookways	T647AJT	Wilts & Dorset	TRX615	Buglers	V189EAM	Thamesdown	V953DDG	Stagecoach West
SJR817Y	Bennetts	T648AJT	Wilts & Dorset	TSO17X	Marchants	V190EAM	Thamesdown	V954DDG	Stagecoach West
SLH42W	Bakers Dolphin	T649AJT	Wilts & Dorset	TSO31X	Marchants	V191EAM	Thamesdown	V955DDG	Stagecoach West
SMY635F	Wilts & Dorset	T728REU	First Badgerline	TSU603	Trathens	V196LFJ	First Western Nat	V956DDG	Stagecoach West
SNJ590R	Currian	T729REU	First Badgerline	TSV302	Hopley's	V200DCC	Castleways	V957DDG	Stagecoach West
SNJ593R	Currian	T730REU	First Badgerline	TTT162X	Plymouth Citybus	V393SVV	River Link	V957EOD	Filer's
SNN158R	Truronian	T731REU	First Badgerline	TTT163X	Plymouth Citybus	V444AJP	A Bus	V958DDG	Stagecoach West
STW33W	A Bus	T761JYB	Bakers Dolphin	TTT164X	Plymouth Citybus	V448DYB	Coombs	V959DDG	Stagecoach West
STW34W	First Western Nat	T762JYB	Bakers Dolphin	TTT165X	Plymouth Citybus	V450FOT	Somerbus	V960DDG	Stagecoach West
SUR284R	Keith Webber	T766JYB	Berry's	TTT166X	Plymouth Citybus	V483XJV	Dawlish Cs	V961DFH	Stagecoach West
SVJ777S	Seawards	T789RDV	First Western Nat	TTT167X	Plymouth Citybus	V651DFX	Wilts & Dorset	V962DFH	Stagecoach West
SVL175W	F T Williams	T801RHW	First Cityline	TTT168X	Plymouth Citybus	V652DFX	Wilts & Dorset	V980XUB	First Badgerline
T2TRU	Truronian	T826AFX	First Southern Nat	TTT169X	Plymouth Citybus	V653DFX	Wilts & Dorset	VAB893R	Taw & Torridge
T7BBC	Bluebird Cs	T827AFX	First Southern Nat	TTT170X	Plymouth Citybus	V654DFX	Wilts & Dorset	VAD141	Pullham's
T12SBK	Swanbrook	T828AFX	First Southern Nat	TTT171X	Plymouth Citybus	V655DFX	Wilts & Dorset	VBC984X	Bakers Dolphin
T30ARJ	Andy James	T829AFX	First Southern Nat	TTY696Y	Tally Ho!	V656DFX	Wilts & Dorset	VBG114V	First Southern Nat
T32JCV	Truronian	T830RYC	First Southern Nat	TVD862R	Berry's	V657DFX	Wilts & Dorset	VBG115V	First Western Nat
T34JCV	Truronian	T831RYC	First Southern Nat	TWH698T	Thamesdown	V658DFX	Wilts & Dorset	VBG118V	First Southern Nat
T35JCV	Truronian	T867RGA	Trathens	TWH699T	Thamesdown	V659DFX	Wilts & Dorset	VBG120V	First Southern Nat
T35RJL	Wilts & Dorset	T868RGA	Trathens	TWN936S	• First Western Nat	V660DFX	Wilts & Dorset	VBG127V	First Western Nat
T59AUA	Bennetts	T869RGA	Trathens	TWS915T	First Western Nat	V661DFX	Wilts & Dorset	VDF365	Pullham's
T64BHY	First Southern Nat	T870RGA	Trathens	UAL103L	Keith Webber	V662DFX	Wilts & Dorset	VDV111S	First Southern Nat
T104JBC	First Southern Nat	T871RGA	Trathens	UAR586W	First Western Nat	V663DFX	Wilts & Dorset	VDV114S	First Western Nat
T105JBC	First Southern Nat	T872RGA	Trathens	UAR588W	First Western Nat	V664DFX	Wilts & Dorset	VDV116S	First Western Nat
T106JBC	First Southern Nat	T920LEU	Bakers Dolphin	UAR589W	First Western Nat	V665DFX	Wilts & Dorset	VDV117S	First Western Nat
T117AUA	Peter Carol	T948UEU	First Southern Nat	UAR590W	First Western Nat	V666DFX	Wilts & Dorset	VDV118S	First Western Nat
T118AUA	Peter Carol	T953RTA	Seawards	UAR595W	First Western Nat	V667DFX	Wilts & Dorset	VDV119S	First Western Nat
T128EFJ	Plymouth Citybus	T979OGA	DAC Coaches	UAR597W	First Western Nat	V668DFX	Wilts & Dorset	VDV120S	First Western Nat
T129EFJ	Plymouth Citybus	TAD24W	Dukes Travel	UBC464X	Marchants	V669DFX	Wilts & Dorset	VDV121S	First Western Nat
T12TRU	Truronian	TAH276W	Western Greyhound	UCT838	Bluebird Cs	V670DFX	Wilts & Dorset	VDV122S	First Southern Nat
T130EFJ	Plymouth Citybus	TAY888X	Bakers Dolphin	UDF936	Pullham's	V671FEL	Wilts & Dorset	VDV134S	First Southern Nat
T131EFJ	Plymouth Citybus	TAZ4992	A Bus	UDL671S	Wilts & Dorset	V672FEL	Wilts & Dorset	VDV135S	Stagecoach Devon
T132EFJ	Plymouth Citybus	TAZ4993	A Bus	UDL674S	Wilts & Dorset	V673FEL	Wilts & Dorset	VDV137S	First Badgerline
T133EFJ	Plymouth Citybus	TAZ6963	Buglers	UDZ1287	Keith Webber	V674FEL	Wilts & Dorset	VDV141S	First Western Nat
T134EFJ	Plymouth Citybus	TDZ3265	First Badgerline	UEL489	Wilts & Dorset	V675FEL	Wilts & Dorset	VDV142S	First Southern Nat
T135EFJ	Plymouth Citybus	TFO319	Western Greyhound	UFX330	First Southern Nat	V676FEL	Wilts & Dorset	VDV143S	First Badgerline
T136EFJ	Plymouth Citybus	THX220S	First Western Nat	UFX857S	Bath Bus Company	V677FEL	Wilts & Dorset	VDV144S	First Western Nat
T137EFJ	Plymouth Citybus	TIB8702	Keith Webber	UFX860S	First Badgerline	V678FEL	Wilts & Dorset	VEU231T	Stagecoach West
T138EFJ	Plymouth Citybus	TIJ687	Quantock	UFX940	First Southern Nat	V679FEL	Wilts & Dorset	VEX288X	First Western Nat
T139EFJ	Plymouth Citybus	TIL1253	Tilley's	UHW661	First Western Nat	V680FEL	Wilts & Dorset	VIB5239	Tally Ho!
T140EFJ	Plymouth Citybus	TIL1254	Tilley's	UHY384	A Bus	V681FEL	Wilts & Dorset	VJI3968	Wilts & Dorset
T158ALJ	Wilts & Dorset	TIL1255	Tilley's	UJI1761	Swanbrook	V682FEL	Wilts & Dorset	VJT138S	Yellow Buses
T159ALJ	Wilts & Dorset	TIL1256	Tilley's	UJI1762	Swanbrook	V683FEL	Wilts & Dorset	VJT139S	Yellow Buses
T160ALJ	Wilts & Dorset	TIL1257	Tilley's	UJI1763	Swanbrook	V684FEL	Wilts & Dorset	VJT140S	Yellow Buses
T163RMR	Thamesdown	TIL1258	Tilley's	UJI1765	Carmel Coaches	V685FEL	Wilts & Dorset	VJT458S	Tally Ho!
T164RMR	Thamesdown	TIL1259	Tilley's	UJI2507	Wilts & Dorset	V686FEL	Wilts & Dorset	VJY921V	Bakers Dolphin
T165RMR	Thamesdown	TIL1260	Tilley's	UJI3791	Bakers Dolphin	V701FFB	First Cityline	VMJ967S	Quantock
T216REL	Wilts & Dorset	TIL1261	Tilley's	UJI3794	Dartline	V732FAE	First Cityline	VNT18S	Bakers Dolphin
T217REL	Wilts & Dorset	TIL1262	Tilley's	UKT552	First Western Nat	V733FAE	First Cityline	VOD125K	First Southern Nat
T218REL	Wilts & Dorset	TIL1263	Tilley's	ULL933	Western Greyhound	V734FAE	First Cityline	VOD594S	First Southern Nat
T270BPR	Yellow Buses	TIL2746	Fosseway	UMR199T	Thamesdown	V735FAE	First Cityline	VOD596S	Western Greyhound
T271BPR	Yellow Buses	TIL2747	Fosseway	UMR200T	Thamesdown	V736FAE	First Cityline	VOO273	First Western Nat
T272BPR	Yellow Buses	TIL3383	Beeline	UOB366Y	First Southern Nat	V737FAE	First Cityline	VPH53S	Quantock
T273BPR	Yellow Buses	TIL9865	Wakes	UOR968T	Thamesdown	V738FAE	First Cityline	VTH942T	First Western Nat
T274BPR	Yellow Buses	TIW7681	Taw & Torridge	UPK138S	Coombs	V801KAF	First Western Nat	VUV246	Wilts & Dorset
T275BPR	Yellow Buses	TJF757	Castleways	UPV487	Bakers Dolphin	V802EFB	First Southern Nat	VVV959W	Western Greyhound
T276BPR	Yellow Buses	TJI3134	First Southern Nat	URF668S	First Western Nat	V802KAF	First Western Nat	VYC852W	Safeway
T277BPR	Yellow Buses	TJI3135	First Southern Nat	URS320X	First Western Nat	V803EFB	First Southern Nat	W2BBC	Bluebird Cs
T278BPR	Yellow Buses	TJI3136	First Southern Nat	URS327X	First Western Nat	V803KAF	First Western Nat	W3TRU	Truronian
T310AHY	First Southern Nat	TJI3137	First Southern Nat	URS328X	First Western Nat	V804EFB	First Western Nat	W4TRU	Truronian
T316KCV	First Western Nat	TJI3138	First Southern Nat	URU651X	Hookways	V805EFB	First Western Nat	W102PMS	Stagecoach Devon
T320NRU	Yellow Buses	TJI4683	First Southern Nat	URU690S	Wilts & Dorset	V806EFB	First Western Nat	W157RYB	Dawlish Cs
T330AFX	Yellow Buses	TJI4838	First Western Nat	URU691S	Wilts & Dorset	V807EFB	First Western Nat	W161RFX	Wilts & Dorset
T331AFX	Yellow Buses	TJI6312	Beeline	USV115	Wilts & Dorset	V808EFB	First Western Nat	W161RYB	Berry's
T335AFX	Yellow Buses	TJI9462	Yellow Buses	USV821	First Southern Nat	V809EFB	First Western Nat	W162RFX	Wilts & Dorset
T419PDG	Bennetts	TJT188X	Yellow Buses	USV823	First Southern Nat	V810EFB	First Cityline	W163RFX	Wilts & Dorset
T469JCV	First Western Nat	TJT191X	Yellow Buses	UTO835S	First Western Nat	V832DYD	First Southern Nat	W164RFX	Wilts & Dorset
T470JCV	First Western Nat	TJT192X	Yellow Buses	UWB183	First Western Nat	V833DYD	First Western Nat	W165RFX	Wilts & Dorset
T471JCV	First Western Nat	TJT193X	Yellow Buses	UWR496	Western Greyhound	V834DYD	First Western Nat	W166RFX	Wilts & Dorset
T472YTT	First Western Nat	TJT194X	Yellow Buses	UWV604S	River Link	V835DYD	First Southern Nat	W259WRV	Dartline
T473YTT	First Western Nat	TJT195X	Yellow Buses	UWV614S	River Link	V852DYB	Wakes	W311SDV	Plymouth Citybus
T565RFS	Buglers	TJT196X	Yellow Buses	UWV619S	Citytours	V938DFH	Stagecoach West	W312STA	Plymouth Citybus
T633AJT	Wilts & Dorset	TJT197X	Yellow Buses	UWW6X	Wilts & Dorset	V939DFH	Stagecoach West	W324UEL	Yellow Buses
T634AJT	Wilts & Dorset	TJT198X	Yellow Buses	UWW7X	Stagecoach West	V940DFH	Stagecoach West	W334UEL	Yellow Buses
T635AJT	Wilts & Dorset	TJT199X	Yellow Buses	UWW12X	Wilts & Dorset	V941DFH	Stagecoach West	W346VOD	Seawards
T636AJT	Wilts & Dorset	TJY761	Yellow Buses	UWW16X	Wilts & Dorset	V942DFH	Stagecoach West	W347VOD	Seawards
T637AJT	Wilts & Dorset	TMW997S	Roselyn Coaches	UWW17X	Wilts & Dorset	V943DFH	Stagecoach West	W371PHY	Coombs
T638AJT	Wilts & Dorset	TND129X	Wilts & Dorset	UWY83X	Andy James	V944DFH	Stagecoach West	W372PHY	Coombs
T639AJT	Wilts & Dorset	TNJ995S	Citytours	UYC860R	Berry's	V945DFH	Stagecoach West	W381UEL	Yellow Buses
T640AJT	Wilts & Dorset	TNJ996S	Citytours	UYD950W	Wakes	V946DFH	Stagecoach West	W382UEL	Yellow Buses

Registration	Operator
W383UEL	Yellow Buses
W384UEL	Yellow Buses
W391JOG	Castleways
W501VDD	Stagecoach West
W504VDD	Stagecoach West
W505VDD	Stagecoach West
W508VDD	Stagecoach West
W509VDD	Stagecoach West
W562RYC	Dawlish Cs
W601PAF	First Western Nat
W601PLJ	Wilts & Dorset
W602PAF	First Western Nat
W602PLJ	Wilts & Dorset
W603PAF	First Western Nat
W603PLJ	Wilts & Dorset
W604PAF	First Western Nat
W604PLJ	Wilts & Dorset
W605PAF	First Western Nat
W606PAF	First Western Nat
W607PAF	First Western Nat
W608PAF	First Western Nat
W609PAF	First Western Nat
W678DDN	James Bevan
W702PHT	First Cityline
W703PHT	First Cityline
W704PHT	First Cityline
W705PHT	First Cityline
W706PHT	First Cityline
W707PHT	First Cityline
W708PHT	First Cityline
W709PHT	First Badgerline
W711RHT	First Badgerline
W712RHT	First Badgerline
W713RHT	First Badgerline
W714RHT	First Badgerline
W715RHT	First Badgerline
W716RHT	First Badgerline
W717RHT	First Badgerline
W801PAE	First Cityline
W802PAE	First Cityline
W803PAE	First Cityline
W804PAE	First Cityline
W804PAF	First Western Nat
W805PAE	First Cityline
W805PAF	First Western Nat
W806PAE	First Cityline
W806PAF	First Cityline
W807PAE	First Cityline
W807PAF	First Western Nat
W808PAE	First Cityline
W808PAF	First Western Nat
W809PAE	First Cityline
W809PAF	First Western Nat
W811PAE	First Cityline
W811PAF	First Western Nat
W811PFB	First Cityline
W812PAE	First Cityline
W812PAF	First Western Nat
W812PFB	First Cityline
W813PAE	First Cityline
W813PAF	First Western Nat
W813PFB	First Cityline
W814PAE	First Cityline
W814PAF	First Western Nat
W814PFB	First Cityline
W815PAE	First Cityline
W815PAF	First Cityline
W815PFB	First Cityline
W816PAE	First Cityline
W816PFB	First Cityline
W817PAE	First Cityline
W817PFB	First Cityline
W818PAE	First Cityline
W818PFB	First Cityline
W819PAE	First Cityline
W819PFB	First Cityline
W821PAE	First Cityline
W821PFB	First Cityline
W822PAE	First Cityline
W822PFB	First Cityline
W823PAE	First Cityline
W823PFB	First Cityline
W824PAE	First Cityline
W824PFB	First Cityline
W825PFB	First Cityline
W826PFB	First Cityline
W827PFB	First Cityline
W828PFB	First Cityline
W829PFB	First Cityline
W831PFB	First Cityline
W832PFB	First Cityline
W833PFB	First Cityline
W834PFB	First Cityline
W921JNF	Liskeard & District
W922JNF	Liskeard & District
WA51ACO	Plymouth Citybus
WA51ACU	Plymouth Citybus
WA51ACV	Plymouth Citybus
WA51ACX	Plymouth Citybus
WA51ACY	Plymouth Citybus
WAF156	Hambleys
WDD17X	Beard
WDD194	Pullham's
WDF946	Pullham's
WDF998X	Marchants
WDF999X	Marchants
WDK562T	Quantock
WDR145	Buglers
WDR598	Tally Ho!
WDZ5236	Duchy Travel
WHW465T	Western Greyhound
WJB490	Wakes
WJI2321	Bakers Dolphin
WJI3490	Bakers Dolphin
WJI3491	Bakers Dolphin
WJI3492	Bakers Dolphin
WJI3493	Bakers Dolphin
WJI3494	Bakers Dolphin
WJI3495	Bakers Dolphin
WJI3496	Bakers Dolphin
WJI3497	Bakers Dolphin
WJI5152	Beeline
WJI6879	Bakers Dolphin
WJI6880	Bakers Dolphin
WJS843X	Keith Webber
WLT713	Boomerang Bus Co
WNL382A	DAC Coaches
WNN734	First Western Nat
WOI8022	Bath Bus Company
WRO430S	Thamesdown
WSV323	Wakes
WSV408	First Western Nat
WSV529	DAC Coaches
WSV537	Western Greyhound
WSV868	Wakes
WTG360T	Bath Bus Company
WTH943T	First Western Nat
WTH945T	First Western Nat
WTH946T	First Western Nat
WTH950T	First Western Nat
WTH961T	First Western Nat
WXI3860	Hookways
WYD103W	Wakes
WYD104W	Wakes
WYV47T	Swanbrook
WYY752	First Badgerline
X70CJT	Turners
X80CJT	Turners
X141CDV	Plymouth Citybus
X142CDV	Plymouth Citybus
X143CFJ	Plymouth Citybus
X149BTA	Seawards
X191HFB	First Southern Nat
X192HFB	First Southern Nat
X193HFB	First Southern Nat
X194HFB	First Southern Nat
X201CDV	Plymouth Citybus
X201HAE	First Badgerline
X202CDV	Plymouth Citybus
X202HAE	First Badgerline
X203CDV	Plymouth Citybus
X203HAE	First Badgerline
X204CDV	Plymouth Citybus
X315WFX	Yellow Buses
X424CFJ	Dawlish Cs
X474SCY	First Western Nat
X475SCY	First Western Nat
X476SCY	First Western Nat
X477SCY	First Western Nat
X478SCY	First Western Nat
X501BFJ	First Western Nat
X502BFJ	First Western Nat
X503BFJ	First Western Nat
X504BFJ	First Western Nat
X506ADF	Stagecoach West
X507ADF	Stagecoach West
X510ADF	Stagecoach West
X511ADF	Stagecoach West
X512ADF	Stagecoach West
X513ADF	Stagecoach West
X564CUY	Beard
X605XFX	Wilts & Dorset
X606XFX	Wilts & Dorset
X607XFX	Wilts & Dorset
X608XFX	Wilts & Dorset
X609XFX	Wilts & Dorset
X687XFX	Wilts & Dorset
X688XFX	Wilts & Dorset
X904ADF	Geoff Willetts
X966AFH	Stagecoach West
X967AFH	Stagecoach West
X968AFH	Stagecoach West
X969AFH	Stagecoach West
X971AFH	Stagecoach West
X972AFH	Stagecoach West
X973AFH	Stagecoach West
X974AFH	Stagecoach West
X975AFH	Stagecoach West
X976AFH	Stagecoach West
X977AFH	Stagecoach West
X978AFH	Stagecoach West
XAA299	Wilts & Dorset
XAK902T	Marchants
XAM152	Wilts & Dorset
XAN431T	First Western Nat
XAN48T	Berry's
XAN48T	Roselyn Coaches
XBF976	Truronian
XBJ860	Wakes
XBU5S	Thamesdown
XBU19S	Thamesdown
XBU20S	Thamesdown
XBZ7729	Thamesdown
XBZ7730	Thamesdown
XBZ7731	Thamesdown
XBZ7732	Thamesdown
XCT251T	Duchy Travel
XDG614	Pullham's
XDV601S	First Western Nat
XDV603S	First Western Nat
XDV608S	First Western Nat
XDV609S	First Western Nat
XEL4	Excelsior
XEL24	Excelsior
XEL31	Excelsior
XEL158	Excelsior
XEL254	Excelsior
XEL542X	Bakers Dolphin
XEL606	Excelsior
XFF283	First Western Nat
XFG25Y	Ebley
XFG27Y	First Southern Nat
XFG30Y	Ebley
XFJ466	Dartline
XHK220X	First Western Nat
XHK221X	A Bus
XHK222X	A Bus
XHK223X	First Western Nat
XHK225X	First Western Nat
XHK228X	First Western Nat
XHK230X	First Western Nat
XIA857	Stagecoach Devon
XIB1907	Beeline
XIB3910	Wilts & Dorset
XJI5457	Bakers Dolphin
XJI5458	Bakers Dolphin
XJI5459	Bakers Dolphin
XJI6233	Beeline
XJI6330	Bakers Dolphin
XJI6331	Bakers Dolphin
XJI6332	Bakers Dolphin
XJI6333	Bakers Dolphin
XLH570	Bakers Dolphin
XLV143W	First Southern Nat
XMW120	Thamesdown
XPG295Y	F T Williams
XSL228A	Wilts & Dorset
XSS332Y	First Western Nat
XSS333Y	First Western Nat
XSS334Y	First Western Nat
XSS338Y	First Western Nat
XSS340Y	First Western Nat
XSS341Y	First Western Nat
XSU910	F T Williams
XXI8502	Wilts & Dorset
XYC248W	Wakes
XYC249W	Wakes
Y1EDN	Truronian
Y2EDN	Truronian
Y5TRU	Truronian
Y14DLC	Dartline
Y36HBT	First Badgerline
Y37HBT	First Badgerline
Y38HBT	First Badgerline
Y39HBT	First Badgerline
Y138RDG	Citytours
Y139RDG	Citytours
Y166GTT	Seawards
Y167FEL	Wilts & Dorset
Y168FEL	Wilts & Dorset
Y169FEL	Wilts & Dorset
Y170FEL	Wilts & Dorset
Y171FEL	Wilts & Dorset
Y172FEL	Wilts & Dorset
Y173FEL	Wilts & Dorset
Y174FEL	Wilts & Dorset
Y175FEL	Wilts & Dorset
Y189KMB	Dukes Travel
Y192YMR	Thamesdown
Y193YMR	Thamesdown
Y194YMR	Thamesdown
Y195YMR	Thamesdown
Y196YMR	Thamesdown
Y197YMR	Thamesdown
Y200BCC	Bennetts
Y201KMB	Dukes Travel
Y227NYA	Bakers Dolphin
Y228NYA	Bakers Dolphin
Y229NYA	Bakers Dolphin
Y263YNB	Liskeard & District
Y300BCC	Bennetts
Y313NYD	Plymouth Citybus
Y314NYD	Plymouth Citybus
Y400BCC	Bennetts
Y411CFX	Yellow Buses
Y412CFX	Yellow Buses
Y413CFX	Yellow Buses
Y414CFX	Yellow Buses
Y415CFX	Yellow Buses
Y416CFX	Yellow Buses
Y417CFX	Yellow Buses
Y418CFX	Yellow Buses
Y446AUY	Citytours
Y644NYD	Plymouth Citybus
Y645NYD	Plymouth Citybus
Y646NYD	Plymouth Citybus
Y647NYD	Plymouth Citybus
Y648NYD	Plymouth Citybus
Y802KMB	Dukes Travel
Y818NAY	Dawlish Cs
Y835NAY	Dawlish Cs
Y906GFJ	Seawards
Y922DCY	Hopley's
YAZ6391	Shaftesbury & Dist
YAZ6392	Shaftesbury & Dist
YAZ6393	Shaftesbury & Dist
YAZ6394	Shaftesbury & Dist
YAZ8922	Beeline
YCV500	Hambleys
YEL5T	Wilts & Dorset
YFB972V	Stagecoach West
YJI8594	Bluebird Cs
YJI8595	Bluebird Cs
YJI8596	Bluebird Cs
YJV806	Stagecoach West
YMW843	Wilts & Dorset
YNW33X	Hookways
YOR456	Roselyn Coaches
YPL78T	Quantock
YPL92T	Quantock
YPL105T	Quantock
YPL420T	Applegates
YRY1Y	Bakers Dolphin
YSU923	Tally Ho!
YTT178S	Taw & Torridge
YVX401X	Grey Cars
YXI2730	Bakers Dolphin
YXI2732	Bakers Dolphin
YYA122X	Safeway
YYD699	South Gloucestershire
YYO685	Tally Ho!

ISBN 1 897990 64 2

© Published by *British Bus Publishing Ltd*, September 2001

The Vyne, 16 St Margarets Drive, Wellington, Telford, TF1 3PH

Telephone: 01952 255669 - Facsimile: 01952 222397

www.britishbuspublishing.co.uk - E-mail editorial@britishbuspublishing.co.uk